FACE–TO–FACE INTERACTION:

RESEARCH, METHODS, AND THEORY

FACE–TO–FACE INTERACTION:
Research, Methods, and Theory

STARKEY DUNCAN, Jr.
DONALD W. FISKE
THE UNIVERSITY OF CHICAGO

 LAWRENCE ERLBAUM ASSOCIATES, PUBLISHERS
1977   Hillsdale, New Jersey

DISTRIBUTED BY THE HALSTED PRESS DIVISION OF

JOHN WILEY & SONS
New York   Toronto   London   Sydney

Lawrence Erlbaum Associates, Inc., Publishers
62 Maria Drive
Hillsdale, New Jersey 07642

Distributed solely by Halsted Press Division
John Wiley & Sons, Inc., New York

Library of Congress Cataloging in Publication Data

Duncan, Starkey.
   Face-to-face interaction.

   Bibliography: p.
   1. Interpersonal communication.   I. Fiske, Donald
Winslow, 1916-   joint author.   II. Title.
BF637.C45D86   301.4   77-1841
ISBN 0-470-99113-5

Printed in the United States of America

To Our Families

Contents

Preface

The understanding of face-to-face interaction is central to the conceptualization and study of human social conduct. A major focus of the book is on how to do research on this topic. How can that research be sound and replicable? To learn about interactions, what is the necessary level of analysis? What methods of data collection and analysis make most effective use of information available in interactions?

A second major focus is on a model for conceptualizing face-to-face interaction. This model draws its components from several social sciences, especially linguistics. Its basic idea is that face-to-face interaction can be construed as having a definite organization or structure, just as language is understood in terms of its grammar. Within that organization, the participant has options that he can exercise, including the option of violating aspects of the organization. A pattern of option choices may be described in terms of the participant's strategy within observed interactions. Some tasks for research are discovery of the elements of this organization and development of adequate ways of describing the organization as a whole.

Much has been written for professional and popular audiences about interpersonal interactions and about specific actions that occur in these encounters. These have included both insightful commentaries based upon general observations and investigations of single behaviors. What this book proposes is a general conceptual framework for guiding empirical investigation. In particular, emphasis is placed on the simultaneous study of a number of acts, searching for the locus of each act within a context of other acts in contiguity to it.

This book was written for researchers and students concerned with face-to-face interactions. It is more a treatise than a textbook aimed at coverage of the large body of prior work on that topic. We present here a definite viewpoint and show how that view can be implemented. As such, this volume may be useful as supplementary reading for courses on nonverbal communication and a variety of social science courses that deal with face-to-face interaction.

In Part I we consider the substantive area and the research strategies appropriate for it. The processes of classifying behavior and of collecting data on face-to-face interactions are examined. What designs can be used for research on that topic? What kinds of research procedures are satisfactory and what kinds are unsatisfactory in this area?

In Part II we describe a large correlational study in which numerous scores for the occurrences of acts in a whole interaction are analyzed. It reports correlations of such scores with scores for other acts of the same participant, with scores for acts of the partner, and with scores from many self-descriptive variables.

In Part III we report a study exploring elements of the organization of several interactions used in Part II and of other interactions. The organization is studied in terms of action sequences. Particular attention is given to actions associated with the exchange of speaking turns and with speaker–auditor interaction during speaking turns.

In Part IV we propose the general conceptual model and outline how that model can be used to guide research.

The research reported here could not have been done without the contributions of labor, ideas, and constructive advice of a number of individuals, and without indispensable financial support. We wish to express our appreciation and indebtedness to those individuals and institutions from whom we have received so much.

Little of the reported research could have been carried out without basic financial support. Initial transcription and analysis of videotapes were made possible by Grants MH-16,210 and MH-17,756 from the National Institute of Mental Health to Duncan. Continuing research support was provided by the Division of Social Sciences of the National Science Foundation Grants GS-3033 and GS-3033A1 to Duncan, Grants GS-3127 and GS-3127A1 to Fiske, and SOC74-24084 to Duncan and Fiske. A pilot study for the work described in Part II was supported by a grant from the Social Science Research Committee, Division of Social Sciences, University of Chicago.

One of the pleasures of doing research in a university setting is the presence of students who give generously of their time, energies, and ideas. The following students gave these, as well as their unique contributions as individuals, to the research team: Lawrence Brunner, Jeanine Carlson, Mark Cary, Alan Fogel, Barbara Kanki, Diane Martin, Ray O'Cain, Thomas Rossen, Thomas Shanks, Cathy Stepanek, and Andrew Szasz. At a turning point in the project, Dr. Anna Katz Lieblich brought a fresh perspective and special research skills as a research associate in the Department of Behavioral Sciences. As indicated in the text, some of the results reported are derived from the research of Susan Beekman and George Niederehe.

Too easily overlooked are the subjects in our studies. For modest or sometimes no financial compensation their good-faith willingness to engage in interactions and to be videotaped provided the basic stuff of our research. We hope that they will judge their cooperation to have led to some constructive results.

This project could not have been undertaken and pursued without the continuing tangible and intangible support of the University of Chicago. This support was most directly provided by David McNeill, Chairman of the Committee on Cognition and Communication; Norman Bradburn, Chairman of the Department of Behavioral Sciences; M. Brewster Smith, Chairman of the Department of Psychology; and Robert McC. Adams and William H. Kruskal, Deans of the Division of Social Sciences.

Essential to any set of developing ideas and methods are the advice and encouragement of one's colleagues in both the visible and "invisible" colleges. Taking the time to furnish thoughtful critiques and suggestions on written products of this project were Allen Dittmann, Paul Ekman, Ralph Exline, Siegfried Frey, Erving Goffman, Adam Kendon, Robert Krauss, Dell Hymes, Norman Markel, Norman A. McQuown, Howard Rosenfeld, Robert Rosenthal, and Emmanuel Schegloff. These scholars have done their best to keep this research ship on a reasonable course and cannot be faulted for any misdirections detectable in the pages to follow.

We wish to mention in this connection the comments of reviewers of research-grant proposals and journal articles. While they cannot be properly acknowledged (their identities being a more or less well-kept secret), their remarks were often constructive and insightful, making possible a substantially improved report.

To say that Janet Records prepared the manuscript cannot do justice to her efforts, executive ability, and tact. She maintained the organization of manuscript preparation, typed with astonishing speed and accuracy, and gently indicated ragged sections and deteriorating usage—all with unfailing equanimity. Thank you, Janet. Barbara Page Fiske read the manuscript and made many valuable suggestions about style and exposition.

FACE–TO–FACE INTERACTION:

RESEARCH, METHODS, AND THEORY

Part I

FACE-TO-FACE INTERACTION:
THE RESEARCH AREA
AND SOME BASIC ISSUES

1

Introduction

Let us consider the everyday world of face-to-face encounters. Commonplace activities in these encounters—greeting, discussing, joking, bargaining, directing, commiserating, getting acquainted, promising, rebuffing, and the like—make up the fabric of an individual's social world. In this monograph we shall be concerned with research on face-to-face interaction. In the course of our discussion we shall propose a research model for identifying various types of regularities in face-to-face interaction, and we shall outline a conceptual framework for interpreting these regularities.

We intend our proposals to be general with respect to type and location of interaction. Any occasion of face-to-face interaction will be considered potentially fair game for inquiry under our research model: conversations, family meals, elevator rides, athletic events, casual greetings in passing, and religious rituals. Nor need the location of the interaction be restricted. The location may be public, such as sidewalks, grocery stores, and airports; semipublic, such as offices, courtrooms, and classrooms; or private, such as homes.

We take for granted the centrality of face-to-face interaction for individuals and society. In Goldschmidt's (1972) words, "Social interaction is the very stuff of human life. The individuals of all societies move through life in terms of a continuous series of social interactions. It is in the context of such social encounters that the individual expresses the significant elements of his culture, whether they are matters of economics, social status, personal values, self-image, or religious belief [p. 59]." It is in this sense that we interpret Sapir's (1968) statement that society "is being reanimated or creatively affirmed from day to day by particular acts of a communicative nature which obtain among individuals participating in it [p. 104]."

It will not be surprising, then, that we find ourselves in agreement with Wilson (1972) when, in his review of Hinde's (1972) *Non-verbal communication*, he evaluates the general study of human communication as "what

3

surely must be one of the most important of all emerging scholarly fields [p. 627]."

By focusing on the process of face-to-face interaction itself, we and others working in this area are intellectually indebted, as Kendon (1975) points out, to Georg Simmel, who placed great emphasis on forms of interaction (Levine, 1971), and to George Herbert Mead (1934), who urged the pursuit of social psychology by "starting out with a given social whole of complex group activity, into which we analyze (as elements) the behavior of each of the separate individuals composing it [p. 7]."

FACE-TO-FACE INTERACTION

As Goffman (1971) and others have pointed out, it is difficult to choose a fully satisfactory term for this emergent area of inquiry. Among the many investigators concerned with various aspects of social conduct there is as yet no consensus on a name for the field itself. Although Goffman speaks of "face-to-face interaction," he chooses "public life" to designate the field he considers in his monograph, *Relations in public*. Others working with the same general sort of phenomena have used such terms as "context analysis" (Scheflen, 1966); "clinical sociology" (Lennard & Bernstein, 1969); "nonverbal communication" (e.g., Duncan, 1969; Hinde, 1972; Mehrabian, 1972); "ethnography of encounters" (Goldschmidt, 1972); "human ethology" or some similar term (e.g., Arensberg, 1972; Blurton Jones, 1972; McGrew, 1972; Eibl-Eibesfeldt, 1970); and "human linguistics" (Yngve, 1975).

Thus we posit our term, less from a conviction of its ultimate desirability than from the necessity of using some single term amid the confusing array of alternatives. More important is the special approach to describing face-to-face interaction, considered in the next section.

"SOCIAL ACTION"

We shall be selective in the manner in which these face-to-face interactions will be described. Acknowledging that the literature abounds with a seemingly endless variety of ways of describing interaction—from physiological indices to models of existential conflict—we approach the study of face-to-face interaction through data based on the relatively specific, immediately observable behaviors, so numerous and varied, of which the larger activities are composed. We refer here to such things as head nods, smiles, hand gestures, leg crossings, eyebrow raisings, voice lowerings, throat clearings, completions of syntactic elements, head scratches, and posture shifts. When human conduct is characterized on this relatively low level of abstraction, judges use only a minimum of inferring in their ratings, and they need not summarize their judgments over time. These points and others are considered in greater detail in Chapter 2.

It is the sort of occurrence mentioned above that Goffman (1971, p.1) has termed the "small behaviors." Our term for them will be acts or actions, a usage anticipated by Mead (1934), who spoke of the "social act."

The terms "act" and "action" are widely used by authors in social science and philosophy. For this reason some distinctions seem needed here. The purpose of these distinctions is to draw rough boundaries around the referent of the terms as we use them. It is hoped that subsequent discussion throughout this monograph further clarifies our usage.

In the first place, by focusing on action in social contexts we use the term "act" in a narrower sense than do the philosophers of human action (e.g., those represented in Brand, 1970, and in White, 1968). The broader concern of these philosophers is with all human action, including such elemental acts as an individual's moving his hand when he is quite alone. But we wish to preserve the widespread distinction between human action and "mere behavior," such as the beating of one's heart, perspiring under the influence of fear (Taylor, 1966), and sneezing. And we believe we use the term "action" in the same spirit as, for example, White (1968), who concludes a point in his discussion by stating that "none of this shows, of course, that human actions must be voluntary, intentional, purposive, conscious, etc. . . . ; but only that they must be the sorts of occurrences of which it makes sense to ask whether they are any or all of these [p. 8]."

As Kendon (1975) points out, this approach to describing face-to-face interaction (and that of many others in this area) contrasts sharply with the approach of Bales (1950), who also uses the term "act." In Kendon's words, the category system used by Bales and others (reviewed by Heyns & Lippett, 1954; and by Weick, 1968) "classifies not so much the behavior itself as the intent that is judged to lie behind the behavior [p. 4]."

MAJOR CATEGORIES OF ACTION

For the sake of convenience, the broad spectrum of acts potentially contributing to face-to-face interaction has been subdivided in a variety of ways. A representative set of categories and terms might include the following: (a) paralanguage (Trager, 1958), covering those elements of vocalization not typically included in the phonological description of language; (b) body motion, or kinesics (Birdwhistell, 1970), or visible behavior (Kendon, 1972a); (c) proxemics (Hall, 1966): use of "social and personal space and man's perception of it [p. 1]"; (d) use of scent (social olfaction); (e) haptics (Austin,

1967): body contact between persons; (f) the use of artifacts, such as dress and cosmetics; and (g) language, as it is traditionally defined. These categories will be briefly described, together with major transcription systems (if any) in each case

Trager's (1958) paper proposing the term "paralanguage" remains a basic reference with respect to those actions. He distinguished *voice qualities*, "actual speech events, phenomena that can be sorted out from what is said and heard [pp. 4–5]," from *vocalizations,* "actual specifically identifiable noises (sounds) or aspects of noises [p. 5]." Examples of voice qualities would be pitch range, resonance, tempo, and vocal lip control. Examples of vocalizations would be intensity (or stress), pitch height (or level of vocal pitch at some moment), extent (or duration of a syllable), laughing, crying, whispering, and several other sounds such as "uh–uh" (English negation), "uh–huh" (English affirmation), clicks, hisses, and the "uh" of filled pauses. While it is true that Trager's system is relatively undifferentiated in many areas it remains remarkably useful for much practical work. Crystal and Quirk (1964) and Crystal (1969) provide valuable theoretical discussions of intonation and paralanguage, as well as their own systems for dealing with these phenomena.

Body motion refers to a wide variety of visible actions. For example, in the study reported in Part III, the body-motion transcription included such actions as head gestures and movements (nodding, turning, pointing, shaking, etc.) and directions of head orientation; shoulder movements (e.g., shrugs); any facial expressions that could be clearly seen; hand gestures and movements of all sorts (each hand described separately); foot movements (each foot separately); leg movements; posture and posture shifts; and use of objects, such as pipe, kleenex, papers, and clip board.

Some relatively comprehensive systems for describing body motion exist. For example, Birdwhistell (1970, 1971) has published two systems, termed "microkinegraphs" and "macrokinegraphs," respectively. These two systems reflect the "etic–emic" distinction often encountered in linguistics. An "etic" descriptive system is one that remains as close as possible to raw physical description of the behaviors involved, as in a phonetic description of speech. A phonetic descriptive system might be designed to be applicable to any sample of speech in any language. Contrasting with an "etic" system would be an "emic" one representing a hypothesis as to the essential elements of particular social codes under investigation. One might, for example, propose a phonemic system for describing English speech. Such a system would constitute a hypothesis as to the essential phonological elements of English speech. Birdwhistell's microkinegraphic system attempts an "etic" description of body motion. Consisting of line drawings, angles, and other symbols, it is extremely fine grained and purportedly independent of the movement practices of specific cultures. The macrokinegraphic system uses symbols that can be found on a typewriter keyboard and is said to reflect the typical movements of "middle majority American movers." To our knowledge, neither system has been used by other investigators. Examples of Birdwhistell's use of the two systems may be found in the references cited above and in McQuown (1971).

Working within the tradition of ethology, Grant (1969) and McGrew (1970, 1972) have published inventories of typical body-motion actions (including facial expressions) they have encountered in the nursery-school children they have observed.

Ekman and Friesen have developed a system for transcribing facial expressions. Called the Facial Affect Scoring Technique (FAST), the system is designed for studies of the recognition of emotion on the basis of facial expression. Unlike the systems of, for example, Grant and McGrew, FAST is not an attempt to describe the set of facial expressions encountered in observed face-to-face interactions. Rather, as Ekman and Friesen explain, the facial categories were those that had proven useful for investigators concerned with judging emotion from the face. The system is based on matching each facial part of the observed expression with one of a series of pictures for each facial part, as posed by models. The system has not, at this writing, been published; however, it is generally described in Ekman, Friesen, and Tompkins (1971). (In addition, it may be noted that Ekman and Friesen, 1969, have published a conceptually based category system for hand movements.)

Ex and Kendon (1969) provide a notation system for the face. A modified version of the system was used by Kendon (1975b) in a study of the functioning of the face in interaction.

It is inevitable that investigators will encounter a somewhat different set of body-motion actions in different interaction situations. For example, Grant and McGrew in their studies of nursery-school children had to describe a set of actions considerably different from those encountered in the study of adult conversations presented in Part III. Studying subjects' actions during a word-association test, Krout (1935) observed a number of actions not reported by other investigators.

It is quite possible that investigators engaged in a given study will find useful categories in several different transcription systems, but no single available system entirely adequate to their needs. In such a case the investigator may devise a system that borrows from others, but also includes new categories necessary to account for observed actions. (Developing this type of transcription system is further considered in Part III.) In time, as more of such systems are developed and published, a highly useful set of categories for body motion may accumulate in the literature.

Hall (1963), who proposed the term "proxemics," has published a system for transcribing actions generally falling under that rubric. His "proxemic notation system" includes a representation of posture, the angle between the shoulders of two interactants, the distance between interactants, the type of touching (if any) that occurs (termed "haptics" by Austin, 1967), the direct-ness of visual contact (if any), the body heat detected by the interactants, the odors detected by the interactants, and voice loudness (a dimension describa-ble through paralanguage). In a later publication, Hall (1966) hypothesizes a set of distance zones that are socially significant for "non-contact, middle-class, healthy adults, mainly natives of the northeastern seaboard of the United States [pp. 109-110]." While there is now extensive literature on spatial arrangements in face-to-face interaction (e.g., Altman, 1970; Edney, 1974; Goffman, 1971; Hall, 1966; Pastalan & Carson, 1970; Pederson & Shears, 1973; Sommer, 1969), there has been virtually no empirical work published on such proxemic factors as touching, heat detection, and social ol-faction for humans.

THE CONTEMPORARY STUDY OF FACE-TO-FACE INTERACTION

As suggested by the many names used to refer to the investigation of social conduct, this research area belongs to no single traditional discipline; it has been interdisciplinary from the beginning. This has been a happy state of af-fairs. As investigators from a wide variety of disciplines have been drawn to the study of face-to-face interaction, this area has benefited from the appli-cation of their respective special insights and skills.

The nonverbal-communication research literature has received contribu-tions from anthropologists, sociologists, and social psychologists seeking techniques for more concrete description of cultural processes and seeing face-to-face interaction as the central medium for the transmission and affir-mation of culture.

Ethologists have been intrigued by the possibility of extending to humans the techniques for discovering and describing organization in the interaction of nonhuman animal species. These ethologists have brought with them a special appreciation of genetically based inputs to interaction.

Personality and individual-difference psychologists have sought in the study of acts alternatives to the traditional intrapsychic concepts such as trait and need, contemplating a reorientation of the description of persons in terms of social action.

Psychologists and psychiatrists studying psychotherapeutic processes and the sources of psychopathology have sensed the possibility of more powerful techniques and concepts for the analysis of these more specialized forms of face-to-face interaction.

Linguists and anthropological linguists have long been aware of the cultur-al context of language use, in terms of the social situation in which language occurs, in terms of other behaviors contributing to the interaction process, and in terms of the many social functions accomplished through the use of language.

And philosophers have involved themselves in the analysis both of natural language and of broader social forms. The list continues to expand.

Amid the rich variety of conceptual perspectives and methodological approaches suggested above, the field has in one sense flourished; but in another sense, floundered. In one sense, it has shown remarkable breadth; in another sense, it has become attenuated. In one sense, it has been tolerant; in another sense, it has been uncritical. In one sense, it has developed multiple facets; in another sense, it is missing a clear direction.

This diverse and largely inchoate state of the field has not, as Kendon (1975) has so perceptively noted, troubled most of its active investigators. Rather, they have enjoyed it, appreciating an increased potential for emergent new directions. But it seems that this appreciation of diversity has carried a quite unnecessarily negative side effect. Stemming in part from the prevailing laissez-faire attitudes, major conceptual and methodological assumptions have not been clearly articulated and actively considered in the academic forum. Issues have not been joined, debated, and potentially sharpened. Weak methods and questionable assumptions have not been scrutinized. Broad theoretical bases for valid empirical findings have not been advanced.

It is interesting to note that Edney (1974), in reviewing the literature on human territoriality, reached much the same conclusions: "Unfortunately, the available information on human territoriality is limited and unsystematic; ideas in the area are loose, definitional problems exist, and theories have never progressed beyond an elementary and informal stage. No particular paradigm characterizes research on the topic, and as yet there is no standard set of principles that can be reliably applied to problems in the area. Available research reports also reveal a diversity of assumptions and starting points [p. 959]."

In the spirit of contributing to incipient discussion in the area of face-to-face interaction, we intend to address these issues and problems directly. We shall be critically examining research assumptions, concepts, and methods. This examination will not, however, include a broad literature review and attempted integration of research results. Given the current state of the field, we believe that such an undertaking is premature. The reasons for this judgment will become increasingly apparent in the course of the discussion.

GUIDING PERCEPTIONS AND CENTRAL THEMES

Investigators inevitably approach their research with some set of basic perceptions and perhaps prejudices regarding their subject matter and the proper approach to it. Clearly, this was the case with us. We wish to state some of these fundamental views in order to provide a broad context for the particular research strategies described below. These views relate to the essential elements of face-to-face interaction, the present state of research in this area, and the orderly and sound development of social science.

Data

As we suggested earlier in this chapter we are convinced that the strongest single aspect of contemporary research on face-to-face interaction is its data base. We refer to the many studies that generate data through observations demanding a minimum of inference by the rater (in part by avoiding the ascription of "meaning" to actions), and virtually eliminating the necessity to sum perceptions over time. In the next chapter we shall examine in greater detail the process of observation through descriptive category systems. But the significance of this strength will continue to be examined from several perspectives in the course of this monograph.

Intermediate-Level Concepts

Just as a system for observing human interaction requires either more or less inference on the part of the rater, so the terms and concepts designed to describe the regularities uncovered by analysis must be pitched at either a higher or lower level of abstraction. We judge that much research in psychology (to implicate only our own discipline) has relied on excessively abstract levels of discourse. Riskin and Faunce (1972), in their review of family-interaction research, have stated this issue perceptively:

> There is, if anything, an overabundance of abstract concepts and theories, e.g., "power," "dominance," "self-esteem," "homeostasis," "conflict," "family rules," "double-bind," . . . etc. And there are many factors requiring minimal inference which can be measured with high reliability, e.g., "who talks," "interruptions," "who follows whom," "amount of silence," "amount of talking," "whose choice 'wins out'," "laughter," etc. Noticeably lacking, however, are the intermediate concepts and steps through which to relate the low-order observational data and variables to high-order abstractions. This lack contributes to the ease with which some writers make great leaps from almost mechanical-level measurements to complex theorizing [pp. 399–400].

In developing an area of inquiry, it is of central importance to establish in the first instance a set of low-level constructs that can be tied directly and explicitly to the data. Based explicitly on these low-level constructs, other constructs at successively more abstract levels can be developed. To state this seems merely to utter a truism, but it has scarcely been a standard procedure in psychology, and perhaps in much of social science.

Structure and Strategy

We believe that any adequate description of face-to-face interaction must take into account both the structure, that is, the social forms for that interaction, and the individual operating within that structure. Any social action may be seen as shaped by both these elements. This view of the Janus-like nature of this area is well articulated by Goodenough (1974) in his description of Geertz's efforts to "describe not just 'grammar' or 'structure' but the 'rhetoric' of life, not just the rules of the game but the many, often conflicting purposes people hope to realize by playing the game and the strategies and tactics (including cheating) by which they try to realize them [p. 435]." This same integrated duality has been deeply considered by Goffman, who has written not only of "rules" and "convention" (e.g., Goffman, 1971), but also of strategy (e.g., Goffman, 1969).

Natural Social Systems

We hold a deep respect for the complexity of natural social systems, including those operating in the two-person conversations we have studied. As stated in the preceding section, we see these systems, at least those applying to face-to-face interaction, as being composed of both social structure and individual (or group) strategies. Each of these two aspects potentially involves considerable complexity. Because of their complexity we believe that they are best approached through careful exploratory studies aimed at the discovery of phenomena and the generation of hypotheses.

If the object of our study is face-to-face interaction as it occurs in everyday life, then the appropriate point of departure for such study is the observation of that interaction in situations as natural as possible. Given sufficient protocols made of the proper sorts of interactions, there will be enough natural experiments, enough instances where an event occurs naturally, to establish preliminary propositions or hypotheses.

Hypothesis Formation

We hold a similar respect for the importance of hypotheses in the development of an area of inquiry in particular, and in science in general. It seems to us that, in general, casual observation and–or personal intuition provide a poor basis for the development of hypotheses even, or perhaps especially, of those hypotheses relating to activities in which each of us participates daily. It seems likely that personal or folk models will prove to be as inadequate for descriptions of face-to-face interaction as they have proven to be of linguistic grammars. We consider it highly desirable to develop hypotheses through broadly based, systematic observation, combined with appropriate analysis of the data generated by that observation. In this manner, it may be possible to develop a set of firm, clearly stated, and empirically based hypotheses. And it seems appropriate to expect that in many cases, the process of hypothesis formation will be made public, just as is the process of hypothesis testing.

SUMMARY OF TOPICS

We perceive the present state of research on face-to-face interaction to be both complex and stimulating. Our discussion will extend from specific issues relating to data generation and analysis, to broader issues relating to strategies of research design, and conceptual frameworks within which to place results. The development of this discussion is briefly summarized below.

In the next chapter we consider both some principles of research design in work on face-to-face interaction, and what we consider to be a central strength of this work: data generation through the description of interaction in highly specific terms. The discussion in Chapter 2 is general with respect to the various types of research considered subsequently. It indicates the principles and techniques that guided the research studies reported in this monograph.

Research issues, both specific and broad, are considered through the presentation of two contrasting but complementary studies. These studies stand as examples of two distinct approaches to the study of face-to-face interaction, respectively labeled "structural" and "external variable" by Duncan (1969). Very briefly, Duncan characterized a structural study as viewing face-to-face interaction as an organized social system something like a language; such a study is designed to discover and to document that system, describing it in terms of rules and the like. An external-variable study takes a more traditionally psychological approach, typically seeking individual and group differences in the use of certain actions by relating the rates and durations of these actions to other variables, such as characteristics of the interaction situation, scores on personality inventories, the reaction of judges to the interaction, or sometimes other actions.

The relationships between structural and external-variable studies are carefully considered, together with an evaluation of the potentialities of each. A central emphasis is placed on explicating their guiding assumptions, methodology, and specific research techniques. On the basis of an examination of both general research issues and the specific results of the two studies, the distinction between structural and external-variable studies is reformulated, and some notions about the future development of research in this field are advanced.

External-variable study.   A fairly large external-variable study is presented in Part II. This study was designed along the same general lines as the typical "nonverbal-communication" study. We view the study as being notable mainly for its size, in terms of number of subjects and interactions recorded and number of actions observed, and for certain design features such as repeated measures on all subjects. Once again, considerable attention is given to such technical aspects as the construction of variables, in addition to the rather voluminous results and their implications.

Structural study.   In the review mentioned above, the "numerical predominance of external variable studies" (Duncan, 1969, p. 134) was noted. It seems fair to say that that imbalance continues to prevail at this writing. In view of the relative infrequency of published reports of structural studies, detailed attention will be given in Part III to the conception and development of the structural study, as well as to each aspect of data generation and analysis. It is hoped that such extended treatment will help to make the rationale and technique of structural studies more accessible to those who are relatively unfamiliar with that particular research approach. For those in fields such as linguistics and anthropology in which there is considerable attention paid to the structure or organization of actions of various sorts, the methods of data analysis leading to the formulation of hypotheses may be of some interest. The structural study was initiated before the external-variable study and was continued concurrently with it.

Conceptual framework.   In Chapter 12, Part IV, an initial statement is made of a conceptual scheme for ordering and understanding the phenomena of face-to-face interaction. This scheme is designed to be directly relevant to research issues, including the interpretation of the results of studies in this area, and the optimal design and execution of future studies. The formulation of this conceptual scheme, while breaking from the attitude of suspended commitment described by Kendon (1974), is intended primarily as a device for stimulating more focused discussion of the issues. In any event, an attempt has been made to integrate this conceptual scheme with the discussion of methodology in an effort to make it maximally relevant to the ongoing development of research in this area.

Concluding discussion.   The final chapter builds both on the experience and results stemming from the two studies presented in Parts II and III, and on the conceptual framework described in Chapter 12. A primary aim is to integrate the practical considerations discussed in Parts II and III with the theoretical developments in Chapter 12 of Part IV. In particular, pains are taken to describe with some specificity the various implications for research deriving from this joint consideration of theory and research practice.

2

Measurement Techniques and Research Strategies

The first tasks in developing a study of face-to-face interaction are those of establishing general principles of research design and of data generation (that is, measurement). Before addressing ourselves to the specifics of each of the two studies presented below in Parts II and III, it seems appropriate to consider certain broad principles of design and measurement at this early point in the discussion. There are two reasons for this judgment. First, these broad principles may be said to apply equally to both of the studies presented below, providing a strong element of communality between them, despite their contrasting aims. Second, many of the principles of design and most of the principles of measurement considered in this chapter appear to be quite broadly held among workers in the field commonly referred to as "nonverbal communication," and in related fields. In this sense, many of the elements of the two studies are scarcely unique to them. It is to these broad sources of communality that we now turn our attention.

MEASUREMENT TECHNIQUES

The generation of data through measurement is a crucially important process in research. It is necessary that measurements be, as far as possible, precise, replicable, and observable by any qualified observer. That is, scientific data should be characterized by intersubjective consensus (cf. Popper, 1959). To the extent that these ideals are approximated in a measurement process, a strong data base is created to serve the initial formulation and later testing of hypotheses.

Rather than reviewing the place of measurement in science, however, our intention in this section is to consider some of the more specific properties and problems of measurement in research on face-to-face interaction. The subsequent process of converting the data resulting from measurement into variables will be taken up in each of the following parts.

Category Systems Producing Acts

Measurement has been defined as the assignment of numerals to objects or events in accordance with certain rules (N. R. Campbell, 1928). In studies of face-to-face interaction the "numeral" is typically a symbol indicating the observed occurrence of an event specified in the category system. (Various category systems for audible and for visible events were mentioned in the preceding chapter. Other systems are described in Parts II and III.)

In this discussion of measurement we consider some general characteristics of category systems. When the category system has certain properties described below, the recorded data are termed "acts" or "actions." Certain minimal properties of category systems in general, such as mutual exclusivity of subcategories, are assumed.

Recognition Rules

The rules for the identification of events as instances of the applicable categories will be termed *recognition rules*. Using the investigator's category system, the task of the rater is in the first place to recognize the occurrence of an event specified by a recognition rule. Once that occurrence is noted, the rater can make a tally if he is counting, activate a timer if timing, or inscribe the appropriate symbol if transcribing the interaction. It is also necessary, of course, to recognize the point at which the categorized event has terminated, a decision based on the same recognition rule. At this point, this is necessary because the rater either resets himself to make another counting increment, stops the timer, or enters an "end of event" symbol in the transcription.

Explicitness of Recognition Rules

One characteristic of recognition rules is the degree to which they are explicit. An example of a fully explicit recognition rule would be that designed by Jaffe and Feldstein (1970) for their automatic speech-processing equipment. The task of this equipment (taking the place of the "rater" or "observer" in their study) was to identify the occurrence of speech in the interactions, differentiating that from nonspeech. The recognition rule in this case was stated in terms of a threshold of sound established for a pair of voice-actuated relays. Any sound level above that threshold was recognized by a digital computer as speech, and any sound level below the threshold was recognized as a speech pause. Building on this initial recognition rule, additional, entirely explicit rules were used to define a set of conversational events to be studied, such as "speaker switch," "pause," "switching pause," and "simultaneous speech."

An example of an almost entirely implicit recognition rule would be a rule generated through ostensive definition, in which one or more examples of the event in question are simply pointed out. The pattern-recognition properties of the observer are then relied upon to identify the distinctive properties of the examples, and, most likely, to make some generalizations about these properties, so that the desired recognitions for new sets of events may be made. An ostensive definition of a recognition rule for a class of events termed "hand gesticulation" would be made simply by pointing out some instances on a film or videotape of what the investigator wishes to be included in that class, along with some instances of what is not included in the class.

Events Classified by Cultural Categories

Although fully explicit recognition rules are a goal for social science, use of implicit rules is not necessarily a major obstacle for the achievement of interjudge reliability and for the generation of useful data. For example, raters may have little trouble in agreeing on what is a smile or a head nod or a hand gesticulation, even when these events are defined implicitly. This agreement is probably found because these classifications approximate those provided by the culture of the raters and thus are used by them regularly, though not necessarily explicitly, in everyday life. (The definitions of these "natural" classifications seem rarely to be explicit.) Thus, the investigator may successfully use implicit recognition rules for defining categories within his classification system to the extent that those categories exist in the culture of the raters. It may be added that the research will be successful only to the extent to which the categories match those existing in the culture of the observed interactants.

Despite the hazards involved in the use of categories having implicit recognition rules, it may be argued that an all-out pursuit of fully explicit recognition is not always an optimal research strategy when the research area is at an early developmental stage, and if the proper precautions are taken (as mentioned above). There may be much to be gained by capitalizing on observers' more complex, implicit rules for recognition of cultural classes of events, as opposed to an uncompromising adherence to fully explicit rules. In any case, however, a high level of agreement between observers should be obtained or immediately sought by discussion among the observers.

A study by Boomer and Dittmann (1962) illustrates the productive use of observers' implicit recognition rules. They studied the ability of subjects to identify correctly the presence of unfilled pauses in different locations in the stream of speech. They defined these locations in terms of the phonemic clause, a unit of language based on intonation (Trager & Smith, 1957). "Juncture" pauses were those that occurred between phonemic clauses, and "hesitation" pauses were those that occurred within phonemic clauses. They found that subjects needed considerably longer pause durations in order to identify the presence of juncture pauses than they needed to identify hesitation pauses. They concluded that "any arbitrary definition of speech pauses in terms of duration alone violates certain underlying linguistic and psychological realities. Pauses cannot be abstracted from their speech context and studied in isolation without discarding useful information [p. 219]."

The realities of which Boomer and Dittmann speak would be, in our terms, implicit recognition rules for cultural categories, these categories being labeled by Boomer and Dittmann as juncture and hesitation pauses, respectively. The implicit recognition rules for these categories presumably include criteria based on the immediate linguistic context of the pause, in addition to its duration. It is this type of natural, implicit criterion that may potentially be used to great advantage by an investigator constructing classification systems for behavioral events.

Recognition Rules Involving Unobservables

But there is a serious error to be avoided in developing relatively natural classification systems for studying interaction. This error occurs when the definition of the recognition rules involves the use of some supposed "meaning" of the act, or some other unobservable entity such as intention, motivation, or the like. Unobservable elements play a dominant and subversive role when classification systems require identification of instances of "empathy," "aggression," "gives information," "asks for opinion," or similar states of meaning, intention, motivation, etc. This type of category has predominated in such research areas as small-group processes, psychotherapy research, and family interaction.

One of the most significant and constructive aspects of the work of many researchers in fields referred to as "nonverbal communication" and "human ethology" is the abandonment of unobservables in their category systems. It may very well happen that two raters agree entirely on the type of action they have observed, while sharply disagreeing in their respective interpretations either of its "meaning" in the stream of interaction, or of the intentions of the participant. Further, as Kendon (1975a) points out, there is a paradox inherent in the use of categories based on unobservables such as meaning, for in effect such categories take for granted an understanding of the very phenomena that are under investigation.

It would seem that better understanding of the impact of various actions on the stream of interaction is the object of investigation, to be approached through careful analysis of data. It is not a task assigned to a rater.

It should be pointed out in the context of this discussion that implicit recognition rules need not involve unobservables. Boomer and Dittmann's (1962) study may again serve as an example. Their subjects' implicit rule differentiating juncture from hesitation pauses presumably involved the observable elements of duration and location with respect to structural units of intonation, these units being identifiable on the basis of phonological parameters.

Nominal and Ordinal Scales

A classification system may consist entirely of nominal categories. That is, the rater may be required to note from moment to moment only the presence or absence of a given class of event, making no further discriminations with respect to it. It would seem reasonable to expect a high degree of interjudge reliability for such a classification system, other things being equal.

Nominal scales have been widely used by investigators in the area of nonverbal communication, and research of this sort appears to have been well served by such scales. There is more than enough information in these scales, properly defined, to provide meaningful data on important issues, especially at this stage of development of the area.

On the other hand, it may be desirable or even necessary to construct a classification system requiring further discriminations beyond the mere presence or absence of the event in question. Let us assume, for example, that we have asked our observers to identify all instances of smiling by an interactant, and that our recognition rule for smiling is defined as retracting and raising the corners of the lips. (This is, of course, not the only possible recognition rule for "smiling.") But we also wish to make a further discrimination between "slight" retractions and retractions greater than "slight." ("Slight" might be defined ostensively.) In this case, the observer's rating task involves a two-step sequence: (a) recognition of lip retracting and raising, and (b) a discrimination between "slight" and "greater than slight." This discrimination requires the drawing, either implicitly or explicitly, of a boundary line dividing the two degrees of smiling. In this case, the classification system includes an ordinal scale nested within a nominal one.

It seems reasonable to expect a somewhat lower degree of interjudge reliability for this type of nested, nominal-ordinal scale. This expectation is based on two considerations:

1.   Two decisions are required rather than one; a decision with respect to the nominal scale, and a decision with respect to the ordinal scale. Thus, the effect of using the two nested scales is to double the number of possible points at which disagreement can occur.

2.   The boundary separating the two ordinal scale points ("slight" and "greater than slight") introduces another possible source of disagreement. In the material to be rated, instances of smiling may be observed in which the degree of retraction is close to the defined boundary between the two points. In these instances, consistent discriminations may be more difficult, with an accompanying increased possibility of interjudge disagreement. To the extent to which such borderline instances of smiling are encountered in the rated interaction(s), reliability may suffer. And of course the problem is aggravated as the number of ordinal scale points is increased.

Despite these potential liabilities of classification systems involving ordinal scales, an investigator may decide that the potential gain in information is worthwhile. Indeed, there are various sorts of actions on which it is impossible to develop useful information apart from ordinal scales. For example, virtually all aspects of paralanguage (Trager, 1958), such as tempo and intensity, require rating in terms of ordinal scales. Even though most vocal events, including speaking, coughing, and laughing, may be rated in terms of tempo and intensity, the typical use of these categories involves speaking. In this case, the initial, nominal discrimination is quite simple: is the interactant speaking or not? But this discrimination yields no information on the various aspects of paralanguage. Thus, ordinal scales are required in order to pursue research on paralanguage.

Similarly, all ratings of parakinesic (Birdwhistell, 1970) aspects of action (relating more to style of movement) would require ordinal scales, if transcription systems for parakinesics were available. While investigators of face-to-face interaction have yet to engage in systematic work on parakinesic phenomena, such phenomena stand in the same relation to movement as paralinguistic phenomena to vocalization.

It may be less apparent that certain body-motion actions commonly investigated, while not properly considered parakinesic, nevertheless involve an ordinal scale nested within a nominal scale. The example of gaze direction in this regard may be unexpected, but it seems to fit. Consider the rating of two-person interactions in terms of whether or not one participant is looking at the partner, a common type of measurement in such studies. In this case, the nominal part of the scale is concerned with whether or not the participant's eyes are open. But in addition, the rater must make an estimation of whether or not the direction of the participant's gaze falls within some area including some parts or all of the partner's body. Once again, a boundary line of some sort must be drawn, and the gaze direction is judged to be either within or out of that boundary. A judgment on an ordinal scale is required. It may be noted, however, that in this case the scale is greatly simplified, having only two points: "on target" versus "off target."

Our usage of the term "ordinal" in this discussion is a broad one. Essentially it refers to a set of two or more coordinate categories for actions differing in degree or in some aspect such as direction. As in all ordered scales, the orientation of the order is quite arbitrary in that it can be taken as starting at either of the two ends. In the case of just two categories, the distinction between an ordered scale and a nominal scale as the terms are being used here is that the nominal scale refers to the presence or absence of some act (such as smiling or gesticulating) while the ordinal scale refers to an aspect of the act (such as the direction of the gesture).

Discrete Decisions

The discussion of ordinal and nominal scales has assumed the use of discrete decisions. Raters are required to make yes–no judgments with regard to whether or not some action falls in a given category of the classification system. This assumption has been made because classification systems of this sort have been used predominantly, if not exclusively, within this general research area. And it seems reasonable to expect that this will continue to be the case for the foreseeable future.

In the case of nominal scales the discrete decision has to do with whether or not a classifiable event has occurred in the interaction. In the case of ordinal scales the occurrence of the classifiable event, such as vocalizing or gazing, is assumed. The discrete decision has to do either with assigning some aspect of the occurrence to one of the available ordinal categories, or, once such an assignment is made, with deciding whether or not some subsequent change in that aspect of the event is substantial enough to constitute a crossing of the boundary between the presently assigned category and an adjacent one.

For example, the rater must decide whether or not paralinguistic loudness is normal or one degree overloud, or whether or not a participant is gazing at the partner. Let us say that in a particular case these respective decisions were that the paralinguistic loudness fell into the "normal" (unmarked) category, and that the gaze direction was at the partner. Once these initial assignments are made, the rater must subsequently decide whether or not some detectable increase in paralinguistic loudness is substantial enough to warrant an assignment to the "overloud" category, and whether or not some detectable change in gaze direction warrants an assignment to the "away from partner" category.

Moment-by-Moment Judgments

In category systems of the type under discussion, the rater is not required to sum his judgments over time. Optimally, the rater's action is immediate upon recognizing the onset of the categorized action, and similarly immediate upon recognizing any subsequent offset. There is no requirement of the rater that he characterize as a whole some stretch of interaction. The extreme of this sort of summing task is presented by self-description inventories that ask the subject (the rater in this case) to characterize his entire life or to indicate the presence or absence of some disposition over some unspecified "present" time. An example closer to research on face-to-face interaction would be the rating of a participant as more or less "anxious" during some five-minute stretch of interaction. The avoidance of the necessity to sum one's experience prior to judgment decisions reduces, once again, the complexity of the rating task, thereby potentially increasing the reliability of measurement.

Narrowed Focus of Attention

One final attribute of the observation of acts deserves mention. The definition of most acts requires of the rater a sharply narrowed focus of attention in order to accomplish the task. This narrowed focus of attention is perhaps most dramatically illustrated in the observation of certain paralinguistic phenomena, such as pitch level. Here, the rater must fix his attention upon a single physical parameter of the speech stream, screening out or minimizing all other aspects of speech, such as other paralinguistic phenomena, content, and syntax. A trained, experienced rater can often transcribe extended stretches of speech for paralinguistic pitch without gaining any clear notion of what was said.

The same narrowed focus of attention is required for the rating of body motion. In this case the focus remains on specific body parts: a single hand, perhaps, if gestures, self-adaptors, and the like are being rated. Even closely adjacent body parts are not simultaneously rated by a single rater. For example, an investigator is not likely to ask a rater to cover both head direction and shoulder shrugs in a single pass of the videotape or movie film. Thus, on a given pass through the tape, a rater is required to attend to only a single type of action in a single body part. This narrowed focus of attention in the observation of acts serves to decrease the complexity of the required judgments, and to increase the accuracy of the obtained ratings.

Reliability

It is not surprising that both interjudge and test–retest reliability are high for category systems having the properties described above. It has been mentioned that the typical study of "nonverbal communication" uses category systems of this sort, and in fact it has become routine to encounter reports of substantial reliability in these studies.

Although an early study by Dittmann and Wynne (1961) cast doubt on the ease of obtaining test–retest reliability for some elements of paralanguage (they found acceptable test–retest reliability for intonation), a number of subsequent studies have shown high reliability for a number of actions. Table 2.1 is a summary of a series of reliability studies reported in some subsequent papers. The table is not presented as an exhaustive survey; it includes all of the "nonverbal" studies reporting reliability known to us. It may, perhaps, be used as an indication of the kind of work that has been done on this issue. It will be noted that investigators have checked the reliability on a variety of aspects of both speech and body motion.

As indicated in Table 2.1, a variety of methods of measuring reliability have been used. Not all of these methods have been optimal. Partly because of the different methods used, actual reliability figures reported in the studies have not been included in the table. Nevertheless, in all of the studies shown, reliability figures have been generally very high, mainly in the .90s and high .80s.

In addition to the studies shown in Table 2.1, a reliability study is reported in Part II for the category system used in the research reported there; and in

TABLE 2.1

Some Reliability Studies of Category Systems Having the Properties Discussed
in Chapter 2

Study	Type(s) of action	Type of reliability		Type of measure
		Inter-judge	Test-retest	
Baxter and Rozelle (1975)	Speech; body motion; posture	X	X	Product-moment r
Duncan and Rosenthal (1968)	Intonation; paralanguage	X		Kappa (Cohen, 1960)
Exline (1971)	Gaze	X		Simple percentage
Libby (1970)	Gaze	X		Product-moment r
Markel (1965)	Paralanguage	X	X	Intraclass (Ebel, 1951); product-moment r
Markel (1969)	Paralanguage	X	X	Intraclass; product-moment r
Mehrabian (1968)	Body motion; posture	X		Product-moment r
Mehrabian (1972)	Body motion; posture	X		Product-moment r
Mehrabian and Friar (1969)	Body motion; posture	X		Product-moment r
Rosenfeld (1966)	Body motion	X		Product-moment r

Appendix A a reliability study is described for one of the category systems used in the research reported in Part III.

Automatic Data Generation

The logical goal of objective data generation is the entirely automatic processing of audible and visible recordings by machines, so that the data are "untouched by human hands." As mentioned above, Jaffe and Feldstein (1970) achieved this end, in their study of speech and silence in conversations. It is in principle possible to measure all aspects of intonation and paralanguage electronically, although we seem to be far from being in a position to do so at this writing. It should be pointed out, however, that the development of a satisfactory set of fully explicit recognition rules for such electronic measurement would be a major research program in itself. In the meantime, dealing with intonation and paralanguage remains a task that raters appear able to do with ease and naturalness.

With respect to body motion, a fully automatic processing system seems to be problematic, even on principle. It seems likely that both body-motion and speech-activity measurements in terms of human judgments will continue for some time.

Machine-Aided Data Generation

While entirely automated data generation in research on face-to-face interaction seems to border on the utopian at this point, there appear to be more practical and immediate ways in which the presently laborious task of data generation can be significantly facilitated by appropriately designed man–machine systems. For example, Ekman and Friesen (1969) have described their VID–R system for automatically retrieving instances of specified actions from a large videotape library.

Futrelle (1973), is, at this writing, developing another type of aid for data generation. This system, named GALATEA, involves a visual display in which the film or videotape image appears simultaneously with, and superimposed on, a (green) computer-controlled image from a cathode-ray tube (CRT), driven by the machine's display processor. The rater works with an electronic "pen" which, when moved about the display, inputs to the system the location, shape, motion, and other features, as desired, of the videotape images. The nature of these inputs and the identification of the data are controlled by the operator, using both the pen and a computer terminal. This information is stored by the computer on a frame-by-frame basis and can be displayed on the CRT.

GALATEA promises to provide a number of advantages which, in combination, offer significant improvement over presently available techniques for data generation. Among these advantages are: (a) the rater's ability to work directly on the film or videotape image; (b) the automatic precision timing of events on a frame-number basis; (c) the automatic and accurate interdigitation or sequencing of acts (such as one participant's head nod, closely following the partner's beginning a gesticulation); and (d) the automatic storage and analysis of these data. Futrelle's system, and perhaps other future systems similar to it, may permit the data-generation process, in studies of face-to-face interaction using acts, to improve both in speed and in quality.

Conclusion: Measurement Techniques

We believe that an excellent data base for a developing social science of face-to-face interaction may be generated through the observation of acts, as we have defined them. The strength of such data lies in their relative objectivity. They are generated through the disciplined observation of categories of action requiring a sharply narrowed focus of attention, minimal levels of inference, discrete decisions, and moment-to-moment judgments, while avoiding the attribution of meaning, intent, and the like to the observed participants.

In stressing these desirable attributes, we do not wish to overstate the case. For this reason, we explored the potential complexities in the use of acts. These complexities, as we see them, principally derive from the use of ordinal scales and implicit recognition rules. However, full appreciation of these potential sources of weakness in data generated through the observation of acts, as that observation is currently practiced, should not serve to obscure either the demonstrable strengths of such data, or the substantial improvement they provide over the more abstract and global categories so frequently encountered in social-science studies of face-to-face interaction.

Finally, no investigator has minimized the laboriousness of present rating procedures that rely almost entirely on human operations. Development of the research area will surely be facilitated by imaginative and appropriate use of machine aids to data generation.

PRINCIPLES OF RESEARCH STRATEGY

Data on face-to-face interaction are, of course, generated within the context of a specific interaction situation and a research design—both chosen by the investigator. It is to some of the issues involved in such choices, issues of research strategy, that we now turn.

Inductive Research

It has already been mentioned that we believe that much of research on face-to-face interaction is at an early developmental stage. It may be argued that a fledgling area of inquiry, or at least a fledgling approach to an area of inquiry, can be developed in the soundest way through systematic exploratory studies aimed at generating strong, empirically based hypotheses. To advocate studies aimed at exploration and discovery is not to comment negatively on the process of hypothesis formation and testing. On the contrary, it is to comment on the state of development of the field, and to recognize and respect the character of hypotheses and their role in scientific endeavor.

It would appear that a number of investigators share to some extent this general view, both of the developmental stage of the field and of the proper construction of hypotheses. Fastidious exploratory work has been a hallmark of studies by, for example, Condon and Ogston (1967), Ekman and Friesen (1968), Jaffe and Feldstein (1970), and Kendon (1967, 1970, 1975). As evidenced both in published discussions and through research practice, it seems agreed by many that the task before us remains that of seeking both promising phenomena and promising questions.

Natural Settings

Consonant with the emphasis on inductive research is the attempt to study interaction in as natural a form as possible. The central purpose of this area of inquiry is to understand the conduct of the social activities of everyday life. It would seem to be of considerable importance that these activities be approached as directly as possible, at least in the exploratory phase of work in this field.

To be sure, it is impractical to take an absolutist approach to naturalness in the study of face-to-face interaction. Limitations on the naturalness of the interactions used for research stem from both research requirements and considerations of ethics. In order that fine-grained observations may be made of a large number of simultaneously occuring actions, such technical accoutrements as sound recording equipment, videotape, or movie cameras are required. And the desire of many investigators to avoid surreptitious observation may dictate that such equipment be used in full sight and with the prior full understanding and consent of the interactants. But the goal is to minimize, within the constraints of research requirements and ethics, intrusion upon the interaction in question.

It is possible, however, to overestimate the intrusive character of recording devices and other research apparatus. In this respect our experience matches that of Gumperz (1972), who has observed that, "although it would seem difficult to induce people to speak normally while a tape recorder is operating, it has been found that when speakers are interviewed in groups, the social obligations among members frequently lead them to disregard the recording instrument and to behave as if they were unobserved [p. 25]."

In addition to the introduction of recording equipment, the interests and purposes of an investigator may lead him to focus his observations on interactions in particular settings, or of a particular sort, or between particular types of individuals. And it may be judged expedient to bring together individuals of the desired type for the purpose of interaction, as opposed to waiting for such individuals to interact on a purely spontaneous basis. Each of these intrusive acquiescences to research convenience carries a high risk of introducing additional and presently unspecifiable influences on the interactions in question. Such a risk may be acceptable to the investigator initiating research on a particular problem if he plans to do later studies that avoid that intrusion and probable influence. Thus, some kinds of intervention in the general context of the interaction seem a practical research necessity. Nevertheless, we believe that holding such intervention to a minimum is a highly desirable goal.

But there are some sorts of experimental interventions that can and should be entirely avoided. The interests of exploratory research in this area do not appear served by providing the interactants with (a) special stimuli, such as deceptive instructions; (b) unusual interaction conditions, such as obscuring the heads of the participants or having them interact through a screen; and–or (c) special and unusual tasks, such as pressing bars at prescribed moments. As suggested by Gumperz (1972), an interactant's own reactions, the actions of the partner, and the developing character of the interaction itself provide the necessary and sufficient research stimuli. And they are, in that sense, the creation of the interactants, not of the investigator.

Experimental Control of Confederates' Actions

The desirability of exploratory research on relatively natural interactions has definite implications for another, more specific research practice in this area: the attempt by the investigator to introduce "experimental controls" in the action of one or more confederates interacting with subjects. This sort of control is typically attempted in one of the following ways, or in some combination of them:

1.   The confederates are instructed to provide two or more different interactional "feeling tones" to different groups of subjects, such as "warm" or "friendly" with one group, and "cold" or "hostile" with another.

2.   The confederates are instructed to hold certain actions constant, most frequently gaze direction.

3.   The confederates are instructed to engage in certain actions either at some specified rate, such as a certain proportion of head nods, or in some specified pattern, such as generally gazing at the subject but occasionally gazing away in a "natural" manner. Once confederates are so instructed, and perhaps trained to a certain extent, the experiment is typically run under the assumption of the confederates' successful maintaining the desired ac-

tion controls, with little or no subsequent checking of the validity of the assumption.

Beyond the deception necessarily associated with the use of confederates, attempts to achieve experimental control over confederates' actions require two presuppositions by the investigator, neither of which may be justified: (a) knowledge of just which actions should be controlled, and the manner in which they should be controlled; and (b) the ability of confederates to achieve the specified control over these actions.

Studies in the area of face-to-face interaction, including those to be described in Parts II and III, suggest that (a) a wide range of actions, both gross and subtle, contribute to the process of interaction; (b) these actions are organized in part by relatively complex systems of rules and the like; and (c) the organization of interaction includes appropriate sequences of action involving both participants (in two-person interactions).

These considerations suggest three relatively independent problems with regard to attempts to control confederates' actions. In the first place, considering the broad range of gross and subtle actions potentially contributing to face-to-face interaction, it may be virtually impossible for a confederate to monitor the requisite actions satisfactorily, much less to maintain continuous conscious control over them. On this point speculation is not necessary. The literature contains a body of research on the effects of experimenter bias (e.g., Rosenthal, 1966), as well as studies providing evidence (a) on the subtlety of actions demonstrably contributing to this effect (Duncan & Rosenthal, 1968; Duncan, Rosenberg, & Finkelstein, 1969); and (b) on the inconstancy of these actions by experimenters from one subject to another. This research evidence should suggest to investigators that it is appropriate to maintain a healthy respect for the difficulties of holding actions "constant."

Second, if there are "rules" applying to appropriate conduct in interaction, then attempts to introduce experimental controls on this conduct, in the absence of thorough knowledge of the relevant rules, would seem to involve a high degree of risk. It is one thing to hold constant certain properties of an electrical current in one part of an electrical system, in order to observe the effects of certain experimental operations on the rest of the system. But what if holding constant an action (such as gaze direction) by a confederate is perceived as clearly inappropriate by other participants—the subjects—in the interaction? Further, and less importantly, it is in violation of the careful inductive development of early knowledge in an area that we have been advocating.

Finally, in Part III evidence is presented suggesting that the organization of interaction includes not merely certain appropriate actions, but also appropriate sequences of actions involving both participants (in two-person .

interactions). If this is the case, then an action by a confederate may be called for in response to an action by the subject. In this sense, an adequate control of the confederate's action may be obtainable only through control of the subject's action as well, a paradoxical situation. In view of these problems, we hold that the practice of attempted control over confederates' actions is undesirable and in any event unlikely to be carried out successfully, regardless of which type of control is attempted.

Despite these and any other possible arguments against the attempt to treat confederates' actions as susceptible to experimental control, it seems unlikely that psychologists will abandon a practice so deeply rooted in their research tradition. (It is of interest that the anthropological literature, for example, seems essentially free of this tradition, being focused much more on the description of naturally occurring cultural phenomena.) In the face of this practical consideration, we would strongly urge that, if control of confederates' actions be attempted, it should be standard practice to observe, analyze, and report the actions of the confederate as carefully as those of the subject.

We wish to make clear that we are calling into question the attempted control of confederates' actions, not the use of all possible experimental controls. It seems to be a much more straightforward matter to arrange to observe interaction of only certain types of individuals, in certain interaction situations, and so on. And it seems a simple, straightforward matter to control physical aspects of the setting in which the observed interactions occur, such as arrangement and type of furniture, decoration of the room, and lighting. Becker (1973), for example, uses a simple control of this type in his study of "jurisdictional" markers of space at library tables. On the other hand, the use of highly unnatural physical devices in the interactional setting, such as blinds or barriers between interactants, masks, and the like, are clearly significant deviations from the conditions of everyday interaction and therefore of doubtful value in its study, at least in this stage of the research.

Coverage of Actions

It has been typical for investigators to study face-to-face interaction by including one or two actions in each study, treating each action as interesting in its own right, or playing off one action variable (such as average duration of mutual gaze) against another (such as distance between participants). One result of this research strategy, as noted above, has been a useful accumulation of solid, replicable findings with respect to these actions. For example, we know that, as a group, females tend to look at their partners in interaction more than males do, and so on.

While productive in some ways, we view this single-variable research strategy as limiting, in that it is capable of shedding little light on the possibly rich interconnections between a wide variety of different actions. A given action by a participant in an interaction may be related to an indefinitely large number of other actions, not only by that participant, but also by the partner. It would seem that a major objective of research on face-to-face interaction at this point in its development should be the discovery of the extent and nature of these potential relationships.

As opposed to research based primarily on single actions, a variety of actions may be treated as potential elements in a system of as-yet-unknown extent and complexity. Although inclusion of a broader range of actions in a study undoubtedly increases its size and cost, our experience has suggested that the actual increase is not as great as might be expected, as compared with a single-variable study. And the potential payoff of broader coverage of actions is great, provided, of course, that the study is properly designed in other respects and the data are properly analyzed. In any event, the studies described in Parts II and III are multiple-variable studies, providing the reader with a more concrete sense of the promise and the pitfalls of such studies.

We are not arguing that every possible action should be included in every study, nor that the investigator should study all possible variables at the same time (a patently impossible task). The argument is that in exploratory studies the researcher should make an effort to cover as wide a variety of actions as is feasible. Such a strategy maximizes the possibility that new relationships between actions may be discovered. However, once such relationships are discovered and hypotheses are formed with respect to these relationships, subsequent cross-validational studies need only consider those actions involved in the hypotheses. This general approach is illustrated in Part III.

Conclusion: Research Strategy

The preceding arguments are based on the assumption that the phenomena to be understood are human actions as they occur in face-to-face interaction in natural settings. At this stage of our knowledge about such interaction, it seems wisest to use research designs that are as close as possible to natural conditions, designs that are maximally representative, rather than systematic (to cast the issue in terms introduced by Brunswik, 1947).

The risks associated with subjects' awareness of being observed and recorded seem unavoidable today. Other threats to internal validity (Webb, Campbell, Schwartz, & Sechrest, 1966), to the confidence with which valid conclusions can be drawn from the data of a given study, should be minimized. Problems of external validity, of generalizing from the research observations to interactions within the general cultural setting, can be handled by replications using different settings and different groups of subjects. While behavior in the laboratory that is reactive to experimentally induced conditions is undeniably real behavior, the understanding of such reactions in the laboratory seems at best an inefficient approach to the understanding of naturally occuring interactions.

We have distinguished between necessary and unnecessary interventions in the interactions being observed. We have argued that necessary interventions be minimized, and that most unnecessary interventions be avoided. Necessary interventions appear to be centered around the process of observing and recording the interaction. These interventions are viewed as potential (but possibly overestimated) threats to internal validity (Webb, Campbell, Schwartz, & Sechrest, 1966), to the confidence with which valid conclusions can be drawn from the data of a study. In this sense, they should be minimized.

Unnecessary interventions appear to center around various sorts of experimental "control" of the interaction situation. Some of these seem acceptable, either as central to the issue under investigation, or as simply a reasonable convenience. Acceptable controls seem confined to naturalistic use of proxemic aspects of the situation, such as arrangement of furniture, use of appropriate props (for example, stacks of books), and the like. Unacceptable controls have to do with attempted programming of confederates' actions. We hold such attempted controls as both inappropriate and impractical.

It would seem that, for the present, research on face-to-face interaction would be best served by exploratory studies based on careful, wide-ranging observation of behavior and subsequent analysis. In time it may be possible to develop, through sound exploratory findings, fruitful hypotheses for experimental studies. But even when these hypotheses become available, the difficulties of "controlling" the actions of confederates remain.

Part II

INDIVIDUAL DIFFERENCES
IN BRIEF CONVERSATIONS

Part I has set the stage for presentation of two contrasting types of empirical study: structural and external variable. It briefly described the general approach of each of these types.

In Parts II and III we report the empirical investigations. In Part II, a correlational analysis of natural acts is described. This study was large scale compared with prior ones. It included several dozen indices of actions for each of two interactions involving 88 subjects. It was correlational over subjects, that is, it observed the covariation of each action for a subject with his other actions and with the actions of the partner in each interaction. Its objective was also a search for correlations with scores from self-descriptive instruments.

The key feature of this study was the use of action indices for the total interaction. Each person was scored for several acts, the indices being for total frequency, total extent, or mean duration. Additional scores of these same kinds were obtained for each person when in the speaking role and when in the not-speaking role. Thus, the objective was to characterize, by these summary indices, the person's actions in each interaction. Each interaction provided a sample of actions, but the sample was clearly not random. It occurred within a specific context provided by the research conditions, the sex of the partner, and the serial position (first or second) of the interaction.

In Part III we examine some of the same actions from a different perspective. Separate acts are analyzed in terms of their relationships to preceding or concurrent acts of the person or his partner. One major section has as a reference the point in time at which one speaking turn ended and the next began. A study of acts in their interactional context, rather than a study of persons, is reported in Part III.

3

A Study of Individual Differences
in Five-Minute Interactions

Since research on interactive actions is laborious and expensive, this study of individual differences in five-minute interactions was designed to serve a number of purposes. First, we hoped to make it paradigmatic. We wanted to indicate what could be done in a comprehensive study involving an extensive list of actions and their interrelationships. Not only can investigators profit from our mistakes, from seeing the inadequacies of this study, but they also can profit, we trust, from our findings.

Second, we report descriptive statistics on our variables, data indicating their strengths and weaknesses. We recognize, of course, that such data cannot be considered as normative because our sample was not representative of any large, well-defined population. It will, however, be possible to compare our findings with those of subsequent investigations examining different populations. Where the findings agree, we will begin to accumulate evidence for the pervasiveness of relationships throughout the culture from which the various samples are drawn. Instances of disagreement will point out the necessity for determining the conditions with which the descriptive statistics vary.

Our objectives were partly substantive. A third purpose was to see whether a person's acts in brief interactions were correlated with his picture of himself. (A pilot study had yielded very promising findings.) We reasoned that how a person sees himself would be related to how he behaves, that is, if a person sees himself as friendly, he smiles and looks at a person to whom he is talking. From the other side, a person who smiles and gazes at others may come to see himself as friendly. Thus, this aspect of our objectives for this study can be illustrated by the hypothesis that persons who describe themselves as friendly will have a higher number of smiles and spend more time gazing at the partner during the total interaction than will persons who do not so describe themselves.

33

A fourth purpose was to explore sex differences, both in descriptive statistics for each variable and in patterns of association with other variables. Another, closely related purpose was to test the hypothesis that a person's actions vary with the sex of the partner. Does a woman act differently, in terms of the actions included in this study, with a man as compared to her actions with a woman? Does a man behave differently when with another man than he does when with a woman? The analyses pertinent to this empirical question have been reported in a separate paper (Beekman, 1973).

Finally, it was obvious that the mass of data collected for the preceding purposes made possible the pursuit of many other questions. What are the patterns of intercorrelations among action indices descriptive of a person's behavior for a five-minute interaction taken as a whole? What are the relationships between the indices for one person and those of the partner? Are there any relationships between such indices and the partner's reported description of himself? Do the person's postsession reports of his reactions to the total situation and to his partner relate to his indices?

It will be apparent that our objectives were broad. We were not attempting to test a series of specific hypotheses. We set out to explore an extensive domain in a broadly conceived study which we hoped would help develop this area of research. Even though our findings could not be definitive, we believed that they could provide leads for further research of a similar multivariate character and for more intensive investigations of subdomains within this topic. For example, in trying to interpret the findings for gazing, we found that it was necessary to rescore our protocols to obtain separate scores for rate of gazing while speaking and rate while not speaking. Fortunately, the coding had been recorded in such a way that these two new indices could be obtained without going back to watch the tapes again.

Unusual Features

Although those familiar with prior research on acts in interactions will recognize several distinctive features of this investigation, it seems desirable to make these explicit. It is somewhat unusual to include both male and female participants and to have each participant interact in two conversations. More unusual is the number of variables (as noted earlier). This study included several families of acts so that their covariations could be observed. We also scored a number of indices for each family of acts to throw light on the most fruitful ways to measure each kind of act: frequency or rate, total duration or proportion of time during which the act occurred, average duration. (These are examined in a later section.) Finally, we distinguished between acts while speaking and acts while not speaking. The same act can have different correlates for its occurrences in these two conditions.

The number of participants was 88, which is also unusually large. Taken all together, more than seven hours of videotapes were analyzed. Since several acts could occur simultaneously, the total of the timed durations was about 22 hours. Approximately 30,000 acts were observed and entered in the record, about 330 for each five-minute interaction, and hence about one act per second for the several hours of taping. It will be obvious that the fine-grained analysis of interactions produces an enormous amount of data.

Design

The design of a research study requires many decisions of the kind that Runkel and McGrath (1972) have explicated. We shall indicate both our decisions and our rationales leading to them.

We decided to have each person participate in two interactions, one with a person of the same sex and one with a person of the opposite sex. This choice made it possible to determine whether behavior varied with sex of the partner. We also wanted to obtain some evidence on the stability of our action indices over interactions. We recognized that two presumed effects were being opposed to each other: the more that a person's actions are affected by the sex of the partner, the less stability over interactions would be observed.

With two interactions for each participant, we were able to assess whether the acts changed as the participants became more familiar with the conditions and adapted to them. To avoid confounding possible order effects with effects associated with sex of partner, we used a balanced design. For half of the subjects, the first interactions were with persons of the same sex and the second were with persons of the other sex; for the other half, the first were with persons of the opposite sex and the second with persons of the same sex. It will be obvious that half of the participants were male and half were female.

Two pairs interacted simultaneously, in different rooms. Then one member of each pair went to the other room for the second interaction.

Subjects

The participants were graduate students in either the Law School or the School of Social Service Administration at the University of Chicago. It was decided to use graduate students because they would be older and more mature than undergraduates, the other readily accessible population, and hence more settled in their ways of behaving and in their views of themselves. Two schools were used so that it would be easier to pair subjects who were unacquainted with each other. Each interaction consisted of one student from each school. We anticipated correctly that the members of such pairs would not have met each other previously. These schools were chosen because they had sufficient numbers of each sex to permit us to obtain the samples we needed.

Names were randomly selected from student directories. Participants were recruited by a letter and a subsequent telephone call describing the research as "an exploratory study of human conversations." The refusal rate was very low. Of those who agreed to participate, most appeared at the appointed time. Hence there was little self-selection. Participants were paid $3.00 for the 90-minute session. All were Caucasian except two Black women, one from each school. The ages of the participants ranged from 22 to 36 years, with a mean of 25.

Procedure

Four students, two male and two female from each school, were brought to the research place at the same time. Prior to any contact with other subjects, each spent 50-60 minutes alone in a separate room taking paper-and-pencil tests: the Adjective Check List (Gough & Heilbrun, 1965), the Thorndike Dimensions of Temperament Scale (Thorndike, 1966), and the Inclusion scales from the FIRO–B Questionnaire (Schutz, 1958). The Adjective Check List was selected because a large number of scales have been developed from it. The Thorndike scale was chosen because we thought that temperament variables, indicating patterns and styles of discharging energy, would be particularly likely to be related to observed behaviors. The Inclusion scales report the desire to be with people and the behavior toward that end.

After completing these tests, the subjects paired off for the recorded interactions as described below. When these were completed, each returned to a separate room to fill out a questionnaire reporting his experiences in the interactions: his comfort before the camera and with the other person, his interest in that person and in the conversation, and his perception of the structure of the interaction (see Table 6.3.) We thought that knowing their perceptions and reactions, both to the general situation and to each interaction, might help us to understand the findings.

The Interactive Sessions and the Recording

The two participants were seated in adjacent chairs turned slightly toward each other, facing a videocamera. Each had a small lavaliere microphone suspended around his neck. A female experimenter gave the following instruction: "I would like the two of you to have a conversation for the next seven minutes or so. You can use the time to get acquainted with each other or to talk about anything else that interests you." She then left the room. When the first conversation was terminated, one member from each dyad exchanged places, the instructions were repeated, and a second conversation was recorded for each of the new pairings.

All interactions were recorded in two "lounges" or waiting rooms in the Law School, one room on each side of the moot courtroom. These rooms were designed as waiting rooms for lawyers and judges participating in trials.

The two rooms were identical in size, decoration, and furnishings, providing a highly convenient arrangement for conducting two simultaneous interactions. The rooms were approximately 36.6 x 70.1 dm in size. They were unusual in that they had five sides instead of four. The fifth side was a wall about 33.5 dm long across what would have been one of the corners of the room. The participants' chairs were placed in front of this wall, and the videocamera in each room was placed in the corner opposite this wall.

There was wall-to-wall carpeting in both rooms, and both carpets and walls were of a light gray color. The rooms were comfortably furnished with couches, arm chairs, end tables, and coffee tables. The lighting in the rooms consisted of an assortment of floor and table lamps. For the purposes of videotaping, this lighting was augmented by a pole lamp in each room. Each lamp had three, 200-Wa bulbs. These bulbs had large, frosted globes of about 15 cm diameter, thus eliminating glare and the need for shades. Also for purposes of taping, a large, dark-green felt cloth was placed on the wall behind the participants.

OBTAINING THE DATA AND INDICES

Coding

The last five minutes of each interaction was marked off for coding. The first two minutes were not included because they would be most likely to show any effects associated with reacting and adapting to the unfamiliar situation and to the stranger.

Each action was coded by a trained rater, rating only one action for each pass of the tape. The raters were encouraged to replay segments of the tape as many times as necessary to record each kind of action or to time it accurately with a stopwatch. Each speaking turn was counted and timed, each nodding of the head was counted, each period of gesturing was counted and timed, etc.

To establish the communicability of the rating system, the main rater trained other raters. For each variable, a second rater independently rated one person in each of 20 interactions. For infrequently occurring actions, this rater scored the entire five minutes. For more frequent actions, only the first 2.5 minutes were scored.

The agreement between the main rater and the second rater was determined by the coefficient of intraclass correlation (Haggard, 1958). This statistic assesses the degree of absolute correspondence between the two raters. The usual product-moment correlation assesses relative correspondence, correspondence of relative position in each rater's array of ratings for the variable; if it had been used here, it would have yielded slightly higher values than those for intraclass correlation. Of the several dozen reliability values, most were in the .90s, many in the high .90s. The three lowest were .76, .77, and .82 (See Table 4.1.)

The Generalizability of Indices for Behaviors in Interactions

Since an individual differences study is reported here, it is desirable to consider the psychometric aspects of the indices. Let us first examine the question of the reliability of our indices. One kind of reliability, or generalizability as the topic is becoming more appropriately labelled, is interobserver agreement. In the next chapter we show that generalizability over raters appears to be excellent for the indices characterizing each person in these interactions: the median correlation between raters was .95.

We also determined the stability of the indices, the correlations between the first and second interactions. These were varied but generally rather low. In terms of these indices, our subjects showed limited consistency across interactions. We are unable to determine the extent to which these consistencies were attenuated by adaptation to the total research setting and by the change in sex of the partner from the first to the second interaction. Note, however, that the objective situation remained constant and that the two interactions took place with only a very brief interval between them. We must conclude that, over all, our indices are not highly generalizable over partners of different sexes. Some exceptions are noted in the next chapter.

A third kind of generalizability in test theory is consistency among responses to stimuli or test items. This concept cannot be readily applied to interactive behavior since we cannot identify sets of specific stimuli which we believe a priori should be followed by responses reflecting a common underlying variable. It becomes apparent that the psychometric concept of internal consistency requires the assumption that the investigator can designate a set of responses which are presumed to be indicants of some attribute shared by all subjects. Such a psychometric view does not fit the orientation of this research. While we assumed that all acts of a given kind, such as all nods by all participants, could be considered a homogeneous class, we began with no conscious, intentional framework of substantive variables (such as acquiescence or approval).

The matter is complicated further by any temporal trends within each interaction as a person becomes more comfortable with the partner and as they begin to become acquainted with each other. Such effects would tend to lower not only the internal consistency of action indices, but also their correlations with other actions.

We can, however, consider the largest observed correlation between an index and any other variable which is experimentally independent of it as a rough lower-bound estimate of the consistency of the indexed action within a single interaction. More generally, an act which correlates with several other variables can be assumed to have sufficient dependability to merit further investigation. Only indices which have no substantial correlations with other measures can be suspected of possessing insufficient dependability.

It is, of course, possible that action indices obtained from longer samples of behavior, especially if these were taken from later periods in interactions, would be more generalizable. We doubt that the additional effort would be justified and would pay off at the present stage of knowledge about interactive actions. We are left with the fact that some of our obtained correlations may well be attenuated by the particular conditions used in this research.

The fundamental psychometric concept of validity applies to our behavioral indices only in a narrow, rather trivial way. Our indices had content validity in that other judges, we are confident, would agree that each index was clearly measuring the kind of act as we labelled it, that is, they would be willing to say that what we identified as nods were nods and that our gestures were gestures. The validity of our study as a whole is a separate matter which need not be considered at this point. We trust that our study had internal validity in the sense that our interpretations of the observed scores and the analyses are warranted. The external validity, the generalizability of our findings beyond these specific data, will be determined by the outcomes of similar studies conducted in the future.

THE ACT VARIABLES

Criteria for Selection

The extensive list of acts selected for coding and analysis was determined on the basis of a number of considerations and criteria. A central requirement was that the act be codable with very high agreement between coders. We are convinced that intersubjective consensus on each basic datum is essential for scientific work. To obtain such high agreement, we chose acts which could be readily identified. While each act was defined in a few words, we tried not to rely on verbal definitions: in principle, each of our acts can be identified by pointing to a few specific instances on a videotape projection and perhaps pointing to some negative examples, acts which were not included in the class. Thus the definitions, implicit or explicit, were usually in physical terms. We wanted to avoid any interpretation by the coder, such as would be required to code approving looks, disparaging gestures, or nervous laughs. We also avoided behaviors that would not have clear beginnings and ends, such as restlessness.

The acts selected as meeting these specifications tended to be of relatively brief duration, many of them lasting only about one second or a few seconds.

Also, each class was measured just in terms of presence or absence of a kind of action for manifested acts. We did not attempt to judge degree or intensity; for example, for this study, we had one class for smiles, with no distinctions between slight and broad smiles.

An exhaustive list of acts observable in interactions would include many which were rare or which applied to only a few subjects, such as twirling one's glasses, making a face. We tried to restrict our list to actions which would be shown by many subjects and which would usually occur several times during the five-minute period of observation. (Some of the acts that were included for other reasons turned out to be of little interest because they were uncommon.)

Another kind of criterion was presumed relevance. We wanted to include acts which could be perceived by the other person, and hence we were not interested in such variables as degree of tension of foot muscles within the shoe. Relevance also meant including variables which prior research, within this research program or in published literature, had indicated to be of importance. We did not, however, utilize all such variables in exactly the same form as they had been measured previously. For example, the coding of eye contact would have required the use of a videocamera directly behind each participant. To avoid such additional instrumentation and intrusiveness, we coded gazing in the general direction of the partner's head: it can be coded more economically, objectively, and accurately—it is difficult even for a participant to determine that the other person is looking directly at his eyes.

Essentially, we emphasized variables which could be identified as physical acts per se. With one or two possible exceptions, our acts were not defined in terms of meanings or possible symbolic values. They were seen as samples of activity, not as signs which had some a priori significance. We wanted the meaning or importance of each kind of act to emerge from its relationships and patterns without prejudgment on our part.

Finally, it is worth pointing out that, although these acts tend to pervade all interactions, and although some such behavior is almost constantly occurring, the participants in interactions are usually attending to the verbal communication and its contents. These actions tend to be out of the center of their attention. Although a person can readily perceive these acts in the other person, and although he can recall observing them if asked to describe the actions of the other, these actions are so familiar, so taken for granted, that they seem rarely to be matters of conscious concern. These acts are much like a number of other acts, such as how we walk, or how we wave to a friend—we simply do not think about them very much.

While this unobtrusive and commonplace quality undoubtedly has theoretical significance, it also has methodological value in that the observation and recording of these behaviors seem less likely to be affected by the presence of the videocamera and the subject's awareness that he is being studied than is the verbal content in his interactions. It seems probable that when a person is concerned with how he is presenting himself, he is more likely to attend to and to modify his words, his posture, and his facial expression than he is to modify his back-channel acts and many other actions in our list. While all of the acts we studied could be affected by strong situational influences, we feel that the mild situational effects in this study had little impact on our action scores. Subsequent investigations may, of course, indicate that our judgment was wrong on this point.

The Variables and Their Families

Our act variables are listed and defined below. They are organized informally by families of two kinds. One kind is a set of related behaviors, such as actions pertinent to speaking turns. The other kind is a set of indices for a particular act, such as smiling or gazing. Acts of the latter type were coded only for onset and offset, for beginning and end points. For many variables, separate indices were obtained for each of the two states, speaking and not speaking, in addition to the indices for the total five minutes that were coded for each interaction.

The kinds of indices used for one or more variables included the following:

1. *Time.* This index refers to the total of all durations of the act obtained by summing the recorded times (in seconds) for the several occurrences.

2. *Extent.* This label refers to the proportion of time that the person was engaged in the act. For example, within the time that he had the speaking turn, during what fraction of it did he smile?

3. *Mean Length.* This index was the average of the several durations of each timed action.

4. *Number.* This index was simply the frequency of occurrence of the act. The count was for the total five minutes unless the index was further qualified by indicating that only the speaking or not-speaking time is being considered.

5. *Rate.* When the count was divided by the time (in seconds) that the person spoke or listened, the resulting index indicated the rate of occurrence of the act.

In the listing of the variables, the full label is given for each: the kind of behavior, and whether speaking or not, if relevant. Where the latter is not indicated, the variable refers to the total interaction. While these labels are, we hope, specific and unambiguous, they are rather cumbersome. In the subsequent discussion, it will often be convenient to use a shortened form of the label, as in instances where there can be no confusion among the variables. For example, Nod Rate may be referred to simply as "Nods" since we used only one index for this act. Similarly, it will sometimes be smoother to refer to "Number of Turns" rather than to "Turn Number."

Turn-taking acts.   A central feature of any conversation between two people is the fact that they take turns talking: first one person speaks, then the other, then the first person speaks again. This aspect of the interaction was coded into the following variables:

   1.   *Turn Time.*   How much of the five minutes did the person spend talking? This index is simply the sum of the durations of all of his speaking turns. (It was almost exactly the complement of the partner's turn time.)

   2.   *Turn Number.*   Number of speaking turns. This index has essentially the same value for the two participants, since each of a person's turns occurs between two turns of the other.

   3.   *Turn Mean Length.*   Average duration of the person's talking turn. This index is computed by dividing Turn Time by Turn Number.

   Other turn-related acts.   Three other variables are related to the turn variables. Interruptions involve attempts to take the speaking turn. Filled Pauses maintain the turn. Social Questions shift the turn to the other.

   4.   *Interruption Rate.*   This variable was derived from the number of times that the person interrupted the other person. Since the opportunity of interrupting depended upon the amount of time the other was speaking, we took this index as a rate: number of interruptions divided by partner's speaking time. An interruption was recorded whenever the person who did not have the speaking turn started speaking while the speaker was still talking, that is, whenever the person and the speaker talked simultaneously. The person interrupting might or might not be successful in taking over the speaking turn.

   5.   *Filled Pause Rate.*   Filled pauses are part of the larger class of speech disturbances. A filled pause is any pause during which the speaker emits sounds such as "er," "ah," "um." Filled Pause Rate is the number of filled pauses divided by the person's speaking time.

   6.   *Social Question Number.*   This is a content variable, defined as the person asking the other a question about him which naturally invites him to take a turn to answer the question. Examples from our interactions are "How about you?" "What d'you . . . ?" and "You're from Michigan?." This content variable required more judgmental interpretation by the rater than any of the other variables.

   Back-channel behaviors.   While one person is speaking, the other can give feedback in several ways. Even though such feedback may be a spoken sentence, like "I agree," it was coded as occurring within the first speaker's turn, not as a separate turn.

   7.   *Nod Rate.*   Number of times a person nods his head while the other is speaking. Each nod or continuing sequence of several nods is counted as one entry. Since the opportunity for nodding is determined by partner's

speaking time, this variable was analyzed as rate of nodding: number of nods divided by the partner's speaking time.

8. *Short Vocal Back-Channel Rate.*   Number of one-word back channels while the partner is talking. Examples are "Yes" and "Mhm." Again, this was analyzed as a rate: the number of Short Back Channels was divided by the partner's speaking time.

9. *Long Vocal Back-Channel Rate.*   Number of back channels longer than one word, such as "That's right" and "I agree." This was also taken as a rate by dividing by the partner's speaking time.

10. *All Back-Channel Rate.*   This is a summarizing index. The total number of nods and verbal back channels (short and long) was divided by the partner's speaking time.

Smiles.   Smiling can occur while speaking and while not speaking. Smiles can be brief or long. Hence, several indices were used:

11. *Smile Number.*   Total number of smiles during the five minutes of observation.

12. *Smile Extent Speaking.*   Total time for smiling while speaking divided by speaking time.

13. *Smile Extent Not Speaking.*   Total time for smiling when not speaking divided by partner's speaking time.

14. *Smile Time.*   Total time for smiling, whether speaking or not.

Laughs.   In interactions like these, laughs tend to be brief and hence the duration of laughs was not scored.

15. *Laugh Rate Speaking.*   Number of laughs while speaking divided by speaking time.

16. *Laugh Rate Not Speaking.*   Number of laughs while not speaking divided by the partner's speaking time.

17. *Laugh Number.*   Total number of laughs during the five minutes.

Gazing behaviors.   Gazing here refers to looking toward the partner's face. It was rated largely from the movement and the orientation of the actor's head.

18. *Gaze Number.*   Total number of gazes at partner.

19. *Gaze Rate Speaking.*   Number of gazes while speaking divided by speaking time.

20. *Gaze Rate Not Speaking.*   Number of gazes while not speaking divided by the partner's speaking time.

These latter two variables were added to some of the last analyses we made, when inspection of the correlational patterns for gaze variables suggested the desirability of such variables. (Agreement, stability, and some other descriptive statistics were not computed for these added variables.)

21.   *Gaze Mean Length Speaking.*   To obtain the average length of each gaze while speaking, the total gaze time while speaking was divided by the number of gazes while speaking.

22.   *Gaze Mean Length Not Speaking.*   Average duration of gazes when not speaking.

23.   *Gaze Mean Length.*   Total duration of all gazes divided by total number of gazes.

24.   *Gaze Extent Speaking.*   Total time spent gazing while speaking divided by time speaking.

25.   *Gaze Extent Not Speaking.*   Total time spent gazing while not speaking was divided by the partner's speaking time.

26.   *Gaze Time.*   Total time spent gazing during the five minutes.

Gesturing.   All gesturing with the hands was included in this one class of acts. Each period of gesturing was counted and timed, even if the kind of gesture changed during the period. Since gesturing occurs almost exclusively while speaking (at least in the participants in this study), it was not coded for the rare instances while not speaking.

27.   *Gesture Time Speaking.*   Total time spent gesturing while speaking. This is the only raw time variable, that is, not adjusted for speaking time, which we included in our analyses.

28.   *Gesture Extent Speaking.*   This variable was obtained by dividing total gesture time by speaking time.

29.   *Gesture Mean Length Speaking.*   Total time spent gesturing (while speaking) divided by the number of gesturing periods.

30.   *Gesture Rate Speaking.*   The number of gesturing periods while speaking divided by the speaking time.

Self-adaptors.   This class includes all self-manipulation: touching clothing, accessories, the face, hair, or other parts of the body. Each period of time during which the person engaged in self-adaptors was treated as one instance, even if the specific kind of self-adaptor changed.

31.   *Self-Adaptor Number.*   Total number of periods of self-adaptors.

32.   *Self-Adaptor Extent Speaking.*   Time engaged in self-adaptors while speaking divided by the total speaking time.

33.   *Self-Adaptor Extent Not Speaking.*   Time engaged in self-adaptors while not speaking divided by the partner's speaking time.

34.   *Self-Adaptor Time.*   Total time engaged in self-adaptors.

35.   *Self-Adaptor Mean Length Speaking.*   The total time spent in self-adaptors while speaking divided by the number of periods of such self-adaptors, hence average duration.

36. *Self-Adaptor Mean Length Not Speaking.*   The total time spent in self-adaptors while not speaking divided by the number of periods of such self-adaptors.

37. *Self-Adaptor Mean Length.*   The total time engaged in self-adaptors, whether speaking or not, divided by the number of all periods of such acts.

Foot movements.   This family included all movements of either foot, except the movements necessarily involved in shifting the leg position. Very short twitches or jerks of the foot were arbitrarily taken as half a second in duration.

38. *Foot Time.*   Time spent moving a foot.

39. *Foot Number.*   Number of times the person moved a foot.

40. *Foot Mean Length.*   Time spent moving a foot divided by the number of such movements.

Postural shifts.   During a conversation, a person may shift the position of his legs or may shift his seat in the chair.

41. *Seat Rate Speaking.*   Number of times the person shifts his seat position while speaking divided by the time speaking.

42. *Seat Rate Not Speaking.*   Number of times the person shifts his seat position while not speaking divided by the partner's speaking time.

43. *Seat Number.*   Total number of times the person shifts his seat position, whether speaking or not.

44. *Leg Rate Speaking.*   Number of times the person shifts his leg position while speaking divided by the speaking time.

45. *Leg Rate Not Speaking.*   Number of times the person shifts his leg position while not speaking divided by the partner's speaking time.

46. *Leg Number.*   Total number of times the person shifts his leg position, whether speaking or not.

47. *Shift Rate Speaking.*   Since there is some similarity between seat position and shifting leg position, and since such shifts are infrequent, we included variables combining those two acts. Shift Rate Speaking indexed the number of seat or leg shifts while speaking divided by the speaking time.

48. *Shift Rate Not Speaking.*   Number of seat or leg shifts while not speaking divided by the partner's speaking time.

49. *Shift Number.*   Total of leg and seat shifts.

Discussion.   It is evident that our list of variables is not comprehensive. We did not code a speaking and a not-speaking index for each type of index in each family. We did not record average durations for all variables. We used some broad classes, such as gesturing, rather than coding each different kind of gesture. Also, as noted before, we coded presence or absence rather than degree, smile or not smile instead of no smile, slight smile, and broad smile. The a priori judgments made about what indices to include were based on earlier experience with some of these families and on what the literature suggested as to the potential fruitfulness of an index or family.

It is, however, obvious that we had to omit many possible indices for purely economic reasons if we wanted to include a number of act families. We had to weigh the desirability of trying out many possible indices against the costs in time, energy, and patience. As it was, it took many months of coding to score the seven hours of tapes on these indices.

We also excluded from some or all analyses certain indices which were available but seemed less promising than those we used. For example, raw times and frequencies were not included when it seemed wiser to use derived scores such as proportion of available time that the person engaged in self-adaptors while speaking.

An interaction is an ongoing process. We analyzed five-minute segments of behavior. Since the duration of the segment is arbitrary, the rate of occurrence of an act is more important than the actual number of times it was observed in the segment. And since the duration of speaking time and its complement, time not speaking, varied from interaction to interaction and was presumably determined in each instance both by the person and the partner, it seemed best to adjust for differences in opportunities to manifest an act by taking rate while speaking, or while not speaking.

For some variables, we used the total number of acts during the five minutes. Such indices are also rates. We did not take the trouble to divide each observed frequency by five minutes since this value was a constant and such a division would not alter the obtained correlations.

Similar considerations apply to the timed variables. While we do not feel it is necessary to discuss all the minor scoring decisions which have to be made, one must be noted because it explains something which could puzzle the reader. Some acts (such as smiles) continue from one speaking turn into the next turn, when the other speaks. In such instances, one smile would be counted as occurring while speaking and also while not speaking, but would be counted only once in the total of all smiles. Similarly, for smiling while speaking, the duration of such a smile was taken as ending at the end of the turn and the duration during the next turn was included in the value for not speaking. Hence, the average durations of smiles while speaking and while not speaking tend to be shorter than the average duration of all smiles. This arbitrary coding rule introduces a slight inaccuracy into some indices for the separate speaking and not-speaking turns. We do not believe that this degree of inaccuracy had any serious impact on the interpretations.

TRANSFORMED SCORES

Inspection of the distributions of scores for the 88 subjects on each index revealed that many were highly skewed in a positive direction. Thus, the mean number of smiles was eight, but one person had 22 smiles. It seemed unwise to use such raw scores in correlational analyses, since a few subjects with extremely high values could have undue effect upon the observed correlations. We also reasoned that the information contained in each additional smile became less as the number of smiles increased. For these reasons, we decided to transform the raw scores into log scores. Logarithms to the base 2 seemed appropriate because that base has been used in information theory, and we believe that an information-theoretic approach is appropriate in this domain. (We recognize that the choice of base for the logs makes no practical difference in our interpretations of our findings.)

Having decided to transform the raw data into log values, we faced the difficulty that many of our observed values were zero. While a common solution to that difficulty is to add one as a constant to all scores, our problem was complicated by the fact that some of our indices were proportions while others had maximum values in the hundreds. After trying a number of solutions, we found that adding the mean to all scores for an index produced reasonable distributions without large gaps between the lowest entry for the transformed zeroes and the next entry with any observed frequency of one or more. These distributions were typically much less skewed than the corresponding distributions of raw scores. Hence we adopted the rules that distributions with zero entries would be transformed by taking the log to the base 2 of the raw score plus the mean of the distribution, and that distributions without zero entries would be transformed simply into values for logs to the base 2.

In the presentation of descriptive statistics for each index, we will give the values of the mean, etc. for the raw scores. For some statistics, we will also give values for the transformed scores. Discussions of group differences on a given index will be in terms of raw scores. All the reported correlational analyses will be for the transformed scores. We did compute some correlational matrices for the raw scores and found the patterns were somewhat different from those for transformed scores.

We recognize that it is desirable to be able to replicate studies, using exactly the same measurement procedures as in the original study. Our study can, of course, be exactly replicated by others, using in the replication the means obtained in this study to obtain the transformed scores. In most instances, however, it seems likely that the pattern of results would be essentially the same in a replication study if the means for those data were used instead of our means.

4
Descriptive Statistics
and Group Differences

In this chapter we present some empirical findings of the individual-difference study. These will include univariate statistics providing information about the distributions on each variable and comparisons of male and female subjects.

As one way to reduce the enormous quantity of data to be assimilated, we decided initially to emphasize the second interaction. We were interested in natural activity, and so it seemed best to direct our attention first to that part of our protocols which was probably closest to such activity. It will be recalled that our ratings were based on the last five minutes of the seven-minute interactions; we omitted the first two minutes to give the subjects an opportunity to adapt to their partners. Similarly, we felt that the subjects would be more at ease in their second interactions, having become familiar with the setting, the camera, and the instruction to have a conversation with the partner (a stranger to them). Our expectation of greater subjective comfort in the second interaction was supported by the subjects' reports on the postinteractions questionnaire. Our decision to emphasize the second conversation turned out to be sound in at least one respect: the level of observed relationships between behaviors and self-descriptions tended to be higher for the later conversations. The basic table of descriptive statistics, Table 4.1, is for second interactions. The two interactions are compared in a later section of this chapter.

The descriptive statistics for distributions presented in this chapter are based on the raw data so that other researchers may more readily compare their findings with ours. Any reference to the transformed scores (based on the transformations discussed at the end of the preceding chapter) is explicitly identified.

CONSISTENCIES BETWEEN RATERS AND BETWEEN INTERACTIONS

Interrater Agreement

The agreement between the two judges in their ratings of 20 persons is given in the first column of data in Table 4.1. These intraclass correlations are generally very high: the median is .95. They have so little variation that they give us minimal information about difficulties in coding specific variables. Yet it would appear that, for example, timing the duration of self-adaptors is more difficult to do reliably than most of the other ratings. There is also some suggestion that totals for the entire five minutes are more reliably determined than corresponding values for speaking or not speaking. For some variables, such better agreement may stem from the larger frequencies or times involved. In other instances, the better agreement may be associated with indices which are simple counts or sums of durations, rather than ratios; the reliability of a ratio is vulnerable to disagreements on either the index in the numerator or that in the denominator, or both. Of course, the facts that these correlations are based on an N of only 20 and only 2.5 minutes for many of the variables mean that they are subject to some sampling fluctuation and we cannot have much confidence in observed differences between them.

Consistency across Interactions

The stability of these acts, their consistency between the first and the second interactions, is indicated in the second column of data in Table 4.1. The outstanding feature of these values is their large range, from .80 down to .00. The median is .40. It is quite apparent that most of these variables reflect characteristics of action which are affected by conditions and not highly stable. On the one hand, the general setting for the two interactions was exactly the same for half the subjects and was much the same for the other half who moved into the other room for the second interaction; also, the second interaction followed the first by only a few seconds. On the other hand, the partner was a different person in the second interaction, and was of a different sex than the first partner. The relatively low stabilities may also reflect differences in manner and direction of adapting to the research procedure. It is evident that highly reliable values for individual persons could be obtained for these variables only by averaging ratings over a series of several observations.

The variables with higher stabilities include Filled Pause Rate, Extent of Smiling While Speaking, and Total Smiling Time. Also high are the Number of Gazes and Total Time Spent Gazing, the Number of Laughs and the

TABLE 4.1
Descriptive Statistics for the Act Variables
Second Interactions [a]

	In-dices	Inter-rater agree-ment	Stabil-ity	Mean	Stan-dard devia-tion	Maxi-mum value	Mini-mim value	No. of zero entries	Skew-ness	Skew-ness trans-formed data
1. Turn Time	Sec.	1.00	.27	150.7	53.8	283	18	0	.00	−1.99
2. Turn No.	No.	.96	.20	13.2	4.9	27	3	0	.41	−.67
3. Turn Length	Sec.	.99	.27	13.5	9.8	71	2	0	3.04	.22
4. Inter-ruptions	Rate	.89	.14	.010	.014	.095	0	29	3.76	.85
5. Filled Pause	Rate	.97	.80	.051	.052	.291	0	6	2.44	1.00
6. Social Questions	No.	.98	.21	3.8	2.6	11	0	7	.72	.02
7. Nods	Rate	.95	.50	.058	.039	.165	0	8	.54	−.20
8. Short Back Channel	Rate	.90	.51	.044	.031	.157	0	4	1.01	.14
9. Long Back Channel	Rate	.88	.31	.013	.012	.061	0	23	1.28	.22
10. All Back Channel	Rate	.95	.55	.115	.064	.319	0	4	.68	−.14
11. Smile No.	No.	.92	.54	8.4	4.3	22	0	1	.35	−.27
12. Smile Extent Speaking	Extent	.87	.71	.13	.12	.60	0	4	1.52	.43
13. Smile Extent Not Speaking	Extent	.87	.45	.12	.10	.43	0	4	1.12	.39
14. Smile Time	Sec.	.94	.72	36.4	27.5	126	0	1	.95	.21
15. Laugh Rate Speaking	Rate	.86	.47	.017	.015	.066	0	19	1.03	.14
16. Laugh Rate Not Speaking	Rate	.92	.30	.010	.012	.053	0	34	1.33	.52

(continued)

TABLE 4.1 *(continued)*

	Indices	Inter-rater agreement	Stability	Mean	Standard deviation	Maximum value	Minimum value	No. of zero entries	Skewness	Skewness transformed data
17. Laugh No.	No.	.92	.52	3.9	3.1	14.0	0	15	.75	−.05
18. Gaze No.	No.	.92	.52	32.6	13.6	66	3	0	.04	−1.50
19. Gaze Rate Speaking	Rate	b	b	.206	.058	.444	.095	0	.98	b
20. Gaze Rate Not Speaking	Rate	b	b	.143	.065	.313	.034	0	.75	b
21. Gaze Mean Speaking	Sec.	.84	.45	3.2	1.2	7.7	1.4	0	1.43	.39
22. Gaze Mean Not Speaking	Sec.	.92	.21	7.8	4.9	29.6	1.9	0	1.99	.25
23. Gaze Mean	Sec.	.97	.25	10.2	12.8	99.3	2.2	0	4.63	1.14
24. Gaze Extent Speaking	Extent	.93	.57	.61	.18	1.00	.25	0	.54	−.29
25. Gaze Extent Not Speaking	Extent	.77	.40	.87	.15	1.00	.31	0	−1.47	−2.42
26. Gaze Time	Sec.	.94	.53	217.3	46.2	299	111	0	−.35	−1.16
27. Gesture Time	Sec.	.98	.31	46.3	30.0	147	2	0	.96	−1.01
28. Gesture Extent	Extent	.98	.42	.31	.17	.75	.04	0	.30	−.90
29. Gesture Mean	Sec.	.99	.38	2.5	1.3	7.1	.8	0	1.29	.23
30. Gesture Rate	Rate	.99	.49	.128	.061	.340	.024	0	.86	−.68
31. Self-Adaptor No.	No.	.88	.40	14.0	5.9	30	3	0	.39	−.77
32. Self-Adaptor Extent Speaking	Extent	.97	.51	.35	.26	1.00	.01	0	.76	.24

(continued)

TABLE 4.1 *(continued)*

	In-dices	Inter-rater agree-ment	Stabil-ity	Mean	Stan-dard devia-tion	Maxi-mum value	Mini-mum value	No. of zero entries	Skew-ness	Skew-ness trans-formed data
33. Self-Adaptor Extent Not Speaking	Extent	.98	.48	.38	.26	1.00	0	1	.56	- .01
34. Self-Adaptor Time	Sec.	.99	.57	108.9	72.1	293	4	0	.66	- .86
35. Self-Adaptor Mean Speaking	Sec.	.82	.20	4.1	2.5	17.5	1.0	0	2.41	1.06
36. Self-Adaptor Mean Not Speaking	Sec.	.76	.30	5.8	3.8	20.7	0	1	1.64	.70
37. Self-Adaptor Mean	Sec.	.86	.26	8.5	7.6	41.9	1.3	0	2.40	.46
38. Foot Time	Sec.	.99	.63	65.4	58.1	268	0	1	1.70	.75
39. Foot No.	No.	.98	.58	23.0	13.3	71	0	1	1.01	.14
40. Foot Mean	Sec.	.93	.39	3.0	3.2	24.3	0	1	4.33	1.97
41. Seat Rate Speaking	Rate	1.00	.40	.003	.005	.019	0	63	1.92	1.26
42. Seat Rate Not Speaking	Rate	1.00	.00	.001	.003	.020	0	76	3.54	2.38
43. Seat No.	No.	1.00	.31	.5	.9	4	0	56	2.06	1.00
44. Leg Rate Speaking	Rate	.87	.13	.005	.007	.036	0	48	1.77	.72
45. Leg Rate Not Speaking	Rate	.99	.13	.002	.004	.013	0	66	1.54	1.30
46. Leg No.	No.	.97	.23	1.0	1.2	4	0	41	1.08	.47

(continued)

TABLE 4.1 *(continued)*

	Indices	Inter-rater agreement	Stability	Mean	Standard deviation	Maximum value	Minimum value	No. of zero entries	Skewness	Skewness transformed data
47. Shift Rate Speaking	Rate	.97	.24	.007	.008	.036	0	63	1.08	.38
48. Shift Rate Not Speaking	Rate	.99	.11	.003	.005	.026	0	76	2.06	1.12
49. Shift No.	No.	.99	.30	1.5	1.6	7	0	56	1.29	.41

[a] All statistics are for raw data, except the last column.

[b] Not computed for these added variables.

Back-Channel Rates. Presumably less oriented toward the social and interactive aspects of the situation are Self-Adaptor Time and Foot Time. Many of the variables with low stabilities have low rates of occurrence.

All of the turn variables have low stabilities. The Number of Turns and, to a lesser degree, the Length of Turns are of course determined to a considerable extent by the partner. It is worth noting that many of the extent and rate variables, which are adjusted for time speaking or not speaking, are more stable than the Turn Length variable itself. (The stability of the complement of Turn Length, Mean Length of Not Speaking Turns, is of course identical with that of Turn Length.) Actions while not speaking tend to have lower stabilities than actions while speaking, presumably because actions while not speaking are more affected by the particular partner, or more exactly by the person's reactions to the actions of the partner.

The indices for total times and extents, that is, for proportion of available time during which a kind of behavior was manifested, are more stable than the indices for rates or mean lengths. This rather marked difference in stabilities is somewhat surprising because total time spent in an action (the numerator in calculating an extent) is the product of rate times mean length. This difference in stabilities may, however, be a function of the particular acts involved: we did not determine all three kinds of indices for all families of these acts.

Consistency of Group Statistics

In spite of the varying stabilities of individual actions across the two interactions and in spite of other differences between the interactions that will be noted later, the group statistics were highly similar for the two times. Most of the differences in means were a few percentage points although a few reached 10%. There were more Seat and Leg Shifts in the first interaction. There were also more Self-Adaptors, although the Extents of Self-Adaptors were lower. The second interactions had slightly more Turns, slightly higher Rates for Nods and All Back Channel, a few more Laughs, longer Extent of Smiling When Not Speaking, and longer Mean Gazes. Thus, the first interaction had a little more of gross movements, the second tended to have a little more of some actions oriented toward the other. This generalization is offered quite tentatively since the differences observed above were not evaluated statistically. (The statistical interactions between order of interaction and sex were, however, evaluated and will be examined shortly in the section on Sex Differences.) The standard deviations and ranges were, for the most part, rather comparable for the two interactions.

Thus, it appears that the two samples of actions for this group of persons obtained from successive conversations were much the same: there was no strong shift in the distributions in spite of the changes in the act indices for the individual persons.

Rather than presenting the distribution for each variable graphically, we are giving a number of indices for each. In addition to the mean and the standard deviation, we are indicating the range by giving the largest and the smallest values for our 88 subjects. Since some of the distributions are J shaped, with large frequencies of no occurrence of the behavior, we have indicated the number of zero entries.

Our several variables ranged from the universal to the rare. Every participant talked, gestured, and gazed at the partner. Most of them smiled, engaged in self-adaptors, provided back-channel feedback, and moved their feet at least once during the five minutes. At the other extreme, many did not shift their seat position or their leg position and those who did shift, shifted rarely.

Like most acts occurring in spontaneous activity, the acts we studied tended to occur from time to time, rather than to persist continuously: for example, the proportions of time spent smiling or laughing were well below half. In such instances, the distributions can be expected to be positively skewed, that is, to have the longer tail extending toward higher values. A somewhat similar tendency can be observed for rate variables, where the minimum is fixed at zero but the maximum is limited only by the physical capacity of the organism. Such variables also tend to be positively skewed. In fact, it will be noted that distributions of raw scores for all our variables were positively skewed with just two exceptions: Gaze Extent When Not Speaking and Total Gaze Time. The first had a mean proportion of .87, thus leaving plenty of opportunity for gazing for smaller proportions of the time, but little opportunity for higher values. Hence, the distribution is skewed negatively. Similarly, the related variable of Total Gaze Time has a mean of 217 seconds out of a possible 300, and it too has a negative skew.

SEX DIFFERENCES

A major objective of this research was the study of sex differences in the various actions investigated. In this section, some findings on such differences will be reported for the separate act variables, emphasizing differences in means. Some differences, those for the patterns of correlations among the behaviors of each participant and with the behaviors of the partner, will be presented in the next chapter. The treatment here will be fairly brief, since a fuller account exists (Beekman, 1973).

Differences in means.   A multivariate analysis of variance was run for the total set of behavioral variables. This statistical technique, a generalization of the more familiar univariate analysis of variance which analyzes only one dependent variable, analyzes more than one dependent variable at the same time. For each main effect and each interaction, it provides a multivariate F pertaining to the total set of dependent variables. When that F is statistically significant, appropriate univariate analyses can be carried out on each dependent variable. The design included factors for sex of the subject, sex of partner, the subject's professional school, and the order with which the subject was paired with male and female partners. The procedure took into account the repeated measures (cf. Bock, 1975).

Taking all the dependent variables together, the multivariate F for sex of subject was significant ($p < .02$) and 13 of the variables had a significant univariate F for this main effect. No other main effect, including sex of partner, was significant. (In this section, "interaction" is the statistical term, not the conversation between two participants.)

The variables with significant differences in means for the two sexes are shown in Table 4.2. The Mean Length of the males' speaking Turns was distinctly longer and their Rate of Filled Pauses was more than twice that for the females: males held the floor longer. Inspection of the means by sex of partner reveals that the length of speaking turns for males interacting with males was distinctly longer than the lengths for the other three sex by sex of partner combinations. Consistent with this interaction is the significant interaction between sex and sex of partner for Number of speaking Turns, with the mean for the male–male pairings being distinctly below the very similar means for the three other pairings. Whatever the source of the males' tendency to hold the floor, it had a stronger effect when they were talking with other males.

The females smiled longer and more often than the males, engaging in smiling for a larger proportion of their nonspeaking time. These sex differences were less in the second conversation than in the first, as Table 4.3 shows. (The significant interactions in this table are actually interactions of sex by sex of partner by order of pairing, this combination reducing to sex by

TABLE 4.2

Significant Sex Differences in Acts

| | Means | | $p <$ |
	Female	Male	
Turn Mean Length	11.2	14.7	.02
Filled Pause Rate	.029	.075	.001
Smile No.	9.6	7.3	.006
Smile Extent Not Speaking	.14	.09	.002
Smile Time	42.2	28.4	.02
Laugh No.	4.74	2.80	.001
Laugh Rate Speaking	.021	.012	.001
Laugh Rate Not Speaking	.012	.008	.03
Gaze Extent Speaking	.66	.56	.003
Gaze Extent Not Speaking	.90	.84	.02
Gaze Time	228.9	207.2	.007
Leg No.	.94	1.52	.03
Seat No.	.46	.83	.02

order of interaction: for example, if the subject was paired first with a male, and the partner was male for a conversation, then that conversation had to be the first one for that subject. The males greatly increased their total Smiling Time, especially when speaking, in the second conversation, while the females reduced their smiling only slightly. Perhaps the increase for the males reflects an increase in their ease in the situation.

The picture is similar for laughing: the females laughed more often, their rates being distinctly higher both when speaking and when not speaking. Only for Laugh Rate When Not Speaking, however, did the males show the marked increase from first to second conversations, as they did for the smiling variables.

The females spent more time gazing at their partner than did the males, the trend holding for both speaking roles. On the other hand, the males shifted their seat position more than the females did. Table 4.3 shows that this greater frequency was significantly related to the order of the conversations: the value is much larger for the first conversation. The pattern of reduced sex differences in the second conversation, due primarily to a change in the male mean, is very similar to that for smiling and laughing although the differences and the change are in the opposite direction. Males also shifted their leg position much more often than did the females. While the overall sex differences were not significant for any foot variable, Table 4.3 shows two sig-

TABLE 4.3
Significant Sex by Order Interactions for Acts

	Conversation No.	Means		$p<$
		Female	Male	
Smile Extent Speaking	1	.155	.094	.003
	2	.132	.125	
Smile Time	1	43.9	24.3	.02
	2	40.4	32.4	
Laugh Rate Not Speaking	1	.013	.006	.05
	2	.011	.010	
Foot Time	1	57.1	75.8	.003
	2	72.1	58.6	
Foot Mean Length	1	2.4	2.8	.01
	2	3.6	2.4	
Seat No.	1	.43	1.07	.03
	2	.48	.59	

nificant interactions between sex and order. For both total time spent moving a foot and average length of such movements, the two sexes practically exchange positions from first to second conversations, the males reducing and the females increasing the average duration of their foot movements.

The significant sex by order of conversation effects raise interesting questions about the nature of the sex differences in these acts. If we accept the view that our subjects were somewhat less at ease in the first conversation than in the second, and the subjects' reports after the session support that view, then some of the sex differences are associated with ways of manifesting discomfort. Our males showed it more by bodily movements, our females by smiling and laughing. It is possible that, for other variables, the course of adaptation is slower; perhaps, when subjects are completely at ease in a very familiar situation, some of the other sex differences would disappear.

(We should remind the reader that, among fifty independent statistical tests, one would expect by chance that two or three would yield results at the .05 level or better. Also, some of the variables discussed above are related to each other, and hence they are more likely to be found together in any set of significant results. We therefore would not be surprised if some of these findings were not replicated in future studies.)

Differences in amount of variation.   Differences in standard deviations, though not as readily interpreted as differences in means, can sometimes be informative. For our variables, the striking finding is that the males showed more variation on about three-quarters of the variables. While many of the differences were small, those for Turn Mean Length and for Rate of Filled Pauses were larger; as noted earlier, the males had larger means for these variables. The standard deviations for males were also much larger for Rate of All Back Channels and for Extent of Gaze While Not Speaking.

More interesting are the differences associated with sex of partner. The standard deviation of Nod Rates was significantly smaller for both females and males in cross-sex pairings than for same sex pairings. Length of all Self-Adaptors had larger standard deviations for both sexes in cross-sex pairs. On the other hand, the standard deviations for both sexes were larger when with male partners for three variables: Lengths of Gaze When Not Speaking and overall, and Seat Shifts When Not Speaking. Leg Shifts While Speaking had more variation for both sexes when with female partners.

For each sex, the variations were significantly different as a function of sex of partner for about one-third of the variables. For females, the larger variation was very generally associated with male partners. Sex of partner did not affect the relative variations consistently in the data for males.

How can such differences in variation be interpreted? Presumably larger variation among individuals' scores are observed when the scores are affected more by the particular individuals themselves and by the particular psychological interactions they have with their partner than they are by the situational influences common to all participants.

Consistency across the two conversations. In general, the two sexes showed, on each variable, about the same levels of consistency between scores for the first and second conversations. There was, however, some trend for the males to have higher values: this was true for 30 of the 47 variables. Only a few of the differences were marked: the males were distinctly more consistent for Short Back Channel and All Back Channel Rates and for Filled Pause Rate; the females were more consistent on Gaze Extent While Speaking. Other differences were between lower levels of consistency. While the more consistent sex also had a significantly higher mean than the other sex for Filled Pause Rate and Gaze Extent While Speaking, there was no general trend for higher consistency to be associated with higher means, for the other variables.

Sex differences and the particular nature of our subject samples. The reader should recall that our subject groups were clearly not random samples from the general population. It has been observed that sex differences in interests tend to be less with higher educational levels. We do not know, of course, whether act differences are similarly reduced. Not only were our subjects in professional schools, but also half of them were in training for vocations not ordinarily associated with their sex: females have been more common among social workers and lawyers have been predominantly males. It is possible that act differences associated with those following traditional vocational roles for their sex would be minimized in our samples. Hence, we would expect more sex differences in random samples of the population than we have observed for our subjects.

DIFFERENCES BETWEEN THE TWO PROFESSIONAL SCHOOLS

As noted earlier, the multivariate analysis of variance did not yield a significant F for the main effect of school. No second-order interaction involving school was significant. Inspection of the means by schools reveals some differences, including a few which would be significant if taken by themselves. The number of these, however, was well within the limits of what would be expected on the basis of chance.

SAMPLE DIFFERENCES

Our selection of subjects and experimental design gave us four groups, each with 22 subjects, each of the two male and the two female groups being stratified by professional school. Each group had its first and its second interaction. The means, variances, and maximum values for each variable were visually compared across the eight groups. Beyond the sex differences discussed above, there was little variation in these descriptive statistics which seemed to exceed that which one would expect from random sampling. In particular, there were no very marked trends for a particular group of subjects to be different from the second group for the same sex. The only exception was the group of males whose first interaction was with other males: in both of their interactions, their Filled Pause Rate was relatively high and their Gesture Time indices were low; they also smiled less in their first interactions.

The variances tended to be related to the means, as often occurs for scores with an absolute zero point. Hence, the differences in variations were not great. For a given pair of variables, their correlation will tend to be higher when variances are higher. So it is undoubtedly true that some of the relatively larger correlations examined in the next chapter are associated with relatively larger variances. This relationship seems of little significance, however, in these data since the variation in variances appeared to be rather restricted.

5
Relationships Between the Acts

Having examined descriptive statistics for each variable separately, we turn in this chapter to relationships between our act variables. Before looking at the empirical findings, however, we have to consider possible ways in which two variables may be related for reasons which are not psychological.

INTERDEPENDENCIES BETWEEN VARIABLES

Dependencies associated with coding procedures. Two variables may be correlated because the coding makes them mutually exclusive. For example, our coding procedure required that almost all of the interaction time be divided between speaking turns for the two participants; either one person or the other was coded as having the speaking turn. (Periods of silence were few and brief. Unsuccessful interruptions were not coded as turns). Since total analyzed time was a constant for all interactions, the negative correlation between a person's speaking time and his partner's speaking time had to be close to -1.00, except for minor errors in timing and in rounding off. Hence the two speaking times did not have to be included as separate variables.

Another coding dependency was present for mutually exclusive acts: by definition, a person who was laughing could not be smiling. In principle, there could therefore be a strong negative relationship between smiling and laughing. In our observations, however, for only a small proportion of the time was a person either smiling or laughing, so that the two could be positively correlated, and in fact were. Similarly, it would be difficult for a person to engage in gesturing and self-adaptors simultaneously: he would have to use one hand for each. Once again, however, the extents of these two actions were sufficiently limited so that only in extreme cases would the duration of one of these actions necessarily limit the duration of the other.

Computational dependencies. One kind of computational dependency occurs when two variables have mathematically related numerators: for example, values for the total interaction will be related to values for speaking turns and for nonspeaking turns where the sum of the numerators for the two states is the numerator for the value for the total interaction. Since total Laugh Number was the sum of the numerators for Laugh Rates While Speaking and While Not Speaking, Laugh Number could be expected to correlate with those rate variables. Similarly, total Smiling Time was composed of the smile times while speaking and while not speaking, these being the numerators for the two Smile Extent variables for those roles, and hence we would expect each extent variable to be correlated with the total Smile Time. Hence the correlation between many total scores and the two role scores contributing to them is a spurious, part–whole correlation. The only utility for such correlations lies in the comparison of the correlational values for the two states, to see which contributed more to the variance for the total score.

Ratios. The majority of our indices were ratios, with one observed value being divided by another. Of these, 15 were rates, where counts were divided by time in a state; seven were extents, in which the time the person was engaged in an action was divided by time in a state. (Each of the nine indices of mean length had a denominator unique to it, so these pose no problem of interdependency.) Mathematically, when two ratio indices are computed with the same variable in the denominator, there is an expectation that they will be related. Thus, one might expect, in principle, that indices for rates during speaking turns would be artifactually correlated with each other. We found no evidence for such misleading effects. The explanation was given by inspection of the relationships between these rate and proportion (extent) variables and Turn Time, the time spent with the speaking turn. While mathematically one would expect a negative relationship between a ratio and its denominator, we observed no tendency for such values. Moreover, the values were often different for the two sexes. We have therefore concluded that our rate and proportion variables are appropriate statistical indices and can be interpreted psychologically without concern about possible mathematical artifacts.

CORRELATIONAL ANALYSES OF THE ACTS

We began our correlational analyses by computing all the intercorrelations of the actions for the total group of 88 men and women. While this matrix yielded many interesting findings, we became concerned about generalizing over men and women together. We then computed separate matrices for the men and for the women. These had enough differences to convince us that the data should be examined by sex of the participant. Then we also became concerned about the possibility that the sex of the partner might affect the correlational patterns, and so we ran four matrices, one for each sex by each sex of partner. These results seemed more meaningful than the preceding analyses. By this point, however, it also became obvious that much greater caution was required in making any interpretations: the original N of 88 had been reduced to 44 for the analyses by sex and was halved again, to an N of 22, for the analyses by sex of subject and sex of partner.

We had originally intended to concentrate on the relationships observed in the second interactions, where the participants were more at home in the situation. We decided, however, that adapting to the situation had little effect upon these relationships. More important was the criterion of replication as a primary basis for our interpretations. Hence, we considered both interactions in determining the relationships to be reported here.

For each matrix of intercorrelations among the participants' actions, we also obtained a corresponding matrix for the correlations of each act with all of the partner's acts in that interaction. Thus, we had the enormous task of interpreting sixteen matrices with about four dozen variables intercorrelated in each one: four matrices provided data on females interacting with females (two for first interactions and two for second) and four were for male pairings; eight matrices dealt with interactions between males and females, four with each sex as the participant under consideration. Note that the same experimental sessions provided the data for males interacting with females and also the data for females interacting with males.

Taking one set of interactions, first or second, by itself, the four separate groups formed by classifying the sex of the two participants are independent groups, except for the complementary nature of the data for males when paired with females and the data for females when paired with males. Each such group unfortunately has just 22 subjects. For that size of sample, a product-moment correlation of .42 or larger is significant at the .05 level, and one of .36 is at the .10 level. Since this was an exploratory study, we began by examining all correlations of .36 or larger. The findings were so complex and were so often confined to a pattern for just one group that we decided to report only findings replicated in several groups. We settled on the requirement that, for one block of the data such as the correlations with other acts of the same person, four of the eight correlations had to be .30 or higher, and of course all four had to have the same sign.

The rationale was based upon probabilities of independent events. For a sample of size 22, a correlation of +.30 or higher has a probability of .11 of occurring in random data, that is, by chance, based on the conservative estimates utilizing Fisher's z transformation. Take such a correlation as a hit. Among a set of eight events, the probability of finding four or more hits is very small, only .0071. The probability of finding four or more negative correlations of -.30 or larger is identical. Hence the combined probability of four or more correlations as large as .30, all positive or all negative, is .0142.

The above reasoning considers the correlation for each of the eight samples as independent of the value for each of the other seven samples. Such an assumption can be questioned. There were four subgroups, each with 22 subjects, and each providing two of the eight correlations, one for its first interactions and one for its second, with partners of different sexes in the two sessions. Suppose the correlations for a sample turned out to be identical in its first and second interactions (being determined entirely by the particular subjects regardless of their partners). We would then have four samples to consider, and four independent correlations. In a set of four events, the probability of finding two or more hits is .062 for positive correlations of .30 or more, and is .062 for negative correlations, or .124 for finding either the positive set or the negative one.

In view of the modest consistencies of the act variables from first interactions to second, we did not expect much consistency between the correlations for the same sample in its two interactions with partners of different sexes. Our expectation was supported: only occasionally did the same correlational pattern appear for a particular group in both its interactions. Hence, the actual situation is between the two extreme cases considered above: among a set of eight observations, the members of each of the four pairs were not completely independent and yet were clearly not highly dependent on each other. We therefore concluded that our criterion of four or more correlations being at least .30 and in the same direction was a reasonable one, corresponding very approximately to the familiar and lenient .05 level of significance.

PLAN FOR PRESENTATIONS

In the main body of this chapter, each coded variable will be discussed in turn, within the context of its act family. To bring together all the material on the variable which may be relevant to its pattern of correlations, the exposition will start with data on the stability across interactions, the interobserver agreement, and the means and variances. Most of this information has already been presented in Table 4.1. References to sex differences are, however, based on data for both interactions together because such analyses were not made for each interaction separately. Similarly, references to means and variances for the pairings by sex and sex of partner are for all interactions. Unless otherwise indicated, these data are for the raw scores, before the transformations. The concluding portion of the chapter considers clusters and patterns involving sets of variables, from the same or different act families.

THE TURN-RELATED ACTIONS

We will begin by examining the findings for the several actions related to turns. These include the three turn variables, Turn Time, Turn Number, and Turn Mean Length. Rate of Interruptions is included because it is turn-taking. Rate of Filled Pauses is grouped with the others because it has sometimes been construed as related to holding the speaking turn. The last of these variables, Social Questions, refers to acts which openly offer the speaking turn to the other.

The turn variables.   These variables were easy to code and had high interobserver agreements (above .95). They are basic variables for the whole study. The most obvious feature of the interaction, obvious to the two participants and to observers, is that the two people are talking to each other, with only one talking at any given moment. They are also basic because many other variables were scored separately for the time the person was in the speaking state and the time he was not in the speaking state. These times were used to compute extent or proportion of time that the person engaged in a particular action.

Although basic to the interaction, the turn variables are also more dependent upon the other person than are any of our other variables. Social convention appears to insist that only one person talk at a time, so that if the other person is talking, a person does not usually talk. Another social convention, for many kinds of conversations, is that someone must be talking. Once the two people have implicitly agreed to have such a conversation, there appears to be strong pressure against having periods of silence. Hence, when the partner stops talking, and especially when the partner relinquishes the speaking turn by inviting a person to talk (for example, by asking a question), a person more or less has to begin talking.

These considerations help to account for the low stabilities of the turn variables, that is, the low correlations between the first and second interactions. The stabilities were lower than for many of our other variables. We feel that adaptation to the research situation played only a minor role in generating these low values. The amount of talking a person does and the number of speaking turns seem to be affected by the behavior of the partner and by the social interaction between the two people. It would appear that a person might be engaged in a rapid interchange in one conversation and, in the other conversation, in a pattern where one person encourages the partner to talk a great deal.

The pattern among the three turn variables.   Turn Time can be viewed as the product of Turn Number and Mean Length (although it was not computed that way): hence, the same total Turn Time can be obtained from a few long turns or from many short turns. Turn Time had high correlations with Mean Length in every analysis. It also had high negative correlations with the partner's Mean Length. These latter are, of course, the same data from the other side: each person's Turn Time was the complement of the partner's Turn Time and would have had a perfect correlation with it, were it not for small effects introduced by the log transformations and any unreliability in the coding.

Turn Length, in addition to that high relationship with Turn Time, was negatively related to Turn Number. This relationship was lowest in magnitude for females talking with males: only in these interactions were Turn Number and Turn Time related (the correlations being positive). Since Turn Number was essentially identical for the partner, Turn Length also had negative relationships with partner's Turn Number.

Turn time. Since essentially all of the five minutes of coded interaction were identified as the Turn of one participant or the other, the mean Turn Time over all participants was 2.5 min. or 150 sec. For this symmetrical distribution of raw times, the large standard deviation (54 sec.) indicates the great variation in individual Turn Times. In the second interactions, the range was from 18 sec. (6% of the total time) to 283 sec. (94%).

To give the reader an opportunity to examine some of the actual correlations between acts, Table 5.1 presents the correlations for Turn Time as observed in each of the eight interactions (the first and second interactions for the four sex pairings). We have included as correlates all variables analyzed individually in this chapter.

The total time that a person talked was related to several other behavioral indices. Turn Time had large positive correlations with Rate of Gazes While Not Speaking, and substantial negative relationships with Gaze Rate While Speaking. Its relationships with gaze times were largely negative. Total Gaze Time had a negative relationship for each sex, this relationship stemming almost entirely from a negative relationship for Extent of Gazing While Speaking, especially for female subjects. Similarly, Turn Time had a negative relationship with Mean Length of Gaze over all and while Not Speaking. Thus, we found that persons who talked a lot did not gaze often or long at their partners when they themselves were speaking; when not speaking, they had many, but short, gazes. These relationships held for each combination of sex of person and sex of partner (of the many values, one value in one interaction was an exception).

Those who talked more had more time to spend gesturing, and Turn Time was related to total Gesture Time, especially for males. Those who talked more did not, however, spend a larger proportion of that time in gesturing. Turn Time had a low relationship to Rate of Interruptions. It also had a positive relationship to Filled Pause Rate and a negative one with Social Questions.

Since transformed Turn Time correlated around -.90 with transformed Turn Time for partner, we would expect that Turn Time would relate to

TABLE 5.1

Correlation of Turn Time with Own Actions[a]

	Females with females		Females with males		Males with females		Males with males	
Order of Interaction	1st	2nd	1st	2nd	1st	2nd	1st	2nd
Turn Number	11	-12	54	54	-23	-38	14	02
Turn Length	75	68	62	74	75	81	58	88
Interruption Rate	33	-03	02	24	42	55	18	30
Filled Pause Rate	40	14	19	42	20	40	02	40
Social Questions	-33	-16	-02	-16	-30	-51	-29	-47
Nod Rate	-35	-03	-21	-40	-05	-19	07	-36
Short Back Channel	-25	-22	05	41	-03	00	01	-22
Long Back Channel	-06	03	02	34	16	-44	09	-21
All Back Channel	-33	-10	-04	04	00	-18	07	-37
Smile Number	-30	21	26	37	-32	-56	08	26
Smile Extent Speaking	-31	-35	-18	27	-16	-47	-07	00
Smile Extent Not Speaking	-25	19	23	28	-12	-35	02	21
Smile Time	-28	-05	12	24	-16	-43	-03	21
Laugh Rate Speaking	-34	-28	-24	25	06	-42	-08	-14
Laugh Rate Not Speaking	02	16	12	29	-20	-27	00	17
Laugh Number	-13	05	11	32	07	-32	06	21
Gaze Number	67	69	60	68	31	51	70	68
Gaze Rate Speaking	-47	-52	-53	-51	-49	-45	-07	-68
Gaze Rate Not Speaking	72	62	79	74	56	70	61	65
Gaze Length Speaking	03	-21	-01	-12	24	18	02	35
Gaze Length Not Speaking	-64	-63	-75	-68	-47	-52	-48	-56
Gaze Length	-65	-73	-60	-66	-44	-50	-59	-69
Gaze Extent Speaking	-39	-63	-43	-51	-15	-22	05	-31
Gaze Extent Not Speaking	-17	-29	09	-06	02	06	-08	20
Gaze Time	-50	-62	-51	-47	-44	-26	-26	-46

Sex of subject and sex of partner

(continued)

TABLE 5.1 *(continued)*

| | Sex of subject and sex of partner | | | | | | | |
| | Females with females | | Females with males | | Males with females | | Males with males | |
Order of Interaction	1st	2nd	1st	2nd	1st	2nd	1st	2nd
Gesture Mean Length	16	-18	03	22	14	04	24	02
Gesture Rate	-30	-24	-25	-37	26	03	-11	23
Self-Adaptor No.	29	-27	-09	10	42	-19	11	09
Self-Adaptor Length Speaking	22	23	09	38	05	-08	-18	34
Self-Adaptor Length Not Speaking	01	01	-53	-26	-05	-42	-05	-19
Foot Time	20	01	-10	-04	25	11	32	-12
Foot No.	08	12	-03	27	16	46	50	06
Foot Length	23	-20	-14	-17	29	-18	10	-22
Shift No.	-23	10	02	45	30	03	12	03

[a] For $N = 22$, $r \geq .36$, $p < .10$; $r \geq .42$, $p < .05$.

partner's acts in more or less a mirror image of the relationships with own acts. That is, the same absolute relationships would appear, but with opposite signs. This expectation was largely fulfilled. Thus, for same-sex pairs, with Turn Time correlating positively with one of a person's acts, the partner's Turn Time should have a negative relationship, since the same persons are involved. On the other hand, if Turn Time for females correlates positively with their own actions when interacting with males, then we would expect male Turn Time to correlate negatively with those acts of their female partners in the analyses for males interacting with females.

Although there were few departures from expectations (for example, when a relationship met our criterion for relationships to own actions but did not quite meet it for relationships to partner's actions), we will rapidly summarize the results for correlations with partner actions. The negative relationship between Turn Time and Partner's Mean Length of Turns was mentioned earlier. Turn Time also had sizable negative correlations with partner's Rate of Gazing When Not Speaking and somewhat lower positive correlations with Rate When Speaking. It had positive relationships with partner's Gaze Length, both over all and when Not Speaking. It was also related to partner's total Gaze Time. The similar relationship with partner's Gaze Time While Speaking was consistently found in the four interactions where the partner was female but not when the partner was male.

Positive relationships with Turn Time were also found for partner's Rates of Nods and Social Questions, and for Length of Self-Adaptors When Not Speaking. The relationships with partner's Filled Pause Rate and total Gesture Time were negative.

Turn Time and Turn Number, unlike the other act indices, are jointly determined by the person and the partner in their interaction. Relationships for these variables may stem from the person's own disposition, from partner's acts, or from some combination. Thus, the relationship between Turn Time and own Gaze Rate When Not Speaking may come from characteristics of the person; on the other side, the partner's nods and social questions presumably encourage the person to talk, perhaps because the partner prefers to listen.

Turn number.   This variable is essentially the same for the two persons in an interaction: each person has a turn after the other person finishes a turn, except at the end of the interaction. Each person contributes to this index. If a person takes long speaking turns, there is time for fewer turns; if a person is very brief each time he talks, there can be more turns.

Within five minutes of the second interaction, each person had an average of 13 speaking Turns. The pace was, however, quite varied, the range being from 3 to 27 turns. Thus at one extreme, there were about six turns during the interaction, while at the other there were nine times as many, about 54. (Since the first speaker was always followed by the other person, except at the end of the interaction, the smallest total number of turns could have been 6 or 7 and the largest, 53 or 54.) Turn Number was determined with high agreement (.96) between raters.

Since Turn Number correlated about .97 with partner's Turn Number, we will consider the two sets of highly congruent relationships at the same time. The negative relationship between Turn Number and Mean Turn Length was large except when females were interacting with males. Turn Number was related to Social Questions and to Rate of Long Back Channels, especially in first interactions. It was correlated with Total Number and Extent of Smiles particularly when females and males were interacting with each other. The relationship with Total Number of Laughs was more general (as was the weak relationship between Turn Number and partner's Extent of Laughing When Not Speaking).

While the relationships with Gaze Rates When Speaking and When Not Speaking were positive, Turn Number had a negative correlation with Length of Gazes When Not Speaking. The corresponding negative relationship with own Extent of Gazing When Not Speaking met our criterion although, in this very rare instance, one positive correlation exceeded .30. Turn Number also had a negative relationship with Length of Self-Adaptors

When Not Speaking, this relationship appearing for all instances where the Self-Adaptors were those of females; it was also for females that the negative relationships with Length of Gazes when Not Speaking and with Gaze Rate When Not Speaking were most consistent.

Turn Mean Length.   Although the average subject had 13 turns of 13 sec. each, the shortest mean length was only 2 sec. and the longest was 71 sec. in the second interactions. Females had shorter turns than males, and hence had more turns in the total coded interaction. The raters agreed almost exactly on this variable.

Unlike Turn Time and Turn Number, the Mean Lengths of Turns for the two participants were not necessarily related to each other by the scoring methods used. Empirically, no relationship was observed for any set of the data. Turn Length was, as noted earlier, negatively related to Turn Time and to Turn Number. These correlations were generally rather large. Time and Number are determined by both partner and self, and it is probably those effects which produced the low stability ($r = .27$) of Turn Length across the two interactions.

Turn Length had negative relationships to Gaze Rate While Speaking, to Gaze Extent While Speaking, and to total Gaze Length. It had a positive relationship to total Gesture Time. This result may have appeared because Turn Length was highly related to Turn Time, and hence opportunity for gesturing. (But see also the analysis of the gesticulation cue in the turn system, Chapter 9.) Turn Length was negatively related to Social Questions (especially for males) and to Laugh Rate While Speaking. Its relationship with Long Back-Channel Rate was also negative. While its positive pattern with Interruption Rate met our criterion, there was a single exception in the other direction among these correlations and also among those for Long Back-Channel Rate.

Turn Length had a number of relationships to actions of the partner. As mentioned earlier, it had a large negative relationship with partner's Turn Time but none with partner's Turn Length. Its very high relationship with Length of partner's Gazes When Not Speaking may stem in part from the partner's opportunity for longer gazes when the participant talked for longer turns. This relationship was also reflected in the correlations with partner's overall Gaze Length. The partner's total Gaze Time was also related to Turn Length. The Length of partner's Self-Adaptors when Not Speaking was another variable with a positive relationship. Turn Length had a positive correlation with partner's Nod Rate and, not surprisingly, a negative one with partner's Rate of Interruptions.

Thus, a person taking long turns did not look at the partner much even though the partner had long gazes at the speaker. While he interrupted, his partner did not. While his partner nodded frequently, he did not encourage his partner to talk by asking social questions or providing long vocal back channels.

Recommendations concerning turn variables.   On the basis of these findings, it is clear that subsequent research on two–person interactions should include all three Turn variables. Although they have substantial interrelationships, each has its separate aspect. These variables indicate much concerning the basic structure of the conversation as it evolves from the literal interaction of the two participants. While Turn Length can vary regardless of the length of partner's turns, the partner's gazing while listening clearly contributes to Turn Length. Other actions of partners probably will be found to have effects within particular sets of conditions.

Interruption Rate.   The next variable, Rate of Interruptions, measures a relatively rare event in our interactions: the mean number of interruptions per subject was only a bit over one; about 35% of the subjects did not interrupt during an interaction and the largest number of interruptions by one subject was four (in a conversation where the partner did little talking). It is likely that the relatively low agreement between coders, .87, was associated with the relative infrequency of interruptions. The consistency of Interruption Rate over the two interactions was very low, only .14; interruptions would therefore seem to be characteristic of particular conditions—the sex pairing, the familiarity with the situation, interactive style of the partner, etc.

Interruption Rate had positive relationships with Turn Time and Turn Length, and also with Gaze Rate When Not Speaking. It was negatively correlated with Gaze Length When Not Speaking and with Nod Rate. None of the relationships was strong. They tended to occur in particular interactions, among the eight types: the two for males interacting with females contributed to each of the relationships.

The only relationship between Interruption Rate and any partner behavior was a negative one with partner Turn Length; presumably the interruption or interruptions tended to shorten the average length of time the partner spoke. (We cannot resist mentioning a curious contrast: in first interactions between females, Interruption Rate had positive correlations with most of the partner's gaze time variables, but in the first interactions between males, it had negative correlations with most of those variables.)

Given the odd distribution of indices for Interruption Rate, these correlations should be viewed with some caution. Such an unusual event as an interruption seems best understood in terms of its immediate behavioral context, that is, in terms of the actions immediately preceding each interruption.

Filled Pauses.   The descriptive statistics for Filled Pause Rate differ in several respects from those for the other variables. It had the highest stability (.80) between the two interactions, a result which is somewhat surprising for a variable with a fairly low number of occurrences: the mean was 8.5 for second interactions. The computed stability, however, is elevated by combining the male and female subjects, whose stabilities are .68 and .44, respectively. This large difference is associated with a large and significant difference in means: 12.1 for men but only 4.6 for women. As often happens, a larger variance (significantly so) was observed with the larger mean. On the other hand, for each sex, the means were similar for male and female partners but the variances were larger for both cross-sex pairs (significantly larger for females with males compared to females with females). It would appear that the number of filled pauses is determined relatively more by the person than are many of our other behavioral variables and such pauses are observed more often in males. Filled Pauses was rated with high agreement between raters.

The above data are for the number of Filled Pauses, frequencies being easier to grasp than rates. The statistics for Filled Pause Rate show corresponding differences. The mean rate for second interactions was .051, about one filled pause every 20 sec. of speaking. While a few persons had no filled pauses, the maximum rate was .29, more than one every 4 sec. of talking.

We have included Table 5.2 showing the correlations with Filled Pause Rate because the pattern of its relationships is somewhat different from those for most of the other act variables. For Filled Pause Rate, the only relationship meeting our criterion is with Turn Time. One reason for its unusual pattern is that its correlations tend to be lower in first interactions (even though the means and variances were similar for the two interactions). Another is that patterns occur for one particular interaction but not for others—for example, the series of negative relationships with back-channel acts for second interactions between males.

A few relationships appeared with partner acts. Filled Pause Rate is positively correlated with Length of partner's Gazes and Length of partner's foot movements. It is negatively related to partner's Gaze Rate When Not Speaking.

Social Question Number. The Number of Social Questions was one of our very few variables based on content. This variable was rated with high agreement between the judges. The correlation between the two interactions was, however, only .21. The mean number of such questions was about four, with a range from none to 11.

Social Questions was correlated positively with Turn Number and negatively with Turn Length and Turn Time. These relationships were more consistent for males than for females. It also had positive correlations with Gaze Rate While Speaking and with overall Length of Gaze.

Social Questions was, of course, correlated also with partner's Turn Number and Turn Time. In addition, it had a positive relationship with partner's Gaze Length, both over all and when Not Speaking.

TABLE 5.2
Correlations between Filled Pause Rate and Own Actions[a]

Order of inter-action	Females with females		Females with males		Males with females		Males with males	
	1st	2nd	1st	2nd	1st	2nd	1st	2nd
Turn Time	40	14	19	42	20	40	02	40
Turn Number	18	07	01	04	05	-41	-02	-06
Turn Length	21	03	20	46	08	49	03	38
Interruption Rate	-19	-42	12	11	52	05	-10	06
Social Questions	04	11	06	00	27	-49	12	-38
Nod Rate	03	-01	14	-20	-05	-09	27	-71
Short Back Channel	-19	-12	04	22	-12	11	23	-42
Long Back Channel	04	-23	-11	34	-31	-61	-04	-22
All Back Channel	-07	-09	09	05	-14	-10	25	-68
Smile Number	-24	-42	-09	22	-26	-44	04	-13
Smile Extent Speaking	-21	-20	-01	02	-09	-47	-14	09
Smile Extent Not Speaking	-20	-20	07	20	-20	-41	04	-14
Smile Time	-21	-24	05	10	-17	-46	-05	-07
Laugh Rate Speaking	-59	-31	-02	23	-01	-06	-09	-26
Laugh Rate Not Speaking	-04	10	-12	18	-27	-17	-11	09
Laugh Number	-41	-18	-05	15	-15	-08	-02	-04
Gaze Number	36	26	17	62	-18	-06	-15	41
Gaze Rate Speaking	22	-03	-23	12	-13	-30	-11	-42
Gaze Rate Not Speaking	23	10	02	28	25	01	-19	51
Gaze Length Speaking	-22	-26	-13	-59	42	07	07	16
Gaze Length Not Speaking	-23	-09	-03	-32	-16	-15	24	-51
Gaze Length	-24	-21	-20	-61	25	-13	16	-43
Gaze Extent Speaking	-04	-30	-33	-51	39	-22	-04	-25
Gaze Extent Not Speaking	-12	00	-04	-23	13	-25	20	-09
Gaze Time	-01	-03	-26	-50	26	-41	12	-33
Gesture Mean Length	14	-01	20	-26	23	-22	-30	-24

(continued)

TABLE 5.2 *(continued)*

| Order of inter-action | Sex of subject and sex of partner | | | | | | | |
| | Females with females | | Females with males | | Males with females | | Males with males | |
	1st	2nd	1st	2nd	1st	2nd	1st	2nd
Gesture Rate	-12	-19	-17	-14	00	04	21	08
Self-Adaptor No.	14	05	-07	10	13	-01	22	-26
Self-Adaptor Length Speaking	28	02	39	04	-27	-21	-21	40
Self-Adaptor Length Not Speaking	-14	02	08	-05	-21	-29	32	-24
Foot Time	00	09	-11	-01	12	-25	-18	-05
Foot No.	16	-05	03	25	03	-04	-24	27
Foot Length	-07	18	-07	-11	44	-29	-09	-29
Shift No.	-17	-19	-04	52	06	-24	-04	04

[a] $N=22$, $r \geq .36$, $p < .10$; $r \geq .42$, $p < .05$.

Thus, Social Questions was associated with a positive Gaze Rate for self while speaking but also, during those same turns, with a positive Gaze Rate for the partner. While the person asking many Social Questions tended to have long Gazes, his partner tended to have short ones. The person asking these questions had less Turn Time and shorter turns during these interactions, which had many turns. Each of these relationships was stronger for males. Among the other correlations for Social Questions, there were more than the typical number of instances in which a moderate correlation in one interaction was found with a moderate correlation of opposite sign in the other, indicating that many specific correlations were a function of the particular groups brought together for the given interaction.

THE BACK-CHANNEL ACTIONS

The next family of actions to be examined are the back channels. These include the Rate of Nods and the Rates for Short and Long Vocal Back Channels. A summary index was also used: the Rate of All Back Channels, including both Nods and vocal back channels.

Nod Rate. The Rate of Nods was fairly stable (.50) across the two interactions. The raters agreed well (.95). In terms of frequencies, the mean was 8.7, with females giving more nods than males, 9.5 and 7.9, respectively. On the average, the listener nodded once every 17 seconds.

With a mean rate of .058, scores varied from 0 (for about 7% of the subjects) to .165, in the second interactions. While the variances for males and females were comparable, both males and females had significantly larger variances when with partners of the same sex.

Nod Rate was related to two other Back-Channel scores: it had high correlations with total Back-Channel Rate, to which it contributed; it also had generally substantial correlations with Short Vocal Back Channels. It was related to total Gaze Time and also to Gaze Length When Not Speaking. Compatible with the latter was its negative relationship to Gaze Rate in the same Not Speaking role. It had a positive relationship, however, with Gaze Rate While Speaking. Finally, it had a low negative correlation with Rate of Interruptions.

Nod Rate was related to partner's Turn Length and Turn Time. It also had a weak relationship with the number of partner's Self-Adaptors.

Short Vocal Back-Channel Rate.   The raters agreed well (.90) in coding this variable, although the agreement is poorer than that for most of our variables. Fair consistency across the two interactions was observed ($r = .51$), the consistency being much higher for males (.73) than for females (.32). With the average participant giving seven Short Back Channels, the mean Rate of Short Back Channels was .044, about one every 23 sec. of Not Speaking time. The maximum rate was one every six seconds. All but 6% gave some Short Back Channels. Females had a slightly higher rate than males although their variance was lower.

Short Back-Channel Rate was highly related to All Back Channels, to which it contributed, and had a substantial relationship with Nod Rate. It was also correlated with Extent of Gaze When Not Speaking and with Gesture Rate.

Short Back-Channel Rate was related to Long and All Back Channels for partner. It was also related to partner's Short Back-Channel Rate for both sexes in interactions between males and females. It was correlated with three of the partner's Smile variables: Rate, Extent When Not Speaking, and total Extent.

Long Vocal Back-Channel Rate.   This variable was rated quite reliably. Its consistency across the two interactions was rather limited—only .31, considerably less than the value for Short Back-Channel Rate. The low consistency is probably associated with the fact that Long Back Channels were rather rare events, the average subject giving only two in each interaction. The mean and variance for females were somewhat larger than the values for males.

Long Back-Channel Rate does not appear to be a fruitful variable for use in studying short interactions. Probably associated with the rarity of Long Back-Channel Behaviors are its few and modest relationships with other variables. It had no correlation with any other Back-Channel variable (except

All Back Channels, to which it contributed). It was related to Turn Number and Length, to Smile Number and Extent When Not Speaking, and to Gaze Rate When Speaking. For partner variables, its correlations with Turn Number and Short Back Channel were positive, but its correlation was negative with the other's Length of Gaze While Speaking.

All Back-Channel Rate. This variable was obtained by adding together the total number of Nods, of Short Back-Channel and of Long Back-Channel acts, and dividing by partner's speaking time. Nods contributed about 50% to that sum, Short Back-Channels contributed about 40%, and Long Back Channels the rest. It was rated more reliably and it was more consistent across interactions than any of its components. Since males were more consistent than females on each of the two major components, they were also more consistent on the composite. The mean for females was a bit higher than for males. Females with male partners had significantly less variance than those with female partners.

All Back-Channel Rate was highly correlated with Rates for Nods and for Short Back Channel and was modestly correlated with Long Back-Channel Rate, these values reflecting the relative contributions which these three parts made to the whole. Its only other relationships were with Smile Number and Gaze Time.

This total Rate was related to the partner's Rate for All Back Channels and also the Rate for Short Back Channels. It was correlated with partner's Smile Rate and two Smile Extents, Total and While Not Speaking. This pattern corresponds to that found for Short Back Channels and presumably reflects the latter variable's contribution to the composite Rate.

Since All Back-Channel Rate does not appear to yield any findings other than those also found for one of its components, it does not seem to be a promising variable.

THE SMILE VARIABLES

The outstanding feature of the correlations for the smile variables is their high degree of intercorrelation. While the Number of Smiles would be expected to correlate with Extents, the Extents of Smiling While Speaking and While Not Speaking also tend to correlate with each other. Also as one would expect, the smile variables tend to relate substantially to the laugh variables. The smile variables are among the most consistent variables over the two interactions.

Smile Number. The raters agreed well (.92) on this variable. The stability was comparatively high (.54), a little higher for males than for females. The average was about 8 smiles, or roughly one every 36 sec. Females smiled significantly more often than males, giving about two more smiles during the 5 min. The frequencies ranged from 22 smiles down to none. Both sexes had larger variances when with partners of the opposite sex, the difference in variances by sex of partner being significant for females.

Smile Number correlated highly with all the Extent of Smiling variables for every pairing in each interaction, all but one of the values being over .65. The correlations with total Smile Time were generally the highest. Smile Number had positive relationships with all three Laugh variables, many being quite high. Those for females with females in second interactions were low to modest, as were three others. These were the only relationships which were generally consistent for both sexes.

Smile Number was related to Number of Turns, the relationship being strongest for interactions between males and females. Its relationship with All Back-Channel Rate was found primarily for male participants. That relationship stemmed in large part from the similar relationship for Long Back-Channel Rate.

One incidental finding was that females had a number of substantial correlations for both sexes of partner in second interactions but not in first: Interruption Rate, Leg Rate While Speaking, Leg Number, Shift Number, and Gaze Extent When Not Speaking, all being positive except the last.

Smile Number tended to correlate with the partner's Smile and Laugh variables although the relationships were quite weak when females were talking to each other. It also correlated with partners' Rates for Short and for All Back Channels, primarily when the partner was male. Its relationship with partner Leg Rate While Speaking and Total Leg Rate was consistent across interactions only for those involving just females. Its low correlation with Extent of Gazing While Speaking was negative.

It seems likely that the results for Smile Number, including the presence of high correlations which were not consistent across groupings or interactions, stem in part from its composite nature. It would seem wise to rate Smile Number separately for the person's speaking and not speaking states.

Smile Extent While Speaking. The Extent of Smiling While Speaking is one of the most consistent variables in those studied: scores for the two interactions correlated .71. It was, however, judged with relatively poor agreement—only .87. On the average, the participants smiled one-eighth of their speaking time, this proportion ranging from more than half the time down to not at all for seven people. Females smiled somewhat more than males and both sexes smiled more when the partner was female (though these trends were not statistically significant). As reported earlier, the large mean difference between males and females in the first interaction almost disappeared in the second interaction (a convergence which was significant). Males had significantly larger variance when with females than when with other males.

Smile Extent While Speaking correlated highly, of course, with Total Smile Time, to which it contributed. It also had generally high correlations with Smile Number and with Extent of Smiling When Not Speaking. It correlated with all three Laugh variables, the values being rather varied.

There was some tendency for these correlations to be higher or lower as a function of the particular group of participants: for example, the group of females whose first partners were females (and whose second were males) had higher relationships with every laugh and smile variable than did the other group of females. Although the patterning was completely consistent, the differences between the pairs of corresponding correlations were typically not significant.

The same tendency for the size of the relationship to be associated with a particular group of people in both interactions rather than with sex of participant or with sex combination appears to a limited degree for other variables. Perhaps as a consequence, most of the other relationships are not consistent for both interactions for both sexes of partner. Thus, for females who interacted with males in their second conversations, Extent of Smiling While Speaking was related to Turn Number, Interruption Rate, and to Length of Self-Adaptors While Speaking; they also had negative relationships with Nod Rate, Total Back-Channel Rate, Gaze Time, all Gaze Lengths, and to Gesture Extent and Rate. This pattern of rapid interactions with interruptions and many short gazes but little gesturing or back channel does not appear elsewhere.

The males talking to these same females had positive relationships between this Smile variable and Social Questions, Rate of Long Back Channel, Leg Rate While Speaking, and Length of Foot Movements; they also had negative relationships with Turn Time, Turn Length, and Filled Pause Rate. This pattern seems largely consistent with that for their female partners as outlined above.

Smile Extent While Speaking correlated with partner's Smile Extent and Laugh Rate While Not Speaking (but not for these variables when Speaking), suggesting temporal overlapping. It also correlated with partner's Total Laugh Rate, Total Extent of Smiling, and Smile Number. The frequency of significant correlations was higher for second interactions than for first: perhaps the participants attended to their partners' behaviors more as they themselves became accustomed to the situation.

The lack of consistencies throughout the correlations for Smile Extent While Speaking is presumably associated with the unusually high level of personal consistency across the two interactions: Smile Extent would appear to be a function of the individual more than of the particular interaction.

Smile Extent While Not Speaking. The Extent of Smiling When Not Speaking was less consistent across the two interactions than the Extent While Speaking (.45 as contrasted to .71). Males were a little more consistent than females. The interjudge agreement was the same for both Smile Extent variables. The actual Extent While Not Speaking was about the same as

While Speaking, for the group as a whole. But once again, females smiled more, and significantly so: .14 as opposed to .08 for males. This larger mean was associated with a larger variance for the females, a common association for variables with an absolute floor or zero point. Sex of partner did not affect these means or variances.

In addition to the expected very high relationship with Total Extent of Smiling and the high relationship with Smile Number, Smile Extent While Not Speaking had substantial correlations with Smile Extent While Speaking and with Rates for Total Laughs and Laughs While Not Speaking. Its relationship with Laugh Rate When Speaking was not as consistent as these others. Its only other relationship was with Long Back-Channel Rate.

This variable was related to all of the partner's Smile variables. Its relationship with partner's Total Laugh Rate was strongest when the partner was female. Smile Extent While Not Speaking was also related to Total and Short Back-Channel Rates of partner, especially with male partners.

Smile Time.   Because Smile Time combines the times while speaking and while not speaking, it has a picture similar to the two Extent variables based on those times. It is as consistent across interactions as Extent While Speaking (.72) and more reliably judged (.94) than either extent. For the data as a whole, females smiled half again as long as males (the difference, 42 versus 28 sec., being significant), the difference being larger in the first interactions and smaller in the second as the two means approached each other. The longest times exceeded 40%; in all the interactions, there were only three observations of no smiling. The means and variances by sex of partner had a pattern derived from that for Smile Extent While Speaking: slightly smaller values when with male partners, the variance for males with male partners being significantly smaller.

Smile Time of course had very high correlations with each of the two turn times of which it was composed and with Smile Number. It had high to modest correlations with all the Laugh variables. In addition, it was related to Number of Turns for each of the four interactions between males and females.

Smile Time was related to all of the partner's Smile and Laugh variables. (The second interactions between females did not, however, have any of these relationships.) It was also related to partner's Rates for Long and for All Back Channels, especially for male partners, and to partner's Leg Rates, Total and While Speaking, especially for female subjects.

THE LAUGH FAMILY

People think of smiling and laughing as related, and our results support this observation. The highest correlations for Laugh variables are with Smiling in the same turn (Speaking or Not Speaking). The Smile variables were discussed first because Smiling was twice as frequent as Laughing in our protocols.

Laugh Rate While Speaking.   The mean rate of .017 indicates that the average participant laughed about 2.5 times while speaking in each interaction. The maximum rate was .066 (roughly 10 laughs) and 11% did not laugh while speaking. The raters agreed reasonably well (.86). Laugh Rate While Speaking was a moderately stable value, the rates correlating .47 between the two interactions. As reported earlier, females laughed significantly more often than males, the difference being large regardless of sex of partner. The variance of the male rates was somewhat lower, perhaps as a consequence of their smaller mean.

While Laugh Rate When Speaking was obviously related to Total Laugh Rate, it was not related to Laugh Rate While Not Speaking: although three of the correlations for male–female interactions were appreciable, those for same sex interaction were all low. Laugh Rate While Speaking was related to all the Smile variables. It had a low negative relationship with Turn Length.

It was also related to partner's Laugh Rate While Not Speaking (and to Total Laugh Rate) but not to partner's Laugh Rate While Speaking. It had relationships with partner's Total Smile Time and Smile Number, although the correlations were not large.

Laugh Rate While Not Speaking.   There were fewer laughs by auditors— about 1.5 per person per interaction. The maximum rate was .053, roughly 8 such laughs; 39% had no laughs when in that role in second interactions, and the picture for first interactions was quite similar. Laugh Rate While Not Speaking was judged reliably (.92). It was less stable over the two interactions (.30) than the Rate While Speaking. Once again, males laughed less than females, especially when the males had a female partner. The difference was large in the first interaction but almost disappeared in the second interaction—the rate for each sex moving toward that for the other. The variances were similar.

Although Laugh Rate While Not Speaking was related to Total Laugh Rate (to which it contributed), its correlational pattern with Laugh Rate While Speaking fell short of our criterion. It was, however, related to Smile Extent When Speaking and even more to the other three Smile variables.

This variable was related to all of the partner's Laugh and Smile variables except Smile Extent When Not Speaking. It was also related to the joint variable, Number of Speaking Turns.

Laugh Number.   This variable is the total number of laughs, summing those in the Speaking role and those when Not Speaking. It was a fairly stable variable over the two interactions (.52) and the judges agreed well on rating it (.92). The average was almost four laughs per person in each interaction, with the females laughing significantly more—almost two laughs more than the males. The variances were similar for the two sexes, with both having somewhat larger variances when with female partners. In these interactions, one person out of six did not laugh at all while the maximum was about four times the overall average (or well over a laugh a minute).

Laugh Number had generally substantial correlations with each of the two Rate variables, it being the sum of the numerators in those ratios. It was also related to all of the Smile variables, the correlations ranging from substantial to modest. It was also correlated with Turn Number, although not in all pairings.

Laugh Number was related to all of the partner's Laugh and Smile variables. The correlations tended to be lower, of course, than those with own acts. These relationships did not appear at all in two of the pairings. It also had a weak relationship with partner's Total Leg Rate.

Even though Laugh Number was a bit more stable than either of the Laugh Rate variables, it does not appear to be a productive variable. The separate rate variables contain all the useful information, with the exception of the relationship with Number of Turns.

Overview of the Laugh variables.   In these interactions, a laugh was a fairly rare event. Laughs tended to be related to Smiles, and to Laughs and Smiles of partners. The results suggest the obvious speculation that a laugh is most likely to occur when a particular person who is predisposed to laughing encounters certain behavioral situations, such as the laugh of the partner. The context of each laugh deserves investigation.

THE GAZE FAMILY

Gazing was defined in this study as looking toward the partner's head. It was the most prevalent of all the actions rated: our subjects gazed at their partners about 60% of the time while speaking and about 87% while listening. The Extents were of course substantially correlated with the Mean Lengths of Gazes. The Number of Gazes was negatively related to the several variables indicating Gaze time; if a person's gazes were long and occupied most of the interaction, he could not have a large number of separate gazes.

Frequency of Gazing

In our initial analyses, the frequency of gazing was indexed by just one variable, total Gaze Number. Subsequently, it became apparent that this variable should be broken down in terms of the Speaking–Not Speaking distinction. While this division brought out the essential independence of the two variables for Gaze Number by turn state, these variables were not entirely satisfactory because they were not adjusted for time in each state. So, still later, we added variables for Gaze Rate While Speaking and When Not Speaking and dropped the two corresponding Gaze Number variables.

Gaze Number.   The total Number of Gazes was judged reliably (.92) and was fairly stable from the first to the second interaction (.52). The mean Number of Gazes was 34, about one gaze every 9 sec. The range was quite large, from as few as three to as many as 66. Females had slightly fewer but longer gazes. Sex of partner had no effect (except that the variance for females was a bit larger with male partners).

Gaze Number had an almost perfect negative correlation with Total Gaze Length. Its relationship with Gaze Length While Not Speaking was very large and negative; the relationship for the corresponding Speaking variable was not quite as large, but still negative. It also had negative correlations with the two Gaze Extents and Gaze Time, the values being quite variable. It was highly related to Rate When Not Speaking, but was not correlated with Rate While Speaking. Gaze Number had a substantial positive correlation with Turn Time and a more varying relationship with Turn Length.

Gaze Number had negative relationships with partner's Turn Time and Turn Length. It was negatively correlated with partner's Gaze Number and Rate While Not Speaking, but positively correlated with partner's Rate While Speaking and Total Gaze Length. In addition, it had a positive relationship with partner's Social Questions and a negative one with partner's Rate of Filled Pauses. The frequency of negative relationships for this variable is striking.

Gaze Rate While Speaking.   This new variable was analyzed subsequent to the major analyses being reported in this chapter. The mean Gaze Rate While Speaking was .21, or roughly one gaze every 5 sec. of talking. It had no relationship with Gaze Rate When Not Speaking (except for one combination out of the eight groupings).

Gaze Rate While Speaking had a weak relationship to Gaze Extent While Speaking and a stronger but negative relationship to Gaze Length While Speaking (the numerator of the Rate variable being the denominator of the Length variable). It had no relationships with other Gaze variables except for a few scattered instances. Gaze Rate While Speaking had negative relationships with Turn Time and with Turn Length, but a positive one with Number of Turns. It also had positive correlations with Rates for Nods, Long Back Channel, and Social Questions.

Gaze Rate While Speaking had a substantial relationship to the partner's concurrent Gaze Rate While Not Speaking (but was not related to partner's Rate While Speaking). It was related positively to partner's Gaze Number and negatively to Total Gaze Time, Total Gaze Length, and Length When Not Speaking. (Its relationships to the shared Turn variables, Number and Time, were mentioned above.)

Gaze Rate When Not Speaking.   The mean Gaze Rate When Not Speaking was .14, or about one gaze initiation every seven seconds. This rate is lower than that while Speaking; it was associated with longer gazes and greater Extent of Gazes.

The correlations for this variable are presented in Table 5.3. This set of correlations is somewhat unusual with respect to the number of large negative values. Gaze Rate When Not Speaking was independent of Gaze Rate When Speaking and showed a somewhat different pattern of relationships. It had very large negative correlations (most in the .90s) with Gaze Length When Not Speaking and substantial negative correlations with partner's Turn Time, variables to which it is arithmetically related. While it had a substantial relationship with Total Gaze Length (to which it contributed), it was *not* related to Length While Speaking. It had negative correlations with Total Gaze Time and Extent While Not Speaking. It had positive relationships with Turn Number, Interruption Rate, and Gesture Time (but not Rate). Its relationships with Nod Rate and with Length of Self-Adaptors While Not Speaking were negative.

Gaze Rate When Not Speaking had a substantial relationship to the partner's concurrent Gaze Rate While Speaking. Most striking were the very high negative correlations with partner's Turn Length. (The common turn variables were mentioned above.) It had positive relationships with partner's Total Gaze Length and Total Gaze Time, and also with Social Questions. Negative correlations appeared with partner's Filled Pause Rate, Length of Self-Adaptors While Speaking, and Total Gesture Time.

In general, these Gaze Rate variables appear to be quite promising. The extent of their negative relationships is noteworthy.

Gazing Time Variables

Mean length of gazes.   We turn now to the other general characteristic of gazes, their length. There is a problem in scoring gaze length for each turn separately: gazes can continue as the subject changes from speaker to auditor, and vice versa. For purposes of computing the mean length of gazes in each turn, any gaze occurring at the beginning of a speaking turn was timed from that point to its cessation, and any gaze occurring at the termination of that turn was timed as if it terminated with the speaking turn. Gazes while not speaking were timed in the same way. As a consequence, the Mean Lengths of Gazes While Speaking and While Not Speaking were distinctly shorter than the Mean Length ignoring turn exchanges (3 and 8 sec. respectively, as compared with 10). This scoring convention has to be taken into account in interpreting the results for Mean Lengths in each kind of turn.

Gaze Mean Length While Speaking.   While this variable was rather stable (.45) from first interaction to second, it was judged with comparatively low agreement (only .84). The mean was 3.2 sec., being about the same in the two interactions and for the two sexes (although females had a slightly larger value than males), and for the two sexes of partners. The variance for males interacting with females was significantly larger than that when interacting with males.

Gaze Mean Length While Speaking had positive relationships with all the other Gaze Time variables and a negative relationship with Gaze Rate While Speaking (and with Gaze Number). Its only other relationship was a low negative one with Smile Number.

It was correlated with the partner's Gaze Mean Length While Not Speaking (that is, the complementary role). It was negatively correlated with the partner's Long Back-Channel Rate.

Gaze Mean Length When Not Speaking. This variable was rated with average agreement between judges (.92). Its stability, however, was only .21, perhaps because the length of time Not Speaking was determined more by the partner than by the participant and the length of time as auditor could influence the Mean Length of Gaze. The mean was 7.8 sec., and order of interaction, sex of participant, and sex of partner had little effect on this statistic. The maximum value, 30 sec., could of course occur only when the partner had unusually long speaking turns. For each sex, the variance when with males was significantly larger than when with female partners.

Gaze Length When Not Speaking was related to all the other Gaze Time variables. It had large negative correlations with Gaze Number. Its negative relationship with Gaze Rate When Not Speaking was very large, and hence had the opposite pattern of relationships with other variables, as reported earlier. The sole exception was that its relationship with Gesture Time did not meet our criterion.

Its relationships with partner variables were not quite as close a mirror-image. Among the Gaze variables, it was related positively to partner's Total Time and Length While Speaking, but negatively with the other's Rate While Speaking. It had positive relationships with partner's Turn Time and Turn Length, together with a negative relationship to Turn Number. (The longer the partner's Turn Length, the greater the opportunity for long Gazes.) It had positive relationships to partner's Total Gesture Time and Leg Rate While Speaking, along with a negative correlation with partner's Social Questions.

Gaze Mean Length. This variable was scored with high agreement (.97). While the raw values were not very stable from first interaction to second (.25), the transformed values used in the correlational analyses were relatively stable (.48). The difference stems from the marked skewness of the raw values. With a mean of 10.2, the range was from 2 to 99 sec. (The largest values are presumably for gazes extending over changes of speaking turn.) The females had a slightly larger mean. For both sexes, the mean was higher when interacting with males and the variance was very much larger.

TABLE 5.3
Correlations between Gaze Rate When Not Speaking and Own Actions[a]

Order of Interaction	Females with females		Females with males		Males with females		Males with males	
	1st	2nd	1st	2nd	1st	2nd	1st	2nd
Turn Time	72	62	79	74	56	70	61	65
Turn No.	64	30	66	77	25	16	71	13
Turn Length	16	14	27	25	16	30	-16	52
Interruption Rate	30	22	04	48	37	63	23	30
Filled Pause Rate	23	10	02	28	25	01	-19	51
Social Questions	06	-06	11	04	04	-24	19	-40
Nod Rate	-52	-12	-40	-40	12	-31	22	-48
Short Back Channel	-38	01	22	32	19	-03	16	-66
Long Back Channel	29	20	14	04	24	-07	50	00
All Back Channel	-42	-04	01	-08	21	-19	27	-60
Smile No.	-02	14	35	54	18	-37	33	15
Smile Extent Speaking	-09	-28	-15	36	11	-12	-01	-06
Smile Extent Not Speaking	-22	25	30	41	24	01	23	-05
Smile Time	-18	-02	14	39	19	-06	11	-03
Laugh Rate Speaking	-34	-15	-01	37	07	-27	11	-30
Laugh Rate Not Speaking	-14	37	21	34	-25	12	27	07
Laugh No.	-18	25	23	42	07	-04	34	00
Gaze No.	77	47	42	80	74	76	84	75
Gaze Rate Speaking	-01	-23	-51	-18	21	05	34	-27
Gaze Length Speaking	-34	-29	-01	-31	-12	-22	-49	-21
Gaze Length Not Speaking	-96	-97	-94	-96	-91	-82	-90	-95
Gaze Extent Speaking	-38	-48	-42	-46	04	-30	-32	-49
Gaze Extent Not Speaking	-50	-30	16	-26	-14	-06	-36	-01
Gesture Mean Length	09	-09	17	03	-16	08	12	-38
Gesture Rate	-40	10	01	-20	31	18	-20	16
Self-Adaptor No.	07	07	-04	-06	23	22	28	02

(continued)

TABLE 5.3 *(continued)*

Order of interaction	Females with females		Females with males		Males with females		Males with males	
	1st	2nd	1st	2nd	1st	2nd	1st	2nd
Self-Adaptor Length Speaking	06	-25	-02	16	-14	-18	-03	21
Self-Adaptor Length Not Speaking	-27	-12	-45	-55	-34	-31	-25	-37
Foot Time	14	07	-27	13	32	12	05	15
Foot No.	05	21	-13	27	50	29	38	29
Foot Length	17	-19	-32	-03	08	-01	-20	-07
Shift No.	-25	20	-14	46	19	30	-12	00

[a]For $N=22$, $r \geq .36$, $p < .10$; $r \geq .42$, $p < .05$.

The relationships with Gaze Mean Length will not be examined in detail because this variable seems less useful than the corresponding variables for the Speaking and Not Speaking roles. Gaze Mean Length had consistent negative correlations from -.90 to -.99 with Gaze Number, the denominator in the ratio forming this variable. It correlated .72 or more with Total Gaze Time, the numerator. Most of its relationships with other Gaze variables were large. Thus this variable overlaps markedly with Gaze variables which have already been discussed.

The fruitfulness of Gaze Length variables is uncertain. Their consistent relationships are almost entirely with other Gaze variables, although Gaze Length When Not Speaking is related to the partner's Turn Time and Turn Length. Their other relationships seem to be associated with particular pairings and in some instances with a particular group of subjects.

Gaze Extent While Speaking. The Extent variables can be viewed as the product of the Number of Gazes and their Mean Length, and hence as composite variables. Gaze Extent While Speaking was judged reliably. It was a rather stable variable over the two interactions, particularly so for the females. The overall mean was .61, the mean for the females being a bit larger. The range was from .25 to 1.00.

All the Gaze variables tended to have high relationships with each other, and this one was no exception. Gaze Extent While Speaking had strong relationships to total Gaze Time (to which it contributed) and to Gaze Length. It had a substantial relationship to Gaze Length While Speaking, of course, and sizable but more varying correlations with Extent and Length When Not Speaking. It had modest relationships to Gaze Rate While Speaking (positive) and to Rate When Not Speaking (negative). It had negative correlations with Turn Time and Length, primarily for females, and with Laugh Time.

Gaze Extent While Speaking was related only to partner's concurrent Gaze Extent While Not Speaking (and, for females, to partner's Turn Time).

Gaze Extent When Not Speaking.   While this variable was fairly consistent across interactions (.40), the agreement in scoring it was relatively poor (.77). The mean Extent was .87, indicating that the auditor looked at the speaker most of the time, the range being from .31 to 1.00.

Gaze Extent When Not Speaking was related in a varying fashion to all of the other Gaze Time variables. While it was negatively related to Gaze Number, it was not related to either of the Gaze Rates. It had a varying, minimum and negative relationship to Turn Number and a minimum positive relationship with Short Back-Channel Rate.

The only partner variable to which it was related was the concurrent Gaze Extent While Speaking.

Gaze Time.   This variable was scored with good agreement (.94), and it was relatively consistent across interactions (.53). The mean was 217 sec., or more than 70% of the interaction. The females had a significantly higher mean. The range was 111–299 sec. (the entire scored part of the interaction).

Gaze Time had very high correlations with Extent When Speaking and most of the values with Extent When Not Speaking were equally high. Its positive relationships with the Length variables were high to very high, except for a few moderate ones, and its negative values with Gaze Number can be described in the same way. While it had a modest negative relationship to Gaze Rate When Not Speaking, it was unrelated to Rate When Speaking. Once again, in view of these high values and in view of the emphasis on scores by Speaking or Not Speaking roles, it seems best to omit any examination of other relationships with Gaze Time.

The Gaze Extent variables (including Gaze Time) appear to be less useful than the Gaze Length variables as indices for gaze time. The Length variables suffer, to be sure, from the arbitrary convention of being terminated when the speaking turn is exchanged and from the consequent relationship to partners' Turn Length in the case of Length When Not Speaking. All the Length and Extent variables are negatively related to Number of Gazes. The major limitations of the Extent variables is their relationship to each of their two multiplied components, Number and Length; the relationships between the Extent variables and variables outside the Gaze family may be viewed as derived from relationships to Length, Number, or a combination of the two.

Overview of the Gaze Family

Gazing is clearly one of the more important acts in the interaction between two people. While our analyses included a considerable number of Gaze variables, we do not feel that our findings for specific variables have greatly clarified the relationships between this act and other actions of participant and partner. Several generalizations do, however, receive some support from our data. First, it appears that gazes while speaking should be considered separately from gazes when not speaking; totals summing over both roles are too complex and not easily understood. Second, rate and time variables for gazing form separate, negatively related classes.

A major difficulty stems from any attempt to consider both of these propositions in identifying appropriate operations for measuring gaze actions. What scoring of rate and time variables is compatible with the speaking turn as the unit within which these are studied?

In scoring our data, several arbitrary conventions were used. A gaze occurring when one speaking turn ended and the partner's turn began was counted as a gaze for both turns. Similarly, the length of such a gaze was measured to the end of the first speaking turn, and that length as truncated was included in the time of gazing for that turn. The duration of the same gaze was measured from the beginning of the second turn to the termination of the gaze, that duration being included in the time of gazing for the second turn. As a consequence of these conventions, the sum of the numbers of gazes when speaking and when not speaking exceeded the actual number of gazes counted without regard for turns. Also, the average lengths of gazes during speaking and not speaking turns were shorter than the average length computed without regard for turns. While these facts now make us somewhat dissatisfied with our gaze variables for speaking and not speaking roles, our scoring records do not permit us to compute any alternative variables.

One small improvement would be to count each gaze extending from one turn into the next as half a gaze for each of those turns. There are other possibilities, all somewhat arbitrary. Each gaze could be counted only for the turn in which it was initiated. There could be a closely related but conceptually distinct variable for number of gazes terminated within a turn. Still another rationale would be to consider separately gazes initiated and terminated within a turn and gazes extending from one turn to the next; the latter variable might need to be further subdivided on the basis of the role in which the gaze began.

While such different conventions might prove fruitful for studying numbers or rates of gazing, the problem of time variables would still remain. Gazes while speaking were shorter and more numerous than gazes when not speaking, so that it would be possible to study the durations of several gazes per speaking turn. It is our impression, however, that the number of gazes initiated and terminated entirely within a partner's speaking turn was very small, and hence studies of the duration of such gazes would be based on restricted and perhaps undependable data.

We believe that these difficulties illustrate the limitations of approaching these actions in terms of scores for total interactions, summing or averaging over total time, or total time in each role. On the one hand, the state of gazing seems important, especially with regard to what other actions are occurring at the same time: for example, can eye contact be presumed because the partner is simultaneously gazing at the subject? On the other hand, more important than number of gazes are the initiations and the terminations. What other behaviors occur at about the same time or just preceding the initiation of each gaze? With what actions is the termination associated? Gazing can best be understood in terms of the interactional context within which each gaze is initiated, continued, and terminated. These contexts are probably different for the three phases of a gaze. Findings pertaining to initiations and terminations of gazes as related to turn exchanges will be reported in a later part of this book. A general model for investigating each act in its interactional context is proposed in the final part.

THE GESTURE FAMILY

Gesturing included all movements of the hands which did not involve touching oneself or one's clothing. Since gestures occurred almost exclusively while talking, the rare instances when not talking were not coded.

Most of the gesture variables had sizable intercorrelations with each other. Gesture Time and Gesture Extent (which corrected for Turn Time) correlated between .72 and .92. Gesture Time also had sizable correlations with Gesture Rate and Gesture Length. Gesture Extent had equally sizable relationships with Gesture Length and higher ones with Gesture Rate. Rate and Length were essentially unrelated to each other (even though a negative relationship might be expected since Number of Gestures is in the numerator of Rate and in the denominator of Length). Given the prevalence of high intercorrelations, it seemed best to limit the analyses to just the two unrelated variables, Rate and Length.

Gesture Rate While Speaking. This variable was computed by dividing the number of gestures by Turn Time. The judges agreed very well (.99). It was fairly stable across the two interactions (.49). The overall mean was .13, roughly one initiation of gesturing every eight seconds while speaking, or 1.5 gestures for each speaking turn. The range was from only a couple of gestures to several dozen. Sex of subject and sex of partner did not affect the means, although females had a larger variance when with males.

Gesture Rate had generally high correlations with Extent of Gesturing and almost as high with total Gesture Time. As mentioned above, it was unrelated to Gesture Length. It had negative relationships with all three Extents of Self-Adaptors and with Length of Self-Adaptors, both Total and While Speaking; these relationships tended to be stronger in second interactions. The negative correlations with variables for the speaking turn may well stem from the fact that if one is gesturing, one cannot also engage in self–adaptors with the same hand or hands. Gesture Rate also had a modest relationship to Short Back Channels.

The only relationships with partner variables were modest ones with partner's Gesture Rate, Time, and Extent. (The correlations were generally larger in first interactions.) It was not related to Length of partner's Gestures.

Mean Gesture Length.   Like Gesture Rate, Gesture Length was judged with very high agreement (.99). It was, however, not as stable across interactions (.38). The overall mean was 2.5 sec. (although females had a slightly longer mean). For each sex, variances were a little larger when with males. The range of mean Gesture Lengths was from less than one second to a bit over 7 sec.

Gesture Length was related to Gesture Time and Extent, most of the correlations being substantial. It had no other relationships. It was not related to any of the partner's variables.

The Gesture variables were disappointing; they had very few relationships aside from those reflecting the difficulty in doing two different things simultaneously with the hands. In contrast, the initiation of a gesture, its termination, and its presence all appear as cues in the turn system considered in Part III.

THE SELF-ADAPTOR FAMILY

Our participants engaged in Self-Adaptor actions, touching themselves or their clothing, about one-third of the time during the interactions. They initiated such behaviors an average of 14 times, the mean Length being 8.5 sec. (Females had very slightly higher rates and total times.) Self-Adaptors, like Gazes, extended from one turn into the next; hence, the Mean Lengths for each turn, timed only while the turn lasted, were shorter than the total Lengths.

High relationships were found among the Self-Adaptor Extent variables and also between the corresponding Extent and Length variables. The Mean Lengths for the Speaking and Not Speaking roles, however, had very low intercorrelations. Hence, they were examined in detail. The Extent variables appeared to have no important patterns not brought out by other Self-Adaptor variables, and so they will not be discussed. The Number of Self-Adaptors was not related to the Mean Lengths but did have moderate correlations with the Extent variables.

Number of Self-Adaptors.   The agreement between judges on this variable, .88, was only fair. It did, however, show rather good stability across interactions (.40). Individual values ranged from 3 to 30 around the mean of 14.

The Number of Self-Adaptors was related to all three Extents of Self-Adaptors, the correlations being modest to high. It had no other relationships. Its only relationship with partner actions was a minimal one with Nod Rate.

Mean Length of Self-Adaptors While Speaking.   This variable was judged with relatively poor agreement (.82) and had little stability (.20). Its mean was about 4 sec.

While it had the expected strong relationship with mean Length of all Self-Adaptors, its relationship with Length While Not Speaking was weak. It was related to all three Self-Adaptor Extents but not to Number. It had negative relationships with Gesture Rate, Extent, and Time, but not Length. Its only correlation with a partner variable, Gaze Rate When Not Speaking, was also negative.

Mean Length of Self-Adaptors When Not Speaking.   Like Length in the opposite role, this variable was judged with poor agreement (.76) and had limited stability (.30). The average Length was 5.8 sec.

Length When Not Speaking was related to all other Self-Adaptor variables except Number. Its negative relationship with Turn Number was limited to females. It also had positive correlations with Length of Foot Movements and Gaze Length While Not Speaking, together with a negative one with Gaze Rate When Not Speaking.

It had low relationships with partner Turn Time (even though not related to own Turn Time), partner's Turn Length, and Length of Self-Adaptors When Not Speaking.

Self-Adaptor variables did not prove fruitful in this study.

FOOT MOVEMENTS

While movements of the hands were recorded in terms of a number of variables, other bodily movements were recorded in more gross categories. Movements of a foot were noted and timed, yielding three variables: Foot Time over all movements of a foot, Number of Foot movements, and Mean Length of foot movements (dividing Time by Number). It will be noted that these variables were not scored separately by Speaking or Not Speaking.

Foot Time had high relationships with Number and Mean Length, indicating the contribution of each to total Foot Time. Foot Number and Foot Length, however, were not related to each other.

Foot Time.   This variable was scored with very high agreement (.99). Its consistency across interactions was relatively high (.63). While the mean for Foot Time was 65 sec., the range was from 2 to 268 sec. Foot Time was not related to any variable outside the Foot family, nor to any partner behavior.

Foot Mean Length.   Foot Length was rated with average agreement (.93), and showed reasonable consistency across the interactions (.39). The mean Length of Foot Movements was 3 sec., the largest mean for any participant being 24 sec. The variance for females was larger when with males.

Aside from its correlation with Foot Time, Foot Length had only one relationship, with Length of Self-Adaptors when Not Speaking. It was correlated with partner Filled Pause Rate for both interactions of the male and the female samples whose first interaction was with partners of their own sex.

Foot Number.   The agreement and consistency of this variable were almost as high as the values for Foot Time. The mean Number of Foot Movements was 23, with a range up to 71. Its only relationship outside the Foot family was a negative one with total Length of Gaze.

Since the number of appreciable correlations for these foot variables was close to chance expectancy, they must be interpreted with great caution. The one relationship with the action of partners must be considered even more tentatively. While these Foot variables did show good consistency across interactions, they do not appear to be fruitful variables in the study of interactions.

THE SHIFT FAMILY

Shifts of the leg or of the seat were rare in our interactions. Roughly speaking, the average participant shifted his legs once during each interaction and shifted his seat once during the two interactions taken together, for a total Number of Shifts of 1.5. Men had higher means than women for each kind of shift. The sex of the partner did not seem to affect the means. There were two to three times as many shifts while speaking as when not speaking. These means reflect the very skewed distributions for these shift variables. Large proportions of the participants did not shift at all, especially when not speaking. The largest frequencies were four leg shifts, four seat shifts, and seven total shifts. All nine shift variables were judged with very high agreement (with one exception). There was, however, little consistency over the two interactions, especially for the scores for speaking or not speaking.

Pearson correlations can be computed as descriptive statistics for variables with skewed distributions. Such correlations must, of course, be interpreted cautiously: in many instances, the value of such a correlation is determined largely by the extreme cases. Given the limited data on these shift variables, it did not seem worthwhile to compute some other measure of relationship on just these particular variables.

For each type of shift, the score when speaking had a low correlation with the score when not speaking. While the correlations between seat and leg shifts tended to be low positive for males (who had higher means), the values for females were essentially zero.

Total Number of Shifts.   To provide a brief look at the correlations for shift variables, the results for Total Number of Shifts were examined. It was recognized that the summing of the two kinds of shifts and the two roles produced total scores with little or no internal consistency. The only reasonable rationale would be that different kinds of shifts were alternative manifestations of the same underlying tendency. The Total Number of Shifts had the practical advantage of having the highest mean and variance of all shift variables.

Number of Shifts was related to all the other Shift variables. Its correlations with Number of Leg Shifts were primarily above .90. Those with Seat Shifts were substantial but not as high, presumably because of the smaller means and variances for Seat Shifts. For each Shift score, Number of Shifts had generally higher correlations with the score for Speaking than for Not Speaking, again associated with higher means and variances. The only other relationship was a low one with Number of Foot Movements. There were no relationships with partner variables, there being only a chance number of the individual coefficients which reached statistical significance.

For other act families, total scores tended to show most of the relationships found for their component scores, though often at lower levels. Hence, it seemed reasonable to omit any examination of other shift variables. An investigator wishing to study body shifts and their relationships to other behaviors would do well to base his scores on periods of interaction several times longer than five minutes.

AN OVERVIEW

Locus of Appreciable Correlations

The number of appreciable correlations, defined as values of .30 or more with either sign, was counted for each of the basic eight pairings—within each interaction, the four pairings of sex of participant and sex of partner. Among the intercorrelations of own acts, there were more appreciable correlations for second interactions. This difference was fully accounted for by the two cross-sex pairings, females with males and males with females. Note that these two sets of correlations are for the same interactions, taken for the males and for the females separately. There were also somewhat more appreciable correlations for males. This trend was fairly consistent across the corresponding pairings by interaction and by sex of partner.

Among the correlations with acts of partner, there also were more appreciable correlations for males. For the total sums, the second interactions had only a few more such values than the first, but the males tended to have more appreciable correlations in their second interactions while the females had slightly less. In both the correlations with own actions and those with partners', the first and second interactions of females with other females had the smallest frequencies of appreciable correlations.

The group or groups with more of these large correlations tended to have higher variances, as one would expect. Thus, for correlations with own actions, for the females with males and the males with females in second interactions, the variances of these two groups were higher than both the same-sex second interactions for 44% of the variables. The higher variances and higher numbers of large correlations were distributed over variables from all the action families. We should also point out that we saw no tendency for a complementary relationship between number of large correlations with own behaviors and number with acts of partner; it did not appear true that an act which correlated relatively highly with own acts had relatively fewer correlations with the partner's, or vice versa.

The interpretation of these differences is not obvious although the larger variances provide a plausible guess: where the variances are larger, the individuals are more consistent in giving either many or few acts of that kind during that interaction. Perhaps such greater consistency comes from taking a particular strategy or way of adapting to the situation early in the interaction and maintaining that strategy throughout. (This usage of the term strategy is somewhat more general than the more specific meaning given to the term in the later parts of this monograph.) Lower consistencies, with consequent lower group variances and lower relative frequencies of large correlations, would be associated with modifying one's strategy during the course of the interaction. Restating the findings of this analysis in these terms, participants generally were more consistent in their strategies in second interactions, males tended to be more consistent than females, and the strategies adopted by those whose second interactions were with partners of the opposite sex were highly consistent in those interactions. The greater postulated consistency of the males may be related to their greater manifested consistency between their first and second interactions. Of course, the particular pattern for these interactions could stem from the particular groups of males and females involved; there is, however, nothing else in the data to identify these subgroups as different from the other sex subgroups. It seems best to interpret the pattern as associated with the more comfortable second interactions and the cross-sex pairing.

Patterns and Clusters

In most of this chapter, we have examined the relationships obtained for each act, taken by itself. In this section, we look for clusters of act variables which seem to covary together and for other patterning in the observed relationships. All of the specific correlations have been mentioned earlier; the purpose of this section is to consider together some sets of prominent relationships. We do not attempt to include all relationships noted above, or even all variables. For example, we omit mention of most total scores for the entire interaction where the total consists of scores for speaking and not speaking. Again, we omit correlations where we feel the relationship is a byproduct of relationships to another variable. (For example, if a variable is highly related to Turn Time, then a lower relationship with Gesture Time is of little interest, especially if it is not correlated with Gesture Extent.)

Rate of exchanging turns.   In these interactions, Turn Number is a key variable which is essentially the same for both participants. Hence, we can use it to identify those interactions with a rapid rate of exchanging turns, where each participant's Turn Length tended to be short. This negative relationship with Turn Number was distinctly smaller, however, for the Turn Lengths of females talking with male partners. The rate of exchanging turns was associated with Long Back-Channel and Social Question Rates, these being separate kinds of speech units, involving several words, which were not counted as speaking turns.

These interactions with frequent exchange of turns were characterized by higher Numbers of Laughs. There were also more Smiles, primarily in the interactions between partners of opposite sexes. The Rates of Gazing While Speaking and While Not Speaking were larger. Curiously, the women, but not the men, in these rapid interactions had shorter Self-Adaptor Lengths. Thus, we find that rate of exchanging turns and its correlates varied with sex and with similarity or difference of sex for the pair of participants.

Turn Length.   While both participants tended to have short turns in the interactions just described, there were also interactions where just one had shorter turns. The Turn Lengths of the two participants were uncorrelated. Turn Length was related positively to own Interruption Rate and negatively to partner's rate. Successful interruptions gain the floor, which can be held longer if the other does not interrupt. Longer Turns were associated with larger total Turn Time.

People with *short* Turns asked Social Questions and gave Long Back Channels, both actions encouraging the partner to talk. When such people spoke, their Rates of Laughing and of Gazing were high, along with the Extent of their Gazing.

The partners of people with long Turns gave many Nods and few Interruptions. While listening, these partners had a low Rate of Gazing but long Lengths of Gazing and long Lengths of Self-Adaptors. It seems as though some of the participants acted to encourage their partners to talk, and perhaps to take longer turns. One wonders whether such encouragement actually preceded the earliest taking of long turns, or whether these partners accepted the long turn-taking when it appeared and found it easier to encourage it than to try to obtain equal time.

Longer Turns led to more Turn Time. Most of the relationships with Turn Time are for variables related to Length or Number. The exception is Filled Pause Rate. All things considered, Length appears to be a more useful variable than total Turn Time.

Short Back Channels. The two Rates, Short Vocal Back Channel and Nods, are an interesting pair of action variables. While their intercorrelation is rather substantial, they have somewhat different patterns of relationships.

Nods were associated with few Interruptions and with both long Gazes and low Rate of Gazing when listening. But when the participant became the speaker, the Rate of Gazing was high. Nod Rate was also associated with partner's Number of Self-Adaptors, Turn Length, and total Turn Time.

Short Vocal Back Channels were related to Extent of Gazing when listening and, curiously, to a high Rate of Gesturing when talking. Short Back Channels were associated with both Short and Long Back Channels of partner, together with many Smiles and high Extents of Smiling When Not Speaking.

Thus, it seems that while Nodding is not related to back-channel acts of the partner, Short Back Channels are. (In the rating procedure all back channels were counted only for the auditor and hence could not occur simultaneously for both participants.) Perhaps Nodding and Short Back Channels are basically similar, although the first is relatively independent of the partner's activity in this area while the second is facilitated by similar action of the partner. Is the partner's smiling itself a kind of back channel, at least in this context?

Short Vocal Back Channels were not related to any of the Turn variables, although one might expect such relationships. Nods, however, were related to partner Turn variables, another contrast between the members of this pair.

Smiling and Laughing. Most of the smiling and laughing variables were correlated with others in this joint family but with little else. Smiling While Speaking, as compared to when Not Speaking, was more related to Laughing While Speaking. It was also more related to the partner's Smiling and Laughing When Not Speaking (that is, for the same turns) than to those behaviors of partner in the other set of turns. Similarly, Laughing While Speaking was correlated with partner's complementary Laughing When Not Speaking. Somewhat surprisingly, it is not correlated with own Laughing When Not Speaking and it was not related to the partner's Laughing or Smiling When Speaking.

Thus, Smiling appears to be a general characteristic of our participants, for each interaction and for the two interactions together, regardless of Speaking or Not Speaking. It is associated with Smiling of partner in the same turn periods. Smiling While Speaking is related to the partner's Laughing While Not Speaking, whereas Smiling While Not Speaking is not.

Laughing seems to be even more specific to being speaker or auditor, although Laughing in each position is related to Smiling in both. All in all, the understanding of laughing and smiling clearly calls for analysis of their sequential appearance in interactions.

In the preceding account we have discussed rates of laughing along with extents of smiling. Scoring and analyses of rates of smiling might clarify our understanding of this joint family. We already know that the total Number of Smiles is related to own and partner Short Back Channel, as noted in the preceding discussion of back channels.

Gazes.   As with Laugh Rates, the Rates of Gazing in the two roles were uncorrelated. Gaze Rate While Speaking was correlated positively with Number of Turns and negatively with Length and total Time. It was related to three rates when Not Speaking: Nods, Long Back Channels, and Social Questions. Perhaps all involve attending to the partner. Gaze Rate While Speaking was related to Gaze Extent While Speaking but negatively to Length of those gazes. A high Rate of Gazing While Speaking was complemented by the partner's high Gaze Rate while listening, though the relationship with partner's Gaze Length While Not Speaking was negative.

Gaze Rate When Not Speaking has a rather unusual pattern of relationships. It had an extremely high negative correlation with Length of such Gazes, only in part because both variables involved the Number of Gazes When Not Speaking. High Rates of Gazes When Not Speaking were associated with large Turn Times in interactions with many turns. In complementary fashion, they were strongly correlated with low Turn Lengths for partner, and with partner's high Rate of Gazing While Speaking. Associated in addition were partner's Social Questions and relative absence of Filled Pauses. In contrast, those with high Gaze Rates When Not Speaking also interrupted and gave few nods.

The pictures for these independent Gaze Rates are not clear; the results in Part III will help to clarify the uses of these variables. What is apparent is that they are important to the interactions between our participants. The pattern of relationships for Gaze Rate When Not Speaking seems to complement the pattern noted above for the partners of those with long Turn Lengths.

The Gaze Rates appear to be more important variables than Gaze times, either Extents or Lengths. Gaze Length While Speaking is related primarily to other Gaze variables for that person. Length When Not Speaking has the exceptionally high negative correlation with the corresponding Rate. Its very large relationship with partner's Turn Length seems to be more than an artifact, more than a relationship with greater opportunity for long gazes; it seem probable that the listener's long gazes encourage the speaker to take long turns.

The Extent variables add little to what the other Gaze variables have brought out. It is worth noting, however, that Extent While Speaking is related to partner's Extent while listening.

Self-Adaptors.   Like other families of actions, the Self-Adaptor family has many intercorrelations, primarily with the Extent variables. In terms of correlations outside the family, the Lengths are of most interest. Length While Speaking was negatively related to Gesture Extent and Rate, possibly because it is difficult to engage in a Self-Adaptor and a Gesture at the same time. Length When Not Speaking was related to few Turns and Long Turns for partner (which may have provided the opportunity for the longer Self-Adaptors). It was also associated with own Foot Length and Gaze Length as listener.

Other families.   The Shift and Foot variables offered no interesting patterns of relationships with variables from other families. Somewhat surprisingly, the same is true for the Gesture variables. Perhaps for all these, and for the Self-Adaptors, it is the sequential location of each ocurrence which is pertinent to the course of the interaction.

Comments on the patterns.   These patterns are not strong sets of interrelationships. In general, we do not find three or four variables which have high intercorrelations. More particularly, each pattern does not appear consistently in four to six of the eight pairings formed from sex, sex of partner, and order of interaction. In contrast, some of the relationships within single families of actions are, as a set, notably stronger or weaker for a single pairing. We may also note that there are not many links between patterns. Finally, the patterns are not associated primarily with the first or with the second interaction.

Concluding Remarks

The correlations that we found among the action variables are about what one would expect: for example, smiling and laughing are associated. Some of the relationships, we must remind the reader again, are a product of the way in which the variables were scored. In particular, total scores are related to the part scores for the separate speaker and auditor periods. There are also relationships which are a function of permitted possibilities: if the mean length of the periods as speaker or as auditor is short, the mean length of some acts in those periods will tend to be short.

That point also illustrates the fundamental nature of the turn variables in these interactions. They provide the basic structure of each interaction. Many of the variables are related in one way or another to length of turns and to the exchange of turns, matters that are examined intensively in Part III. Note, however, that the list of variables chosen for coding and scoring in

Part II was determined only in part by the concerns of the study with turn-related actions in Part III.

We have already pointed out that the correlations tended to be more positive than negative. This trend is particularly strong within action families as a function not only of interdependencies in scoring but also of consistency across the speaking and not-speaking phases of the interaction. It is also found between smiling and laughing, among the back-channel actions, and among the leg and seat shifts.

The most important general finding is the number of correlations between the acts for one person as speaker and the partner's acts as auditor. These relationships are for action within the same segments of the interactions. Subsequent investigation will have to determine whether these pairs of correlated acts occurred simultaneously (as seems very likely for laughs) or in close temporal succession. These complementary relationships were less common for self-adaptors and bodily shifts.

6
Actions, Self-Descriptions, and Reactions

In this chapter, we consider a second major part of our investigation of individual differences in actions coded from the five minutes of interaction. The previous chapter presented the covariations of these actions over participants. This chapter considers relationships between these actions and the participants' descriptions of themselves.

This investigation of relationships to personality variables was one of the main original purposes of this research. It seemed reasonable to expect that a person's personality would be related to his behavior, in this case, his acts in an interpersonal situation. The plausibility of this expectation was supported by the consideration that these acts are generally outside the center of the actor's awareness. The actor ordinarily is attending to what he is saying and to what the other person is saying or doing. This direction of attention should help to reduce the likelihood that these acts would be monitored to create a favorable impression in the eyes of the other person any more than the actor's usual disposition to do so.

Much research has been done on the relationships between nonverbal actions and personality variables (see the "External Variable" section of Duncan, 1969). An unusual feature of the analysis reported below is the large number of action variables and the large number of personality variables which were included.

There are several modes by which personality is measured (Fiske, 1971, Chapter 5). Among these are judgments by others based upon a person's current behaviors and judgments based upon prior behavior of some kind. It seemed to us, however, that the most likely place to find relationships between acts and personality was in measurements of personality obtained from the mode employing self-descriptions of participants. What is expressed in actions is presumably the person as he sees himself. It is also reasonable to hypothesize that a person's actions may contribute to his view of himself.

INSTRUMENTS FOR OBTAINING SELF-DESCRIPTIONS

One major instrument used to elicit self-descriptions was the Adjective Check List developed by Gough and Heilbrun (1965). This procedure presents a list of 300 adjectives in alphabetical order. The subject is asked simply to check those which he considers to be self-descriptive. This test has several advantages: it is relatively easy for the subject to take; it covers a wide range of dispositions; it can be scored for a large number of personality variables (listed in Table 6.1). We also used it because a small pilot study had yielded promising relationships between acts and ACL variables (for reasons that appeared later to be associated with unique features of that particular preliminary investigation).

The acts we were studying are motoric expressions. As such, they may well be determined in part by constitutional makeup, by patterns of physiological functioning, that is, by factors falling under the classical notion of temperament. That term includes not just emotionality; more broadly, it can be construed as referring to the rates and patterns of energy discharges. Activity, reactivity, expressiveness, and similar clusters of dispositions belong in that domain. On the basis of this rationale, we included the Thorndike Dimensions of Temperament (Thorndike, 1966).

Finally, we include two scales developed by Schutz (1958) assessing an aspect of people's Fundamental Interpersonal Relations Orientation. These scales assess the desire to be included in social groups as expressed in action and as a preference for relevant actions by others. Table 6.1 lists the set of self-descriptive variables used in this research, with the definition for each variable.

PROCEDURE

It will be recalled that four persons were scheduled for each session. Their first task was to complete the self-descriptive instruments. Each did so in a separate room, alone. The subjects were then assigned to pairs for the videotaped interactions.

As in the investigation of interrelationships among the acts, several analyses were made of the correlations between each act and each of the numerous self-descriptive variables: one included all subjects in their second interaction, another was by sex for second interactions, and others were by sex and sex of partner, for each interaction separately. In addition, in an effort to obtain more dependable values, we made an analysis, for each sex, in which we threw together the action data from the first and the second interactions. Thus, each person contributed two entries to the array for each correlation, one his action score in the first interaction and one for his same personality score but his different action score from the second interaction. We recognized that entering these interdependent values for the same person reduced our degrees of freedom for evaluating each correlation.

The task of interpreting these correlations was colossal. For each subset of data, several dozen acts were correlated with several dozen personality scores, yielding more than 2,000 correlation values. With the total data grouped into four subsets, we had more than 8,000, and for analyses by sex, sex of partner, and interaction, we had over 17,000. Simply identifying the coefficients of notable size was time-consuming.

In addition, we faced the problem of selecting a criterion for values to be studied. In a set of 2,000 independent correlations, 100 could be expected to reach the familiar .05 level of confidence. But our correlations were not independent. Within the data for any subset of correlations, the various self-report scores themselves had many appreciable intercorrelations. In addition, the subsets were often not independent of each other: for example, the subset of females whose first interaction was with females were the same persons as those in the subset whose second interaction was with males.

In the following presentation of results for these correlational analyses, we shall concentrate primarily on the findings for the four groups formed from classification by sex and order of sex of partner. Thus, one group was composed of those females who interacted first with a female and next with a male, one was the other females (whose first interaction was with a male), and two were the corresponding groupings for males. In these correlations, each person was entered twice, as noted above, the personality score being identical each time.

This particular analysis was chosen for several reasons. It involved only four subsets and hence was a little easier to examine and interpret. Also, it provided a kind of replication: there were two values for each act-personality correlation for each sex, one value for each sex group. If a relationship appeared only for one sex group, it did not seem sufficiently dependable and general to merit close scrutiny. In emphasizing such summarizing correlations, we are essentially ignoring the differences in order of sex of partner: we did not feel confident in attempting to explain why a correlation should be larger for those males whose partners were in the male–female order than the value was for those with partners in the female–male order. It is possible that the male participants found it easier to adapt to the research situation when their first partner was also male, and that as a consequence their actions were more likely to be similar to their usual actions outside that situation, and more related to how they see themselves. Having had this easier introduction to the total situation, the additional complication of interacting with a female of about the same age, in a second interaction, might also be easier. In contrast, those faced in the first interaction not only with the unfamiliar research situation but also with a partner of the opposite sex might engage in actions less representative of their everyday actions.

TABLE 6.1

Variables for Self-Description

Adjective Check List [a]

Number of Adjectives Checked (total).

Number of Favorable Adjectives Checked: Key is composed of the 75 adjectives selected by undergraduate judges as among the "most favorable."

Number of Unfavorable Adjectives Checked: Key is the 75 adjectives selected by undergraduate judges as least favorable or most unfavorable.

Defensiveness: Items differentiating between responses of applicants for counseling whose self-descriptions were unduly favorable and those whose self-descriptions were not.

Self-Confidence: Items differentiating people assessed as high versus low on poise, self-confidence, self-assurance, etc.

Self-Control: Also based on empirical key developed from assessments.

Lability: Empirical key differentiating responses of subjects assessed as high versus low on such characteristics as spontaneity, flexibility, need for change, rejection of convention, and assertive individuality.

Achievement: For this variable and the next 14, the key is based on judgments of psychology graduate students as to self-endorsed adjectives indicating or contraindicating presence of the need as defined by Edwards (1954), "To strive to be outstanding in pursuits of socially recognized significance."

Dominance: "To seek and sustain leadership roles in groups or to be influential and controlling in individual relationships."

Endurance: "To persist in any task undertaken."

Order: "To place special emphasis on neatness, organization, and planning in one's activities."

Intraception: "To engage in attempts to understand one's own behavior or the behavior of others."

Nurturance: "To engage in behaviors which extend material or emotional benefits to others."

Affiliation: "To seek and sustain numerous personal friendships."

Heterosexuality: "To seek the company of and derive emotional satisfactions from interactions with opposite-sexed peers."

Exhibition: "To behave in such a way as to elicit the immediate attention of others."

Autonomy: "To act independently of others or of social values and expectations."

Aggression: "To engage in behaviors which attack or hurt others."

Change: "To seek novelty of experience and avoid routine."

Succorance: "To solicit sympathy, affection, or emotional support from others."

Abasement: "To express feelings of inferiority through self-criticism, guilt, or social impotence."

Deference: "To seek and sustain subordinate roles in relationships with others."

Personal Adjustment: Empirical key based on responses of subjects assessed as high versus low on personal adjustment and personal soundness.

Counseling Readiness: Empirical key based on responses of clients judged as showing a more positive versus a less positive response to counseling.

Thorndike Dimensions Of Temperament [b]

Sociable: "Likes to be with other people, to do things in groups, to go to parties, to be in the middle of things."

versus Solitary: "Likes to be by himself, to do things by himself, to read or engage in other kinds of solitary activities."

(continued)

Ascendent: "Likes to be in the center of the stage, to speak in public, to 'sell' things or ideas, to meet important people; tends to stand up for his rights or his point of view."
versus Withdrawing: "Tends to avoid personal conflict, to dislike being in the public eye, to avoid taking the initiative in relation to others, to accept being imposed upon."

Cheerful: "Seems to feel generally well and happy; satisfied with his relations to others, accepted by others, at peace with the world."
versus Gloomy, Sensitive: "Often seems to feel moody, depressed, at odds with himself; sensitive to the criticism of others; prone to worry and anxiety."

Placid: "even-tempered, easygoing, not easily ruffled or annoyed."
versus Irritable: "Short-tempered, annoyed or irked by a good many things, inclined to 'blow his top.' "

Accepting: "Tends to think the best of people, to accept them at face value, to expect altruism to prevail."
versus Critical: "Tends to question people's motives, expecting self-interest, conscious of the need for each to look out for himself."

Tough-Minded (Masculine): "Tolerant of dirt, bugs, and profanity; enjoys sports, roughing it, and the out-of-doors; uninterested in clothes or personal appearance; rational rather than intuitive."
versus Tender-Minded (Feminine): "Sensitive to dirt, both physical and verbal; concerned with personal appearance; aesthetic interests; intuitive rather than rational."

Reflective: "Interested in ideas, in abstractions, in discussion and speculation, in knowing for its own sake."
versus Practical: "Interested in doing and in using knowledge for practical ends, impatient with speculation and theorizing."

Impulsive: "Carefree, happy-go-lucky, ready to do things at a moment's notice."
versus Planful: "Careful to plan life out in advance, systematic, orderly, foresighted."

Active: "Full of energy, on the go, quick to get things done, able to get a lot done."
versus Lethargic: "Slow, easily tired, less productive than others; likes to move at a leisurely pace."

Responsible: "Dependable, reliable, certain to complete tasks on time, even a little compulsive."
versus Casual: "Often late with commitments, rushes to meet deadlines; has difficulty getting things done, unpredictable."

Fundamental Interpersonal Relations Orientation (FIRO)[c]

Inclusion Expressed: "I initiate interaction with people."
Inclusion Wanted: "I want to be included."

[a] Quotations are reproduced by special permission from *The Adjective Check List Manual* by Harrison G. Gough, Ph.D., and Alfred B. Heilbrun, Jr., Ph.D. (Pp. 7-9). Copyright 1965. Published by Consulting Psychologists Press Inc.

[b] Quotations from Thorndike (1966, p. 6).

[c] Quotations from Schutz (1958, p. 59).

In selecting correlations for examination, we arbitrarily chose values of .30 or higher, either positive or negative. For the data classified by the four subgroups, two male and two female, there were 44 entries per correlation. For an N of 44 independent observations, a correlation of .30 is significant at the .05 level. Since the 44 observations were from 22 persons (each in two interactions), the actual confidence level is somewhere between .05 and .22 (two-tailed test).

The probability of one of these correlations being +.30 or more would be half of these values (that is, between .025 and .11). For a pair of correlations, such as those for the two subgroups of males, the probability of their both being +.30 or more is .012 or less. The same probabilities apply to one and two negative values in that range of magnitude.

THE FINDINGS

A preliminary overview.   In considering the findings, the reader should recall the nature of the two sets of variables being correlated. The various self-report scores can be assumed to be reasonably stable over time. Gough and Heilbrun (1965) report stability coefficients ranging from .45 to .90 (over a period of ten weeks) for the ACL Scales. While Thorndike (1966) does not report any stability values in his Manual for the TDOT, we can assume that they approximate those of similar scales and are above .60. On the other side, the stabilities of the act scores in our data were relatively low: the median of our computed stabilities was .40. If two measurements of a variable, derived from sequential samples of behavior, correlate only .40 with each other, one should not expect such measurements to have many high correlations with other variables, even more stable ones.

In general, we found little relationship between acts and self-descriptive scores. In no case was the substantial correlation found for all four independent samples of subjects. There were some relationships present in both samples of the same sex. Even for the relationships reported below, we have limited confidence. Since the total numbers of values reaching any particular level of statistical confidence usually did not greatly exceed the numbers to be expected by chance if our 44 observation points had come from 44 separate persons, we cannot accept any obtained finding with much assurance.

Smile Number as an example.   To permit the reader to obtain some idea of the nature of the correlations, two sets of correlations for Smile Number are presented in Table 6.2. Smile Number was chosen rather arbitrarily because it was relatively stable across interactions (.54) and because it had a number of large coefficients. Columns 1–4 of Table 6.2 present the findings for the groupings by sex of subject, each sex being subdivided by the order of the sex of the partners. Columns 5-12 present the results for the analysis by sex, sex of partner, and order of the interaction. These correspond to the eight pairings used in the analysis of the relationships between actions, in Chapter 5.

The two sets of analyses involve the same data categorized in different ways. Thus, Columns 5 and 8 (from the second set of analyses) are for the same group of females, Column 5 being for their first interaction (with females) and Column 8 being for their second interaction (with males). The same self-descriptive indices were used in each of the two columns, each subset of the data. The entries used in computing a given correlation in Column 5 and those entries used in computing the corresponding correlation in Column 8 were, in effect, pooled in the computation of the corresponding correlation in Column 1, the column for females whose first interaction was with females.

It will be apparent that the first set of analyses provides a summary integration of the data from the corresponding pair of columns in the second set. Thus, for Defensiveness, the value of .38 in Column 1 of the table summarizes the values of .41 and .37 in Columns 5 and 8; the -.31 in Column 2 is an integration of the .01 and the -.53 values in Columns 6 and 7 of the right side of the table. In general, each value in the left side of the table falls between the corresponding values on the right side, as one would expect when the means and variances for the variables in the two finer analyses (broken down by interaction, on the right side) are quite comparable. It should also be noted that the pairs of values for the same persons as given on the right side of the table are often fairly disparate (for example, the .01 and the -.53 values mentioned above). Such changes can stem from changes in a second interaction when the participants were more acquainted with the total situation, from change in sex of partner, or from other influences, including complex interactive effects. But note also that the corresponding values for the two samples from the same sex, on the left side of the table, also show many large differences. Such discrepancies are best seen as stemming from the total of several influences, including various complex interactions, rather than coming primarily from some one source. It should be recalled that the multivariate analysis of the action variables did not find a significant main effect for sex of partner (see Chapter 4, page 55).

The rows of Table 6.2 are the various self-descriptive variables. They include those from the Adjective Check List and those from the Thorndike Dimensions of Temperament, plus Inclusion Expressed and Inclusion Wanted from the Fundamental Interpersonal Relations Orientation scales. (Added on at the bottom are seven variables from the Postinteractions Questionnaire which is discussed in the last section of this chapter. For the latter questionnaire variables, it should be recalled that the subjects were asked about each interaction separately. Hence, the data entered into correlations for these variables did not usually involve the same values for both interactions, as was the case for the test scores.)

TABLE 6.2

Correlations for Total Number of Smiles with the Self-Descriptive Personality Variables and the Reported Reactions [a]

Sex of participant:	Female								Male			
Sex of partner in 1st interaction:	Female	Female	Male	Male	Female		Male		Female		Male	
Sex of partner in 2nd interaction:	Male	Female	Male	Female		Female		Male		Female		Male
Interaction(s) included	1 & 2	1 & 2	1 & 2	1 & 2	1	2	1	2	1	2	1	2
Column no.	1	2	3	4	5	6	7	8	9	10	11	12
Personality variables (ACL)												
No. Adj. Checked	-25	-05	-25	-06	-28	-03	-06	-24	-19	07	-22	-32
No. Favorable Adj. Checked	30	-46	17	48	25	-13	-68	34	10	57	41	25
No. Unfavorable Adj. Checked	-20	30	-17	-26	-12	42	24	-27	-15	-20	-34	-20
Defensiveness	38	-31	17	41	41	01	-53	37	08	50	33	26
Self-Confidence	-05	-43	-09	38	17	-39	-47	-21	-05	49	28	-14
Self-Control	28	00	29	10	36	06	-04	23	20	11	10	39
Lability	12	-29	-09	16	-13	-21	-34	30	-13	31	00	-03
Achievement	05	-05	-10	29	26	07	-12	-10	-16	41	17	-02
Dominance	-02	-24	-09	31	12	-08	-35	-13	-09	41	22	-09
Endurance	17	21	-05	16	37	31	16	04	-11	25	07	01
Order	09	23	05	07	24	31	19	-02	00	12	01	11
Intraception	35	-25	-08	28	27	11	-48	43	-13	35	21	-04
Nurturance	35	-18	22	52	17	-22	-16	49	17	51	56	27
Affiliation	20	-39	29	50	16	-25	-49	23	24	55	48	36
Heterosexuality	13	-38	18	26	-05	-37	-40	25	11	31	23	25

(continued)

Exhibition	-21	-33	-13	18	-25	-37	-32	-18	-14	30	06	-12
Autonomy	-26	-17	-32	-28	-13	19	-40	-37	-27	-21	-36	-38
Aggression	-34	08	-19	-20	-29	06	10	-40	-19	-12	-31	-20
Change	-01	-35	-13	05	-09	-22	-45	04	-08	15	-05	-18
Succorance	-18	31	-18	-25	-32	11	44	-09	-15	-20	-31	-21
Abasement	23	29	06	-16	14	32	29	30	09	-14	-19	03
Deference	25	34	25	01	15	19	45	33	21	-11	15	30
Personal	28	-29	37	42	20	-13	-40	34	27	41	47	48
Adjustment												
Counseling	-34	23	-02	-40	-12	44	11	-50	-03	-48	-34	-01
Readiness												
(Temperament)												
Sociable	11	-10	53	49	-08	-02	-15	25	-59	43	58	47
Ascendent	-16	-25	-20	-09	-15	-23	-28	-17	-18	-03	-16	-22
Cheerful	21	-18	07	26	22	-24	-16	21	01	19	37	13
Placid	06	-03	11	16	00	-11	01	10	06	-01	36	16
Accepting	20	-08	23	-09	26	-28	04	17	24	-04	-15	22
Tough-Minded	-30	-36	-22	17	-19	-21	-47	-40	-28	04	32	-14
Reflective	21	03	09	-06	21	23	-01	21	17	-22	10	-01
Impulsive	-20	-12	09	16	-26	-03	-17	-17	17	27	06	01
Active	-02	31	-14	-09	21	36	29	-18	-01	05	-25	-28
Responsible	12	13	04	03	31	25	06	-02	-02	01	04	10
(FIRO)												
Inclusion	17	-13	28	46	-05	02	-31	33	31	50	44	24
Expressed												
Inclusion	22	03	35	42	00	22	-01	39	48	46	40	20
Wanted												

(continued)

TABLE 6.2 (continued)

Sex of participant:	Female		Male		Female				Male			
Sex of partner in 1st interaction:	Female	Male	Female	Male	Female		Male		Female		Male	
Sex of partner in 2nd interaction:	Male	Female		Female	Male	Female	Male	Female	Male	Female	Male	
(Postinteractions questionnaire)												
Aware of Camera	34	-11	33	02	15	-26	-03	46	40	12	03	23
Comfort with Camera	52	-18	20	24	-31	-28	-14	-66	-31	23	26	-01
Comfort with Partner	-08	-11	05	34	-12	-30	02	-00	-10	29	44	26
Interest in Partner	09	14	28	05	23	-00	23	05	01	-11	28	47
Interest in Seeing Again	23	28	17	11	16	18	33	29	-10	-09	29	42
Interest in Subject	-19	-00	11	-06	-09	23	-12	-29	-07	-25	24	36
Influence	-09	-03	-03	22	05	-06	-02	-18	05	53	-12	-18

[a] Columns 1-4: $N = 44$, $r \geq .30$, $p < .05$. Columns 5-12: $N = 22$. $r \geq .42$, $p < .05$.

Let us consider this table in some detail. We can begin with Columns 1–4 on the left side and, arbitrarily, consider only pairs of correlations of .30 or higher, both being positive or both negative. For the two groups of females, the first two columns, there is only one relationship which appears in both groups of females: a negative one with Tough-Minded, that is, a positive relationship between Number of Smiles and Tender-Minded or Feminine. For the second pair of columns, there are three consistent relationships in the two male groups: positive ones for Personal Adjustment as keyed on the ACL, for Sociable, and for Wanted Inclusion. In contrast, values of .30 or more but with opposite signs can be noted in the correlations for females (first two columns) for Defensiveness and for Number of Favorable Adjectives. Note that no personality variable correlates .30 or above consistently (same sign) with Smile Number for three of the four groups, and of course no relationship appears in all four groups.

Turning to the right side of the table, we should recall that Columns 5 and 8 involve one sample of females, Columns 6 and 7 involving the other sample; similarly for Columns 9 and 12 and Columns 10 and 11, for males. First, note that there is very little consistency associated with the pairing of the sexes: for example, while for females talking with males, Smile Number has negative correlations with Autonomy and with Tough-Minded in both instances, and positive ones for Deference, there are six instances in which the relationships have the opposite direction in the two cases: Number of Favorable Adjectives Checked, Defensiveness, Lability, Personal Adjustment, Intraception, and Inclusion Wanted. The reader may enjoy speculating about the distinctive patterns of relationships found for these two groups of females talking with males, taking into account the fact that all the negative correlations in each pair of these contrasting relationships were found for the same group of females and also utilizing the information from the other large correlations found only for one group or the other. There is the additional observation that, when these same two groups of females were interacting with females, there is only one value above .30 for any of the variables mentioned above. Hence, the relationships have something to do with talking to a male, but why is Number of Smiles associated with high personality scores in one group and with low scores in the other? It seems unlikely that the ordinal position of the interaction is solely responsible.

Turning now to the values for each group of female participants, the group who interacted first with other females (Columns 5 and 8) had only one pair of positive correlations, with Defensiveness, and one pair of negative values, indicating low Comfort with Camera. The other group of females, in Columns 6 and 7, had pairs of negative values for Self-Confidence, Heterosexuality, and Exhibition.This latter group is the one which was mentioned above, in connection with correlations for interactions with males, as having a number of negative correlations for variables on which the other group had positive correlations.

Now consider the findings for males, in Columns 9–12 of the table. In all four columns, there is a high positive correlation between Smile Number and Sociable. Aside from this relationship, the two interactions with females (Columns 9 and 10) have positive correlations with the two Inclusion variables, while the two interactions with other males have positive values for Affiliation and Personal Adjustment, together with negative values for Autonomy.

Looking at each subgroup of males, we see that those interacting first with females (Columns 9 and 12) have no pair of correlations over .30 (except for Sociable). The subgroup interacting first with males (Columns 10 and 11) has pairs of positive correlations for seven variables and a negative pair for one. Note that for these data on males, there is no instance of a pair of large correlations with opposite signs, positive in one group but negative in the other; furthermore, the values below .30 tend to be consistent in direction with the corresponding larger values.

What tentative generalizations might one formulate from these findings? Smile Number is associated, in males, with self-reports of being Sociable, and in some males with a defensively favorable self-description which includes being Affiliative and Nurturant, and both Wanting and Expressing Inclusion within the group. For females, Smile Number is related to the self-report of being Tender-Minded or Feminine although this relationship is stronger for interactions with men. Other relationships are specific to a sample, especially when the acts are scored from interactions with male partners.

No relationships appear for both sexes, and only a couple for each sex separately. No relationships were found for both sexes when they were interacting with each other, and none were shown for each sex when interacting with others of the same sex. The number of smiles in a five-minute interaction appears to have no relationship to these self-descriptive variables which is common to major sections of the data. The obtained relationships appear to be mediated in a complex way by the several characteristics of the interactions: the sex of the actor, the sex of the partner, the pairing. This picture illustrates the desirability of examining the actual course of the smiling actions in these conversations: who initiates smiles, what actions precede such initiations, what actions are associated with terminations of smiles, etc.

The rest of the Smile family.   Having looked at Smile Number, we next consider the other variables in the Smile family. As a set, the variables in the Smile family were more stable than those in any other family. Smile Time, the total extent of smiling in the interaction, had a set of correlations fairly closely paralleling that for Smile Number. There was no self-report variable with appreciable correlations for all four sex groups. For the two male groups, Smile Time had moderate positive correlations with Sociable and with Inclusion Wanted. For the two female groups, it correlated positively with Tender-Minded.While it also had a positive correlation with Number of Favorable Adjectives in the group interacting first with other females, the correlation was negative in the other female group.

The other correlations of .30 or more appeared primarily in the group of females talking with males first and also in the males who talked first with other males. These values, however, had opposite signs for the two groups: while the male group had positive correlations for Self-Confidence, Lability, Affiliation, and Exhibition, the corresponding ones for the female group were negative.

The trend of the patterns for Smile Extent While Speaking and While Not Speaking is similar to that for Smile Time, which was based on these two part scores. For Extent While Speaking, Sociable again has positive correlations for the male groups, and Number of Favorable Adjectives shows the opposed correlations for the females. For Extent When Not Speaking, Inclusion Wanted joins Sociable in having positive correlations for both male groups, and Affiliation has the same pattern. The few appreciable values for females are scattered.

Thus, for the Smile family as a whole, there is no consistent relationship for both sexes. The males do show a consistent correlation with Sociable, a relationship which is supported by the values for other, similar variables, such as Inclusion Wanted. For the females, the relationships with Tender-Minded are weaker than those for males with Sociable. The only other notable features are associated with particular subgroups. While the more conservative interpretation is that these are associated with chance fluctuations in the sampling of subjects, there is the alternative speculation that these findings stem from the sex of the participants together with the order of the sexes of the partners with whom they interacted.

The Laugh family.   Closely related to the Smile family is the Laugh family. Its variables were moderately stable (.30–.52) across the two interactions. Once again, no relationship appeared consistently in all four sex groups. For the males, there were few values reaching the criterion of .30. Sociable, however, was correlated in both male groups with Laugh Number and with Laugh Rate When Not Speaking.

There were no relationships consistently in the same direction for the two female groups. Once more, the contrasting pairs of correlations appeared, with the intuitively expected positive values present for the females whose first interaction was with females, the other group showing negative values: for example, for Laugh Time, this contrast was found for Number of Favorable Adjectives Checked, Defensiveness, Affiliation, and Heterosexuality. (The contrasting values for Succorance had the opposite signs.) Some of these relationships were also found for one or the other of the Laugh Rate variables. The only additional pattern was that Self-Confidence joined the list of contrasting values for the female groups. Inspection of the correlations from the analysis for each of the eight subgroups (formed from sex, sex of partner, and order) reveals some consistency between the pairs of values for each sample of subjects and supports the tentative interpretation that the above relationships are primarily associated with a set of subjects rather than with a sex pairing.

We find, then, that Laughs have relationships with self-descriptions which are fairly similar to those for Smile variables. This similarity is, of course, to be expected in view of the correlations between the Laugh and Smile scores.

Turn-related actions.   Returning now to the same order of consideration of actions that was used in the preceding chapter, we can look at turn-related actions: the three Turn variables, the Rates for Interruptions and Filled Pauses, and the Number of Social Questions. The three Turn variables had rather low stabilities across the two interactions. These variables, as much or more than any other set, were influenced by the partner: Turn Number was essentially identical for the two partners, and the partner could markedly restrict a participant's total Turn Time. Perhaps as a consequence, the Turn variables had few appreciable correlations with self-descriptions. Turn Number had none for males; among the few for females, only Tender-Minded was consistent for the two groups. Turn Length had very few for either sex, and none were consistent across groups. Among the few for Turn Time, only the values for Autonomy for males were consistent.

Rate of Interruptions had very little stability across interactions. Among its small number of correlations with self-descriptions, none were consistent. Social Questions, another action with low stability, also had very few correlations and no consistent ones.

In contrast with the other variables in this cluster, Rate of Filled Pauses was very stable—it was the most stable of the actions we scored. While it had more correlations with self-descriptions than the variables we have just been considering, the correlations were for specific samples, especially for samples of men. The only consistent relationship was a negative one with heterosexuality for the males, and this appeared for each interaction of each group. If any other personality disposition is associated with Filled Pauses, we did not measure it.

The findings regarding relationships between self-descriptions and these actions related to turn-taking are for the most part negative. Since most of the acts are themselves rather unstable, perhaps nothing else could be expected. On the other hand, a very stable action score, Filled Pause rate, had no particularly promising results even though another stable variable, Smile Number, did show a few consistent relationships.

The Back-Channel actions.   The four back-channel actions had moderate stability coefficients (.50–.55, except for a value of .32 for Long Vocal Back-Channel Rate). In spite of this stability, there were no consistent relationships for all four sex groups or even for either pair of groups of the same sex. There was no pattern in a group for one sex which also appeared in either of the groups for the other sex. Although the males whose first interaction was with other males had a relatively high number of correlations with self-description variables, that pattern was not discernible in the limited set of values for any other group.

Nod Rate had no results meriting comment. While Rate of Short Vocal Back Channels had positive correlations for Number of Favorable Adjectives Checked, Self-Control, and Personal Adjustment in the male group interacting first with males, the corresponding correlations for the other male group were almost as large but negative. (Some of these variables were also involved in diametrically opposed patterns mentioned for other acts, earlier.) The two female groups had opposed signs for their correlations of Long Back-Channel Rate with Order, Active and Responsible. In these instances of opposite patterns, most or all of the values are positive in one group and negative in the other, presumably because of the associations among the self-descriptive variables that are involved. All Back-Channel Rate, the summarizing variable, had no consistencies or contrasts for the male groups and no values as large as .30 for either female group.

The Gaze family.   The stabilities of the Gaze variables ranged from .21 to .57, the Extent variables tending to have higher values than the Length ones. There is nothing to report about their correlations with self-descriptive variables. While there were some of .30 or larger, there was no consistency between pairs of sex groups, and not even any opposed pairs of correlations. Only once in a while was a correlation meeting the .30 criterion in one group matched by a comparable value in a group of the other sex.

The Gesture family.   The Gesture variables were moderately stable across the two interactions, the coefficients ranging from .31 to .49. The values were slightly higher for the male subjects. For both male groups, Gesture Time Speaking had negative correlations with Self-Control and with Deference and positive correlations with Aggression. These relationships were in part a function of the relationship between this raw Gesture Time variable and total Turn Time; Turn Time had similar but lower correlations with Deference and Aggression. When gesture time was measured as Gesture Extent (by dividing raw time by Turn Time), the only consistent relationship remaining was the negative one with Self-Control. Gesture Rate and Mean Length had no replicated relaionships.

The Self-Adaptor family.   These variables had a range of stability values from .20 to .57, the two length variables being the least stable. Self-Adaptor Extent While Speaking had negative relationships with Exhibition in both male groups. In the two female groups, it was correlated with Gloomy, Sensitive (the opposite pole from Cheerful, Objective). For females, the Number of Adjectives Checked had consistent negative correlations with Self-Adaptor Extent While Not Speaking, total Self-Adaptor Time, and Number of Self-Adaptors. The only other consistent relationship was that in the female groups between Self-Adaptor Length When Not Speaking and Defensiveness.

In the male group that interacted first with other males, Autonomy was negatively correlated with all but one of the Self-Adaptor variables. The trend in the other male group was enough in the same direction to produce similar correlations for all males together, for four variables in this family.

Foot variables.   With values from .39 to .63, these variables were comparatively stable across interactions. The only consistent relationships in the groups for the same sex were for males: Mean Length of Foot Movements had positive correlations with Dominance and negative ones with Counseling Readiness. For this same action, the male group and the female group whose first interactions were with males had positive correlations with Affiliation, Personal Adjustment, and Number of Favorable Adjectives Checked.

The several Shift variables.   In our short interactions, there were few shifts of seat or leg position and the several Shift variables had rather low consistencies across the two interactions. No consistent relationships were found for these action variables. The male group which interacted first with other males did have a very large number of relationships with Rate of Leg Movements When Not Speaking, the general association being with negative or unfavorable ends of the self-descriptive scales. This pattern is all the more striking when we observe that the five variables with relationships for the other male group all had correlations in the opposite direction.

Discussion.   The overall picture of the relationships between self-descriptive variables and action scores summarizing each brief interaction is not encouraging. No relationship appeared in all four groups. Only a limited number appeared in both groups for one sex. At best, our data provide only a few hints of low relationships which might eventually be confirmed by replicative studies. For example, there seem to have been more relationships for males than for females. Perhaps the men were expressing a bit more openly their own self-perceptions. Perhaps the women were manifesting their acquired modes of interacting with strangers, following strategies which varied with the partner to whom they were talking.

Why were so few relationships uncovered? It might be argued that our criteria were too high. We do not believe that our approach was too conservative. If other investigators also search for relationships between self-descriptions and these actions in similar interactions, we would expect them to find very few of the relationships appearing in our data, and we would expect the magnitude of these correlations to be low—in the order of .20–.25.

It seems unlikely that associations of that small size will contribute to our understanding of either self-descriptive variables or the actions as scored for total interactions.

It is true that one would not expect to find high correlations involving variables with relatively low stabilities. Self-descriptive variables have moderately high internal consistencies and reasonable stability over periods of weeks or months. Our action scores, however, had lower stabilities: while some were fairly large, others were close to zero. Basic psychometric theory would suggest that we could not anticipate very many substantial relationships with such limited stability of action scores. Such theory would predict that more relationships would be found for the more stable variables than for less stable ones.

Inspection of our findings does not reveal much support for this prediction. One reason, of course, is that many of the actions had few or no relationships with the self-descriptions. More important, we feel, is the consideration that the actions were to a large extent a function of the total context, including the sex of the subject, the sex of the partner, and sometimes, the order of the interaction. Thus, the relationships between self-descriptions and Rate of Filled Pauses were associated sometimes with sex, sometimes with a particular group of one sex, and sometimes with second interactions. If a disposition conceptualized as a self-descriptive variable tends to be associated with an action, the disposition will be manifested only under certain circumstances.

For example, a person may have a disposition that could be manifested by what is identified in Part IV as a strategy. This tendency will be manifested when the person perceives the behavioral context to be appropriate, but not in other situations. If the person experienced the first interaction as calling for the strategy, the person might use it frequently there. But when the second interaction presented the person with a partner of the opposite sex from the first partner, a partner with different characteristics, the strategy might no longer be appropriate. In this way, an act which was not stable across the two interactions could be correlated with a self-reported attribute because the act occurred with high frequencies in just one of the interactions, for persons seeing themselves as high on the attribute.

If an investigator were to pursue further the search for relationships between self-descriptions and total action scores for interactions like these, the most promising lead to investigate would probably be the tendency for observed relationships to be associated with a particular group of subjects. In our data, such differential patterns of correlations do not appear to be associated with obvious psychometric factors such as unusually high variance for the action scores. Inspection of means, variances, and maximum values gave no suggestion that differences among the several distributions contributed to these results. While we feel that random sampling fluctuations are not solely responsible, we have no clue as to other determinants. We have not tracked down the explanation further because we believe that a more fruitful approach is the investigation of individual differences in manifestations of alternative strategies within particular interactive contexts, as discussed in the following parts of this monograph. Such differences could, of course, be related to self-perception as reported on instruments like those we used.

PARTNERS' SELF-DESCRIPTIONS

Among the several possible analyses of the data is that for relationships between a subject's actions and the partner's self-descriptions. As part of our earliest analyses, this set of correlations was computed along with the others. By the time we ran analyses for intercorrelations between actions for each interaction and for each sex pairing separately, we had concluded that there was little to be found in relationships to partner's self-descriptions and did not compute correlations for the eight subgroups. We also did not compute them for the breakdown by the four sex groups used in analyzing the relationships between actions and self-descriptions of the subjects themselves: it did not seem fruitful to incorporate into the same computation of a correlation the self-description of a male partner in one interaction and the self-description of the female partner in the other interaction.

We did examine the correlations for second interactions between own actions and partner's self-description. We had available the findings for all participants together and for each sex separately. We recognized that these analyses threw together the two sexes of partners: thus, among the female participants, half had male partners in these second interactions and half had female partners.

Very little emerged in these analyses. There was no consistency between the correlations for male participants and those for female. A comparison was made, variable by variable, between the number of significant correlations linking actions and partner's self-description and the number of such correlations between those actions and own self-description. The overall picture, as might be expected, was fewer relationships with partner self-descriptions. The occasional exceptions will be mentioned below. We recognize that the pooling of partners of both sexes might reduce the size of the correlations with partner self-descriptions; that disadvantage, however, is largely offset by the fact that the comparable values for own self-descriptions included those persons whose actions occurred when interacting with a person of their own sex and an equal number of persons who were interacting with a partner of the opposite sex. In the exposition below, we will mention only correlations reaching the .05 confidence level (.30 or above). The reader should also know that none of the correlations were large: few exceeded the .01 level (.39).

Let us look now at the relationships that did appear for a few behaviors, in the analyses of second interactions. While Turn Length had no relationships for males, it had several for females: positive correlations with partners' self-attributed Defensiveness, Number of Favorable Adjectives Checked (and negative with Number of Unfavorable), Self-Control, Personal Adjustment, Nurturance, and Affiliation; there was also a negative correlation for partners' Aggression. Thus, Turn Length for females appears to be associated with partners who present themselves favorably and see themselves as friendly and supportive. It is worth recalling that Turn Length had quite a few relationships with the participant's other actions and also with the partner's actions, but no consistent relationships with own self-description.

Five of the above correlates were also found for Turn Time, but only within the female group. Like Turn Length, with which it is highly related, Turn Time had many correlations with own actions and just one with own self-description. In the exceptional instances of these two Turn variables in females, then, there were more correlates with partner self-description than with own.

Again just for females, Filled Pause Rate was correlated positively with partners' Self-Control and Personal Adjustment, as well as with Endurance, Order, and Accepting. Filled Pause Rate was correlated with own Turn Time but with no other action. It also had three consistent relationships with partner actions. Following the trend mentioned above, Filled Pauses had no relationships with own self-description for these females.

Smile Number had relationships for male participants but not for female. Positive correlations were found for partners' Number of Favorable Adjectives Checked, Lability, Nurturance, Affiliation, and Heterosexuality, together with a negative one for Counseling Readiness. Perhaps complementing this set of correlates for males is the previously mentioned finding for females that Smile Number had a number of correlations with own actions in their corresponding second interview.

Laugh Rate When Not Speaking was, it may be recalled, correlated with Smile Number. It had similar correlates for the group of males. It had positive correlations with partners' Number of Favorable Adjectives Checked, Nurturance, and Affiliation, and a negative one with Counseling Readiness. In addition, it had positive correlations with Defensiveness and Placid, and a negative one with Impulsive. (Both Laugh Rate and Smile Number had far fewer correlations with own self-descriptions. They did, however, have a number of relationships with own and partner actions for these males in their second interactions.)

Two Self-Adaptor variables had somewhat similar patterns of correlates, but again only for males. Extent of Self-Adaptors while Speaking was related positively to partners' Self-Control, Personal Adjustment, Endurance, Intraception, Nurturance, and Responsible, but negatively to partners' Autonomy, Aggression, and Impulsive. The overlapping variable of Self-Adaptor

Length While Speaking also had positive relationships with partners' Self-Control, Endurance, Intraception, and Responsible, and a negative one with Impulsive. In addition, the correlation with Active was positive. Again, these lists of correlates are much longer than that for correlates with own self-description.

For the other actions, the number of correlations with partner self-descriptions was lower, uncomfortably close to the frequency that would be expected if all the partner self-descriptive variables were random variables unrelated to each other. The relationships mentioned above deserve brief comments. First, these variables had more relationships with partner self-descriptions than with own, probably because they were selected as those with the largest number of relationships with partner self-descriptions. Second, they can be clustered into three action families, the several actions in each family being correlated with each other. For females, only one family, Turn-related Actions, is involved. For the other two families, the relationships are for males. Third, the self-descriptive variables related to a particular action tend to fall into a few intuitive clusters which also appeared in the intercorrelations of the self-descriptive variables. The major cluster is Defensiveness, Number of Positive Adjectives Checked, (Low) Number of Negative Checked, Self-Control, and Personal Adjustment. The pair, Nurturance and Affiliation, are highly correlated with each other and tend to be correlated with that cluster. Autonomy and Aggression are highly intercorrelated. Thus, the various significant correlations are clearly not independent findings.

From this brief account of the relationships we observed between actions and partners' self-description, the reader can probably understand why we did not pursue these analyses further. We grant that these sets of findings were often for variables which had few or no relationships with self-descriptive variables or with the partner actions that we scored. While it is possible that subsequent investigations by others may establish some relationships between these actions and self-descriptions by partners, we doubt that these will be very general. We found no relationship for both men and women. We would expect that any established relationships would apply only to particular combinations of sex of subject and sex of partner, for a specified context. Even these relationships we would predict to be of relatively small absolute magnitude, accounting for very little of the variance in any action variable.

CORRELATIONS BETWEEN ACTS AND REPORTED REACTIONS

After the second interaction, participants were asked to complete a short questionnaire (see Table 6.3) about each interaction separately. They were asked how aware they were of the presence of the camera (Aware of Camera), how comfortable they felt about interacting in front of the camera (Comfort with Camera), how comfortable they felt with their partner (Comfort with Partner), how interested they were in their partner (Interest in Partner), how interested they were in seeing their partner again (Interest in Seeing), how interested they were in what they and their partner talked about (Interest in Subject), who had the most influence in determining what was talked about (Influence), and three other questions.

In the reports for the first and the second interactions, taken separately, the substantial intercorrelations between Aware of Camera and Comfort with Camera were negative, while those among Interest in Partner, Interest in Seeing, and Interest in Subject were positive. Comfort with Partner had moderate correlations with this latter set of variables. The variation among the correlations between these variables is taken as indicating that the participants took this questionnaire seriously and considered each item carefully, rather than taking a general set toward each interaction and responding positively or negatively to all the items.

These reactions were analyzed for relationships with own actions and with partner actions, separately for first and second interactions and by sex and sex of partner pairings within each interaction. These analyses parallel those for the separate actions, discussed in Chapter 5. For each of the eight sets of correlations, there were 22 observations.

The correlations between Smile Number and these reactions are included in Table 6.2, at the bottom. (This table also includes correlations for the four sex groupings, the participants of each sex being categorized by the order of the sex of their partners. These correlations, in Columns 1–4 of the table, have each subject entered twice, once for his reaction and his Smile Number score for his first interaction and once for his reaction and Smile score for his second interaction. Hence, the 44 observations are not independent for these correlations.)

The correlations of these reported feelings and reactions with the participant's own acts show practically no consistency between the two interactions, between the two sexes, or between the two sexes of partner. (See the bottom of Table 6.2 as an illustration.) We believe that the participants were reporting frankly and openly. Given this belief or assumption, these data indicate that any observed relationships between these reports and the participants' actions are essentially a function of the conditions for each set of interactions. As we have indicated earlier, our participants did seem somewhat more comfortable and at ease in the second interactions. Also, the sex of the actor and whether the partner was of the same or opposite sex were factors in some of the relationships which we have already considered.

The report of being Aware of Camera had more large correlations for first interactions than for second: for females, it tended to be related to various movement variables. For males interacting with females, it tended to be related to Smiling and Laughing. This Awareness had few relationships with

TABLE 6.3 Postinteractions Questionnaire

We would like you to answer some questions about the interaction in which you have just participated (the second of the two conversations).

1. What were your strongest reactions during the interaction?

2. How aware were you of the presence of the videotape camera?

| aware of it all the time | somewhat aware of it all the time | aware of it initially, but forgot about it later | forgot about it most of the time |

3. How comfortable did you feel with the particular person with whom you were paired?

| comfortable | somewhat comfortable | somewhat uncomfortable | uncomfortable |

4. How comfortable did you feel about interacting in front of the videotape camera?

| comfortable | somewhat comfortable | somewhat uncomfortable | uncomfortable |

5. How interested were you in what you and your partner talked about during the interaction?

| interested | somewhat interested | not very interested | uninterested |

6. How interested were you in the person with whom you were paired?

| interested | somewhat interested | not very interested | uninterested |

7. How interested would you be in seeing the person with whom you were paired again?

| interested | somewhat interested | not very interested | uninterested |

8. Who had the most influence in determining what was talked about during the interaction?

| I had more influence | about equal, but I had slightly more influence | about equal, but my partner had slightly more influence | my partner had more influence |

9. How well acquainted were you with your partner before this research took place?

| fairly well acquainted | have talked to him (her) before | have seen him (her) before | have never seen him (her) before |

10. How different were your feelings in the second interaction from your feelings in the first interaction?

| different | somewhat different | not very different | just about the same |

Now we would like you to answer some questions about the *first* interaction in which you participated. Stop a moment to review it in your memory so that you have it clearly in mind, and won't confuse it with the other one.

11. What were your strongest reactions during *that* interaction?

(continued)

TABLE 6.3
Postinteractions Questionnaire *(continued)*

12. How aware were you of the presence of the videotape camera?

| aware of it all the time | somewhat aware of it all the time | aware of it initially, but forgot about it later | forgot about it most of the time |

13. How comfortable did you feel with the particular person with whom you were paired?

| comfortable | somewhat comfortable | somewhat uncomfortable | uncomfortable |

14. How comfortable did you feel about interacting in front of the videotape camera?

| comfortable | somewhat comfortable | somewhat uncomfortable | uncomfortable |

15. How interested were you in what you and your partner talked about during the interaction?

| interested | somewhat interested | not very interested | uninterested |

16. How interested were you in the person with whom you were paired?

| interested | somewhat interested | not very interested | uninterested |

17. How interested would you be in seeing the person with whom you were paired again?

| interested | somewhat interested | not very interested | uninterested |

18. Who had the most influence in determining what was talked about during the interaction?

| I had more influence | about equal, but I had slightly more influence | about equal, but my partner had slightly more influence | my partner had more influence |

19. How well acquainted were you with your partner before this research took place?

| fairly well acquainted | have talked to him (her) before | have seen him (her) before | have never seen him (her) before |

20. Many of us feel more or less uncomfortable in unfamiliar situations such as the one you have just been in.
     Please tell us about any feelings of discomfort you have had during this research.

21. Is there anything else you would like to say about your experience in this research?

partner actions. For first interactions between females, it was related negatively to partner Gaze times. In second interactions of males with females, it was also negatively related to partner Gaze times and, in addition, to partner Self-Adaptor times.

Comfort with Camera offered little. Females whose second interaction was with males did have negative relationships with Smile and Laugh variables; that is, those less comfortable smiled and laughed more. Nothing promising emerged for partner actions.

Comfort with Partner showed no noteworthy patterns with own actions. For females interacting with other females in second interactions, this Comfort was negatively related to the Number and Extent of partner's Smiling and The Extent of partner's Self-Adaptors.

Interest in Partner had a number of assorted relationships for females interacting with males, but different correlates for the first and second interactions. In first interactions, this Interest had positive correlations with Smiling, Laughing, and Gazing, along with negative ones for Self-Adaptors, these values being primarily when in the Speaking role. For second interactions between males, Interest in Partner was correlated with own Smiling and with partner Smiling.

Curiously, Interest in Seeing the Partner again had only a few of the relationships that appeared for Interest in Partner, and the total number of correlates is too low to merit mentioning specific ones.

Interest in the Subject of the conversation had very few relationships with own actions. In second interactions for women, it was related negatively to most partner Laugh and Smile variables for both sexes of partner. It also had positive correlations with partner Gaze times when the partner was male. (These Gaze times were positively related to Interest in the Subject in first interactions between females.)

Influence in determining the subject of the conversation was also unproductive. In second interactions, it was positively related to Smiling for males interacting with females, and negatively related to Self-Adaptor times for interactions between females. For first interactions between females, it was positively related to most Smile and Laugh variables.

In summary, the participants' reports of these particular feelings and reactions had no consistent relationships with the actions of either themselves or their partners. A few patterns of correlation appeared for specific combinations of sex, sex of partner, and order. It is worth noting that there were as many relationships with partner acts as with own acts, whereas for acts, there were more correlations with other acts of the subject than with acts of partner. Perhaps partner acts affected these feelings and reactions more than they affected the subject's own acts.

7

Overview and Critique
of our Studies of Act Scores

In this concluding chapter of Part II, we examine what we did and what we found in our analyses of scores for acts during the brief interactions. We consider what we have learned, and assess the approach and methods employed. This critical evaluation provides a basis for comparison and contrast with the different approach to acts used in Part III. Together, these two parts form some foundation for the model presented in the final Part IV.

THE SUBSTANTIVE FINDINGS

Our substantive findings from our studies of correlates of acts in interaction do not impress us. While the number of observed relationships was large, it formed a small proportion of the total number of correlations computed. In other words, the proportion of large correlations was not greatly above the proportion which would be expected by chance. In fact, for some sets of analyses, the obtained and the expected proportions were so close that we have chosen not to report specific values, having no confidence as to which relationships might appear again in similar, replicative studies.

The studies of correlations between acts of the same participant yielded the largest proportion of consistent relationships. For most actions, however, these appreciable and consistent relationships were primarily with other variables within the same family of acts. Of course, we discount the artifactual dependencies introduced by scoring procedures: for example, where one variable or its numerator, scored for speaking, was included in a second variable scored for the whole interaction. Other relationships are more interesting, such as correlations between scores for the same act (for example, gazing) as speaker and as auditor. These could and did vary in magnitude.

In general, however, we did not find many correlations between actions of the same participant. Given that result, it was not surprising to find even fewer relationships between these acts and scores from the self-descriptive instruments completed just before the interactions. Not only were these latter scores derived from actions (responses) obtained in a different physical context, but also these scores dealt with the participants' self-perceptions, a domain rather different from physical activity in an interaction. In responding to the questionnaires, they were cognizing each item and answering in terms of the recollections and images occurring to them at that point in time; they were summarizing these images of their prior experiences. These summarizing responses were then summarized in the scoring of the questionnaire. In contrast, each act occurred in a specific context characterized by the particular partner but also by the other actions preceding it. The occurrences and durations of these acts were later summarized for the five minutes of the coded interaction. Thus, not only were the two types of participants' actions associated with quite different settings and orientations but also the two kinds of scores finally entered into the analyses represent rather dissimilar kinds of summarizing.

Consistent with these analyses is the lack of findings relating acts to scores on the postinteractions questionnaire. Once again, the levels of description were different. A participant who reported being aware of the camera might act in various ways: he might say little, sit more tensely, or laugh nervously. The correlational analysis would pick up only instances in which the same reported feeling was expressed in the same way by a number of subjects.

Even though these acts were not frequently related to each other or to these inventory and questionnaire variables, they could have been related to the partner's acts. Such relationships would be most likely when an act supplemented or complemented an act of the partner. We did find positive relationships for smiling and laughing. We did not have variables which one would expect a priori to be complementary, such as Social Answers along with Social Questions. (The only possible exception is Turn Time: when a speaker stopped, the other started speaking, with no appreciable periods of silence and only very brief periods of simultaneous talking.)

For the most part, we found little of interest in the specific correlations between own and partner's acts. In general, for our subjects as a group, one act did not covary with an act score for the partner. Similarly, a participant's acts were not related to the partner's self-description. Obviously, these findings should not be taken to mean that the way a person saw himself and the way he acted (in terms of the variables we scored) did not have any effect upon the partner's actions in the interaction. All we can say is that such effects are not linear relationships between total amounts, rates, or lengths of one person's acts and similar indices for the other's acts, on the one hand, or self-report scores on the other.

There is, of course, the possibility that we have committed an extensive Type II error, that we have decided incorrectly that many pairs of variables are not related to each other when in fact they are. Our variables were some-what interrelated and our parallel analyses had the same subjects in some instances. Hence, it was not possible to reach precise estimates of chance expectancies and we may have erred on the conservative side. We do feel, however, that it is most unlikely that subsequent research will reveal substantial relationships between variables we decided were unrelated. Moreover, we did spend a considerable amount of time looking at particular sets of relationships occurring in part of the data, for example, in the data for females but not in that for males. While we found we could develop speculative interpretations in such instances, we could not see ways to check these interpretations from the data on hand. And frequently such an interpretation might hinge on one or two correlations of, say .30, these seeming much too frail a reed on which to hang substantive propositions. Finally, we chose to base our decisions on consistency among groups. Just as consistency between findings from independent research studies is the basic requirement for cautious acceptance by a scientific community, so consistency within a study seems to provide an appropriate criterion, especially in an exploratory investigation with thousands of obtained correlation coefficients.

One general finding may be worth noting: the relationships between acts which did show consistency across groups were typically positive ones. This trend appeared not only within act families but also between families. (The major exception was the Turn family.) The trend might stem from the distributions for the two variables in each correlation: for example, from some persons being extremely high on both. This interpretation seems unlikely since the degree of positive skewness in the transformed scores was ordinarily rather small. It is also possible that some global variable of activity or expressiveness pervaded these scores. Since such dimensions fell outside the objectives of our study, we did not explore this interpretation.

The contrary tendency, toward negative relationships, did appear between gesturing and using self-adaptors while speaking, both acts involving the hands. The relative absence of other patterns of negative associations might suggest that our variables did not include sets with elements which tended to be alternative, or even mutually exclusive, modes of expressing the same disposition. This interpretation appears unsound. Our scores were summaries over a five-minute period. While a person could not, by our rules, be scored as smiling and laughing at the same moment, there were extensive periods when a person was scored as not smiling, these periods leaving plenty of opportunity for the short laughs that did occur. In fact, of course, smiling and laughing were substantially interrelated in our data.

Did we include the right variables?   In this study, a very large number of actions were examined, many more than in the typical experiment on acts of this sort. The set which we used was selected rather arbitrarily, on the basis of promise as estimated from preliminary work. It did not include all types of measures for all acts. Hence, it is possible that we omitted some variables which might have more substantial relationships than the ones we included.

Certainly our set of self-descriptive variables was a biased sample of the heterogenous population of self-report scores which are available. It is possible that other self-report scales or personality measures produced by peers or by diagnosticians might have correlated more highly with these actions. Only future research by others can tell us.

In addition, the reader must remember that we omitted any variables referring to the verbal content of the interaction (with the exception of the Social Question variable). Similarly, paralinguistic measures were not included. It may be that the acts we examined have strong relationships to content and paralinguistic variables.

METHODOLOGICAL CONTRIBUTIONS

A major purpose of this investigation was methodological. We wanted to collect sufficient data on each of many acts so that we could report something about its statistical and psychometric characteristics. To this end, we have presented, for each act index, its mean and several values relating to the shape and extent of its distribution. From these data, an investigator who is considering research with such variables may be able to choose those which will be likely to meet his needs.

A researcher employing these variables and analyzing their relationships to each other and to other types of variables must take into account their distribution in making his decision about an appropriate procedure for determining such relationships. For many of these variables, the distribution of raw scores is skewed positively: the mean of the distribution is well below the midpoint of the range of observed scores. It seems undesirable to compute product-moment correlations between such variables. We resolved this difficulty by transforming the raw scores into logarithms, the resulting distributions being much less skewed. In addition to the technical desirability of making such a transformation, this step was consistent with the measurement of information in information theory, and these acts can be viewed as providing information.

A considerable number of our variables had zero raw scores for some or even many participants. It is probable that the frequency of such scores would be lower in summary scores for longer periods of interaction. As long as there are any zero scores, however, they must be taken into consideration in decisions about the form of the transformations, about the appropriate statistical technique for analyzing associations, and about the interpretations of observed associations.

At least as important as the distributions are the values for consistencies between judges and consistencies between interactions. While the samples

used for estimating interjudge agreement were small, our obtained coefficients probably do indicate which variables are likely to show high agreement and which should be scored with particular care and perhaps extra
training in order to obtain comparably high levels of agreement.

We attach considerable importance to the stability coefficients, the correlations between the scores for the first and second interactions. These values
should reflect the extent to which a given act index is determined largely by
the participant's characteristic style as against determination by characteristics of the partner, by factors stemming from unique interactions between
the two participants, or by change in the participant's adaption to the videotaped situation. We would expect that indices showing little consistency between these two interactions would show even less between our situation and
a different one, such as a conversation with a close friend with no known termination in time closely approaching.

Kinds of Variables.

One conclusion we have drawn from these analyses is that careful consideration should be given to the kinds of variables one selects for studies of acts
in interactions. It has become obvious to us that investigators should measure
separately acts when the person is speaking and acts when not speaking. For
example, Gaze Rate for the entire interaction is a complex variable summarizing two unrelated rates, Gaze Rate While Speaking and Gaze Rate When
Not Speaking. For most of our act families, we had separate variables for
actions in the two states. We did not, however, have all types of variables in
this form: for example, Smile Number was the total for the whole period of
interaction; it should have been scored as rate while speaking and rate while
not speaking. Unfortunately, the original coding from the videotapes was
done in such a way that these rates could not be readily derived post hoc and
we decided not to rescore the videotapes for these new rate variables.

In coding acts for each of the two turns, there is a problem concerning the
extent and duration of variables (as was noted earlier). How does one handle
the actions which extend from one role into the next, such as a smile which
starts when the person is speaking and continues after the other begins
speaking? One good solution is feasible only with long interactions: one can
score the duration of all actions which begin and end within a turn. A long
interaction would provide enough instances to obtain a fairly stable index for
many kinds of acts. Similarly, the total extent of an act during the speaking
or auditor turns could be computed as the sum of these actions.

An additional score could be obtained for important and prevalent kinds of
acts. One could include as one kind of variable those acts which started in a
particular turn and continued into the complementary turn. These might be
found to be so highly related to those acts which started and ended within the
turn that they could be combined with that class.

Rate, Extent, and Duration Types

Our variables were of three types. We had rates, which were the number of occurrences or onsets of the act per unit of time. Although these may be conceived in terms of onsets, they are also the rate of offsets or terminations of the act. We also had durations or mean lengths of time for certain actions. These are obviously periods between onset and offset. Finally, we had the most global type, the total time during which the act was manifested, the total extent. These totals can be thought of as the product of the number of the acts times their average length.

Our analyses make it clear that the differentiation of these three types is distinctly worthwhile. In some families (for example, Smiling), the rate and the time variables are positively related—the more frequent the onsets, the longer the acts and the more total time they occupied. In other families, such as Gazing, the rate variables had negative relationships with time variables, but more so with length than with extent. The pattern of these relationships for an act family may be a function of the relative prevalence of the act: gazing was going on more of the time in our interactions than was smiling.

We found little evidence that any one of these types had characteristics making it more valuable than the other types. They did not differ appreciably on level of interjudge agreement—though the agreement on rates tended to be a bit better and the agreement on lengths tended to be a bit worse. It should be remembered, of course, that we did not have all types of scores for each act family. We scored Filled Pauses only for occurrence (rate), not for duration or extent. Hence, this or other generalizations about the types cannot be asserted with high confidence since type and act family are confounded.

In terms of consistency between the first and second interactions, the extent variables tended to be more stable than the rates or mean lengths. While it is easy to interpret the lower stability for rates in terms of an onset being the consequence of some particular conditions which might vary in their occurrence from one interaction to the next, it is difficult to see why mean lengths should tend to be less stable than total time. One possible interpretation is that length reflects intensity. For example, a hearty laugh is likely to last longer than a chuckle, and an energetic gesture may take more time than a small movement of the hand. This interpretation would also require the presumption that the intensity component would vary more with the particular context than would the frequency.

An examination of the types in terms of frequencies of relationships did not reveal any marked trends. The numbers of relationships with the person's other acts, with the partner's acts, with own self-descriptive variables, and with partner self-descriptions did not indicate that any one type was clearly more promising and deserving of special emphasis in further investigations.

In summary, we believe that the three types of variables provide somewhat different information and that all three should be included in research using summarizing scores to study acts in interactions.

Sex Differences

Our data make it clear that the correlates of an act in interactions such as these often vary with the sex of the person. In terms of the frequencies of appreciable relationships with own acts, males had larger frequencies than females for a majority of our variables. They also tended to have more relationships with partner variables than did females, again examining the patterns by act variable. This tendency was found most clearly for some variables in the back-channel family.

In view of these trends, and in view of the differences in patterns of relationships reported in earlier chapters of this Part, it seems quite clear that analyses of interactions should be done separately for male and female participants. In addition, there is considerable evidence in our data that the analyses should also be made by sex of the partner.

A CRITIQUE OF THE STRATEGY USED IN THIS STUDY

The general approach in this section of our work was exploratory. We wanted to learn about these act variables—about their distributions, dependabilities, and relationships with other acts of self and partner and with self-descriptive variables for self and partner. Thus, our aims were extensive. We sought to survey rather than to probe deeply into particular areas. What we found was perhaps what we should have expected. The patterns of relationship tended to vary with the sex of the participant, with the sex of the partner, and sometimes with the order of the interaction. All our interactions took place under almost identical conditions—the same instructions and the same physical arrangements—and yet we found limited generality of rela tionships. This result emerged in spite of the relative similarity of the various group distributions of scores on these variables.

The fluctuations in the relationships presumably stem from the complexity of the psychological situation for each participant. Coming to the situation with whatever behavioral dispositions and self-characterizations he had acquired during his life, he construed the situation in his own particular way and he found himself interacting with a stranger who also brought residues of his past life to this interaction. His task was to adapt to the demands of the particular conditions. It is quite possible that interactions in familiar circumstances and with familiar people might show more consistent and regular patterns of relationships than appeared in our data (Current investigations of the first author may throw some light on this possibility.)

Since our approach was extensive, we did not attempt to analyze our data in every possible way. One decision which we made early in our work was not to use factor analysis to reduce our large number of variables to a smaller number of abstracted factors. We had a number of reasons for this decision. One was that we were interested in these actions, these molecular acts, for their own sake. We wanted to understand each of them, rather than to develop some more comprehensive variables which might have been interpreted as restlessness, responsiveness, or energy level. It is our belief that much conceptualization and research on individual behavior has been limited to the search for global variables like the dimensions in the laymen's terminology for describing people. We grant that the search for basic general variables is one of the objectives of a science. We believe, however, that such a search must be preceded by the identification and measurement of dependable observational indices, indices which can be assessed with very high intersubjective consensus. A general dimension with intuitive appeal is of little explanatory value in a systematic theory unless it can be related to tangibles and observables. We realize that our viewpoint is not the one most prevalent among researchers in the personality domain or in the area of interpersonal interactions.

A major technical reason for not factor-analyzing our data may be more generally acceptable to our colleagues: our sample of subjects was too small to yield dependable results. Even if we had factored a correlation matrix for all 88 subjects, we would have had a sample of dubious size. Entering both interactions would not have helped. Any such analysis would combine men and women, who often showed different patterns of correlations, and also the four sex pairings, which also had differences in patterning. Any homogeneous group, such as one sex by itself, would have much too small a size.

The number of persons is important both in absolute terms and also relative to the number of variables. We had about 60 act scores before we had finished. Most factor analysts would find our ratio of persons to variables quite questionable. Of course, we could have done a factor analysis on a selected smaller set of variables, but which should be included? As we have seen, the several variables in each act family did not always covary with the same external variables. From within each family, one would have had to select variables which were not experimentally dependent on each other. For example, all the total extent variables would be excluded since they combined data from the extent variables for the speaking and not speaking roles. (A factor analysis of all variables would obviously have yielded several factors, each of which would be centered on an act family, such as the laugh-smile family, or the gaze family, since most of the high correlations were within families.)

Finally, as we proceeded with analyzing and studying our findings, we began to recognize the crucial significance of the act context at the moment of onset for each act. We found that laughs correlated substantially with partner's laughs during the same turns. Thus, Laugh Rate While Speaking correlated with partner's Laugh Rate When Not Speaking. The obvious hypothesis is that the laugh of one person was often followed by a laugh by the other. So we became interested in what actions preceded a particular molecular act, rather than in the original question which had the form; with what other acts is this act correlated, when scores are obtained for each act over the entire five minutes that were coded?

Our strategy implicitly assumed that our scores would reflect the participants' dispositions to engage in these actions within the interaction as a whole. Thus, each score was taken as determined by the person, the person's sex, the partner's acts, the partner's sex, and interactions among these and between these and the person's other acts. But such a loose interpretation does not indicate conditions under which a type of act occurs. What are the antecedent conditions for an interruption or for a gesture? We became convinced that relationships or lack of relationships among the total scores for the five-minute period could tell us very little about the occurrence or nonoccurrence of any one act at a given moment.

UNITS OF DATA AND POOLED OBSERVATIONS

Our basic datum unit was a score obtained by summing acts over an entire period (either the whole five minutes or the time as speaker or as auditor). We sought to determine whether such total scores covaried over persons, keeping constant the total situation and, in subanalyses, the sex of the person and other variables. Thus, each score is associated with a person's acts during a period of time. What unity does such a series of acts have? Without realizing it, we used this scoring practice to indicate some general disposition of the participant for displaying the act, under favorable circumstances for eliciting it. But what are these circumstances? We are unable to answer that question from our correlational data. What we did was to reduce our thousands of specific observations of onsets and offsets of acts into these summarizing statistics which are essentially measures of central tendency, and then attempt to find relationships to other, similarly summarizing scores.

What we did, of course, was to follow a procedure quite pervasive in research on personality and on some other psychological topics, such as nonverbal communication. We lumped together responses without regard to the specific acts preceding them. While we did not interpret these total scores as traits which characterized the participants generally, regardless of situation, we did take a step toward assigning an index to a person as a property of that person, at least within that situation.

Clearly, it is not the total number of laughs which affects the total number of partner's laughs. After all, at any intermediate point in the interaction, not all of the subject's laughs had occurred, so the total number, itself, has no influence. It is obviously the single laugh, at this point, which is experienced by the partner, together perhaps with the accumulated experience of any prior laughs.

Our use of these summarizing descriptive statistics, and their general use by others, stems from several sources. An obvious justification is their greater convenience, the amount of time and labor saved. It might also be argued by some that it is wise to look for general, gross relationships before embarking on more intensive investigation. Still another reason is that psychologists tend to think about people as laymen do, in general descriptive terms. When we think back about a conversation with someone, we may recall that the other smiled a lot, or kept interrupting us, or kept fidgeting with a button. We readily characterize a person's behavior in a particular interaction and then imperceptibly drop the qualification and describe the person as if our descriptive terms applied to him at any moment in any situation. Thus, in our data, we characterized the person as he behaved in the interaction as a whole.

We do not mean to imply, of course, that such total scores are meaningless. For example, some of our data indicate that the total context did affect averages of such scores, such as the convergence of male and female means for some variables, from first to second interactions. At the individual level, it seems true that a person is more likely to smile a lot when he is comfortable and is enjoying the interaction. Yet we cannot infer from frequent smiling that the person is necessarily comfortable and content. In our data, some women smiled a lot when they felt uncomfortable in their first interaction. A context does not necessarily have uniform effects on all persons. If the effects of a context are reflected in several act scores, it is possible that these scores will covary over persons as a function of their perception of the context. If, however, the effects of the context upon actions are not similar, relationships will be obscured. It is important to remember that a context may have a general effect on all subjects or may affect some subjects one way and other subjects in a different way.

While we did not compare act scores across markedly different situations, it does seem as though the effects of the total situation on the individual participants were small. This interpretation seems justified by the relatively low consistencies of these scores from first interaction to second. It would appear that the most important sources of contextual influence were associated with the actions of the individual partner in each interaction. The sex of the person, the sex of the partner, the particular sex pairing, and the order of the interaction had smaller contextual effects.

Thus, our total scores were affected to some degree by ambient conditions associated with the entire five-minute period. In the later half of the interaction, the occurrence or nonoccurrence of an act may well have been influenced by the extent of some act of the partner during the first half. The question is, what was the degree of such influence? Our data suggest that, over all, such remote influence is rather limited. On the other hand, it is possible that the occurrence of a given act is closely associated with the immediate interactive context, with the acts of partner and self which occur within seconds, or even fractions of a second, of the beginning of that act. In Part III we consider molecular acts in their immediate interaction context.

Part III

STUDIES OF THE ORGANIZATION OF FACE-TO-FACE INTERACTION

The research paradigm for the study reported in Part II was that used by the vast majority of studies of nonverbal communication. This has been labeled (Duncan, 1969) the "external-variable" approach to studying nonverbal communication. In an external-variable study, a participant's actions are counted or timed over some stretch of interaction. Variables are based on summary figures for these countings or timings. The variables are then subjected to analyses of group differences and of patterns of covariation.

In Part III we describe a study that approaches face-to-face interaction from a significantly different perspective. The study began with the presupposition that face-to-face interaction is in part an organized, rule-governed phenomenon. The purpose of the study was to develop further information on the nature of this organization or "grammar," as it were. Such a study was described in Chapter 1 as being a "structural" study.

In the study to be reported, the elements of the potential organization were not taken as immediately obvious or as necessarily available to the intuitive scrutiny of one's own experience. Rather, careful transcriptions were made of face-to-face interactions, and these materials were subjected to systematic, exploratory analyses with the aim of discovering and documenting significant regularities in the transcribed actions. The findings of such regularities led to a series of hypotheses relating to various aspects of an organization applying at least to the interactions transcribed. These hypotheses were then subjected to an initial test using a new set of interactions.

In describing this structural study, particular attention is devoted to methodological and conceptual issues. It will be important to consider how a study aimed at discovering rule-governed regularities in interaction might be designed, what research techniques might be used, and what sorts of evidence might be offered to substantiate claims of discovered rule-governed regularities. At the same time it will be important to develop a systematic approach to describing such regularities as may be encountered.

The results of the study are presented in Chapter 11. Prior to that presentation is a consideration of some of the conceptual underpinnings of the research design (Chapter 8) and the specific methods used (Chapters 9 and 10). Design and methods are described in some detail, because reports of structural studies in the literature are relatively infrequent.

8

Presuppositions of Research Strategy

It has been stressed in previous chapters that this study from its inception was considered to be exploratory in nature. The goal was to discover and to document some elements of the organization of social interaction. The desired outcome of the study was the generation of empirically based hypotheses regarding this organization.

As described in Chapter 2, a frequently desirable design feature of exploratory studies is that they be as naturalistic as possible. That is, within the bounds of technical requirements of the study, the investigator attempts to intervene as little as possible in the phenomena under study. And certainly the introduction of experimental controls in their traditional sense is properly made only after the development of hypotheses, if at all.

This initial decision on an exploratory study was determined primarily by two factors: (a) the virtually complete absence of strong empirically based hypotheses regarding the specific area to be investigated; and (b) the broad use of discovery-oriented research in anthropology and linguistics, the research fields perceived to be most closely related to the kind of work envisioned.

Upon beginning the development of this line of research, it quickly became apparent that there had been little prior empirical work in this specific area. A search of the literature at that time (Duncan, 1969) yielded a number of studies reporting correlations and group differences using "nonverbal" behaviors. There was, in addition, a considerable body of theoretical discussions of social organization by social scientists and philosophers, some insightful descriptions of behavior patterns based on unformalized observation, and a few general discussions of methodology. There was, however, a conspicuous dearth of studies reporting actual generation and analysis of data bearing on the organization of interaction. An exception here was Kendon (1967), considered below. The literature was decidedly overbalanced in the direction of theoretical and programmatic writings.

THE NATURAL HISTORY OF AN INTERVIEW

There were, however, exceptions to this general picture, the most important of which was *The natural history of an interview* (McQuown, 1971). The underlying purpose of the materials presented in this work, as articulated by McQuown in his Foreword, was to initiate first steps in a process aimed at the development of "the foundation of a general theory of the structure of human communicative behavior . . . (p. 5). " Both in its conceptualization and its implementation, *The natural history of an interview* served as the foundation of the design of the present study, and indeed, provided much of the motivation for pursuing it. On these grounds *The natural history of an interview* requires careful consideration. (It should be noted that the citation date—1971—given for this work refers to the date that the monograph became publicly available through the University of Chicago Regenstein Library. The actual work on the book, including most of the transcription and the theoretical and methodological chapters by Bateson, Birdwhistell, and Hockett, was essentially completed by 1959.)

Begun in 1955, this often cited and long unpublished monograph represents the culmination of an extended research effort by a group of linguists, anthropologists, psychiatrists, and psychologists, formed through the initiative of the late Frieda Fromm-Reichmann, and later guided under the editorship of Norman A. McQuown. According to the introduction to the monograph, this research group originally included McQuown, Alfred L. Kroeber, Gregory Bateson, Charles F. Hockett, Henry W. Brosin, Ray L. Birdwhistell, and David M. Schneider. As the work continued over the years, the group of contributors came to include Albert E. Scheflen, Felix F. Loeb, Jr., William Charney, William C. Condon, William M. Austin, Raven I. McDavid, Jr., William Offenkrantz, and Starkey Duncan, Jr.

The monograph includes a detailed transcription of speech and body motion of portions of conversations between an interviewer and various members of a family, as recorded on sound film and audiotape. Accompanying the transcription are chapters on Communication by Bateson, Vocal Activity by Hockett, Body Motion by Birdwhistell, Implications for Psychiatry by Brosin, and a description of The Actors and the Setting by Bateson, along with a number of appendices.

The conceptualization of *The natural history of an interview* clearly foreshadows many of the recent developments in linguistics, sociolinguistics, and "nonverbal communication," as well as the research to be considered here. And its empirical work carried it significantly beyond the programmatic papers so frequently encountered in these fields, or in the general area of "human communication." Many of the research principles, as both articulated and exemplified in the monograph, centrally influenced the development of methodology for the present research. These principles are considered below.

Transcription of Actions

Except perhaps when some linguists are dealing with their own native language, and so acting as their own informants (a practice surely too prevalent at certain points in time), the study of a particular language typically begins with a painstakingly detailed transcription of the vocal productions of one or more native speakers. In carrying out one of these phonetic transcriptions, it is important that there be a minimum of a priori judgments as to just which aspects of those vocal productions are part of the language system, as opposed to those aspects that might belong in paralanguage (Trager, 1958). The purpose of the linguistic investigation is precisely to make such a differentiation, and to discover the components and organization of the language system. It would be absurd to posit these prior to careful analysis. Such an empirically based, inductive research strategy would seem particularly appropriate to research aimed at the discovery of elements of the organization of interaction.

In *The natural history of an interview* this eminently sound research principle was adopted, but expanded in two important ways. (a) In addition to speech, the transcription gave full consideration to body-motion actions; and (b) the actions of all participants in the interaction were transcribed, not merely the actions of a single participant or of those persons considered to be "informants."

By including both speech and body motion in the transcription, it became possible to inquire as to the possibility that elements of language, paralanguage, and body motion might function together within a unified communication framework. As Bateson (1971) put it in his opening essay on communication, "A central question, therefore, which we shall have to face when we analyze the data is the extent to which there is a mutual relationship of 'context' between kinesic and linguistic elements [p. 18]. "

In transcribing the actions of all participants, the interactional character of language and other communicative actions was concretely acknowledged. Language, paralanguage, and body motion are used together within an interpersonal framework. Speakers do not declaim in a cultural and personal void. They take turns in speaking with coparticipants in the interaction. And even while one person is speaking, his coparticipants may be reacting in a variety of ways, nodding their heads, shifting posture and gaze direction, and so on. Jakobson (1964) has observed that pure monologues are extremely rare in societies, "unfamiliar to many ethnic and social groups [p. 162], " and where found, exist in highly specialized forms, such as the "cliche monologue, the ready-made ritual performance—a prayer or a ceremonial speech [p. 163]. "

The interactional context of language use would seem to imply that the study of interaction would be a natural aspect of the study of language. And yet, Jaffe and Feldstein (1970) observed: "The serious study of dialogue patterns makes one poignantly aware that the largest unit dealt with in contemporary linguistics is at most the monologue and, more typically, the isolated sentence [pp. 2–3]. "

Collaborators on *The natural history of an interview* moved directly to expand this traditional research domain. As Bateson (1971) noted, referring to two of the participants, "The system which we now study is no longer merely a descriptive synthesis of Doris' body motion and speech, but the larger aggregate of what goes on betwen Doris and Gregory (p. 20)." In including transcriptions of the actions of all visible interactants and in carefully aligning the actions of one participant with those of the others, *The natural history of an interview* set an early precedent for further work in this area.

Elements of Organization in Face-to-Face Interaction

A central (but not the only) task of research on the organization of interaction is that of discovering and documenting the action-based elements (to be termed "signals," "moves," and "units of interaction" below) of the organization and to specify the relationships obtaining between these elements. At this early stage of research in this area, it seems best to consider these action-based elements to be perceived as discrete, and the organization within which they occur to be a hierarchical one.

These early assumptions were emphasized in *The natural history of an interview* by Bateson (1971), who points out in Chapter 1 that,

> From Gestalt psychology, we have accepted a premise of very great importance: that experience is *punctuated*. We do not experience a continuum: on the contrary, our experience is broken up into what seem to us to be events and objects [p. 12] .... Moreover, Gestalt theory presupposes a *hierarchy* of subdivisions characteristic of the process of perception. We do not perceive the firing of unit end-organs but, from the showers of neural impulse started by that firing, we build images of identifiables and larger meaningful complexes of identifiables [p. 14].

In regard to the development of discrete units arranged in hierarchies, linguistics as it is traditionally defined serves as an excellent model. As Bateson (1971) observes, "A major contribution of the linguists is the demonstration that the stream of communication contains positive signals by which its units are delimited [pp. 13–14]. "

Following, then, in an intellectual tradition that includes Gestalt psychology, much of the work in linguistics, and the position of the collaborators on *The natural history of an interview,* the assumption was made in the present research to regard the action-based elements of the organization as discrete, that is, perceived by the participants as either present or absent at any given moment. It was then assumed that these discrete elements (on a given hierarchical level) (a) combine with one another according to specifiable relations (to be termed "rules" below) to form higher-order elements on the next hierarchical level; and (b) were in all probability themselves formed from some combination of discrete action-based elements on an immediately lower hierarchical level. (It is not necessarily apparent, even after considerable research, just what are the upper and the lower bounds of the hierarchical structure under investigation.)

The search for action-based elements (for example, signals) and their combinatorial relations (rules) was a primary objective of the exploratory study. A necessarily prior objective was the development of an appropriate approach to data analysis—a topic to which we now turn.

RULES FOR EVIDENCE

After the initial planning, there are four general stages through which an exploratory study must move.

1. In the first stage, data must be generated. In the present case, this required the transcription of actions observed in face-to-face interactions.

2. The next, and most crucial stage requires discovery itself—the detection of regular patterning among the transcribed actions. At this point, regardless of whatever discovery-facilitating procedures he might use, the investigator is entirely on his own. The exploratory study will have little to show for itself if discoveries of some sort are not forthcoming at this point. It is notable that exploratory studies contrast sharply with hypothesis-testing studies in this regard. The failure to reject the null hypothesis in the latter type of study may in itself be a finding of considerable scientific interest. But the failure to produce some exploratory findings leaves the would-be investigator of structure with little to show for his efforts.

3. Assuming the investigator believes that he has detected some significant patternings in his data, how does he substantiate his perceptions? This is the task for analysis. But behind the analysis lies the set of assumptions regarding rules of evidence for the data. The question is, "What are the rules of evidence by which an investigator is entitled to claim a particular result for his study?" The legal metaphor here is intentional. The issue concerns the admissibility of evidence in the "court" of scholarly opinion. These rules

of evidence will both guide the investigator in analyzing his data and formulating his results, and aid the reader of the research report in evaluating the investigator's claims.

4.   Finally, assuming that rules of evidence are formulated and that analyses based on these rules produce some recognizable results, the exploratory investigator must formulate his results in terms of hypotheses, duly observing such criteria as conceptual completeness and parsimony.

This section focusses on rules of evidence underlying the analysis linking apparent discovery of patterning to formulation of hypotheses. Rules of evidence will, of course, vary somewhat according to the scientific conventions currently accepted in the investigator's field of inquiry, the type of data involved, and the like. But the question is particularly crucial when the study ventures into a relatively new area, as this one did. And in this regard, *The natural history of an interview* provided less of a model, for issues of data analysis received less systematic treatment in that work than did issues of data generation.

Linguistic Model

Methods used in linguistic analysis were a definite possibility for the study. These methods are aimed at facilitating the discovery of basic "units" in the organization being analyzed, and at establishing the nature of the relationships between these units. Birdwhistell (1970, p. 120) provides a statement of linguistic methods in the context of body-motion analysis. (Birdwhistell, 1970, Chapters 17 and 18, illustrates his application of linguistic analysis to the study of body motion.) At issue, however, was not the use of these methods, which might be judged to be useful or not useful on the basis of attempted application.

More problematic was the frequently encountered linguistic practice of simply describing the results of an analysis, accompanying this description with appropriate examples. This practice with respect to rules of evidence did not seem acceptable for a study on the organization of face-to-face interaction. It seemed unlikely that many members of the linguistic and the psychological research communities would be prepared to accept, on the basis of examples, the proposal that highly organized phenomena might be operating in domains of action outside that of language. A simple statement describing the particular regularities detected in the data might not be convincing.

Regardless of the acceptance or nonacceptance by researchers of such statements, it does not seem inappropriate in general to expect of a research report in social science that its findings be accompanied by data permitting an independent evaluation of the reported findings.

Invariant Sequences

One investigator who, prior to the planning of this study, had written extensively on methodology in structural studies of face-to-face communication is Scheflen (e.g., 1966, 1973). In an article largely devoted to methodology Scheflen (1966) wrote:

> The method for ascertaining or identifying the structural unit is based upon its three characteristics, that is, its components, their organization, and the context(s) in which they occur. We begin by inspecting the behaviors and grouping, as a tentative unit, those that occur together in time. We then test this tentative formulation by three tests, reformulating the unit over and over by trial and error until we have determined the relations of components. When we have found the combination that is a structural unit each of its components will occur together every time. They will have consistent arrangement and appear invariably in the same context. If not we must begin again [pp. 272–273].

At a slightly later point, Scheflen is explicit about the nature of the relations required among the components of a "structural unit." "Simply stated, if *A* appears every time *B* appears, and vice versa, and if *A* does not appear when *B* is absent, then *A* and *B* have relations of interdependence and represent an entity [p. 273]."

Brannigan and Humphries (1972), writing from an ethological perspective, appear to adopt a similar, but more ambiguous, position. They state, "Ultimately if we are to talk of signal value in a quantitative, objective way, we suggest that it will be necessary to classify signals not in terms of their supposed emotional causation but in terms of those behavioral relationships which will under certain stated conditions invariably follow the signal . . . (Brannigan & Humphries, 1972, p. 48)." But their use of "invariably" is rendered problematic by a subsequent reference to a signal that "reduces the probability or intensity of a reactor's attack in a given type of situation [p. 48], " and to another action that possesses a "stochastic connection with overt escape [p. 49]. " These subsequent comments suggest that the earlier notion of invariability was inadvertently overstated.

But Scheflen's approach to documenting regularities in interation appeared problematic as the transcriptions in this study began to be scrutinized. In the first place, Scheflen's criterion apparently fails to distinguish (a) the formal statement of some hypothesized organization from (b) the actual operation of that organization amid the dust and confusion of human interaction. That is, on the basis of observing a number of regularities in action, one might wish to propose in formal terms some organization intended to provide an adequate description of the regularities in question. But a statement of such a hypothesized organization would not necessarily carry the implication that every actual performance of actions within the organization be perfect. The demand for perfection within virtually any aspect of human conduct is, on the face of it, unreasonable. Applied to the realm of linguistics, such a demand for perfection would have the effect of, for example, completely invalidating a proposed rule of English syntax, upon the citing of a single instance of an English speaker's violation of that rule, whether intentionally or through human error stemming from psychological and–or physiological stress or the like. No proposed organization, including linguistic grammars, could survive that test.

Scheflen (1966) states that: "In pattern and natural structure, co-occurrence is not probabilistic. We do not bother to assess the probabilities that human beings have hearts or that the word *heart* has an *a* in it [p. 273 n]." It seems important to emphasize, with Scheflen, the distinction between structural and stochastic models for human conduct. But it is equally important to understand that human performance within a proposed organization will rarely be perfect.

Upon further consideration it becomes evident that Scheflen's criterion carries another flaw: it excludes the possibility of hypothesizing optional elements within the proposed organization. The criterion as stated requires that all proposed organizations involve exclusively the rigid repetition of its component elements. One of the most important goals of research in this area is to discover through empirical studies the manner in which conduct may be organized. It seems important to avoid, insofar as possible, any a priori commitment as to the type of organization that will be proposed.

Although the ongoing course of investigation may produce documented examples of the sort of organization required by Scheflen's methodological criterion, the particular organization hypothesized in this research proved to be of a distinctly different sort. It would seem that one's rules for evidence must be both more general and more flexible than those proposed by Scheflen.

Statistical Criteria

In the end, the rules for evidence adopted for this study proved to have no novelty at all. The underlying conception of the research was that a given organization in face-to-face interaction would introduce marked regularities into the actions subject to that organization. If such were the case, then why not evaluate the proposed regularities by appropriate statistical tests? Such tests would provide an estimate of the probability that the regularity in question might have occurred by chance. At the same time, no requirements of perfection would be involved. The statistical tests would easily accommodate imperfect performance, that is, deviations of observed action from that hypothesized by the organization. And the extent of these deviations could be directly evaluated. Further, there would be no necessary a priori commitment to either optional or nonoptional elements within the proposed organization.

Within this unexceptional approach, the proposed organization claims nothing more than it is: a hypothesis based in the first instance on statistical regularities in an exploratory study. Such a hypothesis would be required to hold up under subsequent validation procedures, and be subject to the normal vicissitudes of any other hypothesis in the social sciences. Thus, it is reasonable to expect (a) that the action regularities stemming from the hypothesized organization be adequately documented; (b) that these regularities be replicated in further studies of appropriate interaction contexts; and (c) that the formulation of the organization on the basis of the existing evidence be superior to alternative formulations.

Actual experience with the data suggested one modification of the standard statistical procedure. If we believe that the organization is well formulated and it is being adequately used by the participants in the observed interaction, then it may be reasonable to expect that the resulting regularities in the participants' actions will provide statistical results well beyond those typically accepted as sufficient. That is, p values might prove to be a great deal smaller than such values as .01, typically encountered in social science. The generality of such an expectation for a wider range of phenomena can only be evaluated, however, upon further experience in this line of research.

Conclusion

In view of the background described in this chapter and in Part I, it will not be surprising that the study of the organization of face-to-face interaction as developed had the following characteristics:

1. The study would be initially exploratory and naturalistic in design;

2. The data-generation process would involve (i) a fine-grained transcription of (ii) a broad spectrum of actions, (iii) of all participants in the interaction, (iv) in such a way that sequences of actions, both within and between participants, be preserved;

3. The analysis would focus on the organization of the interaction, rather than the organization of the messages of individual participants, as would be the case in the more usual linguistic approach;

4. The analysis would carry the presupposition that any hypothesized action-based elements found to be contributing to the organization of the interaction, would be treated, at least initially, as discrete;

5. A prime objective of the analysis would be to discover the manner of segmentation of the interaction into some manner of constituent units on at least one hierarchical level.

9
Data Generation

As it turned out, the research program on the organization of face-to-face interaction had two, distinct phases: an exploratory phase and a replication phase. The discussion to this point has centered on characteristics of the exploratory phase. On the basis of this discussion it may be clear that this phase was designed to discover possible elements of the organization of face-to-face interaction, and to develop empirical evidence supporting these claimed discoveries. On the strength of such evidence, reasonable hypotheses with respect to interaction organization might be advanced.

The replication phase was designed to test these hypotheses on new sets of data. In this phase the purpose was not to discover, but to attempt a first verification of the hypotheses. This replication phase was carried out entirely after completion of the exploratory phase.

The specific methods and transcribing procedures for the exploratory and the replication studies are considered in some detail. Each study necessarily is treated separately, not only because of differences in the types of interactions observed, but also because of crucial differences in the respective natures of the studies, having broad ramifications for the way in which data were generated in each.

EXPLORATORY STUDY

Given the preceding considerations, the appropriate beginning was the transcription of one or more relatively natural face-to-face interactions. And so it was done. It is perhaps notable that this transcription was undertaken and pursued over more than a year without even a vague notion of what sort of actions or phenomena in the transcribed data might be "organized" in the requisite manner. That remained to be discovered, Nor was it at all clear during this initial transcribing phase of the research just what methodology would be used to substantiate any claims of discovered organization—the "rules of evidence" considered above. The transcription phase of the research was, all in all, sustained primarily by a conviction that there must be elements of organization in any interaction, and that a properly executed transcription would provide the necessary materials for bringing that organization to light.

Description of Interactions

The first research issue concerned the type of interaction to be studied. It seemed reasonable that research on the organization of interaction might legitimately focus on any aspect of social life. Because any interaction was potentially fair game, it appeared that this decision was somewhat arbitrary, and considerations such as convenience were allowed to exert marked influence on the decision process, as will be described.

Near at hand was the University of Chicago Counseling and Psychotherapy Research Center, where protracted conversations, both between client and therapist and between therapists consulting with each other, were commonplace. Therapists were entirely accustomed to sound (but not to video) recording of their therapy, and to ongoing programs of research based on these recordings. Clients were not required to participate in research programs, but they usually did, apparently because the research was so much a part of the fabric of the Counseling Center operation, and because it was so calmly accepted on the part of the therapists.

The fact of prior experience with psychotherapy research probably influenced initial decisions to use (a) a conversation, as opposed to some other type of interaction; (b) between two persons, the minimal-sized group; (c) who are both adults, mainly to minimize moving about by the participants. All of these elements were part of the everyday adult-therapy interactions at the Counseling Center.

But it also seemed desirable to begin with the interaction of two persons who were previously unacquainted. Such an interaction would minimize the potentially idiosyncratic aspects that might develop in a long-term relationship between two persons. This decision suggested the use, either of the first therapy interview between therapist and client, or of "preliminary" intake interviews at the Counseling Center in which the prospective client discussed with an interviewer (not the eventual therapist) the general reasons for applying for therapy, as well as certain routine information about occupation, family status, and the like.

It was decided to transcribe a preliminary interview for two main reasons:

1.   There would be less potential disruption of the eventual therapy interaction;

2. It was hoped that a wide variety of types of interaction, from more mundane exchange of routine information, to more emotionally charged topics, might be available in the interaction. As it happened, this hope was strongly fulfilled. In addition, the interaction would have fewer of the characteristics associated more specifically with psychotherapy itself.

More generally, the use of interviews at the Counseling Center had a further potential advantage, not necessarily specific to those interviews. The interactions would have occurred regardless of whether or not the research had been undertaken. They were not held purely or even primarily for the purposes of the study.

The individual who typically conducted preliminary interviews with adult applicants was an experienced and mature male therapist, about 40 years old. He readily agreed to participate in the study.

It was decided that the applicant should be female, mainly so that both male and female behaviors would be included in this first transcription. The receptionist at the Counseling Center was given instructions to mention the study to all subsequent female applicants, with the exception of those (a) who had a marked speech disturbance or some other highly intrusive speech mannerism, and (b) whose dialect was strongly and obviously identifiable with any one of Chicago's many ethnic groups. These exceptions were intended to minimize the potentially specialized interaction effects stemming from either pathology or ethnic group. It was desired that the self-presentation of the client be as free as possible of either one of these two characteristics.

It happened that the first female applicant to whom the receptionist spoke with respect to the study agreed to participate, a circumstance entirely unsurprising in light of previous research experience at the Counseling Center. This client proved to be a young woman in her early twenties. She had had about two years of college in Chicago (but not at the University of Chicago) but had quit, at least temporarily, to work as a secretary. It was learned through the transcribed interview that she did indeed come from a distinctly ethnic family and neighborhood in Chicago. She was a native speaker of American English, however, and her dialect was, to these ears, identifiable mainly as a familiar working-class Chicago dialect.

In the following discussion, the client is designated Participant A; the therapist, Participant B; and the interview, Conversation 1.

Once videotaped, a transcription of the speech and body motion actions in Conversation 1 was begun. The conversation lasted about 40 minutes. Of this, the first 19 minutes were transcribed. The end point of the transcription was located at what appeared intuitively to be a major turning point in the conversation at which there was a major topic change, together with a marked shift in the emotional tone of the interaction. This shift was evident from viewing the tape and also was reported by the therapist. The transcription occupied one academic year. The transcribing technique is considered below.

As transcription of this first interaction was nearing completion, preparations were begun to videotape a second interaction. The purpose of gathering data on a second interaction was to provide a partial control for any elements of Conversation 1 that might be specific to it. At the same time, it was not anticipated that more than two interactions would be transcribed for this exploratory phase. This judgment was based on several considerations:

1.   It seemed unwise to continue transcribing for an indefinite period of time, prior to the realization of any concrete results from the transcribing effort; and

2.   The fine detail of the transcriptions was capable of generating a considerable amount of data on the basis of relatively brief amounts of interaction.

It was decided that the second interaction to be transcribed would be a male–male interaction, to contrast with the initial male–female dyad. Further, it was decided that the male therapist used in the first interview should also be included in this second interaction, in order that any shifts in his conduct from one interaction to the next might be observed. (This potential in the data has yet to be exploited because in time the research issue was more clearly defined as focusing on the general organization of interaction, as opposed to individual variations within that organization.)

The second male in the interaction was also a therapist at the Counseling Center and also about 40 years old. The two men had been good friends for a number of years. In this respect also the second interaction contrasted with the first. The general topic of this second interaction centered around a client whom the first therapist had seen in a preliminary interview, and whom the second therapist had seen for a first therapy hour. However, the interaction was also characterized by some joking and kidding between the two men, a most typical aspect of their relationship. The interaction lasted about 30 minutes, of which the first 19 were transcribed, to match the transcription of the first interaction. This interaction is designated Conversation 2, and the second therapist, Participant C.

Room Arrangement

Both conversations were taped in a room in the Psychology Building at the University of Chicago. The room was arranged in the manner of a typical psychotherapy office within the Counseling Center, except that it did not contain a desk. No special lighting was used to supplement the fluorescent lights on the ceiling. The room was decorated with a low occasional table and a table lamp, chairs for the participants, posters on the wall, and drapes for the window. A file cabinet was in one corner. There was a rug under the participants' chairs. A concession to filming technique was a dark green felt cloth placed on the wall behind the participants, covering the area visible on the tape, to increase contrast on the videotape.

The participants' chairs were set at about an 80° angle to each other. The distance between the inside front legs of the two chairs was about .6 m. Thus, the shoulders of the two participants were slightly less than a meter apart. This placed the participants at what Hall (1966) has termed the far phase of personal distance.

Videotaping

It was not possible, of course, to carry out a transcription of actions in face-to-face interaction without a sound and visual recording of the interaction. A transcription covering a wide variety of actions in fine detail requires the capacity to make a larger number of "passes" through the recording of the interaction. It was decided to use videotape, as opposed to sound film, as the recording medium, mainly on the basis of considerations of (a) convenience (videotape requires no special processing laboratories and is not subject to breakage); (b) unobtrusiveness (videotape cameras are entirely silent and require no awkward "blimp" to shield the interactants and the sound track from camera noise, and good results can be obtained from videotape without any special studio lighting fixtures); and (c) flexibility (tapes can be reused). It should be pointed out, however, that a number of investigators making highly detailed action transcriptions, such as Kendon and Condon, prefer sound film as a recording medium. One reason expressed for this preference is the higher-resolution quality of film.

The actual videotaping procedure was as follows. A single camera was placed so that both participants in each interaction were fully visible from head to foot on the tape at all times. No zoom techniques or other special focusing effects were used. The camera was about 2.2 m from the participants. The camera and tape were left running prior to the participants' entry into the room and were not touched again until after the interview.

Despite the fact that a wide-angle lens was used, the camera was necessarily at such a distance from the participants that more subtle details of facial expressions were not discriminable on the videotape. Less subtle expressions, such as broad smiles and grimaces, were readily discernable. In contrast, very small movements of the hands and fingers, for example, were clearly evident on the tapes, so that fine discriminations of these movements could be made and were included on the transcription. A high-quality monophonic audio track was obtained on the videotape.

No effort was made to conceal the camera or microphone from the participants; both pieces of equipment were in full view. (And the participants in both interviews were, of course, fully aware that the conversation would be recorded for research purposes and had given their prior consent.)

For Conversation 1, the videotape recorder was placed in the same room with the participants, but behind a screen. This proved to be an undesirable arrangement, however, for the hum of the recorder was clearly audible, both to the participants and on the sound track, and the screen and recorder were somewhat intrusive within the room. For Conversation 2, therefore, the recorder was placed in an adjacent room. Wires connecting the camera and microphone to the recorder were led through a small conduit that had been placed in the wall for this purpose.

REPLICATION STUDY

On the basis of the exploratory study, a series of hypotheses were generated concerning the exchange of speaking and related phenomena in conversations. These hypotheses were formulated in terms of signals, rules, and other elements relevant to such exchanges. (These hypotheses will be described in detail in Chapter 11.)

Once the hypotheses were generated, it became desirable to attempt an initial test of them. Thus, this study was not exploratory, but designed to test empirically-derived hypotheses. There were, however, no attempts to impose experimental controls on the actions of the participants. The underlying purpose of the research remained that of studying natural interaction, and uncontrolled interactions were used in the same sense as in the exploratory study. However, as might be expected, the design and the data-generation process of the replication were different in several important aspects from those elements of the exploratory study.

Description of Interactions

The study was based on six, two-person conversations of varying length and type. Two of these conversations (3 and 4) were taped in the same room and in the same manner as the two used for the exploratory study. These conversations were selected from a number of tapes made in a somewhat adventitious manner of conversations in this laboratory. The remaining four conversations (5–8) were selected from the set of tapes made for the study of individual differences described in Part II.

All of the tapes used in the replication study were selected on the basis of two criteria: (a) technical adequacy of the video and audio recordings; and (b) a sufficient number of speaking turns in the conversation to justify analysis. The first criterion seems self-explanatory: tapes had to be of sufficient quality to permit the type of transcription of actions that was to be performed on them. The second criterion—number of speaking turns—was a matter of expediency. It happened that various phenomena associated with speaking-turn exchange had become an important subject in the exploratory study. Because a considerable amount of time was required to transcribe a given stretch of videotaped interaction, it was desirable for that stretch to contain a relatively large number of speaking turns in order to provide data for analysis. It should be noted that no special attempt was made to include or to exclude conversations on the basis of such considerations as age or sex of the participants. With regard to factors such as these, the selection of conversations was largely unsystematic.

Each of the conversations in the replication study is described below. Table 9.1 presents some summary information on the six replication conversations used in the exploratory study.

Conversation 3 was between two male college students, one a freshman, and the other a sophomore. They were recruited as they emerged from participating as paid volunteers in another psychological experiment. They were unacquainted, but quickly discovered that they had a number of mutual acquaintances, as well as much in common to talk about. Their interaction was casual and friendly with a moderate amount of joking and laughing. They were paid $2.00 each for their participation.

Conversation 4 was between two female graduate students who worked in the same office as research assistants. They had known each other for about two years. They were recruited as they were conversing in their office. Their conversation was moved to our videotaping room and continued there, seemingly without interruption; and, after some minutes of taping, the conversation was continued once again in their office. Their interaction was most relaxed and centered on shopping in Chicago.

The general context of the taping of Conversations 5–8 was described in Part II. It will be recalled that the study reported in that section entailed videotaping two-person conversations between 88 subjects recruited from the Law School and from the School of Social Service Administration (SSA) at the University of Chicago. All conversations were between a Law School student and an SSA student who were previously unacquainted. Each subject participated in two conversations: one with a partner of the same sex, and one with a partner of the opposite sex. The second conversation immediately followed the first. The conversations lasted seven minutes each.

With respect to the conversations the subjects were requested merely to get acquainted with each other and to talk about anything that was of interest. The topics proved to be of the sort that might be expected in such an acquaintance process between professional-school students: home towns, colleges attended, present courses of study, work experiences, career goals, and the study in which the subjects were participating.

All subjects, prior to their first conversation, had completed several self-descriptive inventories prior to the conversation. For their participation in this series of tasks each subject received $3.00.

TABLE 9.1
Summary of Selected Characteristics of the
Eight Conversations Analyzed in the Turn-System Study

Conversation No.	Duration of trans-cription (min.)	Sex of participants	Previously acquainted?	Paid?	Comments
1	19	F-M	No	No	Psychotherapy intake interviews, participants previously unacquainted
2	19	M-M	Yes	No	Good friends for 10 years
3	5	M-M	No	Yes	Recruited when departing another psychology experiment
4	5	F-F	Yes	No	On-going conversation videotaped
5	7.5	F-M	No	Yes	Recruited; used in individual-differences study (Part II)
6	7.5	F-M	No	Yes	Recruited; used in individual-differences study (Part II)
7	7.5	F-M	No	Yes	Recruited; used in individual-differences study (Part II)
8	7.5	F-M	No	Yes	Recruited; used in individual-differences study (Part II)

From the 88 videotaped conversations, four were selected on a nonsystematic basis, aside from the two criteria mentioned above. Sex composition of the dyads was not taken into account. It is apparently by chance that all four conversations selected were between a female and a male. Similarly by chance, of the four, two were the first conversation the subject had had in the study, and two were the second.

The transcribing procedure and a check of the interjudge transcribing reliability are described in Appendix A. The transcribing procedure and its associated reliability were based on the results of the exploratory study. For this reason, the material in Appendix A may most profitably be read after Chapter 11, in which the exploratory results are described.

TRANSCRIPTION: EXPLORATORY STUDY

Central to the exploratory study was the task of transcribing the interaction. The transcribed actions would be the data on which all analyses would be performed. While it is a truism that analyses can be no better than the data to which they are applied, the nature of exploratory research provided a complication that imparted an additional dimension of criticality to the transcribing process. Prior to the completion of the transcription, neither the basic phenomena to be investigated, nor the specific aspects of actions relevant to these phenomena, were known. It was not possible to focus the transcription on a set of specific actions of interest because what would be "of interest" was not yet defined. The situation was directly analogous to the anthropological linguist who initiates research on a newly discovered language. The procedure in this case is to make a "phonetic" transcription of the language as spoken by informants, including as much fine detail as possible, and minimizing a priori decisions as to which sounds would ultimately prove to be a part of the language structure. It seems strange to draw an analogy between (a) research on an unknown language; and (b) this research on the structure of face-to-face interaction between English speakers. But considering the extent of firm empirical findings on the organization of face-to-face interaction, the analogy does not seem overdrawn. Certainly, when this study was begun, the analogy seemed entirely appropriate in a subjective sense.

Not everything, of course, was unknown. There was considerable available information on English phonology and syntax, and this was used, at least in part, both for the transcription and for the subsequent analysis. But substantial issues remained concerning the contribution of these language elements to a system of interaction between persons, and concerning the manner and extent to which language elements, paralanguage, and body motion played a part in such a system. Once again, these issues could only be addressed by research based on a relatively thorough transcription, not only of language, but also of paralanguage and body motion.

General Organization

The transcription of body motion from the videotape recordings was done by two persons, working together. In order for an event to be transcribed, both persons had to agree upon its transcription. This practice was also used in the transcription of intonation and paralanguage in Conversation 2. Transcription of intonation and paralanguage in Conversation 1 was done entirely by Duncan.

The transcription was written on large (17 x 13-inch) sheets of paper, ruled both vertically and horizontally in the manner of data sheets. Each horizontal line was designated for the entry of one type of action. For example, gestures of the right hand of Participant B were entered on one indicated line. Because the study was focussed on interaction betwen persons as opposed to messages of a single person, all actions of both participants in the conversations were entered on each sheet, for the stretch of time covered by that sheet. The vertical lines facilitated the careful alignment of all the actions.

Speech

Segmental Phonemes

The first transcription task was to record what the participants were saying: their actual words and word-like utterances. To accomplish this, the Trager and Smith (1957) system of segmental phonemes was used. This system was an attempt to represent with a set of convenient symbols, the basic structural elements of one aspect of the English sound system. The Trager-Smith system is capable of providing a reasonably accurate and economical rendering of the pronunciation of speech syllables, avoiding the irregularities and idiosyncrasies of English orthography.

The Trager–Smith system is designed to be sensitive to English dialect differences, but this potential was not used in the transcription. No special attempt was made to record faithfully the subtle differences detectable between the respective dialects of the participants. During the formulation of the study a decision was made not to focus on dialectal differences as potential elements of the organization of interaction.

On the other hand, careful attention was paid in this aspect of the transcription to verbal slips, mispronounced or incomplete words, speech nonfluencies such as stutters, unexpected forms such as failure to add "s" for plurals, and "ed" for past tenses, and the like. Every effort was made to record accurately the speech of the participants at those moments when they were talking at the same time, and the onset and offset of such moments was carefully noted.

Beyond serving as a record of what was said, this aspect of the transcription served another important function: that of providing the events to which the rest of the transcription was anchored. That is, all other elements of the transcriptions, such as the beginnings and endings of hand gestures and head nods, were located in the transcription with respect to the syllables of words or to the spaces between syllables. This practice departed from the more common one of transcribing with respect to some chronological time scale, such as frames of a movie film. By locating all other actions with respect to the speech syllables, the transcribing process was accelerated by eliminating the task of locating these speech syllables with respect to some other referent. The temporal precision afforded by speech syllables seemed, at that time, to be sufficient for the purposes of the study; and, in retrospect, that judgment continues to appear sound.

One potential problem resulting from the use of speech syllables to locate other actions is the occurrence of protracted silences during the conversation. On our tapes it happened that silences were quite brief, occurring mainly during the speech of one participant, as opposed to between the respective speaking turns of two participants.

In addition to the pronunciation of syllables, there is the prosody or intonation of speech. Trager and Smith (1957) termed the elements of intonation, "suprasegmental phonemes." They include the phenomena of pitch, stress, and juncture.

The Trager–Smith system for transcribing intonation was used, with the following exception: While Trager and Smith specify four stress levels, only the heaviest stress (the primary stress) was transcribed. This was another practice adopted for the purpose of speeding the transcription, while retaining potentially valuable information with respect to stress.

Three terminal junctures—rising, falling, and sustained—were transcribed in accordance with the Trager–Smith system. These junctures are composed of contours of pitch, intensity, and duration occurring on the final syllable of phonemic clauses.

As described below, the point of departure for all subsequent analysis in this study was the phonemic clause (Trager & Smith, 1957). A phonemic clause is a phonological unit, defined by Trager and Smith as containing one and only one primary stress, and one terminal juncture. Transcribing primary stresses and terminal junctures automatically identifies the phonemic clauses in the corpus. Thus, the phonemic clause is based entirely on intonation.

Paralanguage

"Paralanguage" refers to the wide variety of events that occur in speech but are not considered part of language, as that domain is traditionally construed. Examples of paralinguistic actions in English would be (a) variations in pitch or in intensity beyond those provided for in linguistic intonation systems; (b) pauses, both unfilled (silent) and filled ("um," "uh," and the like);

(c) nonspeech sounds, such as laughing, grunting, and sighing; and (d) other qualities of speech, such as rasp and resonance.

As mentioned in Chapter 1, highly useful classification systems for paralinguistic actions have been compiled by Trager (1958), by Crystal and Quirk (1964), and by Crystal (1969), among others. These systems are relatively extensive; any single speaker will probably use a small fraction of the actions categorized by the systems.

On the analysis presented in Chapter 2, most categories within a system for paralanguage necessarily involve an ordinal scale nested within the nominal, dichotomous category of "vocalizing" versus "not vocalizing." The ordinal scale is some dimension along which vocalization is perceived to be varying, such as pitch or tempo. Part of the specification of such an ordinal scale is the number of scale points to be judged. Thus, a scale for paralinguistic pitch might have five scale points: one "normal," unmarked point; two degrees of overhigh pitch; and two degrees of overlow. (Some paralinguistic categories, such as "presence or absence of a filled pause," require only a second nominal judgment, after the initial nominal judgment or presence or absence of vocalizing.)

The following categories were used in the transcription of paralanguage for the exploratory study. Each category will be named, together with the anchor points of the dimension along which the vocalization is perceived to be varying, and with the number of scale points used. Less obvious categories are briefly discussed.

1. *Intensity* (overloud—oversoft; 5 points).
2. *Pitch height* (overhigh—overlow; 5 points).
3. *Extent* (drawl—clipping; 3 points). The relative length or brevity of single syllables.
4. *Tempo* (increased—decreased; 3 points). The relative speed with which sequences of syllables are uttered.
5. *Pauses* Classified according to location and type. With regard to location, juncture pauses were defined as those occurring between phonemic clauses; and hesitation pauses were defined as those occurring within phonemic clauses (Boomer & Dittmann, 1962). With regard to type, filled pauses contain some phonation such as "um," or "uh."
6. *Audible inhalations and exhalations.*

The above six types of paralinguistic actions are quite common, being present in most speech samples. The following paralinguistic actions are less frequently encountered, relatively speaking. This observation on their frequency carries no implications regarding their importance.

7. *Laughing, crying, whispering, and the like.* Trager (1958) observes that these actions "can cover large areas of talking, surrounding, as it were, the language material, or they can occur between bits of language [p. 6]." These actions are extremely coarsely described by existing category systems. There are, of course, many ways to laugh and to cry.

8.   *Resonance*   (resonant—thin; 3 points). Variations in this category are probably brought about by variations in size and shape of the supraglottal cavities.

9.   *Vocal lip control*   (rasp—openness; 3 points). There is often a surprising range of variation in rasp over relatively short stretches of speech. Openness, the polar opposite of rasp, is not often heard. An open voice sounds strikingly soft and may give the impression of intimacy. Openness may not be readily subject to voluntary control, although rasp is. Earlier research (Duncan, Rice, & Butler, 1968) suggested that openness can exert a powerfully facilitating effect on therapy process.

10.   *Glottis control*   (overvoicing—undervoicing; 3 points). Undervoicing was sometimes observed in moments prior to and during crying.

Body Motion

In contrast to both linguistic and paralinguistic speech actions, there was for body-motion events no available transcription system that could be readily adapted to the needs of the exploratory study. Existing body-motion transcription systems proved to be either (a) too imprecise in specifying actions; or (b) quite selective a priori, not permitting sufficiently broad coverage of the actions found in the conversations; or (c) excessively fine or course grained for the purpose of the study. This assessment of the situation appeared to require the development of a body-motion transcribing system tailored specifically to the needs of the exploratory study.

An approach to transcribing body motion was developed that was based on the observation that, within a given interaction, an individual uses a rather distinct repertoire of different body movements. The total number of different movements for any one body part is not extremely large, even when the conversation is relatively animated. In addition, there were several possible types of action that simply did not occur in the conversations, despite the fact that there had been no instructions to the participants concerning permissible or impermissible conduct. For example, the participants never moved their chairs from the positions in which they found them. Once seated, the participants remained in their seats until the conversations were terminated. There was no walking about the room. And there was no body contact between the participants, even though they were in easy reaching distance of each other. (Unsurprisingly, these observations were equally true of the conversations used in the replication study, and of the remaining conversations in the individual-differences study.)

Given these circumstances, it was possible to inventory the movements used in Conversation 1, assign either arbitrary or descriptive labels to the different movements, and then to transcribe body motion for the individuals in that conversation. When this approach was applied to Conversation 2, it was found that the category system developed for Conversation 1 was generally adequate, but that some new categories had to be added. In this manner, a transcribing system was established that (a) seemed to provide thorough coverage of the events encountered in the conversations; (b) appeared adequate for the purposes of the study; (c) was firmly grounded in actual observation; (d) was readily expandable to cover new events observed in additional conversations; and (e) additionally met the more general criteria discussed in Chapter 20.

The transcribing system, as it was developed to cover the events in Conversation 2, is briefly described below. In the terms of Chapter 2, the list of categories contains both (a) nominal classes of action; and in some cases, (b) ordinal subaspects of these nominal classes. It will be recalled that the onset and offset of each occurrence of each of these actions was located with respect to a speech syllable or to the pause between two syllables. The transcription system was, of course, applied to the body motion of both participants in a conversation.

While this description should be sufficient to permit use of the transcription system by other researchers, the spirit in which the system was formulated suggests that it may have greater relevance in suggesting a general approach to the development of transcribing systems, potentially facilitating the development of comparable systems by other investigators to cover the particular set of events encountered in the interactions they have chosen to study.

Head Gestures

1. Head nod.
2. Head shake.

Head Direction

1. Toward face of partner.
2. Away from face of partner.

Smiling

1. Broad smiles. (More subtle expressions were not clearly discriminable on the tapes.)

Shoulder Movements

1. Shoulder shrug, both shoulders.
2. Shoulder shrug, left shoulder only.
3. Shoulder shrug, right shoulder only.

Hand and Arm Rest Positions

These positions were transcribed when one or both hands of a participant were not engaged in some gesture-like activity. The hand was transcribed as resting on the:

1. Head.
2. Mouth.
3. Chin (one hand).
4. Chin (both hands, folded together).
5. Lap.
6. Chair arm (elbow on chair arm).
7. Chair arm (hand on back of chair arm, elbow raised above chair arm).
8. Thigh.
9. Knee.
10. Ankle.

Hand and Arm Gesture Positions

Movements of the hand and arm were transcribed as a series of positions, the trajectory of the hand–arm between these positions being assumed. For example, imagine that a participant has both arms resting on the chair. From this rest position, the participant's right hand–arm rises, then (a) executes a pointing gesture toward the partner; then (b) makes a fist, and then returns to the initial rest position. The transcription of this series of actions would proceed as follows:

1.   The initial rest position would be recorded for those speech syllables over which it occurred.

2.   The syllable on which movement was first detected would be indicated. (The left hand and arm would, of course, continue to be transcribed as being at a rest position.)

3.   The position of the hand and arm at the apex of the pointing gesture would be noted, on the syllable(s) during which the apex was reached. The path between the rest position and the apex of the gesture would be assumed. If the hand had actually taken a roundabout route from rest position to gesture apex, requiring a change of direction in order to reach the apex, the position of the hand and arm at the point of direction change would be transcribed, and the syllable(s) on which the change occurred would be indicated.

4.   The fist would be transcribed for those syllable(s) over which it occurred. Once again, the absence of a transcribed position between pointing gesture and fist would imply a reasonably direct route was taken between the two gestures.

5. The syllable on which the hand and arm returned to a rest position would be noted.

At each point at which the position of the hand and arm during movements was indicated in the transcription, the following elements were included:

Distance of Hand From Body

1. Within about 6 inches of body.
2. From 6 inches from body, to outer edge of chair.
3. Beyond outer edge of chair.

Height of Hand

1. At level of chair arm or below.
2. Between chair arm and shoulder.
3. Above shoulders.

Height of Elbow

1. On chair arm.
2. Between chair arm and shoulder.
3. Shoulder level.
4. Above shoulders.

Lateral Position of Hand

1. In front of body.
2. In line with chair arm.
3. Outside of chair arm.

Wrist Position and Movements

1. Down.
2. Straight.
3. Up.
4. Circle (circular motion of wrist that does not end in firm downward movement).
5. Circular Flip (circular wrist motion that ends in a downward movement).
6. Flip.
7. Slicing (hand going back and forth on horizontal plane).

Palm Position and Movement

This set of positions actually refers to the degree of rotation of the fore-arm. It seemed convenient to indicate this in terms of the position of the palm, assuming that the wrist was in a straight position:

1. Up (palm generally in direction of ceiling).
2. Down (palm generally in direction of floor).
3. Side (palm generally in direction of body).

Hand Position

1. Fist (tightly clinched).
2. Closed (not so firmly clenched as a fist).
3. Curled (normal relaxed position, fingers slightly curled).
4. Extended (all fingers straight and also together; a tensed position).
5. Pointing: one finger.
6. Pointing: two fingers.
7. Spread (all fingers extended, as above, but separated from each other.
8. Cupped (palm forms bottom of cup while fingers and heel of palm form sides of cup).
9. Index finger–thumb circle (these two digits touch at their tips, form-ing a circle).

Posture Positions

These elements were included in the description of posture whenever a change in one or more of the elements was observed:

1. Shoulder orientation.
   a. Straight (shoulders parallel to back of chair).
   b. Between straight and partner.
   c. Toward partner.
   d. Away from partner.
2. Sideways lean of torso.
   a. Straight (no lean).
   b. Toward partner.
   c. Away from partner.
   d. Strongly away from partner.
3. Trunk–thigh angle.
   a. Right angle.
   b. Slightly obtuse angle.
   c. Highly obtuse angle.
4. Position of buttocks on chair seat.

This position was transcribed in terms of an imaginary 3 x 3 grid on the chair seat.

5. Leg orientation.
   a. Straight (the leg(s) on the floor generally perpendicular to the back of the chair).
   b. Between straight and partner.
   c. Toward partner.
   d. Away from partner.
6. Leg position.
   a. Both feet on floor.
   b. Legs are crossed knee to knee.
   c. Legs are crossed ankle to knee.
   d. Legs are crossed shin to knee.
In addition, there was a notation as to which leg was crossed.
7. Leg and foot movements.
   a. Lateral movement of the leg, in which the knee is the primary moving part.
   b. Swinging the foot in any direction.
8. Foot positions.
   a. Dorsal flexion.
   b. Dorsal extension.
   c. Lateral bending of the foot.
   d. Rotation of the foreleg, either on the heel or the toes, so that:
      1. some part of the foot is moved toward the partner.
      2. some part of the foot is moved away from the partner.

Notes on Transcription

It is apparent at this point that there are many actions commonly observed in conversations that are not included in the transcription scheme. This omission is based on the fact that the scheme attempts to cover only those events actually encountered in the two conversations studied. Presumably, additional events can be incorporated in this or a similar scheme as required.

The most time-consuming aspect of the transcription was that applying to the hands and arms. Gestures were frequent, often prolonged, and complicated. Each shift in hand and–or arm position required (a) locating that shift with respect to syllables, a task that was not so difficult as tedious; and (b) reassessing the status of each element of the hand–arm transcribing scheme. It was not uncommon for the two hands of a participant to be engaged in somewhat different types of gestures. As will be seen, virtually none of this laboriously acquired detail was ultimately used in the exploratory analysis, but this was, of course, impossible to anticipate.

The second most time-consuming aspect of the transcription was that applying to speech intonation and paralanguage. As opposed to the transcribing of body motion, which required no specialized training, it seems advisable to prepare for transcribing speech by acquiring some specialized skills of the sort given in phonetics courses. It is true that (a) such courses commonly emphasize the segmental aspects of speech, to the relative neglect of intonation, and (b) often ignore entirely paralanguage. But two aspects of phonetic training may still be valuable to the investigator of intonation and paralanguage: (a) exposure to the general phonetic framework for transcribing speech sounds; and (b) supervised practice in focusing the attention narrowly on specific elements of the speech stream, and in making fine discriminations with regard to these elements.

The construction of any transcription system requires a number of decisions. For the system described above, the most crucial decision was that an attempt would be made to cover as many different types of actions as possible and to include virtually all observable changes with regard to those types of actions. The most important remaining decisions had to do with how many ordinal discriminations were to be made within each of the nominal event types. In most cases, such discriminations were held to a very small number. In setting the number of ordinal points for a category, the investigator must often resort primarily to his own intuitions. A member of our research team Tom Rossen has added the term "gastrosemanticity" to our working vocabulary, referring to the gut reactions that often exert such strong influence in the development of transcription schemes. Because exploratory research is concerned, by definition, with largely unexplored areas, the role of investigator intuition in the development of exploratory research seems inevitable and should be openly acknowledged.

Finally, there is the matter of the time-consuming nature of the two transcriptions done for this study. Given the objectives of the study, it is difficult to imagine how this laborious task could have been significantly reduced without the advantage of hindsight. Further, there is the potential complexity of the phenomena of face-to-face interaction. Hymes (1972) has stated the issue with candor: "If one balks at such detail, perhaps because it requires technical skills in linguistics, musicology, or the like that are hard to command, one should face the fact that the human meaning of one's object of study, and the scientific claims of one's field of inquiry, are not being taken seriously [p. 59]."

10

Preliminaries to Analysis

INITIAL STAGE OF ANALYSIS: PREDISCOVERY

In time, the transcriptions were being completed, and analyses could begin. As has been mentioned above, at the onset of analysis it was not known what phenomena would prove to be the focus of the analysis. The discovery of these phenomena was, of course, a major goal of this study. (The development of methodology was another.) This prediscovery phase is built into the very nature of exploratory studies. It is, for investigators, the dark before the dawn, but in a special universe in which the dawn does not necessarily occur.

Despite this metaphorical darkness, there was not a sense of being entirely lost. It was reasonably clear where one must look in order to find the desired phenomena. The reasoning was as follows.

To the extent that interaction is organized, it exhibits regularities; and the notion of regularity implies repetition. But there might easily be legitimate regularities, occurring frequently in the lives of the participants and also in our two conversations, that would be undetectable in this study because they occurred only once or twice in these particular conversations. An example of such regularities might be those applying to the initial greetings between unacquainted persons. (An interesting senior honors thesis by Mark Cary at the University of Chicago indeed suggests regularities, some unsuspected, in these initial greetings.)

Clearly, the data-generation strategy used in this study, based on the analysis of only two conversations, is not appropriate for the discovery of such infrequent or single events in conversations. The fine–grained transcription, extending in each conversation over (a) a wide variety of actions, (b) both participants; and (c) extended portions of two conversations, was better suited for the analysis of more frequently occurring elements of organization, even those involving relatively small events. The plan was, therefore, to

163

search for actions in the transcription that seemed to occur frequently, and to attempt to build the exploratory analysis around any such actions that were found.

But beyond the basic discovery issue, there were two other central issues requiring resolution in this study at this initial stage, that were not built into the nature of exploratory studies. Rather, they were methodological problems for which solutions were needed for studies in this general research area.

One of these issues had to do with justifying a claim that a discovery of some sort had been made. On the optimistic assumption that an interesting set of phenomena would be discovered, it was not known how a claim of such a discovery might be substantiated. What would be the rules of evidence for this material? The various academic disciplines in the social sciences, for example, linguistics, psychology, and anthropology, have each developed their own somewhat distinctive set of rules of evidence. It was not clear that any one of these might be fully adequate or appropriate to the material at hand. In Chapter 8 this issue was briefly outlined and the solution—in terms of statistics—was described. In this chapter this issue will be examined more specifically as it applies to the phenomena under investigation.

Another analytic issue remained unresolved: that of unitizing the transcribed material. It was necessary, prior to a statistical analysis of the material, to segment the stream of the transcribed conversations into some sort of units for the purpose of analysis. It was not clear, as the analysis phase of the study was beginning, just how this unitizing should be done.

In this section the development of the study at this primitive, prediscovery stage of analysis will be described in broad terms.

UNITS OF ANALYSIS

The first task actually undertaken was that of breaking the transcriptions into smaller units. It seems axiomatic that units of some sort are necessary for statistical analysis: one needs to make counts of various phenomena in the data. But it is possible to count the number of such things as head nods or shifts in gaze direction in our transcriptions without considering units. For our purposes, however, units were necessary for counting something else: the number of times some given action did *not* happen, so that rates of occurrence could be calculated. That is, to claim some relationship between a given action and some other event, it is of course necessary to compare (a) the rate at which the action and other event occur together, with (b) the rates at which each occurs without the other. Thus, breaking the stream of interaction into units permits one to count the number of times given actions did not occur, so that rates can be calculated.

In the following discussion, these units are called "units of analysis." Units of analysis are developed strictly for the purpose of analysis; their use does not represent a hypothesis that they correspond to any units actually segmenting the interaction, although presumably the closer units of analysis are to actual units, the more productive of results the study will be.

There are any number of ways in which conversational material can be broken into units. A major research decision has to do with how this unitizing will be done. One might use some measure of time such as seconds, minutes, or movie-film frames. In much research on psychotherapy, the unit of analysis has been what has variously been termed an intervention or a response; we might call it a speaking turn. Also frequently found are units based on elements of linguistic syntax, such as clauses or sentences.

Use of Intonation

From a variety of previous research experiences, it had been anticipated that the unit of analysis for this study would not be based on time, responses, or syntax, but rather on intonation.

The anticipated use of intonation for the creation of units of analysis stemmed from several considerations:

1.   The use of any unit based on time seemed essentially arbitrary, failing to take into account the actual events of the interaction. It seemed more desirable to use these events in the creation of units.

2.   The intervention or response as used in psychotherapy research, while meeting the criterion of being based on natural events in the interaction, appeared to be too large and thus insensitive, relative to the detail of the transcription.

3.   Linguistic grammars appear to be based excessively on "well-formed utterances" or the like, that fail to take into account the fits and starts, the dust and confusion, of ordinary conversations. Thus, the attempt to apply traditional syntactic models to natural conversations results in a surfeit of instances for which the models simply do not fit.

4.   Intonation, in contrast, can readily be transcribed for any speech utterance, whether well or ill formed syntactically. Previous research experience had led to the subjective impression that intonation might well constitute a point of natural contact between language on the one hand, and paralanguage and body motion on the other. That is, it seemed possible that much of both language and nonlanguage elements of interaction might be organized in some fashion around the structure of intonation.

A brief comment on the relation between syntax and intonation is appropriate at this point. It has, from time to time, been claimed (e.g., Lieberman, 1967) (a) that there is extensive overlap between intonation and syntax; (b) that persons transcribing intonation are deeply influenced by the syntactic structure of the language over which the intonation is being transcribed; and (c) that, in any event, transcription of intonation is unreliable. Acknowledging that this statement of the arguments is excessively brief and incomplete, an equally brief and incomplete response might be made to them:

1.   There is, indeed, considerable coincidence of intonation and syntactic boundaries in transcriptions of speech. This coincidence, however, is far from complete; both for well- and ill-formed utterances; and it is precisely at those points at which intonation and syntax do not coincide that speech analysis becomes particularly interesting. It was at these points that the intonation boundaries, as opposed to the syntactic ones, were used.

2.   The transcription of intonation seems most likely to be a complex process, taking into account nonlinear combinations of pitch, loudness, and duration variations. It is quite possible that considerations of syntax exert an influence on this process at certain points, particularly those at which the rater is experiencing difficulty in making decisions on the basis of purely phonological criteria. Much remains to be understood about the subjective criteria for transcribing intonation, and this study does not contribute to that understanding. It may be pointed out, again, that there are points at which syntactic and intonation boundaries clearly diverge, and that intonation transcription can be readily applied to stretches of speech in which the syntax is in a state of disarray.

3.   Good reliability has been obtained for transcriptions of intonation in a variety of ways.

The approach to transcribing intonation was based on the Trager and Smith (1957) system, as described in the last chapter. Transcribing in terms of this system automatically produces a set of phonemic clauses, defined as containing (a) one and only one primary stress; and (b) a terminal juncture. Thus, the terminal junctures, in effect, mark the boundaries between successive phonemic clauses. These clauses are, in themselves, a unitizing of the material.

To give a general idea of the length of a phonemic clause, as transcribed in this study, the clauses varied from a minimum of one syllable to a maximum of about eight or nine syllables, with an estimated modal value of about four syllables. During the 19 minutes transcribed for Conversation 1, there were 668 phonemic clauses in the speech of Participant A, and 375 in the speech of Participant B, or a little less than 1 per second.

Intonation-Marked and Intonation-Unmarked Phonemic Clauses

It had been planned, however, not to use the phonemic clause itself as a unit of analysis, but rather a unit based on the clause and somewhat larger than it. The notion of this larger unit derived from the observation of patterns of pitch and terminal contours in the intonation.

In the course of reviewing transcribed speech materials of a variety of native speakers of American English, it was noticed that phonemic clauses could be dichotomized on the basis of intonation patterns. On the one hand were those phonemic clauses having a variation in pitch from the intermediate level (Level 2 in the Trager-Smith system), and–or a rising or falling terminal juncture (transcribed as↗ or↘). Phonemic clauses containing this sort of variation in pitch level and–or terminal juncture will be termed "intonation-marked" clauses. Examples of intonation-marked phonemic clauses may be found between the following points in Fig. 10.1, below: 1–4, 12–13, and 27–28. (The clause extending between Points 14-18 is a special case that will be considered in a later section.)

Contrasting with intonation-marked clauses were those in which the intonation pitch level remained constant at the intermediate level throughout the clause, and in which the terminal juncture was neither rising nor falling (transcribed as⟶). Such clauses will be said to be "unmarked" in intonation. Examples of unmarked phonemic clauses may be found between the following points in Fig. 10.1: 5–8, 9–10, 19–23, and 24–26.

Given this simple dichotomy, sequences of clauses were frequently observed in which one or more unmarked clauses were followed by an intonation-marked clause. An example of such a sequence may be found between points 5 and 13 in Fig. 10.1. This general unmarked-marked sequence of clauses was being considered as a likely candidate for defining the unit of analysis in the transcribed material for this study. Of course, an intonation-marked clause might also immediately follow another intonation-marked clause. In those cases in which there was a succession of two or more immediately adjacent intonation-marked clauses, each of these clauses would comprise a unit of analysis.

Speaking-Turn Exchanges and Concurrent Actions

An inspection of the transcription was undertaken to test in an intuitive way this basis for unitizing the material. In addition, during this inspection a list was kept of actions that appeared to occur frequently in the transcription. In the process of this turning through the pages of the transcription, a surprisingly extensive list of recurring actions was quickly developed and primary attention in the inspection was shifted to these actions. The material was reviewed a number of times, resulting in both additions to and deletions from the list, and revisions of the definitions of the actions listed. This screening of actions and revisions of definitions was to continue throughout the exploratory analysis, both in this prediscovery stage and in the more formal analysis.

As the list of recurring actions was being developed, it was noticed that at certain points, many of the listed actions tended to occur, either simultaneously or in tight sequences spanning only a few syllables. The most immediately prominent point at which this clustering occurred was at the end of speaking turns. When this observation was made, it was clear that the first element to be explored in the organization of two-person, face-to-face conversations would be the process of exchanging speaking turns.

It should be emphasized that the notion of the orderly exchange of the speaking turn between participants in conversations had not previously been explicitly considered to this point in the study. That is, it had never been questioned, just how it might be that participants were often able to accomplish such orderly exchanges of the turn. This phenomenon had certainly not been previously considered as a possible object of analysis in the study. (The several references in the literature to this phenomenon either appeared or were gathered subsequently.) It was, nevertheless, a fairly obvious phenomenon and, for several reasons to be considered below, a fortuitous one on which to initiate an investigation.

Inspection of the transcribed material was resumed, focusing both on those actions that appeared to be present most frequently at the points of speaking-turn exchange, and on actions that intuitively seemed to have the quality of ending or punctuating a turn, such as paralinguistic drawl. The list of regularly recurring actions became transformed into a list of actions that were found with some frequency at the points of speaking-turn exchange. None of these actions had been subjected to systematic analysis. Each of the actions, however, appeared to be prime candidates for such systematic analysis.

Final Unitizing Procedure

But systematic analysis of the exchange of speaking turns was not possible until the original problems of unitizing the transcribed material was solved in some manner. Because the listed actions occurred not only at the ends of speaking turns, but also at various points during speaking turns, it was decided to use the occurrence of the listed actions as a basis for unitizing, rather than depending solely upon intonation-marked phonemic clauses as a basis. (These clauses were not abandoned, however, for they comprised one class of the listed actions.)

It must be confessed that the reasons for deciding to define the units of analysis on the basis of the occurrence of the listed actions cannot be fully recalled. It is clear that these actions were the center of interest at that point in the analysis. Further, it was intuitively appealing to use a variety of actions as a basis for units, rather than focusing more exclusively on any single action. And there was a strong subjective sense that the actions were marking units of some sort. But in retrospect, it seems likely that the decision was predominately a subjective one, not elaborately rationalized. As it happened, the decision proved to have several advantages for the analysis that could not have been anticipated at that time. These advantages will be described at the appropriate points below.

To facilitate the description of units of analysis, Fig. 10.1 is provided. This figure shows the transcriptions of the listed actions for a speaker in three separate stretches of speech. The transcribed actions are reproduced exactly, with the exception of three simplifications: (a) English orthography is used instead of the Trager and Smith (1957) phonemic symbols; (b) actions are not shown that were transcribed but not used for drawing unit boundaries; and (c) the information on the shape of the gestures is not included: the figure shows merely whether or not one or both hands were engaged in gesticulation. To aid in locating specific points in the transcription, each syllable and audible inhalation (symbolized as ⟩) is numbered. These three stretches were chosen because of the wide variety of examples that they provide for the discussion below. They do not, however, illustrate every possible situation or configuration of actions that may be found in the transcriptions.

(It will be recalled that the numerals used in the transcription of an intonation pattern—1, 2, 3, and 4—refer to the Trager and Smith (1957) phonemic pitch levels, "1" being the lowest, and "2" being the "normal" level. The three arrow symbols— →, ⤵ , and ⤴ —refer to their terminal junctures: sustained, falling, and rising, respectively. The Trager–Smith symbols for these were | , ⫤ ⊨, and || .)

The following procedure for unitizing the material was developed. The transcriptions were segmented in terms of the actions of the participant who was speaking. Thus, in the course of the entire transcription, units were based on the actions of both participants, but on only one participant at a time. The simultaneous talking that occurred in the conversations was quite brief, rarely lasting more than three to four syllables, and more often lasting one or two syllables. This observation is in line with Jaffe and Feldstein's (1970) finding that the mean duration of simultaneous speech in the conversations they studied was slightly more than .4 sec (compare their Tables D-5 and D-6).

In general, the boundary of a unit of analysis was considered to be located (a) at the onset of the first syllable; (b) following the end of a phonemic clause (not necessarily an intonation-marked one); (c) during or immediately after which at least one of the listed actions occurred.

Certain details are necessary to supplement this general procedure. Boundaries were not drawn at the onset of filled pauses or sociocentric sequences by the speaker (both described immediately below), or at the onset of back channels (Yngve, 1970), such as "yeah," or "m–m," or a head nod, by the auditor. Further, a new unit of analysis was begun at the onset of each new speaking turn, regardless of the actions that preceded that new turn.

The listed actions used in the definition of units of analysis are described below.

Language

1. *Intonation:* the presence of an intonation-marked phonemic clause.

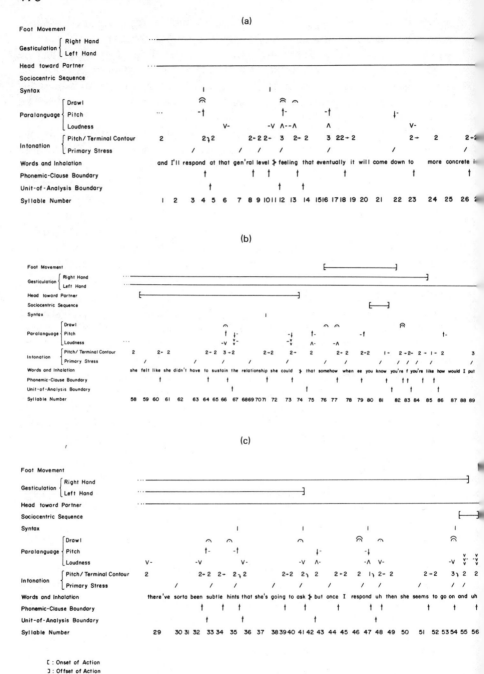

FIGURE 10.1   Illustration of Units of Analysis

For the purposes of this and later stages of the study, an intonation-marked clause was defined as one in ion-marked clause was defined as the 2 2→ pitch/terminal contour pattern on the last two syllables of the clause (or on the single syllable of a monosyllabic clause). The requirement that the deviation occur on one of the last two syllables was instituted to exclude from the class of intonation-marked clauses, those clauses that showed a 3 2 2 → pattern on the last three syllables. The desirability of excluding clauses showing such a pattern was an entirely subjective judgment made at this early stage of the study, but it proved to be productive when more systematic analyses were made of the data.

Boundaries of intonation-marked clauses occur at the onset of the syllable following points 4, 12–13, 27–28, 35, 41, 47, 54, 66, 85, and 89–90 in Fig. 10.1. An example of the 3 2 2 → pattern may be seen on syllables 15–16–17.

One other special situation with respect to intonation may be mentioned. It sometimes happened that two adjoining clauses showed the following pattern: 2 2 3 → 2 1 ➘ or some highly similar variant. In such cases it seemed that the higher pitch level on the first clause was closely associated with the lower pitch level and downward terminal contour on the second clause. The two clauses, considered together, appeared to form a single, more complex pitch-level–terminal-contour pattern. In these cases the unit boundary was placed at the end of the second clause, rather than at the end of both clauses. No example of this particular phenomenon is shown in Fig. 10.1.

2. *Speech content:* uttering one of several stereotyped expressions, termed "sociocentric sequences" (Bernstein, 1962). Examples of sociocentric sequences from our transcription are: "but uh," "or something," and "you know." When used, these expressions typically followed a more substantive statement. Sociocentric sequences occur at Points 55–56 and 80–81 in Fig. 10.1. Sociocentric sequences were never set apart in units of their own. When a sociocentric sequence immediately followed a phonemic clause at the end of which a unit boundary would have been drawn on the basis of the occurrence of other unitizing actions, that sociocentric sequence was included in the preceding unit. Both instances of sociocentric sequences in Fig. 10.1 illustrate this rule. Intonational and paralinguistic phenomena occurring on sociocentric sequences were not used in the drawing of unit boundaries.

3. *Syntax:* the completion of a grammatical clause, involving a subject-predicate combination. The following points in Fig. 10.1 were considered to be those at which the utterance was grammatically complete: 4, 10, 28, 35, 41, 54, 71, and 90. The reason for not drawing a unit boundary at point 71 will be described in connection with the paralinguistic pitch/loudness actions (Number 5 below).

Paralanguage

4. *Drawl:* on the final syllable or on the stressed syllable of a phonemic clause. Examples of drawls that played a part in the drawing of unit bounda-

ries may be found at Points 4, 12, 13, 28, 35, 41, 47, 54, 66, and 82. The drawls at Points 33, 76, and 77 were not used for reasons described in connection with paralinguistic pitch/loudness immediately below. The drawl at Point 48 was not used because it occurred on a filled-pause, as described in connection with false starts (Number 8 below).

5. *Pitch and–or loudness:* a decrease in paralinguistic pitch and–or loudness, either across an entire phonemic clause, or during its final syllable or syllables. When one of these two paralinguistic actions decreased, but the other increased, no unit boundary was drawn. The subjective impression of the decrease would be generally that of "lowering the voice," or of "trailing off." Examples of this sort of decrease in Fig. 10.1 may be found at Points 6–10, 22/23–28, 29–32, 36–41, 48–54, and 67–73. An example of a decrease in paralinguistic pitch not used for drawing unit boundaries occurs at Points 43–47. Over this same stretch of speech the paralinguistic loudness increases, producing a vocal effect quite different from "trailing off" or "lowering the voice."

In some cases decreases in paralinguistic pitch and–or loudness were transcribed over two or three phonemic clauses, and each of these clauses was relatively brief—four or five syllables or less. In these cases, these clauses would be held together within the same unit, even if they would otherwise have been separated by unit boundaries on the basis of other actions or on the basis of the paralinguistic decrease itself. Examples of this sort of situation may be found at Points 23–28, 36–41, and 67–73. At some points in the transcription a decrease in paralinguistic pitch and–or loudness was observed to continue over more extended stretches of speech. In this case, this action was used to draw a unit boundary at the first appropriate point; the action was not used to draw further boundaries as it continued. This situation is not well illustrated in Fig. 10.1, but it may be seen in part at Points 58–66, where the paralinguistic oversoftness had been continuing for a number of phonemic clauses prior to those points.

6. *Audible inhalation.*   It is entirely possible to inhale, whether immediately before an utterance or during it, in such a way that it is virtually inaudible. An inhalation becomes audible probably through increasing the rate at which the breath is taken in and–or through constricting the supraglottal passages through which the breath is taken in. Like sociocentric sequences, audible inhalations were never set apart in units of their own and were included in the units which they followed when those units had been created on the basis of other actions. Examples of audible inhalations may be found at Points 11, 42, 57, and 74 in Fig. 10.1.

7. *Unfilled pause.*   An unfilled pause (Maclay & Osgood, 1959) is a speech hesitation during which there is silence. If some phonation, such as "um," or "uh," occurred during the pause, it is considered a filled pause. There are no examples of unfilled pauses in Fig. 10.1; a filled pause occurs at

Point 48. Filled pauses were not used in the drawing of unit boundaries. The "uh" phonations often occurring as part of sociocentric sequences were treated as sociocentric sequences and not as filled pauses, for the purposes of this study. An example of this situation may be found at Points 55–56.

8. *False start.*   False starts, whether retraced or not (Maclay & Osgood, 1959), were included in the units that they followed and were placed in separate units when one false start followed another. False starts may be found at Points 72–73, 82–83, and 84–85. Stutters were not considered in drawing unit boundaries. (There are no examples of stutters in Fig. 10.1) In this connection, the utterance at Point 79 is difficult to interpret and was not used in the unitizing process.

Body Motion

9. *Gesticulation:*   termination of any hand gesticulation (Kendon, 1967), or the relaxation of a tensed hand position (e.g., a fist), such that both hands are at rest (not gesticulating) and relaxed. That is, a unit boundary was not drawn if both hands had been simultaneously gesticulating and only one of them was brought to rest; and similarly for the tensed hand position. An example of the occurrence of the required termination of hand gesticulation may be found at Point 55 in Fig. 10.1. Examples of the termination of gesticulation by one hand but not by the other may be found at Points 28, 41, and 84.

It is, in general, difficult to provide a fully explicit definition of a gesticulation, although it is a simple task for raters to achieve excellent reliability on gestures with a minimum of training. It is perhaps sufficient for the time being to define gesticulations negatively, as all hand movements that are not classified as self-adaptors or object-adaptors (Ekman & Friesen, 1969). It is somewhat easier to provide a passable definition of self-adaptors, as hand movements in which the hand comes in contact with one's own body or apparel, often with the appearance of grooming. Examples of self-adaptors observed in our conversations would be: rubbing the chin, scratching the cheek, smoothing the hair, brushing off the pants leg, and picking lint (real or imaginary) from the socks. Highly similar actions, termed "self-manipulatory gestures," were also studied by Rosenfeld (1966). Examples of movements considered to be object-adaptors in our conversations would be maintaining one's pipe, rubbing the arm of the chair, adjusting paper on a clipboard, and taking a Kleenex.

10. *Head direction:*   turning the head away from the partner, from a position in which the head had been pointing at the partner. Examples of this action may be found at Points 57 and 74 in Fig. 10.1.

11. *Foot movement:*   a relaxation of the foot or feet of the speaker from a marked dorsal flexion. Examples of this action may be found at Points 57 and 81.

Discussion of the Definition of Units of Analysis

The units defined in the manner described above will be termed "units of analysis" in all further discussion of this study.

The use of the described actions and their associated rules for drawing unit boundaries in the transcriptions was developed entirely on a subjective basis, after some scrutiny of the transcriptions. The procedure was designed to reflect subjective impressions of the points at which it seemed reasonable to draw unit boundaries. Elaborate rules and definitions were not developed, and where ambiguity arose in the process of drawing unit boundaries, decisions were made on the basis of subjective reasonableness. Certainly, the rules described above are not sufficiently elaborate to cover every situation arising either in our transcriptions or in those made by others. They may, however, suggest the general approach taken, together with some of the more important decisions made.

As stated above, these units of analysis were created in order to divide the stream of interaction into units, prior to intensive, systematic analysis. Because the discovery of an empirically based set of interaction units was one of the purposes of the study, there was no pretense that the early, impressionistically based units of analysis were other than rough, naive, temporary, and faulty. Their creation was viewed merely as a necessary step prior to analysis.

As described above, units of analysis were defined in terms of the occurrence of at least one of a variety of different actions. As a result of analysis, some of these actions were subsequently hypothesized to be part of one signal or another. In contrast, other actions, also used to draw unit boundaries, played a part in none of the subsequently hypothesized signals. For this reason, in the analysis of a given signal there were always a number of units of analysis that were unmarked by the display of that signal. This state of affairs yielded an unanticipated benefit for the study: there was in most analyses a stable estimate of the various relevant events associated with the absence of the signal in question. That is, it was possible to present evidence on what things did or did not happen when the signal in question was not displayed, as well as on those things when the signal was displayed.

It is worth noting in the transcriptions shown in Fig. 10.1 that there are few units of analysis having boundaries drawn on the basis of a single action. The piling up of unit-generating actions, either in simultaneous clusters or in immediate succession, was a characteristic phenomenon in the transcriptions. An extreme example of this phenomenon may be observed in the interval bounded by Points 54–57. In this stretch of three syllables and an inhalation, nine of the eleven unit-generating actions occur; only a false start and an unfilled pause are missing.

As mentioned earlier in this chapter, the definitions of units of analysis were never fully formalized, so that an exhaustive account of these definitions cannot be given. The preceding discussion has another purpose: to describe the general research approach. Clearly, the most difficult phase of an exploratory study is that described in this chapter: the prediscovery phase. It is hoped that this extended description of the activities undertaken during this phase may be of some value to investigators contemplating similar exploratory studies.

Rules of Evidence

As mentioned in the preceding chapter, it had not been clear, either at the onset of the study, or at the completion of the transcription, how to substantiate a claim that some aspect(s) of the organization of face-to-face interaction had been discovered. Mere reporting of the discovery did not seem to suffice, perhaps especially in the psychology literature. It seemed reasonable that readers would want to have more precise information about the frequency of the claimed regularity, and about the extent to which the regularity exceeded that which might be expected on the basis of chance.

As it happened, the early stumbling upon speaking turns provided a rather obvious first approximation to a solution for the substantiation problem. The research issue would be framed in the following way: to what extent is it possible to find regularities in the transcription that (a) account for the occurrence of smooth exchanges of the speaking turn; and (b) differentiate occasions of smooth exchanges from those of simultaneous talking? In general, these seemed reasonable criteria for justifying a claim that observed regularities with respect to speaking turns had been observed. The success in meeting these two criteria might easily be evaluated by applying appropriate statistical tests. (In time, as notions regarding various turn-related phenomena developed, the notion of "simultaneous talking" was changed to that of "simultaneous turns. " The reasons for this shift are described below.)

There was considerable relief experienced upon making these decisions. The way appeared to be cleared for the analysis phase of the study to proceed directly, free of the background concern that, after discoveries were made, there would be no adequate way to evaluate them. There was, however, a recognition that all problems in this regard had not been solved. It seemed reasonable to expect that there might be a number of phenomena in the organization of interaction, for which no readily available, clear-cut criteria—such as smooth exchanges of the turn, and simultaneous talking—might be available. Thus, it was sensed that, while the criterion problem appeared to be solved in a most convenient fashion for the moment, it was not a sufficiently general solution.

This uneasy sense was, in fact, confirmed as formal analysis proceeded beyond the consideration of speaking turns. An expanded solution for the criterion problem is considered at the point in the next chapter at which it is required.

11

The Turn System

The "discovery," in a subjective sense, of the phenomena of speaking turns marked a shift in the exploratory study, providing a focus for subsequent analysis. To be sure, no actions had been demonstrated in any substantive way to have a relationship to the exchange of speaking turns. And if no such actions could be found in the transcription, the study would still have nothing to show for the efforts that had been placed into it.

But at the same time it was true that the study had entered a more familiar and routine phase: systematic data analysis. As described above, the initial tasks of the analysis were defined as those of (a) accounting for the smooth exchange of speaking turn between the participants in the two transcribed conversations; and (b) differentiating these smooth exchanges from simultaneous talking. The most obvious approach to accomplishing these tasks was to focus the analysis on those actions frequently observed in the near vicinity of smooth exchanges of the turn. As described in the previous chapter, a list of actions appearing to have potential for the analysis had been developed.

Finding one or more actions related to speaking-turn phenomena was, of course, only part of the task. The other part was to develop a model for the organization of turn exchanges. As mentioned in Chapter 8, part of this model had been implied in much of the transcription itself: that the actions were to be considered as discrete, that is, either present or not present in the transcription at any one moment. Scanning the transcription had suggested two other elements of the model: (a) that speaking-turn exchanges might be served by several different actions, rather than any single one; and (b) that the exchange of turns appeared to be a permissive phenomenon, not a coercive one. That is, in most cases there did not appear to be points at which the partner was obliged to take the turn, but rather points at which he might appropriately act to take the turn, if he were so disposed. Both of these elements of the model were subjected to more rigorous testing, but it was true that they figured prominently in the study, both before analysis and during its early phases. In any event, strong emphasis in the analysis had to be placed on testing both actions and model.

For clarity of exposition, the final set of actions found to be related to the exchange of speaking turns, and the model for their operation will be presented below in their final form. Results for both the exploratory and the replication study will be shown. Accompanying this description of final results, a brief section will describe some of the more important actions and models that were tested and rejected in the process of formulating the final set of results.

The model as a whole has been designated the "turn system." The turn system, as presently defined, consists of the following general elements: (a) two sets of postulated states, one of these sets applying to the respective participants in an interaction, and one set applying to the interaction itself; (b) a set of hypothesized "transition-readiness" states for each participant; (c) a set of hypothesized signals that aid participants in conversations in the coordination of action with respect to the states, among other things; (d) a set of hypothesized rules that apply variously to different aspects of the system; (e) a set of hypothesized "moves"; and (f) two types of units hypothesized to segment the interaction. The rules will be described in an informal manner in conjunction with the aspects to which they apply.

TURN-SYSTEM STATES

Postulated Participant States

The turn system, as presently formulated, requires each participant to consider himself to be either a speaker or an auditor at each moment in the interaction. At each such moment a *speaker* is a participant who claims the speaking turn. An *auditor* (Kendon, 1967) is a participant who does not claim the speaking turn at a given moment. These two postulated states are considered to be discrete and, within each participant, mutually exclusive. The speaker and auditor states are clearly classifications each participant applies to himself and can be known to others only through his actions.

Postulated Interaction States

The turn system was developed in an effort to describe some phenomena found in two-person interactions, as opposed to single persons acting independently. Thus, it is desirable to be able to describe the state of the interaction at any given moment, in addition to the respective states of each of the participants. With regard to speaking turns, the state of the interaction at any given moment can be obtained simply by jointly considering the speaker-auditor state of each participant at that moment. Following logically from the two participant states, there are four possible speaking-turn interaction states:

1. *Speaker–auditor.*   One participant claims the speaking turn; no such claim is made by the other participant. In this interaction state, the current speaker continues his turn, neither yielding it to the partner, nor being interrupted.

2. *Auditor–speaker.*   This interaction state is identical to the one above, except that the participants have exchanged the speaking turn. The participant who had previously been the speaker has now switched to the auditor state, and vice versa. When this exchange is accomplished without passing through the interaction state of simultaneous turns (Number 3 below), a *smooth exchange* of speaking turn is said to have occurred.

3. *Speaker–speaker (simultaneous turns).*   Both participants simultaneously assume the speaker state, claiming the speaking turn. This interaction state represents a breakdown of the turn system for the duration of the state.

"Simultaneous turns" is used here instead of the more usual term "simultaneous talking." Within the turn system there may be two types of simultaneous talking not considered to be simultaneous turns. As is described below, the auditor's responding in the back channel (Yngve, 1970), such as "m-hm," or a head nod, does not constitute a speaking turn or a claim of the turn. An auditor back-channel response, when it overlaps with the speaker's verbalizing, would therefore be a case of simultaneous talking by the two participants, but not of simultaneous turns. In addition, when the beginning of a new speaking turn overlapped only with the previous speaker's sociocentric sequence, the overlap was considered to be an instance of simultaneous talking, but not of simultaneous turns.

4. *Auditor–auditor.*   The previous speaker may display a turn signal and cease talking, thereby apparently relinquishing his turn; but the previous auditor may fail to claim the turn. The result would obviously be silence for the duration of that state. Experience suggests that this fourth logical possibility of the two participant states does occur in conversations, but because it was not observed in either the exploratory conversations or the replication conversations, it will not be considered further in this discussion. Thus, the observed conversations provide only partial evidence on the frequency of this interaction state. It may be encountered, even frequently, in other types of conversations.

Hypothesized Participant Transition Readiness

As opposed to the postulation of the speaker-auditor states, the transition-readiness state of each participant is hypothesized on the basis of the results described below. For this reason, the transition-readiness state may be more fully described after the results are presented and accordingly will be considered in greater detail at that point.

It may suffice to say here that *transition-readiness* refers to each participant's felt and–or ostensive inclination to move to the next unit of the interaction. These units are also hypothesized below on the basis of results. Two distinct types of units are hypothesized to operate on adjacent hierarchical levels within the turn system.

One of these interaction units is the speaking turn itself. With respect to the speaking turn, transition readiness refers to a participant's inclination to exchange the speaking turn. As the turn system is presently formulated, each participant's reading of his own transition readiness refers to a participant's inclination to exchange the speaking turn. As the turn system is presently formulated, each participant's reading of his own transition readiness is one essential factor in the process of framing a course of action with respect to speaking-turn phenomena at any given point in the interaction.

In further contrast to the speaker-auditor states, transition readiness is hypothesized (a) to be a single state continuously operative throughout the interaction within each participant; and (b) to have values on a continuous scale. The value of a participant's transition readiness is presumably free to vary from moment to moment in the interaction and is influenced by many factors. There must, however, be a distinct transition-readiness state for each hypothesized interaction unit.

DEFINITION OF SIGNAL DISPLAY AND ACTIVITY

A signal in the turn system is considered to be discrete. That is, each signal is considered to be either displayed or not displayed at any given point in the interaction. In general, each signal is defined in terms of two elements: (a) the state of the participant (speaker or auditor) eligible to display the signal; and (b) a set of cues based on actions.

Speaker–Auditor State

A given signal may be defined as being displayable only by speakers, or only by auditors, or by either speakers or auditors. For example, the signal associated with the yielding of speaking turns is considered to be displayable only by speakers. Auditor actions were not systematically scrutinized for the occurrence of this signal because it is meaningless within the turn system to think of the auditor as yielding the speaking turn, in that the auditor state is defined as being held by a participant who does not claim the speaking turn.

On the other hand, it is entirely possible to observe both participants simultaneously displaying a signal defined as being displayable only by speakers. It will be recalled from the discussion of interaction states immediately above, that both participants may simultaneously assume the same interaction state. Such a situation is far from meaningless within the turn system.

Action-Based Cues

Each signal in the turn system is defined as being composed of a set of one or more action-based cues. The display of a turn-system signal is defined as the display of at least one of its constituent cues. (This approach to defining signal display is empirically based, not a priori.) The greater part of the definition of signal display has to do with the definition of the cues comprising the signal. Like the signals themselves, the display of each cue is considered to be discrete.

There are, in general, three elements in the definition of a given cue: (a) the actions comprising the cue; (b) those locations in the stream of interaction at which the indicated actions must occur in order to be considered a cue display; and (c) the stretch of interaction over which the cue is considered to be active once it has been displayed.

Actions

Of the three elements of cue definition, the first seems self-evident. The actions comprising turn-system cues will be described in a manner similar to the description in Chapter 9 of the actions used in the creation of boundaries of units of analysis. An action comprising a cue will be termed a "cue-relevant action."

Location Restrictions

Some cue-relevant actions are considered to be cues only when they occur at certain specified points in the stream of interaction. For other cue-relevant actions, such location restrictions are not included in the definition. When action location is an element of cue definition, it is described.

Cue Activity

Each occasion of an appropriately located cue-relevant action is considered a *display*, both of the relevant cue, and of the signal of which the cue is a constituent. Such a physical display is not, however, sufficient to describe the hypothesized functioning of cues in the observed interactions. It is necessary to provide some supplemental concepts.

We may begin by observing, in anticipation of the findings presented below, that there is significant variety in the duration of cue displays. It will be seen that the display of some cues, such as gesticulating, can continue over a substantial stretch of interaction. The display of other cues, such as paralinguistic drawl, can by definition occur only over single syllables. The display of still other cues, such as termination of a gesticulation, or shifting one's gaze away from the partner, are defined as occurring only at some instantaneous point in the interaction.

Let us consider first the case of cues involving briefer displays: those extending over only an instant of time or over one or two syllables. The results suggest that the effects of these cues on the interaction extend beyond the duration of their brief displays. It thus becomes necessary to define some period, longer than the display itself, over which each cue is considered to be active in the interaction. This *active period* for a cue is considered to begin at the point at which the cue is displayed. Because the cue displays are considered to be discrete, it will be said that the cue is "switched on" or "activated" at the moment of its display, and that the cue is "switched off" at that later point at which it is considered to be no longer active in the interaction. The stretch of interaction over which the cue is switched on may be termed its "active period." It will be seen that there is some variation from cue to cue in the extent of their respective active periods.

Cues having displays that can extend over substantial stretches of interaction (for example, gesticulating) are considered in the turn system to be switched on for the duration of their actual display.

It is important to note that in the turn system, active periods for cues are never defined in terms of time, but rather in terms of other interaction events. That is, an active period for a cue is defined as extending from the point at which it is switched on, to some other interactional event. This approach contrasts with, but does not necessarily conflict with, (a) other studies that have carefully attended to temporal parameters of interaction (e.g., Jaffe & Feldstein, 1970; Matarazzo & Wiens, 1972); (b) consideration of temporal properties of signal display (Schliedt, 1973); or (c) other authors who have drawn attention to "chronemics" as one element of the organization of interaction (e.g., Poyatos, 1975).

RULES

Although the object of this study is often referred to in the literature as that of "rule-governed behavior" or the like, it may be seen that rules per se make up only one aspect of the turn system. Other aspects such as signals, and participant and interaction states have been considered above, and further aspects are introduced below.

The term "rule" will be used here somewhat broadly to refer to any statement describing the hypothesized relationship between two or more elements of the turn system. For example, a rule may relate a given signal by a participant to a given state of that participant; or a rule may describe the effect of one signal upon some other signal when both are concurrently switched on;

or a rule may describe the hypothesized relationship between a signal by one participant and some subsequent action by the partner.

In general, there is not extensive discussion of the various senses in which the term "rule" will be used. Furthermore, rules are simply described in words, without formal notation. This relatively informal approach to a potentially complex set of phenomena in face-to-face interaction is motivated by the judgment that further research in this area is needed before the statement of rules becomes highly formalized, as well as by the desire to avoid excessive jargon.

However, there is one distinction regarding types of rules that seems desirable to make for the purpose of clarity. *Signal-definition* rules will be distinguished from *interaction* rules. A signal-definition rule will describe the relationship between (a) a given signal; and (b) either a turn-system state, or another signal. Interaction rules will describe permissible sequences of action within the turn system, given (a) the currently active signal(s); and in some cases (b) certain preceding moves by one or both participants.

MOVES

The turn system is built primarily around a special set of actions that are hypothesized to be "signals" on the basis of research results. Another special set of actions, termed *moves,* is also hypothesized to be part of the turn system. The distinction between signals and moves may perhaps best be described by an example. A ship about to get underway may signal that fact by sounding one long blast on its whistle; the actual getting underway is a move. Although it is appropriate in this case for the signal to accompany the move, either may occur without the other. The ship may signal that it is getting underway, yet fail to do so; or it may get underway without signalling. Moves may or may not have signals associated with them. A move in a chess game would be a move in the sense used here; apart from the signal "check" there are no signals that accompany chess moves.

UNITS OF INTERACTION

The hypothesized units of interaction are described at the end of this chapter. They may best be understood after a presentation of the other elements of the turn system.

SUMMARY OF TURN-SYSTEM DESCRIPTION

Table 11.1 summarizes the various elements included in the description of the turn system.

TABLE 11.1
Elements in the Description of the Turn System

I. Postulated States
   A. Participant States
   B. Interaction States
II. Hypothesized Participant States
III. Signals: Display and Activity
   A. Speaker-Auditor State(s) required for signal display
   B. Cues
      1. Actions comprising the cue.
      2. Location restrictions. (Where the actions must occur in order to be considered a cue.)
      3. Active period. (Stretch of interaction over which a cue is considered to be active, once it is displayed.)
IV. Rules (Statements of relationships between two elements of the turn system.)
   A. Signal-definition rules. (Relationships of a given signal to a turn-system state, a move, or another signal.)
   B. Interaction rules. (Permissible sequences of action within the system, given some specified state of affairs.)
V. Moves
VI. Units of Interaction

SUMMARY OF TURN-SYSTEM SIGNALS

In anticipation of the discussion of turn signals below, Table 11.2 summarizes for each hypothesized signal, its proposed constituent cues and its observed relationships to other events. More detailed information will be provided in the discussion of each signal.

The signals will be presented in approximately the order in which they were discovered and documented. This chronological pattern of presentation seems desirable because it reflects the actual development of the turn system, and because it permits a clearer description of the conceptualization and analysis of each signal.

SPEAKER TURN SIGNAL

As described above, this signal was hypothesized in an attempt to account for the smooth exchanges of the speaking turn in the conversations observed, and to differentiate these smooth exchanges from instances of simultaneous claiming of the turn by both participants.

Definition of Display and Activity

The turn signal is switched on when the speaker displays at least one of six constituent cues. Following a display of one or more turn cues, the signal is switched off when all displayed cues are switched off. Thus, for any single

TABLE 11.2
Speaker and Auditor Signals Hypothesized for the Turn System

Name of signal	Constituent cues	Related to subsequent:
Speaker turn	1. Intonation-marked clause	1. Auditor attempt to take turn
	2. Sociocentric sequence	
	3. Grammatical completeness	
	4. Paralinguistic drawl	
	5. Decrease in para-linguistic pitch and-or loudness on sociocentric sequence	
	6. End of gesticulation	
Speaker gesticulation	1. Gesticulation	1. Suppresses auditor attempts to take turn
	2. Tensed hand position	
Speaker state	1. Turning of head away from partner	
	2. Begin gesticulation	
Speaker within turn	1. Grammatical completeness	1. Between-unit auditor back channel
	2. Turning of head towards auditor	2. Speaker continuation signal
Between-unit auditor back channel	(5 different types, both audible and visible, observed)	
Early auditor back channel	(same as between-unit auditor back channel)	1. Speaker continuation signal
Speaker continuation	1. Turning of head away from auditor	

occurrence of the turn signal, its active period lasts from the display of the first cue in that occurrence, until all cues in that occurrence are switched off.

The six constituent cues (and others) of the signal are described in some detail above in the section on actions used to create units of analysis. Each turn cue is described more briefly below, together with applicable location restrictions and the point at which it is considered to be switched off following its display.

1. *Intonation-marked phonemic clause.* An intonation-marked clause was defined as one in which there is a deviation from the 2 2 → pitch-terminal contour pattern. Location restriction: the deviation must occur no earlier than the last two syllables of a phonemic clause. As was the practice with units of analysis, two adjoining intonation-marked clauses were combined and treated as a single cue when those two clauses appeared to form a single intonation pattern. Switch-off point: this cue was considered to be switched off at the first boundary of a unit of analysis following its display. (The drawing of boundaries of units of analysis is described on page 169).

2. *Sociocentric sequence.*   One of several stereotyped expressions, such as "you know," and "or something." (It will be recalled that sociocentric sequences are never set apart in units of their own.) Switch-off point: the first boundary of a unit of analysis following its display. Location restrictions: none.

3. *Completion of grammatical clause.*   Location restrictions: none. Switch-off point: the first boundary of a unit of analysis following its display.

4. *Paralinguistic drawl.*   Location restriction: the drawl must occur on the final syllable or on the stressed syllable of a phonemic clause. Switch-off point: The first boundary of a unit of analysis following its display.

5. *Termination of any hand gesticulation or the relaxation of a tensed hand position (e.g., a fist).*   This cue was not considered to be displayed unless both hands were at rest and relaxed following a gesture termination or hand relaxation. Location restrictions: none. Switch-off point: the boundary of the third unit of analysis following its display.

6. *Decrease of paralinguistic pitch and–or loudness on a sociocentric sequence.*   This decrease must be in contrast to the comparable paralinguistic actions on the syllable(s) immediately preceding the sociocentric sequence. Location restrictions: the decrease must occur either across the entire sociocentric sequence, or during its final syllable or syllables. Switch-off point: the first boundary of a unit of analysis following its display.

Fig. 11.1 is designed to illustrate the active periods hypothesized for turn cues. In this constructed example, Participant A begins with the speaking turn. After what would correspond to roughly 4–6 sec of speech by Participant A, Participant B responds with a vocal back channel, following which Participant A utters a sociocentric sequence. Finally, Participant B initiates a new speaking turn. Opening brackets indicate the earliest point at which each turn cue could have been displayed, in order to remain active at the beginning of the new turn, given the cue's definition, location restrictions, and switch-off point.

Turn Signal: Interaction Rules

Within the turn system the auditor may claim the speaking turn during the active period of the turn signal, subject to the verbal-overlap restrictions described below. In proper operation of the turn system, if the auditor so claims the turn in response to the signal, the speaker is obliged to relinquish immediately his claim to the turn. When the turn signal is not active, auditor claims of the turn are inappropriate within the context of the system, leading in most cases to simultaneous turns.

The turn signal is permissive, not coercive. The auditor is not obliged to claim the speaking turn in response to the display of the signal by the speaker. The auditor may alternatively communicate in the back channel (Yngve, 1970), or remain silent. In this sense, the auditor possesses real options with

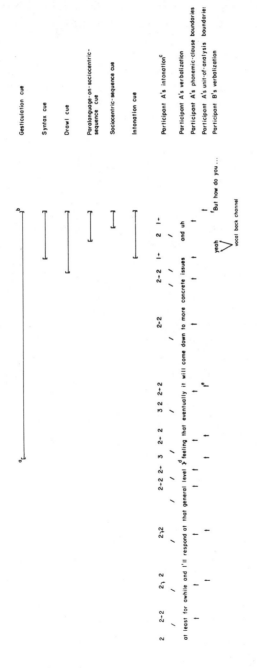

FIGURE 11.1 Active Periods for Turn Cues

Gesticulation cue

Syntax cue

Drawl cue

Paralanguage-on-sociocentric-
sequence cue

Sociocentric-sequence cue

Intonation cue

Participant A's intonation[c]

Participant A's verbalization
Participant A's phonemic-clause boundaries
Participant A's unit-of-analysis boundaries
Participant B's verbalization

2   2-2   2-2   2-2 2- 3   3 2 2-2   2-2   2-2 2- 2 I-
     2-1 2   But how do you ...
at least for awhile and I'll respond at that general level feeling that eventually it will come down to more concrete issues   and uh

yeah
vocal back channel   But how...

[a] [: earliest point at which cue may be displayed, in order to be considered activated at participant B's turn beginning ("But how...")
[b]]: cue considered switched-off
[c] intonation symbols from Trager and Smith (1957)
[d] audible inhalation
[e] this unit-of-analysis boundary not drawn on basis of intonation
[f] beginning of new speaking turn

186

respect to his appropriate response to the speaker's display of the turn signal. (It will be seen that this property of optionality with respect to a participant's response is an important one, both for the formulation of the turn system, and for the development in Chapter 12 of a more general model for face-to-face interaction.)

During the active period of the turn signal, an auditor claim of the speaking turn must be made in such a way that the syllables of the new turn do not overlap with the syllables of the preceding turn. Any perceptible overlap involving the two turns, even when the overlap occurs over only a portion of a single syllable, is treated as an instance of simultaneous claiming of the turn ("simultaneous turns") by the two participants and is so indicated in the data.

It will be recalled that turn cues are switched-off at boundaries of units of analysis. These boundaries are drawn at the onset of the first syllable following the end of a phonemic clause during which at least one of the listed boundary-defining actions occurred (Chapter 10). Boundaries were not drawn at the onset of sociocentric sequences, filled pauses, or audible inhalations but rather on the first syllable of more substantive speech following these vocal phenomena.

As mentioned above in the description of interaction states, an exception to the no-overlap rule is made with regard to sociocentric sequences. When syllables of the new turn overlap with syllables of a sociocentric sequence, the overlap is not considered to be an instance of simultaneous turns, but rather an instance of permissible simultaneous talking. Similarly, overlap of the new turn with the previous speaker's filled pauses and audible inhalations is considered to be permissible simultaneous talking.

Another instance of simultaneous talking considered to be permissible within the turn system has to do with vocal auditor back channels. Because these back channels are not considered to be speaking turns, the overlap of vocal auditor back channels with syllables of the previous speaker's turn is not treated as an instance of simultaneous turns.

Thus, during the active period of the turn signal, the interaction rule requires that the auditor act to take the turn only during some gap, however brief, in the speaker's speech. (This gap, during which the turn signal is active, appears to be a specific example of a "transition-relevance place . . ." hypothesized by Sacks, Schegloff, and Jefferson (1974, p. 703). In the turn system, the gap is not located in the manner they suggest.) Within the context of the turn system, this gap might be caused by a filled or unfilled pause, an audible or inaudible inhalation, or a sociocentric sequence. Jaffe and Feldstein (1970) found the average "switching pause" for their subjects in various experiments and conditions to range from .733 to 1.555 sec. (In their data speaking turns and back channels are not differentiated.) Thus, the gap required does not seem to be a large one, and it can be filled with certain vocal phenomena.

Beyond the general rules applying to the turn signal, brief mention may be made of the handling of certain situations in the transcriptions for purposes of data analysis. First, it must be clear in the transcription that the display of at least one turn cue by the speaker occurred before the auditor acted to initiate a new turn. For example, in a unit of analysis containing no preceding turn cues, an auditor might initiate a new turn simultaneously with the first syllable of a sociocentric sequence. That new turn would have been treated as being preceded by no turn cues. Because it overlapped with a sociocentric sequence, however, it would not have been treated as an instance of simultaneous turns.

It sometimes happened that a speaker would display the turn signal, and the auditor would appropriately initiate a new turn, not overlapping with the preceding turn. After a few syllables of the new turn (roughly one to four), the previous speaker would abruptly begin speaking again, as if continuing the preceding turn. This situation was treated as an instance of simultaneous turns following the display of a turn cue. It is as if the previous speaker reneges on the turn signal just given. The frequency of this type of situation in our data is shown in the lower, right-hand cell of each of the two tables in Table 11.5.

SPEAKER GESTICULATION SIGNAL

It was found necessary to hypothesize a second signal, termed the "speaker gesticulation signal," to account for certain aspects of speaking-turn exchange observed in the transcriptions. The gesticulation signal will be described, prior to the presentation of results on speaking-turn exchange.

Gesticulation Signal: Display and Activity

The speaker gesticulation signal is hypothesized to be composed of a single cue: one or both of the speaker's hands being engaged in gesticulation or in a tensed hand position. Gesticulations and tensed hand positions are discussed in greater detail in the section on definition of units of analysis. Self– and object–adaptors are not considered to be elements of the gesticulation signal.

There are no location restrictions applying to the gesticulation signal. The signal is switched on at the point of its display and is switched off when neither hand is gesticulating or tensed. Thus, the active period for the signal is identical to its actual display.

Switching off the gesticulation signal automatically constitutes the display of a turn cue (termination of any hand gesticulation, etc.).

It may be noted that much speech is not accompanied by gesticulation, and therefore neither the gesticulation signal nor its coordinate turn cue would be applicable for that speech.

Gesticulation Signal: Signal-Definition Rules

The gesticulation signal serves to inhibit any turn signal concurrently being displayed. When the gesticulation signal is displayed during the active period of the turn signal, auditor claims of the speaking turn are strikingly reduced. (The gesticulation signal was termed the "attempt-suppressing" signal in Duncan, 1972.)

RESULTS: SPEAKER TURN AND GESTICULATION SIGNALS

Data from the exploratory study and from the replication study on the speaker turn and gesticulation signals are shown in Tables 11.3 and 11.4. (For description of the exploratory study and the replication study, see Chapter 9.)

Speaker Turn Signal

The hypothesis of the speaker turn signal was based on results from the exploratory study that suggested the signal's relative success in (a) accounting for smooth exchanges of the speaking turn, and (b) differentiating smooth exchanges from simultaneous turns. The success of the signal in meeting these two criteria was evaluated in the following manner:

1. *Smooth exchanges accounted for.* This criterion was applied to the signal simply by dividing the number of smooth exchanges when the signal was switched on, by the total number of smooth exchanges in the transcription.

2. *Smooth exchanges versus simultaneous turns.* While it was necessary for any proposed signal to account for a large percentage of smooth exchanges of the speaking turn, it was also considered necessary for the signal to be effective in differentiating these smooth exchanges from instances of simultaneous turns. For any given cue subset this differentiation may be straightforwardly evaluated by chi square performed on a 2 x 2 contingency table in which the columns represented (a) number of smooth exchanges of the turn; and (b) number of simultaneous turns; and the rows represented (a) number of units of analysis in which at least one of the turn cues under consideration was switched on; and (b) number of units in which none of the cues was switched on.

As reported by Duncan (1972), the speaker turn signal was capable of accounting for 100% of the smooth exchanges of the turn in the exploratory study. That is, if a smooth exchange occurred, it occurred when the turn signal was switched on. When the auditor attemped to take the speaking turn when the turn signal was switched off, the interaction state of simultaneous turns inevitably resulted.

It should be pointed out that, within the exploratory framework of the study the signal was designed precisely to account for as many of the smooth exchanges as possible in the conversations analyzed. The main significance of the results just reported is that a signal could be defined in terms of the actions studied, such that all of the smooth exchanges could be accounted for. It may also be noted that most of the actions used to define units of an-aylsis were tried as potential cues for the turn signal, and those not ultimately included in the signal were explicitly rejected because they did not contribute to the signal's capacity to meet the required criteria.

An initial test of the turn-signal hypothesis generated by the exploratory study was provided by the replication study. The speaker turn signal was applied to the six replication transcriptions in a manner identical to that for the exploratory transcriptions. Table 11.4 shows that, for the 183 smooth exchanges in the replication study, 180 of them (98%) occurred while the turn signal was switched on. Of the auditor turn attempts when the signal was switched off, 88% resulted in simultaneous turns.

A more stringent test of the hypothesis is provided by the chi-square, pitting (a) the occurrence of a smooth exchange or of simultaneous turns, against (b) the turn signal being switched on or off. Table 11.5 shows the respective 2 x 2 contingency tables for the exploratory and replication studies, derived from Tables 11.3 and 11.4.

As reported in Duncan (1972), chi-square applied to the exploratory data yields a value of 52.31, corrected for continuity, $df = 1$, p < .00001. The chi-square applied to the comparable replication data yeilds a value of 56.33, corrected for continuity, $df = 1$, p < .00001.

In these and subsequent chi-square analyses, observations from more than one conversation are pooled; in each conversation, each participant provides observations both as speaker and as auditor. Ordinarily, it is not considered advisable to pool the data from several different individuals in the same analysis because the relationship being tested might hold for only one participant as speaker, or for only one conversation, but not for other participants or conversations. The chi-square analyses presented here were computed on pooled data for several reasons. First, the signals and rules were intended to hold for all participants and conversations studied. Second, the specific data for each person as speaker or as auditor were somewhat limited. For example, the "No turn signal switched on" row for the replication study in Table 11.5 contains 25 observations from six conversations, each with two participants acting as speaker, or about two observations per subset. Finally, the data for each participant in each conversation were examined separately and each subset of data showed the same general pattern of relationship found for the pooled data, although the patterns for the subsets were, as one would expect for reduced sample sizes, of varying degrees of strength. A similar issue concerning correlational analyses is considered below.

TABLE 11.3
Auditor Turn-Taking Attempts and Resulting Simultaneous Turns
as a Function of Number of Active Turn Cues and Activation of
the Gesticulation Signal: Exploratory Study

No. Cues conjointly active	Speaker turn-cue display — No. Units having display (A)	Auditor turn-taking attempts — No. of attempts (B)	Proportion[a] (C)	SE[b]	Simultaneous turns resulting from auditor attempt — No. of simultaneous turns (D)	Proportion[a] (E)	SE[b]
No gesticulation signal active							
0	52	5	.10	.04	5	1.00	.00
1	123	12	.10	.03	2	.17	.11
2	146	25	.17	.03	2	.08	.05
3	89	29	.33	.05	2	.07	.05
4	47	15	.32	.07	0	.00	.00
5	9	4	.44	.17	0	.00	.00
6	2	1	.50	.35	0	.00	.00
Σ	468	91			11		
Gesticulation signal active							
0	56	7	.13	.04	7	1.00	.00
1	109	0	.00	.00			
2	138	0	.00	.00			
3	105	2	.02	.01	1	.50	.35
4	6	0	.00	.00			
5	3	0	.00	.00			
Σ	417	9			8		
ΣΣ	885	100			19		

[a] Column B/Column A.
[b] Standard error of the proportion = $\sqrt{PQ/N}$.
[c] Column D/Column B.

Further findings on the speaker turn signal are described after presentation of the basic findings for the speaker gesticulation signal.

Speaker Gesticulation Signal

The primary issue with respect to the gesticulation signal has to do with its effectiveness in suppressing the auditor's attempts to take the speaking turn. On the basis of the results of the exploratory study, this suppression effect was hypothesized to operate regardless of (a) whether or not a turn signal was concurrently switched on by the speaker, or (b) the number of cues in the turn signal, if it was switched on. It will be recalled that the active period for the gesticulation signal is identical to its display. That is, the hypothesized effect of the signal is not considered to extend beyond its actual display.

TABLE 11.4

Auditor Turn-Taking Attempts and Resulting Simultaneous Turns
as a Function of Number of Active Turn Cues and Activation of
the Gesticulation Signal: Replication Study

Speaker turn-cue display		Auditor turn-taking attempts			Simultaneous turns resulting from auditor attempt		
No. Cues conjointly active	No. Units having display	No. of attempts	Proportion[a]	SE[b]	No. of simultaneous turns	Proportion[c]	SE[b]
	(A)	(B)	(C)		(D)	(E)	
No gesticulation signal active							
0	63	24	.38	.06	21	.87	.07
1	311	64	.21	.02	14	.22	.05
2	369	80	.22	.02	13	.16	.04
3	150	47	.31	.04	2	.04	.03
4	29	9	.31	.09	0	.00	.00
5	9	4	.44	.17	0	.00	.00
Σ	931	228			50		
Gesticulation signal active							
0	20	1	.05	.05	1	1.00	.00
1	104	7	.07	.02	3	.43	.19
2	77	4	.05	.03	4	1.00	.00
3	13	2	.15	.10	2	1.00	.00
4	2	1	.50	.35	0	.00	.00
5	1	0	.00	.00			
Σ	217	15			10		
$\Sigma\Sigma$	1148	243			60		

[a] Column B/Column A.
[b] Standard error of the proportion = $\sqrt{PQ/N}$.
[c] Column D/Column B.

Data on the display of the gesticulation signal during units of analysis are shown in Tables 11.3 and 11.4. For purposes of analysis, display of the gesticulation signal was evaluated in the transcription according to the following rules:

1. If, during a unit of analysis, there was no auditor attempt to take the speaking turn, the gesticulation signal was considered to be displayed in that unit if the signal was active at least at the end of the unit. This rule was necessary because the termination of a gesticulation signal constituted a display of a turn cue, as described above. Therefore, if a gesticulation signal terminated before the end of a unit of analysis, that turn cue was considered to be active at the end of the unit.

2. If an auditor turn attempt occurred at any point during a unit of analysis, it was simply noted whether or not the gesticulation signal was active at the moment of the attempt.

TABLE 11.5
Smooth Exchanges of the Turn and Simultaneous Turns
Resulting from Auditor's Turn-Taking Attempts
When the Speaker Turn Signal was Switched on or Not Switched on

Turn signal switched on	Smooth exchange of turn	Simultaneous turns
Exploratory study		
No	0	12
Yes	81	7
Replication Study		
No	3	22
Yes	180	38

Table 11.3 shows that in the exploratory study there were 417 units of analysis during which the gesticulation signal was considered to be displayed according to the above rules. There was an auditor attempt to take the speaking turn associated with 9 of these 417 units (2%). In contrast, there were 91 auditor turn attempts (19%) associated with the 468 units in which no gesticulation signal was considered to be displayed. (These figures disregard the presence or absence of the turn signal.) The chi-square in this case would be applied to a 2 x 2 contingency table in which (a) the rows represent the display versus nondisplay of the gesticulation signal; and (b) the columns represent attempts versus nonattempts by the auditor. For such a table constructed from the exploratory data, a chi-square yields a value of 64.03, corrected for continuity, $df = 1, p < .00001$.

From Table 11 4, comparable figures may be derived for the replication study. There was an auditor attempt to take the turn associated with 7% of the units of analysis during which the gesticulation signal was considered to be displayed. In contrast, there were auditor turn attempts associated with 24% of the units in which no gesticulation signal was considered to be displayed The chi-square for the indicated contingency table constructed from the replication data yields a value of 31.54, corrected for continuity, $df = 1, p < .00001$.

There was an interesting finding with respect to the respective overall rates of display of the gesticulation signal in the two studies. In the exploratory conversations, the gesticulation signal was considered to be displayed in 47% of the units of analysis, while the signal was considered to be displayed in only 19% of the units in the replication conversations. This finding is mentioned here primarily in order to raise the issue of its interpretation. It is maintained that the finding reflects upon the propensities of given individuals to use a particular signal, rather than upon hypotheses regarding (a) the existence of the signal; and (b) its function within the turn system. This point will be further considered in the discussion section of this chapter.

Auditor Turn Attempts
When Both Turn and Gesticulation Signals Are Active

An interesting situation exists when a speaker concurrently activates both the turn and gesticulation signals. The results described immediately above suggest that a gesticulation-signal display tends to suppress an auditor attempt to take the speaking turn. But what if an auditor should ignore a gesticulation-signal display and make a turn attempt in response to the concurrent turn signal? Does the turn-signal activity permit a smooth exchange of the speaking turn?

The exploratory conversations yielded insufficient data (only two such attempts) relevant to this issue. In the replication conversations there were 14 such attempts. The data in Table 11.4 indicate that, for units in which only the turn signal was active (no concurrent gesticulation signal), 86% of the auditor turn attempts resulted in smooth exchanges of the turn. In contrast, when both turn and gesticulation signals were considered active in a unit, 36% of the auditor attempts resulted in smooth exchanges. Considering only units in which the turn signal was active, a 2 x 2 contingency table can be constructed in which the columns represent smooth exchanges of the turn versus simultaneous turns; and the rows represent gesticulation-signal display versus no gesticulation signal display. A chi-square applied to this table for the replication data yields a value of 19.47, corrected for continuity, $df =$ 1,p = .00007.

Thus, in the replication study, there was a significantly greater probability that an auditor turn attempt will result in simultaneous turns when both the turn and gesticulation signals are active, than when only a turn signal is active.

Number of Turn Cues Active
in a Unit and Probability of Smooth Turn Exchanges

In the course of data analysis for the exploratory study it was noticed that a positive correlation existed between (a) number of turn cues (0–6) active in a unit of analysis; and (b) probability of an auditor turn attempt associated with that unit. Thus, as the number of active turn cues in a unit increased from zero to six, there was a corresponding linear increase in the probability that the auditor would act to take the turn associated with that unit. This relationship was observed only when the gesticulation was not active.

Duncan (1972) reported that for the exploratory study, the correlation between number of active turn cues and percentage of auditor turn attempts was .96. This finding was not supported in the replication study, where the comparable correlation was only .42. This lower correlation in the replication study stemmed primarily from the relatively larger percentage of auditor attempts when no turn cues were active. (It will be recalled that 88% of these attempts resulted in simultaneous turns.)

Unreported by Duncan (1972) was a correlation of .99 between (a) number of active turn cues (with no conjoint gesticulation-signal display); and (b) percentage of smooth exchanges. The comparable correlation for the replication study was .98. It appears, therefore, that the evidence supports the notion of a positive linear relationship between number of active turn cues and smooth exchanges of the turn, rather than between number of active turn cues and auditor turn attempts.

While the strength of these correlations is strikingly and clearly in support of the general hypothesis of the turn signal, it is of great importance to point out that the correlations may be properly interpreted only as indirect evidence with respect to the organization of the turn system. Although it seems generally true that there is an an orderly increase in the probability of an auditor attempt to take the turn as the number of active turn cues increases, it seems entirely possible that the manner of this increase might vary from one conversation to another depending on a number of factors, such as the personal interaction styles of the two participants, the nature of their relationship, and the nature of the conversation. For example, one participant as auditor might aggressively leap at the slightest indication (for example, the switching on of a single turn cue) that the speaker is prepared to yield the speaking turn. Another participant might tend to defer an attempt to take the turn until there is a clear and perhaps repeated switching on of three to five cues. Thus, the correlations have the potential for reflecting more the way that participants operate within the general turn system, than the way that that system is organized.

Thus, the hypothesized turn system is one that permits the participants to exercise significant choice in the manner in which they conduct themselves, while still conforming to the system. Insofar as different individuals exercise this permitted optionality in consistent and different ways, these consistencies may be characterized in terms of "interaction strategies." This point will be considered in greater detail in the discussion section for this chapter and in subsequent chapters.

It is also of interest, though premature, to note that the correlations just described, while involving the relating of one participant's actions to those of the partner, are of a very different sort than those correlations described in Part II that also involve relating one participant's actions to those of the partner. The correlations in Part II were uniformly based on summing the frequencies of the respective actions, across an entire conversation. As described in Part II, this procedure results in the loss of information concerning the actual sequences in which the respective actions occurred in the conversations. This information was not lost when the probability of auditor turn attempts was related to number of active turn cues. Rather, the correlation of these two actions was based on the observed sequence of events in each unit of analysis in the transcriptions.

Finally, it may be noted that the correlation itself is difficult to apply to single conversations in the transcriptions because it is necessary (a) to remove from the analysis all units for which the gesticulation signal was considered active; and (b) to segment the remaining units into six or seven parts (depending on the maximum number of active turn cues). When applied to the transcriptions of single conversations, these operations have the effect of seriously reducing the reliability of the estimate for each data point in the correlation. Nevertheless, the general positive, linear function linking probability of auditor response to number of active turn cues was observed in each conversation. It is clear that there are several approaches to solving this particular methodological problem. For example, it is possible to analyze more extended stretches of single interactions, and–or to combine numbers of active turn cues to create data points, such as 0, 1 and 2, 3 and 4, etc.

TRANSITION READINESS AND SPEAKING TURNS

On the basis of the results for the speaker turn and gesticulation signals, it is possible to consider in greater detail the transition–readiness state hypothesized for each participant. The issue here is to explain the speaker's display of signals and the auditor's attempting or not attempting to take the speaking turn at various points in the conversation. That is, within a system allowing for various options for each participant, why would a participant bother to display a signal or attempt to take the turn?

One approach to the needed explanation is through the hypothesis of one or more internal states for each participant. These hypothesized states may be described in terms directly relevant to the turn system. With respect to the turn and gesticulation signals, it is possible to hypothesize for each participant at each moment in the interaction some tendency to desire either an exchange of the turn or a retention of the current speaker–auditor status quo. This desire may be hypothesized in terms of a *transition–readiness state*. In view of the various results described above, it seems necessary to consider this tendency to be, not discrete, but more like a scale of values, minimally ordinal in character. Such a scale seems necessary in order to take into account (a) the variation in the number of speaker turn cues activated from time to time, (b) the auditor's differential response to these differing numbers of cues, (c) the use of the gesticulation signal by the speaker, and (d) the auditor's attempts to take the turn when no turn cues were active, as well as failures to make an attempt when a maximum number of turn cues were active.

At this general stage of the research in this area it seems more important to hypothesize that some sort of transition–readiness state exists than to invest great energy in devising some detailed model for its operation. For a

more detailed model, it seems desirable to have more empirically documented occurrences of this sort of phenomenon. However, an example of such a
model may be given. Application of this model is limited to the phenomena
on which some evidence exists. It suggests some possible details of transition
readiness with respect to speaking turns, together with a possible algorithm
for auditor decisions on whether or not to attempt to take the turn.

Transition—Readiness Hypothesis for Speaking Turns

We may begin by assuming that one participant is in the speaker state and
the other participant is in the auditor state. Let us say that the transition
readiness for each participant is represented by an ordinal scale, readable by
that participant. On this scale a high reading represents high transition readiness, and vice versa.

Through periodic signal activation the speaker can represent his current
status on transition readiness. Specifically, through activating or not activating turn cues the speaker can indicate a point on the scale from zero to six
(or whatever the maximum number of turn cues proves to be). Moreover, by
activating the gesticulation signal, it appears that the speaker can indicate a
zero value for transition readiness (regardless of concurrent turn-cue activation), or perhaps a negative value.

The auditor has a similar ordinal scale representing readiness to shift to
the speaker state. Unlike the speaker, however, the auditor cannot, apparently, indicate through signal display the current reading of the transition readiness scale. Instead, the auditor can only act or not act to take the turn. (Further research may discover ways in which the auditor can indicate transition
readiness.)

It is possible to suggest an algorithm for the auditor's decision on whether
or not to attempt to take the speaking turn. It should be emphasized, however, that this algorithm is strictly a tentative one, presented mainly as an example. The algorithm is described in specific terms, using six as the maximum number of turn cues that can be activated:

1. Let us say that the auditor reads his own felt transition readiness on
an ordinal scale that runs from some negative value through zero to some
positive value in the vicinity of, but possibly in excess of, six.

2. Concurrently, the auditor reads the speaker's transition readiness
through turn-cue activation: positive values from zero to six depending on
the number of turn cues activated with no concurrent gesticulation signal.
When the gesticulation signal is activated, the transition-readiness reading is
automatically shifted either to zero or perhaps to some negative value, regardless of the number of active turn cues.

3. The auditor then adds his own transition-readiness value to the value
of the speaker's cue activation: if the sum is greater than or equal to seven,
the auditor acts to take the turn. (This algorithm states nothing, of course,

about what the interaction consequences of that auditor act will be. These consequences have already been considered above.)

Fig. 11.2 illustrates the scales proposed in the algorithm. It can be seen that even if the speaker activates six turn cues, the auditor's reading might be equal to or less than zero. Thus, the requisite magic number—seven— would not be met, and the auditor would not act to take the turn. This situation conforms to the finding that auditors do not necessarily act to take the turn even when the maximum number of turn cues is activated by the speaker. On the other hand, the auditor's reading of his own transition readiness might be seven or more, leading to his attempting to take the turn when no speaker turn cues are active, or even when the gesticulation signal is active. Further, the algorithm would permit the probability of auditor attempts to increase, linearly, with the number of turn cues activated, other things being equal; and so on.

FIG. 11.2
Transition-Readiness Values for Speaker and Auditor

Speaker transition-readiness representation							
Gesticulation signal switched on:	No gesticulation signal; Number of turn cues switched on:						
(-)	0	1	2	3	4	5	6
	Auditor transition readiness						
$-n \ldots -1$	0	1	2	3	4	5	6 ... n

Clearly, other algorithms can be developed for these same data, and further findings on the speaking-turn phenomena might suggest an altered set of conditions that an algorithm for auditor response must meet. The important points of this discussion, however, are (a) that some sort of hypothesized mechanism must underlie the observed sequences of speaker signal display and auditor action; and (b) a relatively adequate hypothesis can be advanced for this process.

Transition readiness is considered further below, as additional results are reported.

Turn Signal: Rejected Models

Before proceeding to describe other elements of the hypothesized turn system, it might be well to mention that the model proposed for the speaker turn and gesticulation signals was not at all the first one entertained by persons working on this project. Some of the earlier models are described briefly, together with some of the reasons for rejecting them.

Personalized Cues Sets

It was thought possible that individuals might have somewhat idiosyncratic sets of turn cues—a sort of interactional idiolect—that would be learned, probably quite quickly, by both participants when not previously acquainted with each other. This notion was quickly rejected because no learning effects could be detected in our materials involving unacquainted persons. The turn taking in these conversations seemed to function as well at the immediate beginning of the interaction as at any later point. Instances of simultaneous turns were distributed throughout the conversation. The model itself is implausible in that it ignores the notion of culture itself, in the sense of pools of knowledge shared by the members. Rather than being idiosyncratic, turn-system cues are considered to be culturally shared. Individuals might, however, vary in the manner in which they drew upon this general set of cues.

Cue-Display Thresholds for Auditor Response

An early hypothesis was that, in general, auditor turn attempts primarily followed speaker turn signals involving some critical number of cues. For example, as a group, auditors would tend strongly to attempt to take the turn only when three or more turn cues were active. This hypothesis was quickly abandoned when it was found that a positive linear function fit very well the curve of auditor response to speaker cue activity.

Superordinate Cues

The notion of "superordinate" turn cues referred to the possibility that a speaker's switching on of any one of a set of special cues was inevitably followed by an auditor attempt to take the turn, regardless of whether or not other cues were concurrently active. This notion, tested in the analyses, was abandoned for four reasons:

1.   The cues tentatively identified as "superordinate" seemed rather idiosyncratic to particular individuals.

2.   These cues were identified in terms of relatively specific actions, rather than of general properties of acts.

3.   The number of times "superordinate" cues appeared to be operating in the interactions was quite small, providing a narrow data base upon which to form the hypothesis.

4.   The hypothesis of regular turn cues, as described above, was able to account for every turn exchange in the exploratory study, thus rendering the superordinate-cue notion superfluous.

Further research may produce evidence supporting the hypothesis of something like superordinate cues, but that hypothesis was not needed to account for the data presented here.

Special Cue Combinations

As hypothesized above, each turn cue operates on an independent basis, either being displayed or not displayed at any given moment. The switching on of any single cue is sufficient to switch on the turn signal. And the finding of increased auditor response to the switching on of larger numbers of cues was obtained by simply counting the number of cues active at any given moment, disregarding the particular cues involved in that display.

It was believed, however, that use of specific combinations of cues might play a special role in the turn system. Such a combination might be associated with a higher rate of auditor responsiveness than that which might be expected solely on the basis of number of cues. Perhaps an auditor turn attempt almost always followed the switching on of some subset of two or three cues, and this fact was obscured in our analyses because a random assortment of other cues was also being displayed along with the essential two or three.

A weaker form of the special-cue-combination hypothesis was that one or more single cues were more strongly related to auditor turn attempts than other cues in the hypothesized set.

The pattern of auditor response in our exploratory materials, both to the display of single cues and of specific combinations of cues by the speaker, was carefully analyzed from several different perspectives. No distinguishable pattern—or other characteristic—of auditor response to such specific displays could be discovered, much less a pattern yielding overall results comparable to those obtained for the linear-function hypothesis.

SPEAKER–AUDITOR INTERACTION DURING SPEAKING TURNS

After hypotheses on the speaker turn and gesticulation signals had been developed, attention was directed toward exploring speaker–auditor interaction during the course of speaking turns. It was clear in the transcriptions that, as a speaker continued his turn, the auditor did not typically remain quiescent. There were a variety of movements such as posture shifts, self-adaptors, and head nods, as well as intermittant vocalizations such as "m-hm," and "yeah." The question for research was whether or not regularities might be discovered in sequences of speaker–auditor action during speaking turns, similar to sequence regularities hypothesized in connection with the exchange of turns.

In a sense, the work on speaker–auditor interaction during speaking turns had been anticipated prior to the study of the turn and gesticulation signals. In order to study the exchange of speaking turns it had been necessary to survey all auditor vocalizations and to classify each one either as a turn beginning or as a "back channel." This initial classification of back-channel actions, together with their differentiation from turn beginnings, was aided by the astute observations and research results of Dittmann and Llewellyn (1967, 1968), Fries (1952), Kendon (1967), and Yngve (1970).

Upon completion of the exploratory study of the turn and gesticulation signals, the general research plan was to shift consideration to those actions classified as being in the back channel. It seemed necessary to test the validity of placing various types of actions, both vocal and visual, in a single "back-channel" class, and to seek actions of the partner related to the back channels.

Terminology

It should be mentioned early on that a variety of terms have been used to refer to various subsets of "back-channel" actions. Fries (1952), in a study based on telephone conversations, used the term "conventional signals of attention to continuous discourse." Kendon (1967), in a study of English subjects in conversations, found a general class of "accompaniment signals" that was divided into two subclasses: (a) an "attention signal proper in which p appears to do no more than signal to q that he is attending and following what is being said [p. 44]"; and (b) a " 'point granting' or 'assenting' signal. This most often takes the lexical form of 'yes quite' or 'surely' or 'I see' [p. 44]." Dittmann and Llewellyn (1967, 1968) used the term "listener response."

The term used in this paper was suggested by Yngve (1970), who discussed the "back channel, over which the person who has the turn receives short messages such as 'yes' and 'uh-huh' without relinquishing the turn [p. 568]."

Signal Display and Activity

Following informal exploratory analysis of the transcriptions, the following five types of action were initially classified as alternative forms of communicating in the back channel, as observed in the transcriptions. Consistent with the formulation of other signals in the turn system the back-channel signal is defined as the display of at least one of the set of its constituent forms. In the examples that follow, "S" stands for "speaker"; and "A," for "auditor."

1. *m-hm.*   This expression is used to stand for a group of readily identified verbalizations. Included in the group are such expressions as "m-hm.," "yeah," "right," and the like, and Kendon's (1967) examples of "yes quite," "surely," "I see," and "that's true." Most of the m-hm back channels may be used either singly or repeatedly in groups, as in "yeah, yeah."

2. *Sentence completions.*   Not infrequently in our materials an auditor would complete a sentence that a speaker had begun. In such a case he would

not continue beyond the brief completion; the original speaker would continue with his turn as if uninterrupted. Sentence completions have been independently reported by Yngve (1970). Example: S: "... eventually, it will come down to more concrete issues ..." A: "As she gets more comfortable." S: "and I felt that. ..."

3. *Request for Clarification.* Contrasting with sentence completions are brief requests for clarifications. Such requests were usually accomplished in a few words or in a phrase. Example: S: "... somehow they're better able to cope with it." A: "You mean these anxieties, concern with it?"

4. *Brief Restatement.* This back-channel action is similar to the sentence completion, except that it restates in a few words an immediately preceeding thought expressed by the speaker. Example: S: "... having to pick up the pieces;" A: "the broken dishes, yeah;" S: "but then a very ..."

5. *Head nods and shakes.* Head nods and shakes may be used alone or in company with the verbalized back channels. Head nods may vary in duration from a single nod to a rather protracted, continuous series of nods.

On the basis of modality used, we may distinguish the vocal back channels (1–4 above) from the visual back channel (5).

It is not appropriate, of course, to claim that the list of back-channel actions given above is an exhaustive one. There may be relatively obvious types of back channels occurring in other conversations that simply were not used by the participants in the transcribed conversations. More interestingly, there may be in the transcriptions more subtle types of back-channel actions that were not recognized as such and consequently were not included in the analyses. It seems entirely possible that the notion of communicating in the back channel includes a large and potentially complex set of actions that at present is neither clearly identified nor well understood.

Location restrictions. No location restrictions are placed on the occurrence of back-channel signals.

Active period. The active-period for the back-channel signal is considered to be coincident with its display. Thus, the back-channel signal is considered to be switched on at the beginning of the vocal and–or visual display and is considered to be switched off when that display is ended. When m-hm back channels are used repetitiously in groups, each successive vocalization immediately following upon the preceeding one (as in "yeah, yeah"), the sequence is considered to be a single display.

Back Channel: Signal-Definition Rules

The auditor's use of the back channel is generally taken to indicate continuing attentiveness of one sort or another to the speaker's message. The back channel appears to provide the auditor with a means for participating actively in the conversation, thus facilitating the general coordination of action by both participants, within the structure of the conversation.

While the analyses presented below are concerned exclusively with auditor back channels, it should be noted that a back-channel signal may be displayed by either speaker or auditor, although the auditor back channels were substantially more frequent in the transcriptions. The definition of the signal in terms of its constituent forms is the same, regardless of which participant displays it.

In the transcribed materials, the speaker's use of the back channel most often occurred in either one of two situations. First, a brief back channel such as a head nod or m-hm might immediately precede the beginning of a speaking turn, acknowledging the partner's turn. Further consideration of this situation is provided in connection with the speaker-state signal, discussed below. Second, it was not unusual for a longer auditor back channel to be acknowledged by a speaker back channel. For example, if the auditor responded in the back channel with a brief restatement, the speaker might acknowledge that response with a head nod or "m-hm" before proceeding with the speaking turn.

In any event, among those who have commented directly on the issue (i.e., Fries, 1952; Kendon, 1967; Yngve, 1970), there has been unanimity in the judgment that back-channel actions, in themselves, do not constitute speaking turns. Further, in the present study an auditor back-channel action, in itself, is not considered a claim of the speaking turn.

It was not uncommon in the transcriptions for syllables of a vocal auditor back channel to overlap with the syllables of the speaker's turn, thus producing an instance of simultaneous talking. Because the back channel was not considered a turn, however, such instances are not considered to be instances of simultaneous turns.

Back Channel: Interaction Rules

When the auditor uses a back channel, there seems to be a mutual understanding between the participants that the speaker retains the turn throughout the duration of the back channel, and that the speaker will continue the turn immediately upon the completion of the back channel. By the same token, a speaker's back-channel acknowledgement of an auditor back channel is not considered to be a relinquishment of the turn. Thus, there is no sense in which an occurrence of back channels, in itself, alters the respective state (speaker or auditor) of the two participants.

It appears that both participants perceive a vocal auditor back channel as ending automatically at the completion of the relatively brief utterance involved. In contrast, a speaking turn may properly be continued until that point at which both (a) the speaker displays a turn signal; and (b) the auditor acts to take the turn.

Results: Auditor Back-Channel Signal

In the early stages of investigating back-channel signals, some basic issues required consideration:

1.   To what extent may the various types of actions tentatively identified as back channels be regarded as a single class of action?
2.   To what extent may the auditor back channels be regarded as a class of action distinct from auditor attempts to take the turn?
3.   Are auditor back channels related in any systematic way to actions displayed by the speaker? These issues are deeply interrelated.

Findings reported throughout the remainder of this chapter are relevant to these issues; and most single findings are relevant to more than one issue.

It should be noted that the more clear-cut criterion available for the turn analyses—that of smooth exchanges versus simultaneous turns—was not available for the studies of speaker-auditor interaction during turns. It is precisely the point for the latter analyses that the turn is not exchanged. Instead, the criterion becomes one that is both more subtle and more general: the nonchance occurrence of sequences of action involving both participants. The issue is: given some action by one participant, is that action preceded more frequently than would be expected on a chance basis by some other action, either by that same participant, or by the partner? Thus, the goal is to discover strong regularities in sequences of action during speaking turns, and it is from such regularities that the hypothesis of signals will be derived.

The analyses began with a scrutiny of the location in the stream of interaction of auditor attempts to take the turn, and of the various types of auditor back channels.

Location of Back Channels
and of Turn Attempts by the Auditor

An initial question for analysis concerned the relative distribution of auditor attempts to take the speaking turn, as compared to auditor back channels. Inspection of the transcriptions for the exploratory study suggested that back channels were distributed more widely throughout the units of analysis, while turn attempts seemed to cluster predominantely at the "proper" place: in the speech pause, however brief, between the final syllable prior to the boundary of a unit of analysis and the boundary itself (the onset of the first syllable of the next unit).

For purposes of making this comparison, each type of back channel and each turn attempt by the auditor was identified as occurring in one of four positions with respect to units of analysis:

1.   *Postboundary.*   The auditor vocalization occurs on or soon after the first syllable of the next unit of analysis.

2. *Speech overlap.* The auditor vocalization overlaps with one or more syllables of the substantive speech of a unit of analysis, other than those first syllables defined as being in the "postboundary" position. (The term "substantive" is used here merely to exclude sociocentric sequences.)

3. *Sociocentric sequence.* The auditor vocalization overlaps with one or more syllables of a sociocentric sequence, when a sociocentric sequence is part of a unit of analysis; or the auditor vocalization occurs in the brief pause, if any, between the final substantive syllable of the unit and the sociocentric sequence.

4. *Pause.* The auditor vocalization occurs during the brief pause, if any, between the final syllable (regardless of whether of substantive speech or a sociocentric sequence) of a unit of analysis, and the first syllable of the next unit. (This position was termed the "proper" one above.) Fig. 11.3 illustrates the definition of these positions in terms of a constructed example similar to that used in Fig. 11.1.

In addition, it was noted whether or not the speaker gesticulation signal was being displayed at the time of the auditor back channel or turn attempt. The results of this tabulation for both exploratory and replication studies are shown in Table 11.6. These data were used for the analyses described below.

Before comparing the distribution of all back channels to that of turn attempts, it is appropriate to check the relative distribution of various types of back channels. Within the subset of vocal back channels, the distribution of m-hm back channels was compared with sentence completions, brief restatements, and clarifying questions (considered together to avoid small expected frequencies).

Analyzing the exploratory and replication studies separately, the data in Table 11.6 can be cast in the form of a 2 x 4 contingency table in which the columns represent the m-hm back channels versus the combined three longer forms; and the rows represent the four positions with respect to units of analysis. For the exploratory study, a chi square applied to this 2 x 4 table yielded a value of 3.25 $df = 3$, $p = .36$; for the replication study, chi-square = 2.92, $df = 3$, $p = .59$. Thus, the results indicate that in both the exploratory and replication studies, the distribution of the m-hm back channels across the units of analysis did not differ significantly from that of the longer vocal back-channel forms.

Next, a comparison may be made between the distribution of all vocal back channels (considered as a single class), and visual back channels (head nods and shakes). Once again, the data were arranged in a 2 x 4 contingency table in which $df = 3$. For the exploratory data, a chi-square applied to this table yields a value of 4.06, $p = .25$. For the replication data, chi-square = 1.34, $p = .72$. Thus, data from both the exploratory and replication studies fail to support the hypothesis of a nonchance difference between vocal and visual back channels in their respective distributions across units of analysis.

These two analyses, considered together, provide evidence supporting the conclusion that the various types of auditor back channel do not differ in

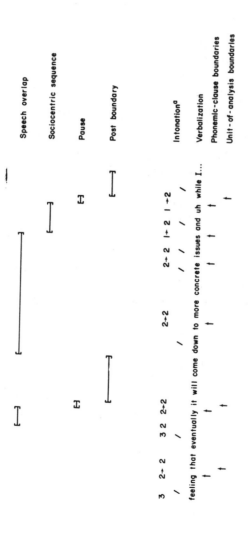

FIGURE 11.3 Illustration of the Definition of Positions Used to Locate Auditor Turn Attempts and Back Channels with respect to Units of Analysis

TABLE 11.6A

Location and Observed Frequencies of Five Types of
Auditor Back Channels and of Auditor Attempts to Take the Turn:
Exploratory Study

Location	Types of Back Channels					No. Back Channels	No. Speaker turn claims	Row total
	m-hm	Sentence completion	Brief restatement	Clarifying question	Head nod			
Exploratory study: Gesticulation signal not active								
Speech overlap	20	3	2	0	18	43	7	50
Pause	29	3	1	3	19	55	77	132
Sociocentric sequence	9	0	0	0	12	21	6	27
Postboundary	8	0	0	0	8	16	1	17
Total	66	6	3	3	57	135	91	226
Exploratory study: Gesticulation signal active								
Speech overlap	11	2	2		20	35	3	38
Pause	32	4	0	2	28	66	5	71
Sociocentric sequence	4	0	1	1	4	10	0	10
Postboundary	3	0	0	0	6	9	1	10
Total	50	6	3	3	58	120	9	129
Grand total: exploratory study	116	12	6	6	115	225	100	355

TABLE 11.6B

Location and Observed Frequencies of Five Types of
Auditor Back Channels and of Auditor Attempts to Take the Turn:
Replication Study

Location	m-hm	Sentence completion	Brief restatement	Clarifying question	Head nod	No. Back Channel	No. Speaker turn claim	Row total
Replication Study: Gesticulation signal not active								
Speech overlap	27	3	3	2	34	69	39	108
Pause	151	13	4	14	130	312	178	490
Sociocentric sequence	12	0	0	0	8	20	7	27
Postboundary	20	3	0	0	23	46	4	50
Total	210	19	7	16	195	447	228	675
Replication study: Gesticulation signal active								
Speech overlap	15	0	0	0	11	26	7	33
Pause	27	1	0	0	36	64	5	69
Sociocentric sequence	2	0	0	0	2	4	0	4
Postboundary	12	0	0	1	14	27	3	30
Total	56	1	0	1	63	121	15	136
Grand total: replication study	226	20	7	17	258	568	243	811

their distribution across units of analysis. This evidence thus favors the treatment of all forms of auditor back channel as a single class.

It is now possible to contrast auditor back channels as a class with auditor attempts to take the speaking turn, once again with respect to respective distributions across units of analysis. Table 11.7 presents data necessary for this contrast, for both the exploratory and replication studies. A chi-square applied to the exploratory data yields a value of 39.13, $df = 3$, $p < .00001$. The comparable value for the replication data is 20.49, $df = 3$, $p = .00032$.

In general, the results show that auditor turn attempts tended to occur more frequently than expected in the pause position (that is, in the "proper place"), while back channels tended to occur either relatively early or late. This finding confirmed the impressions derived from the more informal inspections of the exploratory transcriptions.

Auditor Back Channels and Speaker Gesticulation Signal

In view of the sharp suppression of auditor turn attempts by the speaker gesticulation signal, it is of interest to ask whether or not auditor back channels are similarly suppressed.

Once again considering the exploratory and replication studies separately, 3 x 2 contingency tables were created from the data in Table 11.6 in which the columns represent the display versus nondisplay of the gesticulation signal; and the rows represent (a) m-hm back channels; (b) sentence completions, brief restatements, and clarifying questions (summed to avoid small expected frequencies); and (c) head nods. For the exploratory study, a chi-square applied to this table yielded a value of 1.34 $df = 2$, $p = .52$. Thus, for the exploratory data, display of the gesticulation signal by the speaker had no significant effect on display of the various forms of the back-channel signal by the auditor.

For the replication data, a chi-square applied to the comparable table yielded a value of 8.87, $df = 2$, $p = .012$, Most of this chi-square value (83%) was contributed by the fact that the distribution of the combined sentence completions, brief restatements, and clarifying questions ran counter to distributions for the m-hm back channels and to the head nods. The sentence completions, brief restatements, and clarifying questions tended to occur less frequently than expected during display of the gesticulation signal, and more frequently during nondisplay of the signal. While significance of this chi-square is not at the level accepted as significant in this research, it should be noted that the longer auditor back channels tend to be more suppressed by the gesticulation signal than do the m-hm and head-nod back channels. This finding may be interpreted as suggesting that classification of these longer utterances as either back channels or turns may not be optimally accomplished on the basis of verbal form alone. The speaker-state signal, described below, may provide a useful additional basis for discrimination.

TABLE 11.7
Observed and Expected Frequencies of Auditor Back Channels
and of Auditor Attempts to Take the Speaking Turn in Four Locations
With Respect to Units of Analysis.

	Auditor back channels		Auditor attempts to take speaking turn		
Location	Observed	Expected	Observed	Expected	Total
A. Exploratory Study					
Speech overlap	78	63.21	10	24.79	88
Pause	121	145.82	82	57.18	203
Sociocentric sequence	31	26.58	6	10.42	37
Postboundary	25	19.39	2	7.61	27
Total	255		100		355
B. Replication Study					
Speech overlap	95	98.75	46	42.25	141
Pause	376	391.51	183	167.49	559
Sociocentric sequence	24	21.71	7	9.29	31
Postboundary	73	56.03	7	23.97	80
Total	568		243		811

Regardless of this finding, it is not surprising to find that auditor back channels contrast sharply with auditor turn attempts in their respective rates of display in the presence of the speaker gesticulation signal. If we collapse all back-channel signals, including the longer ones, into the single set: "back channel," a 2 x 2 contingency table can be created, using back channels versus turn attempts for the rows; and gesticulating versus not gesticulating for the columns. For the exploratory data, a chi-square applied to this table yielded a value of 43.35, $df = 1$, $p < .00001$. The data for both studies were entirely consistent in that the back channels occurred more often than expected during the display of the gesticulation signal, and less often than expected when the gesticulation signal was not being displayed. The opposite was true for turn attempts.

Speaker Within-Turn Signal

The preceding analyses presented some evidence that most of the actions identified in the transcriptions as "auditor back channels" were similar to each other, and different from auditor turn attempts, with respect to certain properties of their distribution (location) in the stream of interaction. Because of this evidence that back channels tended to hold together as a class of action, it became of interest to search the transcriptions for speaker actions associated with the subsequent display of auditor back channels. It seemed possible that auditor back channels might tend to occur following certain speaker actions.

More precisely, the research question was framed in the following way: Is there in the transcriptions some set of speaker actions that consistently precedes the display of the auditor back-channel signal (or some subset of the signal)? If such a set of speaker actions can be found, then they may be hypothesized to be cues in a signal marking appropriate points in the interaction for an auditor back channel, in the same sense that the speaker turn signal was hypothesized to mark appropriate points for auditor attempts to take the turn. As mentioned above, the sequential criterion involving consistent precedence of the speaker actions was, in general, the only one available for speaker–auditor interaction during speaking turns. The smooth-exchange/simultaneous-turns distinction does not apply to auditor back channels.

Definition of Display and Activity

The within-turn signal is considered to be switched on when the speaker displays at least one of a set of two constituent cues, described below. Following a display of one or both within-turn cues, the signal is considered to be switched off when all displayed cues are switched off. Thus, for any single occurrence of the within-turn signal, its active period lasts from the display of the first cue in that occurrence, until all cues in that occurrence are switched off. The two within-turn cues are:

1. *Shift in head direction toward partner.* This cue is based, not on the direction of the head itself, but on a shift of the head toward the partner, from a position in which the head had been pointing away from the partner. (Given better image resolution than was available on our videotapes, it may be possible in future studies to define this cue in terms of eye direction rather than head direction.) Location restrictions: none. Switch-off point: the boundary of the third unit of analysis following its display.

2. *Completion of grammatical clause.* This cue is identical to that mentioned as a speaker turn cue. Thus, this cue is common to both the speaker turn and within-turn signals. Location restrictions: none. Switch-off point: the first boundary of a unit of analysis following its display.

It should be noted that, in accordance with the logic of the analysis of auditor back channels, the definition of boundaries of units of analysis was changed in one respect from the definition used in the analysis of turn exchanges. When an auditor back channel occurred, the boundary of the unit of analysis preceding that back channel was drawn at its onset, regardless of whether the back channel was vocal or visual or both.

Fig. 11.4 illustrates the active periods hypothesized for the speaker within-turn cues, using the same constructed example of transcribed interaction used in Fig. 11.1.

Within-Turn Signal: Interaction Rules

As described in greater detail below, both visual and vocal auditor back channels occuring in the pause and postboundary positions tended to occur following the speaker within-turn signal. Like the turn signal, the within-turn signal is permissive, not coercive. The auditor is not obliged to respond in the back channel upon display of the within-turn signal.

Results: Speaker Within-Turn Signal

The relationship between the speaker within-turn signal and auditor back channel was examined in the same general manner as was the relationship between the speaker turn signal and auditor turn attempts. The following indices were calculated: (a) percentage of auditor back channels occurring during the active period of the speaker within-turn signal: and (b) chi-square for activity or nonactivity of speaker within-turn signal versus presence or absence of subsequent auditor back channel.

In calculating the two indices mentioned above, all instances of auditor back channels in the transcriptions were included. Thus, the analysis included the situation in which an auditor back channel is followed within the same unit of analysis by a turn attempt. (illustrated in Fig. 11.1). In that situation the cues active at the onset of the back channel would be analyzed. However, units of analysis that were followed (or interrupted) only by an auditor turn attempt were eliminated from the analysis because turn attempts and back channels were considered, for present purposes, to be two alternative and mutually exclusive auditor tactics at any given point in the interaction. Thus, an occurrence of the turn attempt excluded, at that point, the possibility of a back channel.

Table 11.8 shows the results for the speaker within-turn signal, both for the exploratory study on which the hypothesis of the signal was based, and for the replication study.

In the exploratory study, when vocal and visual back channels were considered together, 88.8% of the pause and postboundary auditor back channels occurred following the display of at least one of the two speaker within-turn cues. The chi-square for the associated 2 x 2 contingency table was 39.31, corrected for continuity, $df = 1, p < .00001$.

As shown in Table 11.8, similar results were not obtained for auditor back channels occurring in positions classified as "speech overlap" and "sociocentric sequence" with respect to the unit of analysis. Auditor back channels occurring in these positions were not associated with any set of speaker cues examined.

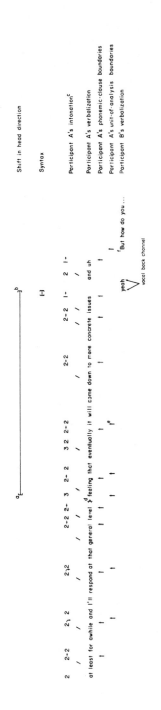

FIGURE 11.4 Active Periods for Within-Turn Cues

Shift in head direction

Syntax

Participant A's intonation[c]

Participant A's verbalization
Participant A's phonemic-clause boundaries
Participant A's unit-of-analysis boundaries
Participant B's verbalization

But how do you ...

yeah

vocal back channel

at least for awhile and I'll respond at that general level feeling that eventually it will come down to more concrete issues and uh

[a] [: earliest point at which cue may be displayed, in order to be considered activated at participant B's back channel
[b]]: cue considered switched-off
[c] intonation symbols from Trager and Smith (1957)
[d] audible inhalation
[e] this unit-of-analysis boundary not drawn on basis of intonation
[f] beginning of new speaking turn

TABLE 11.8

Relationships Between Display of Speaker Within-Turn Cues,
and Subsequent Display of Auditor Back-Channel Signals

No. cues active	No. units having display	Proportion of units with back channel following display	Percent back channels following display of at least 1 cue	x^2
A. Exploratory Study				
Pause and postboundary vocal and visual back channels				
0	286	.049		
1	326	.172	88.8	39.31[a]
2	173	.318		
Speech overlap and sociocentric-sequence vocal and visual back channels				
0	304	.128		
1	327	.107	50.6	3.70[b]
2	154	.032		
B. Replication Study				
Pause and postboundary vocal and visual back channels				
0	187	.134		
1	376	.338	92.5	55.26[a]
2	342	.535		
Speech overlap and sociocentric-sequence vocal and visual back channels				
0	210	.214		
1	359	.084	51.6	35.32[a]
2	334	.054		

[a] Corrected for continuity; $df = 1$, $p < .00001$.
[b] Corrected for continuity; $df = 1$, $p = .05154$.

In the replication study, 92.5% of the pause and postboundary auditor back channels occured following the display of at least one of the two within-turn cues. The chi-square for the associated 2 x 2 contingency table was 55.26, corrected for continuity $df = 1$, $p < .00001$.

As with the exploratory study, similar results were not obtained in the replication study for speech overlap or sociocentric sequence back channels.

Transition Readiness and the Speaker Within-Turn Signal

The relationship between the speaker within-turn signal and certain types of auditor back channels appears similar in several respects to that between the speaker turn signal and auditor attempts to take the speaking turn. In both instances, if the auditor response occurred, it tended strongly to occur after the speaker signal. In both instances the speaker signal was permissive, not coercive, with respect to auditor response.

These parallels between the findings for the two signals suggest the possibility of some sort of transition-readiness state underlying speaker activation of the within-turn signal and subsequent auditor response in the back channel. Such a transition-readiness state is hypothesized in the Discussion section of this chapter, after some additional results necessary to the hypothesis are described below.

SPEAKER-STATE SIGNAL

Following the chronological development of the turn system, it is appropriate to consider next the speaker-state signal.

One of the first projects in the exploratory analysis was to discover actions that might indicate that the auditor would subsequently attempt to take the speaking turn. Such adumbrating actions were never found. However, at a much later point in the exploratory analysis, a hypothesis was formed concerning actions that might operate to differentiate auditor back channels from claims of the speaking turn.

Within the turn system, there are only three general courses of action an auditor can take: (a) respond in the back channel; (b) attempt to take the speaking turn; and (c) neither respond in the back channel nor attempt to take the speaking turn. By definition, all speaking turns involve verbalization. (This is not to say that all interactions require verbalization.) Similarly, a large subset of back channels involves verbalizations. Further, as described above, responding in the back channel is, in itself, considered to be neither a speaking turn nor an attempt to take the turn.

For these reasons, it seemed desirable to find some signal, closely accompanying the onset of verbalization by an auditor, that would serve to resolve the potential ambiguity with regard to whether that verbalization is a back channel or the beginning of a speaking turn. The auditor's use of such a differentiating signal would permit the speaker to recognize immediately an auditor action as either a turn beginning or a back channel; more complex judgments based on the verbal form of the utterance would not be required. On the basis of the information provided by the auditor's signal, the original speaker would be able to frame a course of action appropriate to the nature of the auditor's action. In this manner, the signal would constitute an element in the organization of conversations, potentially facilitating the participants' coordination of their respective actions.

Finally, if such a signal were found, it would be relevant both to the process of speaking-turn exchange, and to the differentiation of speaking turns from back channels as separate types of auditor response.

Logically, a signal differentiating back channels from turn beginnings might be associated either with back channels or with turn beginnings, or each type of event might have its own distinctive signal. However, exploratory inspection of the transcriptions led to the observation that actions potentially serving the desired differentiation frequently occured in association with turn beginnings. Consequently, continued exploratory analysis turned increasingly to the pursuit of actions that might be distinctively associated with turn beginnings, as opposed to back channels.

Speaker-State Signal: Definition of Display and Activity

The speaker-state signal is considered to be switched on when the auditor displays at least one of a set of two constituent cues, in connection with a vocalization. Once switched on, the signal is considered to be switched off only at that point at which the participant displaying the signal shifts to the auditor state. The two cues are described immediately below. Identical location restrictions apply to both cues. These restrictions will be discussed following the description of cues.

1.   *Shift away in head direction.*   This cue is considered to occur when the auditor's head shifts away from pointing directly at the speaker. The cue is based on the shift away in head direction, not the mere fact of prevailing head direction.

2.   *Initiation of a gesticulation.*   The cue is based on the auditor's beginning a gesticulation, after having both hands at rest. The definition of a hand gesticulation, and its differentiation from self- and object adaptors, is exactly as described above in connection with other signals. It is possible that a tensed hand position, as in a fist, should be included in the definition of this cue, but such a position was not observed to occur at the beginning of the speaking turns in the exploratory study.

Location restrictions for the speaker-state cues are as follows. To be considered a speaker-state signal, the indicated cues must occur within a stretch of speech extending from one unit of analysis (of partner's speech) preceding a verbalization by the auditor to the onset of the first word following the syllable carrying the primary intonation stress within the first phonemic clause of that verbalization. In a few cases this first phonemic clause of the verbalization consisted entirely of a phrase such as "Well, uh." When this occurred the location restriction was relaxed so as to extend through the primary-stressed syllable of the second phonemic clause of the verbalization. However, this relaxation of the location restriction was not applied when the first syllables of the new turn were a back channel. Fig. 11.5 illustrates the basic restrictions.

It should be noted that, because the signal is hypothesized to differentiate the two types of auditor verbalization, the location restrictions require the

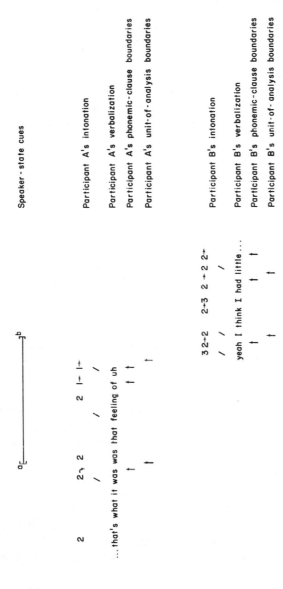

Speaker-state cues

Participant A's intonation

Participant A's verbalization

Participant A's phonemic-clause boundaries

Participant A's unit-of-analysis boundaries

Participant B's intonation

Participant B's verbalization

Participant B's phonemic-clause boundaries

Participant B's unit-of-analysis boundaries

2

2↘ 2   2 ⌐→ ⌐↑

...that's what it was was that feeling of uh

3 2→2   2→3   2 → 2 2↑

yeah I think I had little....

^{a}[: earliest point at which cues may be displayed in order to be considered a speaker-state signal
^{b}]: latest point for speaker-state signal display

FIGURE 11.5   Location Restrictions for Both Speaker–State Cues

signal to accompany closely a verbalization. Cue actions by the auditor, such as looking away, that do not accompany such a verbalization, are not considered to be speaker-state cue displays.

Speaker-State Signal: Signal-Definition Rules

Display of the speaker-state signal indicates that the auditor is at that moment switching from the auditor to the speaker state, thereby claiming the turn. For purposes of exposition, let it be said that the (erstwhile) auditor displays the speaker-state signal, despite the fact that the signal is hypothesized to indicate, at the moment of its display, a shift to the speaker state. When a speaker-state signal accompanies the beginning of a new speaking turn, that turn will be said to be "claimed" by the speaker. The phrase "attempt to take the speaking turn," used extensively above, refers to all new turn beginnings, regardless of whether or not they are claimed.

Speaker-State Signal: Analysis and Results

Location of Signal Display

Because turn beginnings must be vocalized, only vocalized auditor back channels were included in the analysis. Instances of simultaneous turns were not included because it was desired to consider initially only those turn beginnings in which the turn system was apparently operating in its proper manner.

The location restrictions for this signal described the stretch of interaction within which the speaker-state cues were required to occur, in order for them to be considered to accompany an auditor vocalization. For purposes of analysis there was one modification of these restrictions. Some auditor verbalizations were very brief back channels, such as "yeah," and "right." In such cases, the location restriction was relaxed so as to extend one or two syllables (by the previous speaker) beyond the end of the back channel. This modification was intended to compensate for the fact that the first stressed syllable of a longer verbalization (for example, a turn) often does not occur within the first one or two syllables of that verbalization. Thus, the modification was designed to avoid the possibility that the location restrictions would discriminate against back channels by specifying, in effect, a shorter stretch of interaction for them. It should be pointed out, however, that, if phrases such as "Well, uh" are ignored, there were only two occasions in the exploratory transcriptions in which speaker-state cues occurred as late as the end of the third syllable of the verbalization. On both occasions the cue was a gesticulation, and it occurred between the third and fourth syllable of the verbalization.

It may be mentioned that when exploratory analysis began, the location restrictions were defined to include a stretch of four units of analysis: the two units immediately preceding the initiation of a turn beginning or of an auditor back channel, and the two units immediately following such verbalizations. However, it soon became clear that the candidates for speaker-state cues were clustered much more closely around the initiation of turn beginnings. Therefore, the more stringent location restrictions were adopted.

Hypothesis Generating and Testing

For the analysis of this signal, the procedure was changed somewhat from that used for all other signals in the system. An exploratory analysis was applied to Conversation 2 alone. The results of this single-conversation exploratory analysis were then subjected to an initial replication, using the data from Conversation 1. Subsequently, the hypotheses were further tested using the data from the six replication conversations. This procedure contrasted with the usual one of generating hypotheses from the data of both Conversations 1 and 2, and then testing the hypotheses solely on the basis of data from the six replication conversations.

Results

Table 11.9 presents the findings on the speaker-state signal for (a) the exploratory study on Conversation 2: (b) the initial replication on Conversation 1; and (c) the further replication on Conversations 3–8.

Because Duncan and Niederehe (1974) presented findings on two other tentative speaker-state cues—audible inhalation and paralinguistic overloudness—comparable findings from Conversations 3–8 are included in Table 11.9. Briefly, the audible-inhalation cue was defined as a sharp, audible intake of breath. Instances of inhalations, visible on the videotape but not clearly audible on the sound track, were not considered as instances of the inhalation cue. "Paralinguistic overloudness" refers to what Trager (1958) termed "overloud intensity." This cue was considered displayed at points at which the initial speech syllables involved in auditor back channels or in turn beginnings had been transcribed as having at least one degree of overloudness. Transcriptions of paralinguistic overhigh pitch were not considered to be instances of this cue.

Results for each of the four potential cues are presented in each of the three fields of Table 11.9. The line in each field labeled "Any one or more of the four cues" shows the results for the signal defined as the display of at least one of the four cues considered. The line in each field labeled "Head shift and–or gesticulation" shows the results for the speaker-state signal as described above.

TABLE 11.9
Display of Potential Speaker-State Cues
in Conjunction with Turn Beginnings
and with Auditor Back Channels

Cues Active	Turn beginnings marked by cue display		Back channels marked by cue display		X^{2d}	p
	N	$\%$	N	$\%$		
Conversation 2: Exploratory analysis[a]						
Head shift	17	85	10	12	41.71	< .00001
Inhalation	10	50	0	00	41.35	< .00001
Gesticulation	10	50	4	05	24.96	.00002
Overloudness	11	55	6	07	24.00	.00002
Head shift and-or gesticulation	19	95	12	14	47.09	<.00001
Any one or more of the four cues	19	95	16	19	38.92	< .00001
Conversation 1: Initial replication[b]						
Head shift	21	34	0	00	12.33	.00079
Inhalation	3	05	0	00	0.43	.52
Gesticulation	21	34	1	03	9.72	.0023
Overloudness	12	20	3	09	0.97	.68
Head shift and-or gesticulation	38	62	1	03	27.80	.00001
Total: conversations 2 and 1	63	78	19	16		
Conversations 3-8: Second replication[c]						
Head Shift	114	62	27	15	82.85	< .00001
Inhalation	29	16	15	08	4.05	.04
Gesticulation	39	21	9	05	19.47	.00007
Overloudness	11	06	3	02	3.48	.06
Head Shift and-or gesticulation	128	70	34	19	92.96	< .00001
Any one or more of the four cues	134	73	48	27	76.11	<.00001

[a] Turn Beginning $N = 20$;   Back Channel $N = 85$.
[b] Turn Beginning $N = 61$;   Back Channel $N = 32$.
[c] Turn Beginning $N = 183$;   Back Channel $N = 179$.
[d] Corrected for continuity; $df = 1; p (.001) = 10.83$.

All four potential cues, considered both individually and as a four-cue set, showed relatively strong results in the exploratory analysis of Conversation 2. However, both replication studies failed to confirm the exploratory results for the paralinguistic-overloudness cue and the audible-inhalation cue.

In general, the two replication studies show considerable consistency in their results. The head-shift and gesticulation cues show strong results, both when considered individually and when considered as a two-cue signal. In Conversation 1 the two-cue signal was active at 72% of the turn beginnings, and at 9% of the auditor back channels, with an associated chi-square of 30.61 corrected for continuity, $df = 1$, $p < .00001$. In Conversation 3–8 the two-cue signal was active at 70% of the turn beginnings, and at 19% of the back channels, with an associated chi-square of 92.96, corrected for continuity, $df = 1$, $p < .00001$. Thus, the hypothesis of a speaker-state signal, defined as the indicated two-cue set, appears to have received confirmation in both replication studies. (Consideration of the possible sources of signal displays counter to the hypothesis may be found under the heading "Limitations" in the Discussion section at the end of this chapter.)

Simultaneous Claiming of the Turn

As described above, the data in Table 11.9 do not include instances of simultaneous claiming of the turn by the two participants. Exploratory analysis suggested, however, the possibility that cues within the speaker-state signal might play a part in the resolution of instances of simultaneous turns. In this context, "resolution" refers to the process by which one of the two participants "wins" an instance of simultaneous turns, that is, which one emerges with the speaking turn. This issue had not been previously examined in this research because it had been assumed that variables related to relative status of the participants and other similar factors might deeply influence such resolutions, rather than the actions occurring in the interaction.

The research question was framed in the following manner: To what extent is the resolution of instances of simultaneous turns in the transcription predictable from the respective switchings on by the two participants of cues within the turn and speaker-state signals? For initial examination of this question, transcriptions of Conversations 1 and 2 were jointly considered because of the small number (19) of instances of simultaneous turns in those conversations. As with auditor back channels and turn beginnings, all instances of simultaneous turns had been noted in the transcriptions prior to the conception of the analysis.

A scoring system for cue activity associated with simultaneous turns was formulated as follows: For each participant a value of +1 was assigned to the display of the gesticulation signal and to each of the two speaker-state cues. Similarly, a value of -1 was assigned to the display of each of the turn cues. The assigned plus and minus values were then summed for each participant, in each instance of simultaneous turns. For each such instance, the respective sums thus obtained for the two participants were then compared. The participant with the greater sum was predicted to win the conflict over the turn.

No exploratory analysis of the transcriptions with regard to simultaneous turns was undertaken prior to the foundation of this scoring system. The system was developed on an a priori basis, suggested both by a similar scoring system devised in previous research (Duncan, Rosenberg, & Finkelstein, 1969; Duncan & Rosenthal, 1968) to predict the direction of experimenter bias (Rosenthal, 1966), and by the additive effect of turn-cue display on the probability of auditor attempts to take the turn, mentioned above. The active period for relevant cue display in this case was defined as extending from one unit of analysis prior to the onset of simultaneous turns, through the last syllable of the simultaneous turns.

As a result of applying the summing procedure to the 19 instances of simultaneous turns in Conversations 1 and 2, it was found that there was one case (5% of the total) in which the sums obtained for the two participants were equal, thereby permitting no prediction. Of the remaining 18 instances (95% of the total) in which a prediction could be made, all 18 predictions were correct.

These predictions may be compared with those made simply on the basis of the respective speaker and auditor states of the two participants immediately prior to the onset of each instance of simultaneous turns. The participant who has been in the auditor state prevailed on 12 of the 19 instances (63%).

In Conversations 3–8 there were 59 instances of simultaneous turns. Applying the scoring system to these 59 instances, it was found that 48 (81%) were predictable, the two participants receiving different scores. Of the 48 predictable instances, 40 (83%) were correctly predicted. Compared to the proportion of correct predictions expected on a chance basis (50%), the obtained proportion of correct predictions has an associated probability of less than .00003. It should be noted, however, that both the proportion of predictable instances, and the proportion of correct predictions found in Conversations 3–8, decreased from those found in Conversations 1 and 2.

SPEAKER CONTINUATION SIGNAL

With regard to speaking turns, evidence has been presented suggesting that the hypothesized speaker-state signal marks the beginnings of new turns. The speaker continuation signal appears to play an analogous role in speaker-auditor interaction during speaking turns. While, in general, it appears to be accepted by the participants that a speaker is continuing his turn following an auditor back channel, the continuation signal is hypothesized to mark the beginnings of new "units" within the ongoing turn. These units will be considered in some detail in the general discussion following presentation of the turn-system signals, but it may be noted at this point that the hypothesized new units are intended to replace the rough "units of analysis" devised at the onset of this research. In this section, evidence will be presented linking display of the speaker continuation signal to prior display of (a) the speaker within-turn signal; and (b) auditor back channels.

Speaker Continuation Signal: Definition of Display and Activity

The continuation signal is considered to be switched on when the speaker displays a single constituent cue: a shift of head direction away from the auditor. This cue is identical to the "head-shift" cue in the speaker-state signal.

Because no signals have been discovered that tend systematically to follow the speaker continuation signal, the switch-off point for the signal must be defined on logical rather than empirical grounds. It may be said, therefore, that the active period for the signal is coincident with its display. The signal may be said to mark the beginning of a new "unit" within a single speaking turn, and that new unit may be said to remain in effect, either until the beginning of another such unit is marked, or until the exchange of the speaking turn.

The location restrictions applying to the speaker continuation signal are similar to those applying to the speaker-state signal. A difference in the two sets of location restrictions lies in the fact that the speaker-state signal is restricted with respect to the beginnings of auditor verbalizations, while the speaker continuation signal is restricted with respect to the boundaries of units of analysis within turns. To be considered a continuation signal, the speaker's looking away must occur within a stretch of interaction extending from one phonemic clause preceding a boundary of a unit of analysis, to the onset of the first word following the first stressed syllable following that boundary. Fig. 11.6 illustrates the restriction.

Speaker Continuation Signal: Signal-Definition Rules

As indicated above, the speaker continuation signal is hypothesized to mark the beginnings of new units of interaction within a single speaking turn.

Speaker Continuation Signal: Analysis and Results

The speaker continuation signal was hypothesized consequent to exploratory analysis of a variety of speaker actions observed in the transcriptions during the course of speaking turns. These actions were, in general, similar

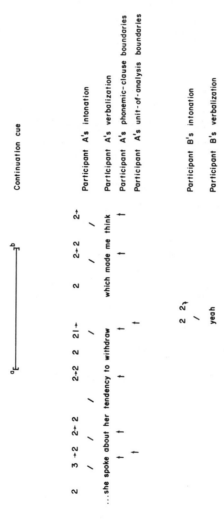

FIGURE 11.6 Location Restrictions for Speaker Continuation Signal

to those analyzed in connection with the speaker-state signal. Analogously to the speaker-state-signal analysis, actions considered for the continuation-signal analysis were required to occur near the beginning of units of analysis. It was noted that actions occurring in that position might be preceded by two types of signals: (a) speaker within-turn signals; and (b) auditor back channels. Further, either one or both or neither of these two signals might precede a speaker continuation signal in any given instance. Thus, all of these possibilities had to be taken into account in the analysis.

Units of analysis that were immediately followed by an auditor attempt to take the speaking turn were not considered in analyses of the speaker continuation signal. Also, auditor back channels classified as "postboundary" were not included in the analyses. This exclusion of postboundary back channels from the analysis was based on the fact that in most cases their position (on or soon after the first syllable of the next unit of analysis) coincided with the position at which a continuation signal would have to be displayed, given its location restrictions, in order to follow the back channel. Thus, the "lateness" of the postboundary back channels tends to leave little opportunity for display of the continuation signal, given its location restrictions. Finally, based on the findings on auditor back channels, those classified as "sociocentric sequence" were combined with those classified as "speech overlap." This combination of positions is termed "early" in the discussion below.

The basic question asked of the data was this: Does the display of the speaker within-turn signal and—or the auditor back-channel signal have the effect of significantly increasing the probability of subsequent display of the speaker continuation signal? This question was one specific form of the general issue in this study: the nonchance occurrence of sequences of action.

In general, the analysis proceeded in the following way. First, a "base rate" for display of the continuation signal was established. This base rate was defined as the rate of continuation-signal display when it was preceded by neither speaker within-turn signal nor auditor back channel. Chi-square comparisons were then made between this base rate, and the rates of continuation-signal display preceded by display of a within-turn signal alone, an auditor back channel alone, or both of these signals. With respect to auditor back channels, separate comparisons were made for those occurring in the "pause" and in the "early" positions.

The data on rates of signal display and the results from comparisons of these rates are shown in Table 11.10, separately for the exploratory and the replication studies. Line 1 shows the base rate for the exploratory study (4.7%), and Line 7 shows the base rate for the replication study (8.1%).

Speaker Continuation Signal and Speaker Within-Turn Signal

The relationships between speaker within-turn and continuation signals may be most directly assessed through analysis of those instances in which the within-turn signal was displayed and was not followed by an auditor back

TABLE 11.10
Rates of Speaker Continuation Signal Display
Following Speaker Within-Turn Signal and-or
Auditor Back-Channel Signal, or Neither

Line	Speaker within-turn signal display	Auditor back-channel display and position	N units having display	Proportion of units with continuation signal following display	x^2 contrast with base rate	p	Continuation signal accounted for(%)
Exploratory study							
1	No	No display	256	.047	(Base rate)		096
2	Yes	No display	372	.169	20.48	.00006	504
3	No	Pause	12	.000	.00		000
4	Yes	Pause	74	.243	24.46	.00002	144
5	No	Early	36	.278	20.95	.00005	080
6	Yes	Early	35	.629	95.41	<.00001	176
Replication study							
7	No	No display	160	.081	(Base rate)		075
8	Yes	No display	484	.188	9.35	.0026	523
9	No	Pause	21	.048	0.01	.92	006
10	Yes	Pause	171	.228	12.37	.00077	224
11	No	Early	31	.323	12.09	.00086	057
12	Yes	Early	38	.526	40.65	<.00001	115

channel of any sort. Results for these instances for the exploratory study may be found on Line 2 of Table 11.10, and for the replication study on Line 8. For these instances, in the exploratory study about 17% of the within-turn-signal displays were followed by a continuation signal, representing a highly significant increase over the base rate. A similar proportion (19%) of the within-turn signals were followed by continuation signals in the replication study. However, the increase over the base rate (8%) was significant at a level considered to be highly marginal for this study. Therefore, in this respect there was only ambiguous replication of the exploratory findings.

Speaker Continuation Signal and Auditor Back Channel

As mentioned above, analyses were carried out separately for back channels in the pause and in the early positions. The effect in the observed conversations of auditor back channels upon subsequent display of the speaker continuation signal may be most directly assessed through analysis of those instances in which no speaker within-turn signal preceded the back channels. Such instances were somewhat infrequent in the transcriptions because of the previously reported relationship between the speaker within-turn signal and auditor back channels in the pause position. But there were sufficient instances to analyze.

In the exploratory study, no continuation signal followed an auditor back channel in the pause position, when that back channel was not preceded by a speaker within-turn signal. This result is shown on Line 3. In the replication study the same situation produced a rate of 4.8% continuation signals (Line 9). In both studies the respective rates of continuation-signal display in this situation were highly similar ($p = .99$) to the respective base rates for continuation-signal display. These consistent results from both studies led to the conclusion that when auditor back channels (a) are in the pause position, and (b) are not preceded by a speaker within-turn signal, those back channels have no effect on the rate of display of subsequent speaker continuation signals.

Markedly different results were obtained for auditor back channels in the early position. When early back channels were not preceded by a speaker within-turn signal, the rate of subsequent continuation-signal display was 27.8% in the exploratory study (Line 5), and 32.3% in the replication study (Line 11). Both these rates produce significant chi square contrasts with relevant base rates. Thus, it appears that prior display of an auditor back channel in the early position is, in itself, sufficient to increase the rate of continuation-signal display.

Prior Display of Both Speaker Within-Turn Signal and Auditor Back Channel

Finally, examination may be made of those instances in which both a speaker within-turn signal and an auditor back channel were displayed. Does this ordered, two-signal sequence have the effect of producing a significant increase in the rate of subsequent speaker continuation signals?

When both speaker within-turn signal and auditor back channel signal were displayed, and the back channel was in the pause position (Lines 4 and 10), the rate of subsequent continuation-signal display was significantly increased over the base rates in both the exploratory and replication studies. In addition, for both studies, the rate of continuation-signal displays following both within-turn signal and auditor back channel was somewhat higher than that rate following within-turn signals alone. But this increase was significant in neither study.

The highest rates for continuation-signal display were observed following display of both a within-turn signal and an auditor back channel in the early position. These results are shown on Lines 6 and 12. It may be noted that in these instances it was required that the within-turn signal precede the early back channel, just as was the case for the auditor back channels in the pause position.

Summary: Results for Speaker Continuation Signal

In general, the results for the replication study paralleled those for the exploratory study. A strong relationship was found between early auditor back channels and subsequent speaker continuation signals. Highly significant increases in the probability of a continuation signal were found when early back channels were displayed alone, without a preceding within-turn signal. These results became somewhat stronger when both a within-turn signal and an early back channel were displayed.

As noted above, the findings with regard to the within-turn signal, when not followed by a back channel, were significantly replicated, but not at a level generally considered acceptable in this research. More solidly replicated were the results showing an increase over base rate of continuation-signal display, following display of both speaker within-turn signal and auditor back channel in the pause position.

Thus, the results may be interpreted as suggesting that the two most prominent antecedents of the speaker continuation signal are (a) a within-turn signal, followed by an auditor back channel in the pause position; and (b) an early auditor back channel. In the exploratory study, 90% of the continuation signals followed at least one of these two antecedents; the comparable figure for the replication study was 92%.

DISCUSSION: THE TURN SYSTEM

In this chapter, results have been presented relevant to the hypothesis of each of six distinct but interrelated signals. For each signal two sets of results were reported: (a) results from an exploratory study that led to the hypothesis of the signal; and (b) comparable results from a subsequent replication study that provided an initial test of each hypothesis. Described for each proposed signal were its definition, general rules applying to its use, and its relationship to other conversational phenomena, such as other signals or the smooth exchange of the speaking turn.

The results in the exploratory and the replication studies stemmed from discovery of certain regularities in the actions transcribed for those studies. In general, these regularities tended to be rather strong ones, as evaluated by routine statistical procedures. Significance levels of .05 or .01, typically found in much psychological research, were not in general considered acceptable for either the exploratory or the replication study.

The strength of the observed regularities lends empirical support to the initial faith that motivated this line of research: that in face-to-face, two-person conversations between adults, there are highly organized elements, beyond those related directly to language. These elements appear to provide the participants with an orderly means by which to coordinate their respective actions with regard to speaking turns and related phenomena.

More specifically, in this discussion we consider the following aspects of the results and associated hypotheses: (a) the general properties of cue and signal display; (b) the limitations of the results and related hypotheses; and (c) the implications of the results for understanding the organization of face-to-face, two-person conversations between adults.

Description of Turn System

Before the discussion focuses on more specialized topics, it may be well to summarize the elements considered necessary to describe the turn system as presently formulated. As presented in this chapter the turn system is described in terms of states, signals, moves, and rules.

States

Two sets of states are postulated in order to give meaning to the signals that were subsequently described. The components of each set are considered to be discrete and mutually exclusive. The first set is composed of "participant states": speaker and auditor. These should need no further elaboration at this point.

The second set contains four "interaction states," representing simply the four possible combinations of the two participant states (when there are two participants in the interaction): speaker–auditor, auditor–speaker, speaker–speaker (also termed "simultaneous turns"), and auditor–auditor. These four interaction states are needed to describe the state of the interaction at any given moment, in terms of the respective states of the two participants.

The signals and rules of the turn system presumably operate to aid in the coordination of the two participants with respect to these states, for example, avoiding the occurrence of the speaker speaker state.

In addition to the postulated states are the hypothesized transition-readiness states applying to each participant. These states refer to each participant's inclination to move to the next "interaction unit." Because there are two types of interaction unit hypothesized—a unit relating to speaking turns, and a unit relating to interaction during turns—separate transition-readiness states were hypothesized to apply to each of these units. Interaction units are considered in greater detail below.

Signals

Signals are hypothesized to provide the partner with various sorts of information about the participant displaying them. There are two elements in the description of signals: participant state and constituent cues.

With respect to participant state, each signal is defined as displayable only by speakers, only by auditors, or by either speakers or auditors. Note that a signal said to be displayable, for example, only by speakers, may nevertheless be displayed concurrently by both participants, if both participants are at that moment in the speaker state.

With respect to cues, each signal is defined as being composed of a set of one or more "cues." The display of each signal in the system is uniformly defined as the display of at least one of its constituent cues. There are three elements in the definition of a cue: (1) the actions comprising the cue display; (2) the location restrictions on those actions; and (3) the active period of the cue.

1. *Cue-relevant actions.* The actions required for the display of a given cue are described. General characteristics of this description are considered in some detail in later sections of this discussion.

2. *Location restrictions.* Some cue actions are considered to be cues only when the actions occur at certain specified points in the stream of interaction. For example, for the drawl cue within the turn signal, the location restriction required that the drawl occur on the final syllable or on the stressed syllable of a phonemic clause. Some cues do not carry locational restrictions.

3. *Cue active period.* The stretch of interaction over which a cue is considered to be active in the interaction is not necessarily coincident with its actual display. Some cues are considered to be "switched on" at the point of their display, and "switched off" at some later point. In this research such cues were considered to be switched off at a specified boundary of a unit of analysis. The active period of other cues was considered to be coincident with their display. It was pointed out that in the turn system active periods were always defined in terms of some interaction event, never in terms of time. This manner of definition proceeds from empirical considerations, not theoretical ones.

Moves

In addition to the signals, certain actions are characterized as "moves" within the turn system. An example of a move would be the auditor's attempting to take the speaking turn. In proper operation of the system, such a move would be accompanied by the speaker-state signal. But this need not be so, and thus the need at certain points for distinguishing moves from signals. In contrast, such a distinction is not made for communicating in the back channel. The back-channel signal is linked to the auditor's remaining in the auditor state, but there is no further overt move with which the signal is associated.

Another move hypothesized within the turn system as it is presently formulated is, paradoxically, the auditor's doing nothing. It has been said that the auditor has three options at any given point in the interaction: act to take the turn (a move, ideally accompanied by the speaker-state signal), respond with a back channel (a signal), and doing neither of these. Thus, neither taking the turn nor responding in the back channel is a real option for the auditor, the taking of which is a positive act exerting its own specific influence on the course of the interaction, and interpretable in the light of preceding speaker actions.

The third hypothesized move is that of the speaker relinquishing the speaking turn in response to an attempt by the auditor to take the turn. As mentioned above, this move appears to involve nothing more than simply becoming quiet.

Rules

Description of the turn system includes a number of "rules," each of which states the hypothesized relationship between two specified elements among the states, signals, and moves. For example, a rule describes the speaker-state signal as indicating a participant's shift from the auditor to the speaker state. A rule describes the gesticulation signal as inhibiting a concurrent turn signal. A rule describes the manner of combination of concurrently activated turn cues. A rule describes the sequence of events required within the turn system to effect a smooth exchange of the turn; and so on.

General Properties of Cue and Signal Display

In describing the hypothesized signals, three properties common to their composition and organization were emphasized: (a) cues for the signals were found in a wide variety of actions; (b) the signals and their constituent cues were treated as discrete entities; and (c) for signals having more than one constituent cue, the display of a single cue was considered sufficient to establish a display of its respective signal. These three properties need not be considered further. However, three other properties, common to the formulation and analysis of these signals have particular relevance to the underlying organization of the turn system.

First, the cues were described in terms of general properties of actions. In the speaker turn signal, for example, it was not a specific intonation pattern that served as a cue, but simply any deviation from the 2 2 → pattern; not the cessation of a specific gesticulation, but of any gesticulation, or the relaxation of any tensed hand position; not a specific paralinguistic pattern, but a drop from the preceding pattern in pitch and–or loudness; and so on. In this manner the cues were able to encompass a wide variety of individual communicational styles, while still functioning as clearly discriminable, discrete events.

Second, for signals with multiple cues, there was a common approach to analyzing the effects on the conversation of the use of more than one cue within any single signal display. One interesting property of the analysis was that, in displays of one or more cues, each cue in the display was simply assigned the weight of one, and these weights were added to obtain a sum for that display. Considering the strength of the relationship between (a) sums for each display; and (b) the probability of a specified type of partner response, it seems unlikely that an alternative weighting procedure would yield demonstrably superior results for these data.

One implication of this weighting procedure is that no special preference is accorded to cues occurring in any one of the major types of action (paralanguage, body motion, and language) over cues occurring in the other types. There appears to be more democracy in the operation of these signals than might be expected from some programmatic discussions found in the literature. For example, although future research may suggest that gestures may be found to serve primarily to modify aspects of language, such was not the case within the turn signal. The weighting procedure underscored the more general point that no cue within the system served in a secondary capacity.

Evidence for a weighting procedure identical to that reported here was found in a somewhat different aspect of face-to-face interaction: the unprogrammed communication of an experimenter's expectations to his subject (Duncan, Rosenberg, & Finkelstein, 1969; Duncan & Rosenthal, 1968). In that case the proposed cues were in intonation and paralanguage.

Finally, there is another interesting aspect of the final analytic procedure used for combining cues within signal displays involving more than one cue. In consideration of the distinctive-feature analysis model for language (Jakobson, Fant, & Halle, 1952), a concerted data analysis was directed toward the possibility that the signals were composed of unique combinations of cues, as contrasted to being composed of indiscriminate aggregates of cues (including single-cue displays). This effort, briefly described above in the section of rejected models, failed to produce positive results. No unique combination of cues and no single cue indispensible to signal display could be found. In general, the process of summing over equally weighted cues appears to contrast sharply with the distinctive-feature model and represents a considerably simpler principle of organization.

Limitations

Before proceeding to further discussion of some implications of the results, it seems appropriate to mention some of their limitations. It should be emphasized that no claim is made (a) that these signals necessarily represent an exhaustive inventory of signals relevant in general to speaking-turn phenomena; (b) that the cues proposed for these signals are similarly exhaustive; or (c) that the management of turns and related phenomena is essentially the same in all conversations involving competent adult speakers of American English.

In its intensive analysis of a limited number of two-person conversations, this study was designed to discover and to document some elements of interactional structure operating in these conversations. It would require a broader survey of conversations to explore the extent to which, for example, (a) further signals operate in connection with speaking turns; (b) there should be additions to any proposed cue set and–or alteration in any cue definition; and (c) further rules apply to the management of turns. The management of speaking turns may be found to differ among contrasting interactional dialects and–or interactional situations, as well as in conversational groups of differing sizes.

Limitations such as these on the generalizability of any results were clearly recognized at the onset of the study. The study was designed as a voyage of discovery; it did not return with a complete charting of the terrain.

Within the confines of the study itself, there was another kind of limitation. Despite the general strength of the regularities observed, the results were not perfect for any signal. For example, a smooth exchange of the turn did not result every time the auditor attempted to take the turn in response to the speaker's display of a turn signal; and in the replication study three smooth exchanges resulted from such auditor attempts when no prior turn signal was displayed. Similarly, not every turn beginning was marked by a speaker-state signal; and some auditor back channels were marked by the signal.

While failure to obtain perfect results is not surprising in any study, it is interesting to consider the possible sources of imperfect results in studies of this type. Assuming that future research continues to support the hypothesized signals operating in specifiable types of two-person conversations, five sources of error immediately come to mind.

1.   There may be errors in the transcription itself. Perhaps an intonation contour was mistranscribed, or the end of a gesticulation misplaced by a syllable. A transcribing error of either sort would have been sufficient to cause a given speaker-auditor transaction to be misinterpreted in the data.

2.   There may be errors in the initial classifications of auditor actions. Some of those classified as back channels (especially the "brief restatements") may have been speaking turns, and vice versa. These classifications were made, it will be recalled, on an intuitive basis at an early stage of the research and were not changed post hoc as further information on the speaker-state signal was developed.

3.   As mentioned above, not all of a signal's component cues, as displayed in the transcribed conversations, have been discovered. Even if some hypothesized signal had produced perfect results, it would be impossible to claim that the proposed set of cues for that signal is exhaustive. On the other hand, this argument cannot be used as an excuse for imperfect results. A claim that the cue list for a given signal is incomplete becomes interesting only at the point at which further cues are documented.

4.   A participant is committing a performance error. For any one or more of a multitude of possible reasons, a participant simply makes a mistake with respect to signal display. Although such errors might occur in an isolated manner from time to time for any given participant, systematic repeated errors of this sort would be expected to promote general miscommunication and possible disruption in the conversation. Indeed, as the elements of the organization of interaction are progressively discovered and documented, it may be possible to locate and describe with great specificity many of the sources of communication difficulty or breakdown.

5.   A final cause of imperfect results would be the deliberate violation of the interaction rules by one or both participants. Such violations might be expected to occur not infrequently when the sanctions applying to the violation are minimal, as appears to be the case, for example, with the occurrence of simultaneous turns. The notion of rule violation is considered in greater detail in the next section and in Chapter 12.

Optional Sequences of Action

It should be noted that, with one exception, the findings reported above were based on regularities in sequences of action involving both participants in the conversations. Consistent with the study's emphasis on interaction, the regularities were found between (a) the display of some action (interpreted to be a "signal") by one participant; and (b) some subsequent action or signal by the partner. The nature and implications of these observed sequences deserve further consideration.

(The single regularity involving only one participant was that found in the exploratory study between the display of a within-turn signal by a speaker and the subsequent display of a continuation signal by that same speaker. Unfortunately, as described above, this exploratory finding was the one receiving the weakest replication, thus rendering its status problematic.)

It is interesting that the sequences of action initiated by a given signal are, for the most part, optional sequences. The signals are generally not in the nature of a traffic signal in which both the green and the red light carry a strong obligation on the motorist to proceed or to stop. (Adam Kendon suggested this analogy.) For example, the data presented in Tables 11.3 and 11.4 indicate that, even when a maximum number of turn cues (five or six) were displayed by a speaker, the probability of a subsequent attempt to take the turn by the auditor was between .44 and .50. Similarly, Table 11.8 indicates that the probability of an auditor back-channel response to the maximum number of speaker within-turn cues (two) was between .32 and .54.

(The single signal that appears not to involve the property of optionality is the speaker gesticulation signal, which is hypothesized to inhibit auditor attempts to take the turn.)

The data suggest that both the speaker turn and within-turn signals mark points in the course of a turn at which the auditor may appropriately respond but is not obliged to do so. The auditor retains considerable discretion over both the type and placement of his responses.

The example of auditor response to the speaker's turn and within-turn signals is representative of the entire turn system. The phenomena observed in this study were truly based on sequences of *inter*action. Each stage of an interaction sequence, including the initial signal display, contains several real options for the participant concerned. At each stage, a participant either ratifies or fails to ratify the immediately preceding actions of the partner (Goffman, 1967, 1971).

Rule Violation

In addition to the options provided for within the turn system, there appears to be a further, more special option available to a participant with regard to the system: to disregard the prevailing rule(s), either momentarily or on a more systematic basis.

Within the framework of the turn system there were a number of points in the observed conversations at which rule violations occurred. For example, auditors attempted to take the speaking turn while the gesticulation signal was being displayed. Speakers refused to yield the turn after (a) displaying a turn signal; and (b) the auditor claiming the turn. And auditors attempted to take the turn in the absence of any turn signal by the speaker. Actions such as these are clear-cut violations of the turn system as presently formulated.

Lacking an empirically based, higher-level formulation of conversational etiquette, it is difficult to evaluate the effect of apparent violations of the turn system on the total conversation. There is no reason to assume a priori that appropriate observance of the turn-system rules is the most important aspect of a conversation, although such observance is apparently one aspect of the conversation. There is no reason to view the turn system as the only such rule system applying to a conversation. It seems reasonable to expect that there are a relatively large number of such rule systems, perhaps interrelated, each one applying to some distinctive aspect of conversational conduct. And, given our limited knowledge of the larger picture, it seems imperialistic to attempt to place the turn system at the center of the conversational microcosmos. Thus, a more fundamental evaluation of turn-system violations awaits development of further empirically based understanding of other aspects of conversational etiquette.

But it is possible to observe the immediate effects of a turn-system violation within the context of the turn system itself. For example, an auditor attempts to take the turn in the absence of a turn-signal display by the speaker. For a fraction of a second, there may be a flurry of speaker-state signals and the like by both participants. And after this micronegotiation of the controversy, one participant emerges with the speaking turn, the other relinquishing his claim. In short, we have simply observed a special case of an interaction sequence in which options are available to each participant at each stage of the sequence. The speciality of the case resides in the fact that it involves a rule violation.

Units of Interaction

In an earlier chapter, mention was made of the assumption of the contributors to *The natural history of an interview* (McQuown, 1971), that experience is punctuated. Bateson (1971) was quoted in his comment that "the stream of communication contains positive signals by which its units are delimited [p. 14]." On the basis of this and similar comments by others, a major purpose of the study was to discover units in the conversations that are not necessarily identical to known linguistic units, but rather marked by a variety of actions in language, paralanguage, and body motion. Further, consonant with the interactional emphasis of the study, units were sought that might serve to punctuate the interaction itself, as opposed to punctuating the messages of individual participants.

As described above, virtually all the findings of the study pointed to regularities in sequences of action and response by the two participants. These sequences lend themselves readily to the hypothesis of units of interaction, as were sought.

In a sense, the study began with a unit of interaction: the speaking turn. However, it was not until after data analysis that notions were developed as to how a speaking turn might be smoothly exchanged. The results described above suggest that in the observed conversations such an exchange requires the appropriate, coordinated action of both participants. This coordinated action involves an ordered sequence of three events: (a) the speaker activates the turn signal (and does not conjointly activate the gesticulation signal); (b) the auditor switches to the speaker state, activating the speaker-state signal; and (c) the previous speaker switches to the auditor state, thereby relinquishing the turn. (This last step appears to involve nothing more than simply becoming quiet, at least momentarily. That this does not always occur is attested by the entries in Tables 11.3 and 11.4 showing simultaneous turns resulting from auditor attempts in response to the activation of at least one turn cue in the absence of a gesticulation signal. This is one example of the general principle that the omission of any one of these three steps results in no exchange of the speaking turn and–or simultaneous turns.) In any event, the proper execution of the indicated three-step action sequence may be termed a *turn interaction unit*. A series of these units may be considered a series of steps in the progression of the conversation on a given hierachical level—the turn level—in its organization. Sacks, Schegloff, and Jefferson

(1974) voice an essentially identical view of turns as a unit created by the interaction of two co-conversationalists.

The notion of interaction units may be applied to the findings on speaker-auditor interaction during speaking turns. In this case, the auditor contributes to the interaction unit through communicating in the back channel. Through the back channel he may acknowledge his receipt and understanding—or lack thereof—of the speaker's message.

The findings suggest that the following ordered, three-stage sequence of actions may be hypothesized to constitute an interaction unit during speaking turns: (a) speaker within-turn signal; (b) auditor back channel in the pause position; and (c) speaker continuation signal. This action sequence appears to create units in the conversation on a hierarchical level immediately lower than that of the speaking turn. This lower-level unit may be termed a *within-turn interaction unit*.

The results further suggest that a within-turn interaction unit may be created in at least one other way. This alternative sequence would involve only two steps (but still both participants): (a) an early auditor back channel; and (b) a speaker continuation signal.

The hypothesis of a two-step within-turn interaction unit is based on the finding that early auditor back channels had the effect of significantly increasing the probability of a subsequent speaker continuation signal, whereas a pause auditor back channel did not. This increased probability of a continuation signal was found, regardless of whether or not the early back channel was preceded by a speaker within-turn signal. In contrast, Table 11.10 shows that, in our transcription, when pause auditor back channels were not preceded by a speaker within-turn signal, these back channels were almost never followed by a speaker continuation signal (Lines 3 and 9).

It appears that both the occurrence of an auditor back channel and its location may play a part in speaker–auditor interaction. That is, an early back channel may not be merely misplaced, but rather it may carry significant information for the interaction.

On the basis of the results, one may speculate that an early auditor back channel may indicate, not only that the auditor is following the speaker's message, but also that the auditor is actually ahead of it. Accordingly, it would be appropriate for the speaker to proceed directly to the next unit, regardless of whether or not he had displayed a within-turn signal. This "skipping-ahead" action by the speaker is not, however, automatic. It depends, apparently, both on the auditor's early back channel, and on the speaker's assessment of the situation.

In contrast, a pause auditor back channel would indicate that the auditor is following the speaker's message as it is developing. Therefore, it would not affect, either positively or negatively, the probability of an ensuing continuation signal.

By the same logic, a postboundary auditor back channel would indicate some auditor acknowledgment, but also that he is not quite following the speaker's message. No analyses were brought to bear on this possibility because postboundary auditor back channels occupy the same position at which continuation signals are typically displayed. It was not possible, therefore, to test the probability of ensuing speaker continuation signals. It is of interest, however, to note that a postboundary auditor back channel does tend to "squeeze out" the possibility of an ensuing speaker continuation signal, given the location restrictions for the continuation signal. That is, the position of the postboundary auditor back channel has the effect of blocking the occurrence of a speaker continuation signal, thus blocking the movement of the interaction to the next within-turn interaction unit. This effect is entirely consistent with the speculation that the postboundary back channel indicates that the auditor is not quite following the speaker's message.

Transition Readiness

It is now possible to return to consideration of the hypothesized transition-readiness state for both participants. Transition readiness refers to a participant's readiness to move to the next unit of the interaction. Because two different interaction units were hypothesized, each on a distinct hierarchical level in the organization of the interaction, two distinct transition-readiness states must be hypothesized.

One transition-readiness state must relate to turn interaction units. This transition-readiness state has been considered in some detail in the section of this chapter describing the results for the speaker turn signal. In this case, the "readiness" refers to each participant's readiness to move to the next turn unit. Such a move would, of course, involve the exchange of the speaking turn. An algorithm was considered for auditor decisions on whether or not to exercise the option to attempt to take the speaking turn.

A comparable transition-readiness state for each participant may be hypothesized for speaker–auditor interaction during speaking turns. In this case, the readiness refers to each participant's inclination to move to the next within-turn interaction unit.

It was said for transition readiness on the turn level that the speaker was able to indicate his degree of readiness through the number of turn cues activated and the use of the gesticulation signal. It is possible that a comparable degree of readiness may be signalled by the speaker on the within-turn level, though more limited in range, in that the maximum number of within-turn cues discovered was two. In this case, it may be well to defer a firm decision (and the construction of an algorithm) until further results on the within-turn signal can be obtained.

With respect to turns, it was said that the auditor cannot indicate through signal display his current level of transition readiness. However, it would be at least partially apparent through the location of an auditor's attempts to take the turn, for example, an attempt in response to zero, one, or two turn cues would indicate a high transition-readiness level. An attempt in response to a large number of turn cues would provide less information because such an attempt might result from either a high or a low transition readiness level.

Roughly the same situation exists with regard to auditor transition readiness and within-turn units. A high auditor readiness on this level would be indicated by an early auditor back channel—the "skipping-ahead" effect discussed above. Once again, if the speaker readiness is at a low level at the time of an early back channel, then he may withhold the speaker continuation signal, presumably failing to ratify the skipping ahead.

In any event, the notion of transition readiness for each participant is hypothesized as the phenomenon underlying both the display of signals and the choice of one of the several options available to the relevant participant at each step in action sequences.

Logical Model of the Turn System

Fig. 11.7 presents a logical model of the turn system, as it is presently hypothesized. Drawn to be read like a computer flow chart, the figure is designed to show the hypothesized organization of the system, in terms of the development of a single speaking turn. Each diamond represents a perceptual decision as to whether or not the indicated discrete signal is being displayed. As a result of that binary decision, a path is chosen leading from the diamond. Paths crossing vertical boundaries (shown as double lines), drawn to separate the actions of one participant from those of the other, connect signal displays that must occur in the indicated ordered interaction sequence. Paths not crossing such boundaries carry no implication of ordered interaction sequences.

No claim is made that the diagram represents a model of the actual perceptual and decision processes employed by the interactants. In particular, not represented are the transition-readiness states and possible associated algorithms hypothesized to underlie the various actions.

The starting point, shown at top left, assumes that one of the participants (A) holds the speaking turn, uncontested. The outcomes shown at the far right are based on those phenomena that have been actually observed in the interviews subjected to analysis.

DYNAMICS OF INTERACTION

As mentioned above, the creation of units of interaction on either the turn or within-turn levels requires the coordinated action of both participants in appropriate sequences. The process by which interaction units are created (or fail to be created) may be seen as one specific example of the exercise of options by both participants in sequences of action.

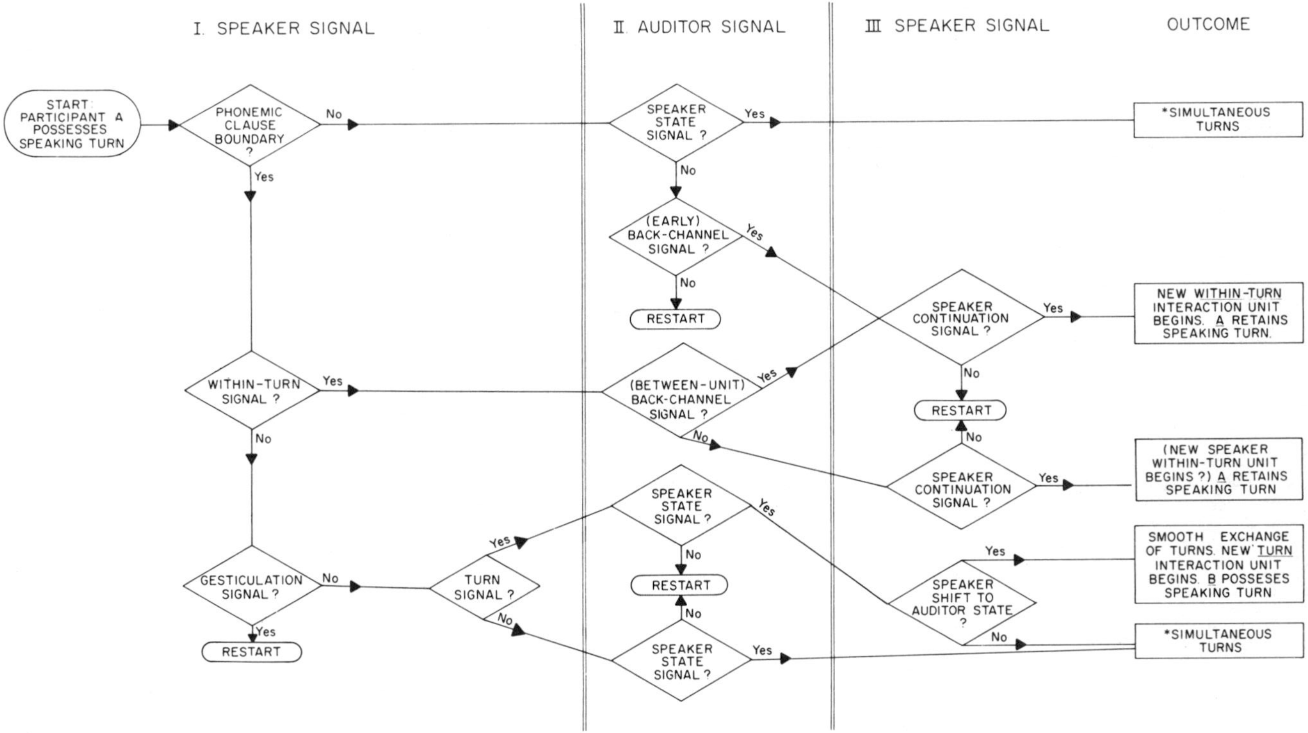

FIGURE 11.7 Logical Model of Hypothesized Turn System.

240

Because of the ongoing nature of an interaction, and because of the presence of real options, an action by a given participant is both a response and an initiative: a response in the sense of taking into account (or failing to do so) the preceding actions of the partner, and an initiative in the sense of representing a positive choice in the presence of alternatives.

Within the turn system, the alternative options are not equivalent in their effect. A participant's choice of one option from a set of possible alternatives at some point in the conversation directly influences its immediately subsequent course. Under this analysis a given action by a participant (more specifically, the exercise of a given option or the violation of a rule) has the general effect of defining the implications for the conversation of the partner's next action. That is, a participant's action sets the immediate context for the partner's next action. Contrasting actions by a participant, at least within the turn system, create demonstrably contrasting implications for a given subsequent action by the partner. And because of these contrasting implications, the participant's action exerts influence on which of the available options is subsequently chosen by the partner.

These general effects may be illustrated by an example. We may begin by considering the effects of an auditor turn claim, or lack thereof, on the speaker's ensuing actions.

It may be said that, after each syllable or word, the speaker has at least the theoretical option either to continue in the speaker state or to switch to the auditor state. Let us imagine that at some point in the conversation the turn signal is not active, and there is no claim of the turn by the auditor. If the speaker suddenly switches to the auditor state, there seems to be an excellent chance that the conversation will lapse at least temporarily into an auditor–auditor state: a situation that appears to be quite undesirable in the conversations observed, in that it was entirely avoided by the participants. On the other hand, the speaker's continuing in the speaker state has the effect of merely continuing the conversation in a normal manner and has an associated probability of 1.00 in the data.

A distinctly different situation is created when the auditor suddenly "interrupts" by claiming the speaking turn in the absence of an active turn signal. This action by the auditor has an immediate and significant effect on each of the options available to the speaker: it changes the interactional implications of the option, as well as the probability that it will be taken. The speaker's switching to the auditor state would have the effect of permitting an exchange of the speaking turn and would imply an acquiescence to the auditor's interruption. In contrast, continuing in the speaker state would entail both a prolongation of simultaneous turns and a momentary conflict over the turn, a conflict that might not be won. In the exploratory conversations the speaker continued with the turn after only 37% of the occurrences of the simultaneous turns (42% in the replication study), a distinct drop from the 100% continuation observed after no auditor turn claim.

The same effects can be traced by observing the effects of speaker signal display on the auditor. For example, the situation in which no turn signal is displayed can be contrasted with the situation in which a turn signal is displayed containing five turn cues (and there is no concurrent gesticulation signal). In this case, the speaker's signal display both defines the implications attaching to an auditor turn claim (simultaneous turns versus smooth exchange), and influences in the probability of such a claim (in the exploratory study 10 versus 44%).

In this manner, a participant's choice of action at each point in the conversation both imparts meaning to, and exerts influence on, the immediately ensuing action of the partner.

The implication of this conclusion for research is that the careful analysis of sequences of action is the proper subject matter for studies of interaction. The result of focusing on a single participant's actions, disregarding their natural placement in action sequences, has the effect of discarding precisely that information which permits an accurate interpretation of the implications of those actions.

Viewed from a broader perspective, the findings support the conclusion that in the observed conversations neither participant, regardless of the momentary allocation of the speaker and auditor states, is in full control of the interaction. The ongoing course of the interaction with respect to speaking turns may be seen as a continually modifiable resultant of the actions (or lack thereof) by both participants. This type of organization has the advantages of both flexibility and sensitivity. It is possible within the system to achieve a continual adjustment of the conversation, taking into account the momentary internal states of both participants. In the case of the present study, this type of adjustment—tuning, as it were, or perhaps negotiation—has been observed in relation to one aspect of the conversation: that having to do with speaking turns. The question naturally arises as to the possibility that other aspects of interaction discoverable through systematic exploratory study, perhaps operating within a specifiable organization having properties either similar to, or contrasting with, those described above.

It is certainly a truism that (dyadic) interaction cannot be fully understood, apart from full consideration of the respective actions of both participants. It would, however, seem to be a characteristic of the study of interaction structure, that it permits the rendering of this truism in highly concrete terms.

INDIVIDUAL DIFFERENCES

When optionality of action exists within some set of rules, as is hypothesized for the turn system, there is opportunity for individuals and–or groups to show distinctive patterns in the manner in which the available options are exercised. Consistent with the discussion to this point, these patterns would have to be described in terms of a participant's characteristic response to preceding actions by the partner.

For example, individuals may characteristically differ as auditors in the frequency of turn attempts in response to the display of a given number of turn cues. Some auditors may immediately attempt to take the turn cue when even a single turn cue is displayed, while other auditors may tend to defer until a larger number of cues, perhaps four or five, are displayed. Similarly, individuals may vary as speakers in the number and range of turn cues characteristically displayed.

Within an organization allowing for optionality in response, the study of individual differences in characteristic response to specific preceding events becomes a natural complement to the study of the organization itself. Research on individual differences within interaction is considered further in Part IV.

Part IV

A PROPOSED METATHEORY
AND RESEARCH APPROACH

The research reported in Parts II and III described some regularities found in the transcribed actions of participants in videotaped, two-person conversations.

The external-variable study reported in Part II was based on summary scores for the frequency and duration of a participant's acts over the course of a two-person conversation. These summary scores lent themselves naturally to analyses of group differences and of patterns of covariation. While it was remarked that the study as a whole was not as productive of results as might be hoped, it is nevertheless true that there were certain clear-cut and meaningful results. And it was noted that there were a number of points at which our results were fully consistent with those reported for external-variable studies by other investigators.

In the structural study reported in Part III, the variables were based on sequences of action involving both participants in the observed conversations. A systematic exploration was made for sequential regularities in the participants' actions related to a possible organization applying to the conversations studied. Such regularities as were tentatively found were subsequently evaluated through routine statistical procedures. Results of the exploratory study led to the development of hypotheses regarding the nature of some aspects of the organization operating in the conversations. These hypotheses were framed using terms such as "signal," "move," "rule," "unit of interaction," and the like.

Let us assume for the moment that the results reported in Parts II and III possess some validity, or at least that the results of some other studies like them possess some validity. The immediate question is, Why? How are we to interpret these results? What is their basis? Why are the observed correlations in Part II as significant as they are? And, at the same time, why are they not higher? Why should females laugh, smile, and gaze at the partner more than males? Why should there be more gazing at the partner by auditors than by speakers? What, really, are signals? What can one say about the generality of the results on the signals and rules?

We cannot proceed to deal with questions of this sort strictly in terms of the studies themselves. As Taylor (1966) points out, "scientific explanation usually does not now mean simply explanation based upon and verifiable by observation, but rather, explanation fits into a certain general conception of what reality ought to be like. The framework is, in other words, not simply a method of discovery, but rather a fairly large metaphysical hypothesis [p. 5]."

It is time to consider a larger conceptual framework within which the results reported in Parts II and III may be understood. This conceptual framework will not be in the nature of a theory; it will not hypothesize specific relationships between, say, sex of participants and amount of gazing, or between a given signal activation and subsequent action by the partner. Instead, the framework is designed as a metatheory of face-to-face interaction, in terms of which it begins to make sense to talk about such things as signals and individual differences. Further, such a metatheory should help give direction to research on face-to-face interaction. Research design may be sharpened through the clarification of basic issues. The orderly development of concepts from results may be facilitated. And studies such as the ones reported in Parts II and III may be set in perspective by pointing out the aspects of face-to-face interaction that they do not cover.

Finally, it must be emphasized that the proposed metatheory is scarcely being advanced as a final statement. It is intended as something of an outline, a relatively primitive statement aimed at contributing to the discussion of metatheoretical issues by researchers in the area.

Convention

The general notion of convention is frequently found in the literature, sometimes referred to by different terms. "Custom" is frequently used by anthropologists (e.g., Malinowski, 1944). Goffman (e.g., 1971), together with many other social scientists, uses the term "norm." Scheflen (1968) has referred to much the same sort of idea in his discussion of "programs." And "rules" or "rule-governed behavior" is often used by philosophers of human action (e.g., Hayek, 1962; Searle, 1969), as well as throughout linguistics. All of these terms may be taken as referring to the same general sort of phenomenon, although meaningful differences exist in their respective referents when used by different authors.

The signals, rules, and other elements mentioned in Part III are identified with the operation of convention(s) in the conversations observed, with respect to speaking-turn phenomena. (Presumably, there are many other conventions operating in such conversations.) It will be held that empirical evidence for the "turn-system" rules and other elements was obtained because the conventions jointly used by the participants introduced pronounced regularities in their respective actions.

It will be held that there is a decided advantage to be gained through the use of conventions: the coordination of action by the participants in interactions. Conventions are typically brought into play whenever coordination of action among persons is desirable. Conventions are applied to repetitive instances of situations requiring coordination.

Interaction Strategy

Conventions have the effect of regularizing actions in certain important respects (Shwayder, 1965, p. 260), but not in all respects. No convention constrains all aspects of the actions to which it applies. Interaction strategy is possible in part because of the degrees of freedom allowed by convention. Interaction strategies are describable in terms of the ways that individuals and–or groups actually use these degrees of freedom. We hold that such strategies arise only within the framework of convention and are interpretable only within that framework.

As opposed to conventions, which serve only to facilitate coordination of action, interaction strategies may serve any human purpose, such as competition, deceit, ingratiation, and, of course, coordination.

Because of considerations such as these, the study of interaction strategy is seen as complementary to the study of convention. Both convention and interaction strategy must be included in any complete description of face-to-face interaction.

Like convention, notions closely related to interaction strategy as described below are often found in the literature. For example, Whitten and Whitten (1972) have reviewed the anthropological literature relevant to "social strategies." Goffman (1969) has devoted a monograph to "strategic interaction." Ervin-Tripp (1972) speaks of "performance strategy." (It may be noted in this regard that the correlations and group differences reported in Part II are not interpreted as stemming directly from interaction strategy. Rather, those results are seen as reflecting indiscriminately and incompletely the operation of both convention and interaction strategy in the conversations observed. A more focused and descriptively adequate approach to research on interaction strategy is proposed in the next chapter.)

In Chapter 12 the notions of convention and interaction strategy are developed in generally abstract terms, although the lines of the development itself are very definitely oriented toward research issues. In Chapter 13 the conceptual framework outlined in Chapter 12 is applied to a series of specific research issues. The studies reported in Parts II and III are interpreted in terms of that conceptual framework. General issues of procedure for research on face-to-face interaction are considered, and the conduct of research on convention and interaction strategy is discussed in detail.

Terminology and Usage

Before the discussion proper is begun, some notes and cautions need mentioning:

1.   To facilitate exposition, all interactions are discussed in terms of two-person interactions. This practice has been adopted partly because the studies conducted by the authors have dealt exclusively with two-person interactions. Also, it is inconvenient to indicate repeatedly that a given participant in an interaction might have either one or more partners. It must be emphasized, however, that the discussion is meant to include groups of any size in which face-to-face interaction occurs.

2.   Although reference is made to "a given convention" or "a convention," the definition of the limits of any single convention is in part an arbitrary matter. On the basis of what is known about the organization of language, and on the basis of the results obtained on speaking-turn phenomena, it seems likely that many or all conventions are organized in a hierarchical system or set of systems. Thus, "a convention" would simply indicate some defined location within such a system, whether it be the entire system, one hierarchical level in it, more than one adjacent level, some component(s) within a single level, or the like. For example, we may refer to the entire turn system as a convention, or to the turn signal and its associated rules as a convention, or to the effect of the gesticulation signal upon a concurrent turn signal as a convention.

12

A Metatheory For Face-To-Face Interaction

CONVENTION: SOME BASIC CHARACTERISTICS

In order to approach issues of research on convention, it seems advisable to begin with an account of some of the basic characteristics of convention itself. For this reason, the discussion proceeds from the general to the more specific.

The initial, more general discussion of convention is in the nature of a sketch, intended to include sufficient background material to form a context for more detailed consideration of research issues to follow. More extensive and technically complete consideration of the basic elements of convention may be found elsewhere (e.g., Lewis, 1969; Shwayder, 1965). The present account is indebted primarily to Lewis. Because his elegant treatment of the subject is difficult to condense without omitting crucial points, the present account is more descriptive, relying primarily on examples (many derived from Lewis, 1969, and from Schelling, 1960) and on general commentary on these examples, without extensive proof or justification. The latter may be obtained in Lewis (1969). Lewis is, of course, not responsible for the substance of the present discussion or for any points at which it might depart from his treatment.

Coordination of Action

In the first place, convention has to do with cooperation between persons in situations in which that cooperation is required to achieve a result that is in some sense mutually beneficial to those participating in the situation. It is useful to speak of these situations as presenting "coordination problems" to the participants. Conventions are said to arise as solutions to these coordination problems. The term "solution" here is intended to denote a way of solving a problem, in the mathematical sense. Thus, one can say. "A solution exists for problem X," and the like.

An example of a primitive coordination problem may be derived from Schelling (1960, p. 54). A husband and wife become inadvertently separated from each other in a large department store. We shall assume that this problem is entirely novel for them. They have never been in this store before; they do not have a prearranged meeting point for such a situation; they do not have a generalized contingency plan for such a situation; nor have they become separated in this way in the past. Each is aware of being separated, and each is actively looking for the other. The coordination problem is solved, of course, by their both arriving at the same meeting place at roughly the same time. This example is developed further in later sections of this discussion.

For the purposes of describing conventions it is not necessary to specify why or in what sense each participant in a coordination problem perceives some particular way of solving the problem (convention) as personally beneficial; it is important only that that solution be so perceived. Similarly, it is not necessary to be concerned with the degree of complexity of the actions required for solution or with the extent to which these actions have been explicitly stated. Coordination through convention may range from complicated situations that require extensive, explicit planning on the part of many individuals (such as the development of communication procedures for contact between astronauts and ground control in a manned space flight, or the management of a large bureaucracy), through situations so routine that participants may not think of them as involving coordination per se. Here possible examples might be: greeting a friend, the management of speaking turns in a conversation, the taking of one's position in an elevator, and the avoidance of running into another person on the sidewalk. This second type of situation, together with the conventions applying to it, appears to be pervasive in society.

Further, it is not required that conventions apply to situations involving pure coordination. Even persons in conflict may find it expedient to coordinate their actions in some respects. Simple examples of conflict subject to convention would be games, such as chess and football. Here conflict is carried out within a rather strict framework of conventional rules. Schelling (1960) provides a more dramatic example:

If we are driving toward the same intersection on perpendicular roads on a desert where no legal system determines right-of-way, and dislike and distrust each other and recognize that there is no moral obligation between us, the one approaching on the other's left may nevertheless still slow down to let the other through first, to avoid emergency stops at the intersection; and the other driver may anticipate this. The conventional priority system lacks legal or moral force; but it is so expedient when coordination is needed that the one discriminated against may yield to its discipline, recognizing that he should be grateful for an arbiter, even though it discriminates against him, and recognizing also that he is trapped by the other's acceptance of the signal and expectation that both will comply [pp. 300–301].

Thus, it is not necessary to require that the operation of conventions be confined to situations in which coordination is the only factor involved. It seems possible that within a hierarchical organization for action there may be conflict situations (such as in the somewhat simple example of an athletic contest) nested within the context of coordination through convention (rules for the game). Or perhaps within an overall conflict situation there may be pockets of conventions applying to special instances. For example, belligerents in a war may mutually refrain from using biological and chemical weapons.

We may say, then, with Lewis that conventions serve as solutions to problems for which coordination is both required and, in some sense, mutually desired.

Preferable Solutions

Lewis (1969, pp. 21–22) points out that, to avoid triviality of the coordination problem, it is necessary to stipulate that the problem have at least two solutions, each of which is preferred by the participants over any other possible solution. Thus, there must be at least one degree of freedom with respect to preferred solutions. This stipulation obviously does not deny the possibility of constraints operating upon the creation of preferred solutions to coordination problems. It simply maintains that any such constraints must not permit only a unique solution.

There seem to be at least three general sources of constraint operating on the solution of coordination problems. One of those is biological, including perhaps genetically based behavioral predispositions, human information processing characteristics, and the like. Another possible type of constraint operating on the solution of coordination problems would be the matrix of conventions existing at the time of solution of the problem and recognized by the participants. That is, if the set of conventions being used by the members of a society is not entirely fixed over time, some conventions being abandoned and others being newly created, then it seems reasonable to expect that most newly created conventions would have to be at least roughly consistent with other, related conventions existing when the new conventions are created. Existing conventions might limit the range of possible preferable solutions for some new coordination problem. Finally, and most obviously, there may be physical constraints imposed on the solution of the problem merely on the basis of the limits of the technology that is available to the participants.

For reasons such as these the range of possible preferable solutions to a given coordination problem may not be indefinitely large. This is not of great consequence to this discussion. It is necessary only to eliminate the case of unique solutions. Only coordination problems having at least two preferable solutions will be considered from this point forward.

Coordination of Expectations

We may return to consideration of the predicament of the couple separated in the department store, under the conditions stipulated. How do they solve their coordination problem? Most definitely, the solution to the problem does not lie in each guessing where the other would go, as in, for example, the husband's simply asking the question, "What would I do if I were she?" This strategy is appropriate only if one of the partners is unaware that a search situation exists, and thus cooperation is not involved.

Rather, an effective strategy must involve the coordination of their mutual expectations. In Schelling's (1960) words, the effective question (e.g., for the husband) is: " 'What would I do if I were she wondering what she would do if she were I wondering what I would do if I were she. . . ?' What is necessary is to coordinate predictions, to read the same message in the common situation, to identify the one course of action that their expectations of each other can converge on [p. 54]." As Schelling (1960) points out, "It is likely that each will think of some obvious place to meet, so obvious that each will be sure that the other is sure that it is 'obvious' to both of them [p. 54]."

This apparently awkward line of reasoning aimed at the convergence of mutual expectations may be illustrated through our careless couple. Let us say that upon considering the problem both husband and wife recall that they had discussed visiting the book section while at the store. Each believes that this may be the solution that will be expected by the other. Accordingly, each proceeds toward the book section in the hope of meeting the other there.

Among authors considering convention there seems to be virtually unanimous agreement that solutions to coordination problems are most effectively reached through the process of coordinating mutual expectations as described above. Each participant in the solution of a coordination problem must know both what actions are expected of himself, and what actions he may expect of the other participant(s). It is through the firmness of such mutual expectations that conventions arise. This is considered in greater detail in the next section. More extensive consideration of the operation of expectations in conventional action may be found in, for example, Goffman (1967), Gross, Mason, and McEachern (1958), Lewis (1969), Schelling (1960), and Shwayder (1965). The notion of coordination of mutual expectations seems to be an essential element of conventional action and will be an underlying assumption for the following discussion.

Precedent

Schelling (1960) has shown that individuals can frequently solve coordination problems that they have never before faced, even when they are not allowed to communicate with each other. The possibility of such solutions was one point of the example of the careless couple.

But it is much more typical to face coordination problems that are highly recurrent in life. Individuals solving these problems are rarely forced to operate within an entirely novel context. The problems are at least familiar, more often routine. In this case, we can invoke a powerful aid to solution: precedent. We recall times in the past when the same or similar problems were solved, or perhaps we recall having heard of a solution. If we can reasonably expect that the person with whom we are seeking coordination has experience with a similar precedent, then this shared experience of related previous solutions serves as a forceful element in our solution of the problem.

As Lewis (1969) points out, the means by which we may arrive at a common precedent are extraordinarily flexible. For example, the problem previously solved need not be identical to the one to be solved—only similar enough that we are moved to draw an analogy from one to the other. We do not have to have personal experience with a prior solution—we may have only heard about it, and that story may not even be true. Our coparticipant need not have experience with the same prior solution—he need only be acquainted with prior solutions that agree sufficiently with ours to enable him to draw the same analogies. And it does not matter why the prior solution worked, even if it worked only by luck. The fact that it did work—or that we believe it did—is sufficient to establish the precedent.

What is required for the establishment of precedent is the perception of a regularity in the solution of past coordination problems that we deem to be analogous to each other and to the present problem.

From this perception of regularity in the solution of past coordination problems, we may reasonably extrapolate to both present and future problems. In time we may develop a "general belief, unrestricted as to time, that members of a certain population conform to a certain regularity in a certain kind of recurring coordination problem for the sake of coordination (Lewis, 1969, p. 41)." "Our experience of general conformity in the past leads us, by force of precedent, to expect a like conformity in the future (Lewis, 1969, p. 41)."

"Once the process gets started, we have a metastable self-perpetuating system of preferences, expectations, and actions capable of persisting indefinitely (Lewis, 1969, p. 42)." It is this phenomenon, as roughly outlined here, that Lewis labels "convention."

We may now complete our example of the careless couple. As husband and wife are proceeding to the book section on the basis of their (correctly calculated) mutual expectations, they happen by chance to see each other near the main entrance to the store. It is possible that this meeting, even though it occurred by chance, may serve as a precedent for them. If so, this precedent will provide the basis for the couple's conventional solution to that particular coordination problem, should it ever arise again.

Convention and Regularities in Action or Behavior

It has been stressed that conventions provide an important source of observed regularity in human action. It is not held, however, that conventions are the only source of such regularity. It may be useful in further differentiating the notion of convention to mention some other possible sources of regularity in human behavior that are not considered to stem from conventions. The ensuing list is derived primarily from the discussions of Lewis (1969) and Shwayder (1965).

1. *Physiological factors.*   Examples: involuntary responses, such as behavioral reactions to drugs, piloerection in response to cold, and some eye blinks.

2. *Perceptual–motor abilities.*   This category refers to the description of the abilities persons must have in order to perform given tasks in a predictably successful manner. Examples of perceptual–motor abilities might be riding a bicycle and the actions of a worker on an assembly line.

3. *Natural hazards.*   Regularities in the actions of persons that are introduced by prudent safety practices applied to dangerous endeavors. Lewis's example here is the refraining from smoking by workers in an explosives factory.

4. *Heavy social sanctions.*   Regularities might be introduced into actions that are a result only of extraordinary social consequences of those actions. For example, it is not a convention that prisoners do not attempt to escape from a concentration camp; absence of escape attempts is a result of the fact that guards have the practice of shooting prisoners making such attempts.

5. *Reinforcement schedules.*   Behavior entirely under the control of reinforcement schedules, if such can be demonstrated for humans, would not be conventional on this analysis.

6. *Solitary habits.*   This is a more ambiguous category, discussed briefly below in the section on "number of slots" for situations. In any event, an example here would be the routine followed upon waking up in the morning by a person who lives alone.

7. *Genetically coded behaviors.*   This is another uncertain category, the discussion of which would best be left to ethologists and related investigators. An example might be the tendency of infants to smile in response to stimuli having certain characteristics of the human face.

It can be argued that each of the above types of regularity in behavior or actions, to the extent to which it exists, does not possess the essential characteristics of convention, as sketched in this chapter.

One other possible source of regularity in action is discussed in some detail later in this chapter. This type of regularity, termed interaction strategy, is not considered to be a convention but is stated to be closely related to it.

SIGNALS

A prominent aspect of conventions is that of signals used in their enactment. Signals may be said to facilitate the coordination of action between the participants in the convention. In addition, the signals themselves are conventional, arising through the same force of precedent as the convention they serve.

Terms and Distinctions

Contingency Plans

In the ensuing discussion it will be convenient to follow Lewis in speaking of a conventional solution to a coordination problem as involving a set of contingency plans, one for each participant in the convention. At its simplest, each such plan within the set for a convention would stipulate for some specified participant(s) that, if a given set of affairs obtains, then a certain move (not Lewis's term) should be made and–or a certain signal should be activated.

Communicator–Audience

The discussion of signaling will also assume a simple distinction between a communicator (that participant who, according to the convention, displays a signal at some point), and the audience (that participant who receives the signal). Of course, each participant (in a two-person interaction) will normally be a communicator from time to time, as each participant signals to the other; and similarly, each participant will be the audience as the partner displays signals.

Moves versus Signals

For the sake of exposition it is convenient to distinguish signals from moves within some conventions. An example of this distinction would be the turn system, in which a distinction was drawn between beginning a speaking turn, and signaling via the speaker-state signal that a turn was beginning. In this case, beginning a speaking turn was a move within the turn-system convention; this move might or might not be additionally marked by the signal. The signal, however, serves to clarify what the speaker is doing.

It is entirely possible for a convention not to include signals. For example, in some social circles it is part of table etiquette that, in passing the salt, it is not to be passed hand to hand, but rather it is to be placed on the table near the intended recipient, who will then pick it up. The reason given for this practice is that it helps avoid bad luck for the recipient. This convention involves, not the request for the salt, but the manner in which it is passed, regardless of whether it was requested or not. In this sense, the convention involves only a move.

On the other hand, it is possible for a convention to involve only signals. Here perhaps an example would be the initial exchange of greetings between persons. For the purposes of the example, we may say the greetings help to bring the participants into a state of talk.

One-Sided and Two-Sided Signaling

As Lewis (1969) points out, there may be conventions that involve "one-sided" signals, used to facilitate the coordination "either between communicators or between members of the audience [p. 130]." That is, one-sided signals are those used by participants who are on one and the same side of the communicator–audience dichotomy.

As an example of a signal used to facilitate coordination between communicators, Lewis cites the practice of drivers of horse-drawn wagons to yell "gee" when they want the team to turn right, and "haw" when they want the team to turn left. In this case, "the men are the communicators and the horses are the audience, and both act according to complementary contingency plans. But the coordination problem of choosing contingency plans, and the convention that solves it, exist only among the men. The horses are only beasts, and they react as they have been trained to react. The men must coordinate in order to keep the horses trained and in order to take advantage of their training (Lewis, 1969, p. 130)."

Another example illustrates the use of a signal to coordinate the actions of only members of the audience. In a certain town all men who sought odd jobs as handymen would congregate on a vacant lot near the river, providing a conventional means by which they and potential employers could easily make contact. After the pairing of an employer and a worker through some process of mutual selection, they would proceed to the job site. On the way they would stop at a grocery store and check the price per pound of pork chops. That price would be the hourly wage of the worker. In this case, the coordination problem is that of setting the hourly wage. The signal for facilitating that coordination is the price of pork chops. Both employer and worker are members of the audience. The contingency plan is simply that both

parties agree to the price as the hourly wage. There is, however, no communicator, neither the price itself nor the butcher who set the price. There is no
contingency plan for the price itself or for the butcher. The price is just a
conventional means by which the setting of the wage is mediated.

This discussion is primarly concerned with what Lewis calls "two-sided"
signaling in which coordination between communicator and audience is involved. The example here is derived from Lewis' example of Paul Revere and
the sexton of the Old North Church. In this case, the sexton is the communicator, Paul Revere is the audience, and the lantern is the signal. The contingency plan for the sexton is as follows: (a) if the Redcoats are observed to be
staying at home, display no lantern in the belfry; (b) if the Redcoats are observed to be approaching by land, display one lantern; and (c) if the Redcoats are observed to be approaching by sea, display two lanterns.

The contingency plan for Paul Revere is: (a) if no lantern is observed in
the belfry, go home; (b) if one lantern is observed, warn the countryside that
the redcoats are approaching by land; and (c) if two lanterns are observed,
warn the countryside that the redcoats are approaching by sea. This particular set of plans is not a convention, in that it represents a single situation. If,
however, the situation recurred, and no new arrangement of signals and–or
contingency plans is needed for each recurrence, then the respective contingency plans, together with the accompanying signals, would be conventional.

Contingency-Plan Branching and Audience Responses

In the example above there is a one-to-one correspondence between the
sexton's contingency plan and Paul Revere's. This need not be the case. Just
as the contingency plan for the communicator's signal depends upon the
state of affairs that he observes, so the audience's contingency plan may take
into account, not only the signal displayed by the communicator (and thus
the state of affairs observed by the communicator), but also any other element of the situation observable by the audience. In the latter case, a participant's contingency plan may be relatively complex, involving a series of
branching paths, each of these paths deriving from some observed state of
affairs. A simple example here would be the turn-system contingency plan
(not labeled as such in the preceding chapter) for the auditor's attempting to
take the speaking turn or not so attempting. As hypothesized, this contingency plan required the auditor to base his action on the joint consideration of
two types of information: the number of turn cues activated by the speaker,
and the auditor's own "transition-readiness" state.

Regardless of the degree of complexity of a contingency plan, each such
plan leads eventually to some action by a participant. This action may be relatively direct, as in a locomotive engineer's setting the train in motion upon
receiving the proper signal from the conductor (and upon observing the appropriate state of affairs to obtain with regard to the operating condition of

the engine, the tracks ahead, and so on). On the other hand, the action entailed by a contingency plan may involve further signaling, as was the case for Paul Revere. In any event, alternative actions and–or signals of any sort provided for in a contingency plan will be termed "responses," following Lewis.

Further Characteristics of Signaling

Several aspects of Lewis's approach to signaling appear entirely obvious but may nevertheless be briefly noted. First, the choosing of contingency plans is a coordination problem. The communicator's and the audience's respective plans must match in order to achieve the desired solution. (In the case of Paul Revere and the sexton, the desired solution was the appropriate warning of the countryside.)

Second, the actual signals used might have been different. Some signaling medium other than lanterns might have been used; and, using lanterns, some other correspondence between number of lanterns and observed states of affairs might have been used (such as "two if by land, and one if by sea").

Third, there is a straightforward reason for adopting the two-sided signaling system: certain information, highly useful for solving the coordination problem, can be observed by the communicator but not by the audience. Lewis states this situation with generality and precision: "... it is common knowledge for the communicator and the audience that: Exactly one or several states of affairs $s_1 \ldots s_m$ holds. The communicator, but not the audience, is in a good position to tell which one it is (Lewis, 1969, p. 130)." The sexton in his earlier perambulations had quite intentionally placed himself in a position to observe the Redcoats' movements; this was information that Paul Revere did not have. In contrast, many states of affairs relevant to solving coordination problems involved in face-to-face interaction may be more subtle: the internal states of the communicator, such as willingness to exchange the speaking turn and the like. It is these more subtle states that appear to be of primary interest in research on face-to-face interaction.

Finally, the example provides another instance in which a distinction may be drawn between the actions required to achieve the solution of a coordination problem, and the signals used by participants to facilitate that solution. It is possible that Paul Revere might have taken the appropriate action, even if the sexton had fallen asleep and thus failed to provide the signals, or had gotten the signals mixed up and given the wrong one. But the chances of a solution in these cases are in general diminished.

From the primitive beginnings exemplified by Paul Revere and the sexton of the Old North Church, Lewis proceeds to develop his theory of signaling, in an attempt to encompass the phenomena of language. It will not be necessary for present purposes, however, to follow this further development. It is proposed that Lewis' approach to convention in general, together with its special case of signaling, provides an excellent conceptual framework within which to set the hypotheses presented in the preceding chapter. This application is described briefly in the next section. Following that, further specific aspects of convention and accompanying issues for research are considered.

Convention, Signaling, and the Turn System

We are now in a position to cast the turn-system hypotheses in the terms of the conceptual framework just described.

The turn system is considered to be a convention operating at least in certain face-to-face, two-person conversations between adults. This particular convention serves as a solution to the general coordination problems of avoiding simultaneous turns, and otherwise managing the development of the conversation with regard to both speaking turns and the presentation of information within turns. Similarly, the hypothesized signals are conventional in Lewis's sense. Both speaker and auditor have signals by which their states relevant to the convention may be communicated. That is, both speaker and auditor may be communicators within this specific signaling system.

In the conversations observed, the hypothesized turn system as a convention appears to be a fairly democratic one. It takes into account the states of both participants, and gives somewhat greater weight to the relevant states of the speaker, regardless of which participant happens to be the speaker at any given moment. (In contrast, it is easy to imagine other conventional solutions to the general management of speaking turns and the like that are quite different, both in the signals used and in the organization of the convention. For example, in a conversation between an admiral and a seaman, the applicable conventions may strongly favor taking the relevant states of the admiral into account.)

The proposed signal-definition rules, together with the description of the "behavioral composition" of the various signals, comprise the signaling system. Descriptions of behavioral composition serve to identify the signals in relatively physical terms (for example, paralinguistic drawl, termination of a hand gesticulation, and sociocentric sequence). Signal-definition rules serve in part to tie each signal to some state of affairs observable by the communicator (for example, degree of speaker's transition readiness indexed by number of speaker turn cues activated).

The so-called interaction rules are, in Lewis's terms, elements of the contingency plan, providing for courses of action (involving signals and–or moves) when specified states of affairs obtain. In the turn system, these interaction rules were described in terms of permissible sequences of action. As mentioned above, the set of interaction rules (or the contingency plan) for the turn system is relatively flexible in that, for most signals, the audience's response is determined not only by the signal activation (the ostensive state of the communicator), but also by the current, relevant state of the audience.

Finally, the signaling in the proposed turn system has some degree of sensitivity in that for some signals there appears to be provided a means for communicating the relative intensity of a state (termed transition readiness in Chapter 11).

SITUATION

It was noted in the discussion of convention that it must not represent a unique solution to a coordination problem. The notion of convention applies only when two or more "preferable" solutions to a given coordination problem are available. In the simplest case, convention operates to provide a single, common solution to the problem.

But there is no reason why, within a given society, there may not be more than one conventional solution to a given coordination problem. And that is in fact what we commonly find in everyday life. For example, in one's social world there may be more than one way in which individuals may greet each other.

But we also find that not all such alternative conventional solutions to a coordination problem are interchangeable. To continue the greeting example, some greetings are appropriate in some interaction situations and not in others. In any particular greeting situation, my choice of an appropriate greeting from the many available may depend upon a number of factors, such as whom I am greeting, the location of our interaction, the time of day, other persons present, and the sort of interaction I expect to have (playful, respectful, hostile, etc.).

Factors such as addressee, location of the interaction, and type of social occasion, are often said to form the "context" for the appropriate use of a given convention. In this discussion, the term "situation" will be used in the place of "context." The reasons for this replacement and a more specific definition of "situation" will be provided in the next section.

Consideration of situation is essential, not only for a participant's choosing appropriate conventions to perform in a given interaction, but also for others' interpretation of that participant's performance. It is impossible to evaluate or to assign significance to a conventional act apart from knowledge of the situation in which the act occurred. A delightful example by Goffman (1971) illustrates the wide variety of potential interpretations of what would seem to be a highly straightforward event—driving through a red traffic light—when changes in various elements of the situation surrounding the event are taken into account:

> Take, for example (with apologies to Austin), an act that is tolerably clear: a man driving through a red light. What is he doing? What has he done? (1) Where he comes from they have signs, not lights. (2) The daylight was bad and he couldn't see. (3) He's lately become colorblind. (4) He was late for work. (5) His wife is giving birth in the back seat and he'd like to get to a hospital. (6) The bank robber in the front seat is holding a gun on him and has told him to run the light. (7) He's always done this when no cops are around, figuring that the occasional cost can be distributed across the times when he isn't caught. (8) It's four o'clock in the morning, and no one is ever on the street at this hour, and in addition, he's taken a close look up and down the street to make sure his running the light is completely safe. (9) It's raining, and it's safer not to try to stop on the oil slick. (10) A policeman has waved him through. (11) His brakes gave way. (12) He just plain forgot to look at the light. (13) He's part of a funeral procession. (14) No one is about to challenge him; he's known too well for that. (15) He's an inspector testing the vigilance of the cops on duty. (16) He's driving (he claims) under a posthypnotic trance. (17) He wants to get in a race with the local cop. (18) The cop on the corner is his brother and he is putting him on. (19) Those are diplomatic plates he has. (20) The light was stuck on red, and he and the other motorists finally decided to go through it. (21) The light was changing at the time. (22) He was drunk, high. (23) His mother has a lamentable occupation, and he has a psychiatrically certifiable compulsivity in regard to red lights. (24) There was a police ambulance immediately behind, sirening to go through, and the other lane was blocked with a line of cars.
>
> So our man passed through a red light. But at his hearing when the judge asks him what he was doing running a red light, he will provide an argument as to what was really happening [p. 102 n]."

Terminology

In considering the notion of situation it will be assumed with Tyler (1969) and his fellow cognitive anthropologists that "each people has a unique system for perceiving and organizing material phenomena—things, events, behavior, and emotions [p. 3]." It is in terms of the component elements of this system for a given culture that a member of that culture will (a) decide upon appropriate actions to take; and (b) interpret the actions of others.

A set of terms is needed for discussing cultural systems. Werner (1972) has recently pointed out that an adequate working metalanguage for discussing context, or situation, has not been developed. A useful beginning, however, has been made by Geoghegan (1971). Because his carefully formalized model provides a precise definition of the terms that he proposes, these terms are adopted in the discussion to follow. The terms themselves can be briefly introduced without duplicating Geoghegan's formal treatment. In discussing the terms, examples will be drawn from Geoghegan's example based on Bisayan forms of personal address, and from other studies. Geoghegan (1971) states that "Bisayan (or Visayan) is a Philippine language in wide use among

Christian Filipinos on Mindanao and the central group of islands known as the Visayas [p. 29 n]."

Geoghegan (1971) points out that his formulation

> ... depends heavily on a basic commitment to certain ideas about how people think and about their capabilities and limitations in organizing and processing specific kinds of information. This commitment involves such fundamental notions as the itemization of information (i.e., the cognitive representation of information as discrete units and not as continuously variable magnitudes), the sequential processing of information, the tendency toward efficient cognitive systems, limitations on the amount of information, that can be processed at one time, recoding, contrast beween the states of an assessment (Axiom 1), and so on [p. 29].

With Geoghegan (1971) the discussion of terms begins with the notion of an *entity*, defined "very broadly as referring to any phenomenon that possesses a set of properties [p. 8]." Geoghegan's examples of entities within a cognitive system are Alter or addressee, social occasion, social relationship with Alter, and language used (in a bilingual or trilingual society).

Classification schemes applied to entities are termed *categorizations*. Each categorization is made up of a set of categories. In Geoghegan's Bisayan example, categorizations (together with their respective categories) applied in connection with address terms to the entity Alter are (a) relative age (younger, older, or same); (b) sex (male or female); and (c) absolute social status, or wealth (middle class—poor, or high class—wealthy). Thus, a given entity may be classified in terms of a number of categorizations.

An *assessment* involves the process of applying a categorization to an entity. For example, we may assess an Alter in terms of that Alter's relative age. All potential results of an assessment are a *state* of the assessment. The state of an assessment of the entity Alter in terms of the categorization "relative age," would be "younger," "older," and "same." The actual outcome of an assessment, expressed in terms of categories (for example, "older"), is termed a *correspondence*. Thus, ". . . a state of an assessment is interpreted as a potential result of that assessment, while a correspondence is the actual result. Or, in other words, an assessment is a kind of variable; its states are the values it may take; and a correspondence is its current value (Geoghegan, 1971, p. 11)."

The key term *situation* may now be introduced. A situation is simply the set of actual results derived from applying a set of assessments to a set of entitites. That is, a situation is a set of correspondences. In this sense, the term "situation" will replace the more familiar term "context." A situation is the result of an individual's classifying one or more entities in terms of one or more categorizations used in his culture. A situation will be said to be "formulated" or "developed" by an individual because the perceiving and classifying process is an active one.

The same sort of perceiving and classifying process defined by Geoghegan has been discussed by Gumperz (1972) in more general terms as "a two-step process in which the speaker first takes in stimuli from the outside environment, evaluating and selecting from among them in the light of his own cultural background, personal history, and what he knows about his interlocutors [p. 15]."

Geoghegan's formulation is very general, being applicable to all entities and their attendant categorizations to be found within any given cultural system. It seems entirely possible that some entities and their attendant categorizations found within a culture will not be applied by members of that culture to situations involving face-to-face interaction. An example might be a set of entities such as plants, with their categorizations (plant taxonomies). Strictly speaking, a series of terms might be introduced to refer to members of that subset of entities and categorizations that are used to develop situations applying to instances of face-to-face interaction. For example, we could speak of "interaction entities" and "interaction categorizations." However, because this discussion is concerned exclusively with face-to-face interaction, such special terms are not used, but rather understood, in the discussion to follow.

There is, however, one exception to this practice. Geoghegan's terms apply to elements of the classification scheme used by a member of a culture to perceive and organize material phenomena he encounters, as mentioned above. For the purposes of this discussion it is convenient to use a special term to denote those material phenomena that provide the stimuli for classifications of various aspects of face-to-face interaction. The term *interaction event* is used for this purpose. "Interaction event" refers to the physical aspect of face-to-face interaction. Depending on the classification scheme applied to them, elements of an interaction event might include such phenomena as (a) our member of the culture himself (Ego or participant), together with his appearance, adornment, and actions; (b) other persons perceivable by the participant, and their appearance, adornment, and actions; (c) aspects of the physical setting in which the participant finds himself; (d) the time at which the interaction event occurs (for example, a special or holy season, day or hour), and so on. These elements of the interaction event are perceived and organized in terms of appropriate entities and classifications, yielding a situation. Thus, a situation is the result of a process of classification. An interaction event is that which is so classified.

Situational Requirements

As mentioned above, more than one convention may be available within a culture to handle some aspect of the interaction (such as the greeting, or proxemic arrangement, or topic of conversation). When there is more than one such convention, the alternative conventions may not always be equally appropriate in all interactions. It is necessary, therefore, to specify for each convention those times, places, etc., when it may be appropriately used.

Accordingly, each convention will be said to have a set of *situational requirements,* describable in terms of a set of entities, categorizations, and specific categories within those categorizations. For each convention, these situational requirements state those entities, categorizations, and categories that must apply to an interaction event, in order for the convention to be appropriately used in that event.

For example, using some of Geoghegan's Bisayan categorizations and categories, assume that in a two-person interaction a given greeting is appropriately used by a participant only when both participant and partner are of the same relative age and are of the "high class—wealthy" social status. The sex categorization does not apply nor do other categorizations having to do with social setting, time, etc. The situational requirements for that particular greeting therefore consist of two entities (participant and partner, or Ego and Alter in Geoghegan's terms) and two categorizations (absolute social status, and relative age) with their respective categories: (a) participant: absolute social status (high class—wealthy); (b) partner: absolute social status (high class—wealthy); and (c) partner: relative age (same).

Choice of Appropriate Conventions

With the aid of the proposed terminology, it is now possible to consider the issue of how a participant or potential participant, confronted with some interactional event, decides on an appropriate course of action to take. (The participant need not be aware of this process, of course.) In broad outline, this decision might involve an ordered, two-step process:

1. The participant perceives and classifies the elements of the interaction event in terms of applicable entities, categorizations, and categories, thereby developing a situation for that interaction event.
2. The participant then chooses from his total repertoire of conventions some convention or set of conventions having situational requirements compatible with the situation.

An "appropriate course of action" as judged by other members of the culture would require that our participant make both an acceptable formulation of the situation, and an acceptable choice of convention(s) in terms of situational requirements.

The resulting convention-guided actions, together with the similarly based actions of the other, copresent participants, would constitute a face-to-face interaction.

Specifying Participants in Conventions

Participants and Situation

It has been stressed that a participant's developing a situation for an interaction event involves classifying a number of aspects of the interaction event. Obviously, one of the most important aspects of the interaction event has to do with the individuals participating in it. Each participant, as he formulates a situation for that interaction event, must classify two essential entities: himself and his coparticipants. Because of the classifying process involved, situations are formulated in terms, not of specific individuals, but rather of types of persons, defined according to the categorizations applying to persons in the culture.

Slots: Situational Requirements for Participants

Just as it seems necessary that a participant classify himself and his coparticipant in his formulation of the situation, so a necessary subset of the situational requirements of each convention are those requirements stipulating those persons who may appropriately use that convention. The term *slot* is adopted here to apply to that set of categorizations and categories that describe an appropriate participant in a convention.

Let it be said that there is a slot for each participant for which a convention provides. For example, a convention such as the turn system that applies to two-person conversations is stated to have two slots. Thus, the number of slots for a given convention equals the number of participants for which that convention provides. The number of slots for a convention need not, however, always be expressed as a single number. For example, a convention may apply to the handling of speaking turns when there are three to nine participants.

It seems reasonable to expect that some slots would be extremely broadly defined, including perhaps all members of the culture, while other slots would be quite narrowly defined, with the limiting case being a slot that can be filled only by a single member of the culture, such as a king or chief. Similarly, all slots for a given convention may be defined identically, so that all the appropriate participants in the convention would carry the same categorizations and categories. Such conventions might be said to have symmetrical slots. Other conventions may have asymmetrical slots, that is, slots specifying different categorizations and–or categories. A hypothetical example of a convention having asymmetrical slots (given above) was that applying to speaking turns in a conversation between an admiral and a seaman.

Conventions, Slots, and the Turn System

These notions may be applied to the formulation of the turn system described above. First, it would be an error to identify the slots for that convention with the designations "speaker" and "auditor." These designations are states of the participants which the convention is presumably designed to coordinate. This particular convention was described in terms of two slots (that is, for two-person conversations). The two slots appear to be symmetrical in that they appear to involve identical sets of categorizations and categories: the signals and rules were the same regardless of which participant was speaker or auditor. It was not necessary to tailor the turn system individually to each of the three participants who were originally studied, nor, apparently, to any of the twelve further participants who were subsequently observed in the replication study.

It is not possible at this point, however, to construct an adequate description of the turn-system slots in terms of categorizations and categories. A much larger sampling of interactions involving the proposed convention would be necessary for such a description. It is, nevertheless, possible to make some observations, based on our results and on the persons included in the study, on the sort of categories that do not apply to the convention. The convention as it stands makes no provision for such categories as (a) male–female; (b) new acquaintance–old friend; (c) undergraduate student–graduate student–faculty–university staff–nonstudent; or (d) peer–nonpeer. (Note, however, that not all possible pairings of these categories were observed.)

There are other possible categorizations of persons for which interaction data were not analyzed in terms of this convention. For example, none of the participants was kin to the other. All participants appeared to define themselves in some important sense as peers, with the exception of the therapist–client interaction. Many other sorts of asymmetrical relationships were not observed.

It seems reasonable to expect, however, that the speaking-turn convention, as it is formulated here, is not universally applicable within the culture. For example, there may be other speaking-turn conventions in which certain persons have prerogatives to speak such that they may begin a turn at any point, with the previous speaker immediately reverting to the auditor state, regardless of the presence or absence of any indication by him that he is ready to do so. Or perhaps there are conventions in which only one participant is permitted to be a speaker, all other participants being confined to communicating in the back channel. And so on.

As researchers discover contrasting conventions applying to the same general type of coordination problem (such as managing speaking turns), it will become increasingly important to define with care the slots for each such convention.

Slot, Position, and Role

The notion of slot, as developed here, refers to the specification *for a single convention* of the categorization and categories applying to an appropriate user of that convention. Slot, therefore, is not in any sense synonymous with typical usages of the term "role."

"Role" is often used to refer to some characterization of an incumbent of a position within a social structure. Gross, Mason, and McEachern (1958) observe that this characterization has been made by authors variously in terms of normative culture patterns, or patterns of behavior, or the expectations of significant others.

Gross *et al.* (1958) propose a series of definitions that differentiate the various usages of the single term "role," as well as a number of other concepts. Most relevant to this discussion are their definitions (a) of "position," as "the location of an actor or class of actors in a system of social relationships [p. 67]"; (b) of "role," as "a set of expectations applied to an incumbent of a particular position [p. 67]"; and (c) of "role behavior," as "an actual performance of an incumbent of a position which can be referred to an expectation for an incumbent of that position [p. 67]."

Although a position is primarily defined by Gross *et al.* (1958) in terms of its location within some social system, it should be possible to describe a position in terms of categorization and categories in exactly the same manner in which a slot would be. For example, it should be possible to describe the categorizations and categories that must apply to an individual at some given point in time in order for that individual to fill a specified position, such as President of the School Board in a given community, or Priest in the Roman Catholic Church, or leader of a specific street gang. These categorizations and categories for some position would define the type of person eligible to fill that position, while the social categorizations and categories describing a slot would define the type of person eligible to use a given convention.

It seems entirely possible that being an incumbent of a position may be one of the categories describing a slot for a convention. For example, within the street gang there may be prerogatives enjoyed only by the leader. Because both position and slot are specified in terms of categorizations and categories, it becomes theoretically possible to cross-index the two. To the extent that research has provided adequate descriptions of both slots and positions in terms of social categories, it would be possible to develop both (a) a list of conventions available to incumbents of a given position (given further information on partner(s), location, etc.), and (b) a list of positions whose incumbents are eligible to fill a given slot within a given position.

A cross-indexing of slots and positions would obviously and perhaps significantly be limited by two factors:

1.   A given slot might contain all the same categories as a position but also a set of further categories. In such a case that position's incumbent

would not necessarily be eligible to fill that slot. Similarly, a position might contain more categories than some slot, so that an individual eligible to fill that slot would not necessarily be eligible to fill that position.

2.   The appropriate enactment of a given convention requires not only the proper filling of one participant's slot but also the proper filling of all other slots, as well as other situational requirements of that convention.

Studies of Social Entities and Categorizations: Forms of Address

A number of studies have been designed to discover and describe elements of the situation for specific conventions. One interesting line of such studies concerns the appropriate use of various conventional forms of address. This line of research is usually considered to have begun with Brown and Ford's (1961) study of forms of address in American English. Geoghegan's example from Bisayan was based on data from a study of this sort.

Another interesting example of such a study is Friedrich's (1972) investigation of social entities and categorizations (he and others have not used these terms) applying to the appropriate use in Russian of the two second-person pronouns *ty* ("informal") and *vy* ("formal"). Friedrich gathered his data from a corpus of nineteenth-century Russian novels. He found that topics of discourse, age generation, sex and kinship status, dialect, group membership, relative jural and political authority, emotional solidarity, and other factors, were all categorizations involved in the appropriate selection of either *ty* or *vy*.

Friedrich's acute and sensitive analysis based solely on the use of only two personal pronouns suggests the wider possibilities of charting interpersonal dynamics on the basis of a more inclusive analysis of paralanguage and body motion, together with language, when the conventions applying to such behaviors are more firmly established.

Ervin-Tripp (1972) has similarly studied the categorizations and categories applying within her academic circle to the use of various forms of address, such as those involving title and last name, kin title and first name, first name, and no address term. She found about thirteen categorizations, including those relating to consideration of kinship status, relative age, generation, rank, and relationship to Ego.

Geoghegan suggests that an efficient means of portraying the formulation of a situation, as well as the matching of situation to convention, is through a flow-chart diagram of the type used for computer programming. A progressively specific formulation of a situation may be followed by reading the diagram in the same direction as the arrows.

Situation Markers

It appears that an interesting class of social phenomena exists that serves, among other things, to aid participants in their formulation of situation. In this sense, an important function of these phenomena is to aid participants in arriving at a set of appropriate conventions to bring into play in a given interaction. These phenomena may be termed *situation markers*.

Certain details of clothing, hair style, cosmetics, and other personal adornment may be especially significant in applying classifications to persons. "Uniforms" are, of course, not confined to those with formal uniform regulations, such as military or post office personnel, waitresses, or bell hops.

Similarly, the bearing and gait of a person may provide clear indication of that person's age category, state of health, specific social status, and the like. For example, the swagger of the British military officer may distinctively indicate his status to those familiar with the British military.

Appropriate or desired classification of locations may be aided by signs, architectural design, the type and arrangement of furniture, table settings, and the like. For example, the arrangement and decoration of a courtroom in the United States do not suggest to members of the culture, even to those unfamiliar with courtrooms, that informal discussions among peers or athletic contests would be typical activities within it.

A wide variety of situation markers are effectively illustrated by photographs in Ruesch and Kees (1956).

Because situations are formulated on the basis of an active classifying process by the participants, it is not possible for situation markers to determine aspects of the situation; they may only aid a participant's development of the situation. On most occasions, formulation of a situation may agree fully with the classifications suggested by the situation markers, but this is not necessarily the case. A defendant in a trial may, quite pointedly and effectively, indicate that his formulation of the situation does not agree with that of the others present. And in the evening after all others have departed, a janitor might improvise a skit or a series of impersonations for his co-workers, using the judge's bench as a stage.

It is important to note that situation markers, whether they involve the adornment or action of a person or the decoration or arrangement of objects, are themselves conventional. Situation markers meet the definitional requirements of convention. For example, they aid persons in the coordination of their respective actions. In the case of situation markers, the coordination problem is presumably that of two or more participants arriving at acceptably similar formulations of the situation. Equipped with similar formulations of situation, participants in an interaction will be able to draw from the similar repertoires of conventions.

It follows from these considerations that in two respects situation markers may be viewed as a specialized type of signal. First, situation markers seem specially adapted to the solution of a particular subset of coordination problems: that of achieving a mutually acceptable matching of respective formulations of situation between the two participants. It will be mentioned below that all signals betray, at least in part, a formulation of situation through a referencing process leading from signal to convention to situation. Nevertheless, situation markers appear somewhat specialized for this particular function.

Second, an interesting distinguishing characteristic of situation markers as signals is that they have the potential to facilitate the matching of participants' formulations of situation prior to their actually engaging in interaction and prior to their observing any other persons engaged in focused (Goffman, 1967), face-to-face interaction. Further, once an interaction begins the situation markers may continue to provide a signal independently of that interaction. In contrast, other signals, such as those used by Paul Revere and the sexton, as well as those proposed for the turn system, require for their use the assumption that the two participants are already joined in interaction.

Finally, it may be noted that situation markers may be either one-sided or two-sided signals. A situation marker may be a one-sided signal facilitating coordination of action between members of the audience. An example of such a one-sided situation marker might be the decoration and arrangement of a courtroom, as designed by the architect. These features presumably help facilitate the proper selection of conventions by participants in the judicial proceedings, all of whom would be the audience in this case. However, the decoration of a participant's home or the manner of a participant's attire may be considered to be situation markers that are two-sided signals in which the participant is the communicator.

Variation Among Conventions
in Terms of Their Situational Requirements

It will become apparent that there may be variation among the respective situational requirements of different conventions. Brief consideration is given here to three mutually independent continua along which conventions may vary in terms of their situational requirements. These three continua are: (a) members of the culture included in the situational requirements; (b) number of slots for which the convention provides; and (c) specificity of the situational requirements.

Local versus General Conventions

It is typical to think of conventions as highly general practices involving all members of the culture, such as language and kinship systems. However, consistent with the analysis presented in this chapter, conventions may arise among members of subcultural groups, as large as those composed of moieties or of major socioeconomic groups; or as small as work or social groups, neighborhoods, and families, with the limiting case being a single two-person group within a culture.

Thus, one may speak of situational requirements of conventions as ranging along a continuum relating to the percentage of members of the culture included in the situation, that is, percentage of members of the culture to which the convention applies. The anchor points for such a continuum may be labeled "general" and "local."

It is not difficult to imagine conventions potentially limited to some single two-person group within a given culture—that is, conventions at the extreme local end of the continuum. To illustrate such an entirely local convention, Lewis (1969) cites Hume's (1893) example of two persons rowing a boat. In this case, suitable progress can only be made if both adopt the convention of rowing in rhythm. Once they have mutually hit upon a suitable rhythm (regardless of how they managed to do it), a precedent is established. At that point mutual expectations, together with the mutual advantage to be derived from maintaining the rhythm, may take over to establish the convention.

Personal experience suggests that small children often initiate and take pleasure in establishing small-scale, conventional routines with each other or with adults. Some of these conventions may be highly idiosyncratic, that is, localized. Consider the following report from a father:

> Every time my 2½ year-old son sees me coming down the stairs with a basket of laundry to be washed, he asks, 'Can I watch you?' and I say, 'Yes.' He then goes with me into the laundry room and is hoisted up to sit on the dryer (next to the washing machine).
>
> He and I then proceed to put the laundry into the washing machine. As I measure out the soap, he asks and is permitted to put the 'sugar' into the machine. I then set the controls, and he pulls the knob that starts the water flowing into the machine. After I close the lid, he crawls on the washing machine to inspect the fishing rod that is stored behind it. He then stands and, reaching up, pulls the cord that turns on a near-by light. He then asks me if I want it turned off again, and I say 'Yes.' After he turns it off, he climbs from the washer onto my back and is carried out of the laundry room.

It would be surprising if this informally described convention is not an entirely local one. In addition, it did not last very long: roughly six months. (There is, or course, no necessary relationship between the degree to which a convention is localized and its tendency to change or disappear over time.) It is perhaps of some interest that this particular convention was reported to be thoroughly disrupted when there was a significant deviation from it. For example, on one occasion when liquid, instead of powdered, soap was used, and the child was not allowed to put it in, he seemed to forget all the successive steps in the convention (except for being carried out). Experience suggests that similar conventions, sometimes referred to by parents as "rituals," often arise with small children in association with frequently repeated actions, such as taking baths, getting dressed, and going to bed.

A large subcultural group of particular interest is the family. Most of family interaction may be based on relatively general cultural conventions. On the other hand, it is entirely possible that there may be considerable variation among families in the conventions adopted to handle recurring family situations. For example, Gross, Mason, and McEachern (1958) cite Roberts's (1951) conclusion from his work on Ramah Navaho households, that "the hypothesis that every small group defines an independent and unique group-ordered culture has been supported [p. 77]." It is a matter for empirical research to document the extent to which such local variation occurs, and the differential implications of these local conventions—along with the more general ones—for such aspects of family life as the stability of marriages and the course of child rearing.

Conventions that are highly localized may have great importance for such phenomena as processes of face-to-face interaction in longer term relationships, and in such areas as more idiographic research on individual differences. But for statistically oriented research involving either individual or group differences, it would appear that highly localized conventions might often constitute a confusing source of variance.

Logically, it seems reasonable to assume that more local conventions may be related in two major ways to more general ones: (a) a more local convention may simply represent some modification on a more general convention; and (b) a more local convention may be analytically independent of more general conventions, either having arisen to meet a relatively idiosyncratic local situation, or being a relatively novel solution to a coordination problem. This distinction is entirely logical; it remains for empirical investigation to validate its meaningfulness.

Number of Slots

A second continuum along which conventions may be arranged in terms of their situational requirements is that related to the number of slots for which the requirements provide. This continuum would range from two-person groups on one end, to very large gatherings on the other. This continuum is not to be confused with that of local versus general conventions. For example, a convention may arise to handle coordination problems encountered only in two-person groups, but this convention is employed by every two-person group occurring in the culture. It, accordingly, would be considered among the most general of conventions, even though it applies to the minimum-sized group.

A special case is the possibility of a rule-governed regularity in action of a single person. In addition, this regularity may be highly localized. For example, an observer of animal behavior devises a private system of notation to use in rapidly recording his observations. Or, an individual who lives alone follows a regular sequence of actions from the point of waking up in the morning, through the completion of breakfast. On the other hand, the regularity may be a general one in the culture and not local. Chapple (1970) provides an example of such a single-person, general convention: "When an Eskimo fashions a harpoon head out of walrus ivory, the technology prescribes the order of actions and no other person need necessarily be involved [p. 18]."

It is not entirely clear whether or not such single-person regularities may be properly included within the general notion of convention. They would not be so included on the analysis presented here. Shwayder (1965) argues that they should be. In any event, it is clear that regularities of this sort are common and are of potential interest to researchers.

Diversity versus Specificity

This continuum relates to the number of different interaction events to which the convention applies. Some conventions may be found to be highly diverse, operating wherever persons interact with each other (in a given culture), while other conventions may apply only to highly specific situations, such as Ascot race track when the Queen is present. Careful description of the situational requirements for a given convention, as these requirements are documented, seems to be crucial to the proper understanding of convention-based actions. It goes without saying that investigators expecting to find regularities in actions introduced by a given convention will be disappointed if they seek those regularities in situations in which the convention does not operate.

The Dynamics of Situation

It has been suggested that a participant, drawing on a potentially wide variety of types of information, develops an initial formulation of situation, possibly prior to any specific interaction with his partner. This situation would presumably involve classifying himself, his partner in the interaction, the type of relationship between them, their location, others present, and other elements.

On the basis of his respective situation, each participant selects from the repertoire of conventions available to him an appropriate set to use in that particular interaction. And at some moment one participant initiates the first convention-based action. Our participants are now in interaction. This interaction may be viewed from the specialized perspective of situation.

Disclosure and Ratification of Situation

Given the situational requirements of conventions, it is inevitable that disclosure of a participant's formulation of the situation begins at the moment of his first convention-based action. As soon as that convention is accurately recognized by the partner (presumably immediately in most cases), the situational requirements for that convention also become apparent, thus revealing some part of the participant's situation. In this manner, from a participant's first convention-based act through the termination of the interaction, that participant's classification of various elements of the social event is continuously being displayed.

Upon disclosure of a participant's situation, an immediate issue has to do with whether or not there is acceptable matching of the respective situations by the two participants. The definition of "acceptable" with respective to this matching, may be made in terms of the participants' subjective reactions, as manifested in their actions in the interaction. Just as disclosure of a participant's situation begins with his first convention-based action, so his partner's acceptance or rejection of that situation, as well as the partner's own situation, begins at the moment of his first response to that action.

For example, let us assume that a participant's first convention-based actions in an interaction consist of a greeting that includes some form of address. These actions should be recognizable by the partner as elements of specific conventions. Recognition of the operative conventions initiated by the participant carries two important implications for the partner:

1.   The participant has chosen a specific slot within the convention, leaving another specific slot to the partner.
2.   The participant has formulated the situation in terms of a specific set of entities, categorizations, and categories.

An obvious indication of the partner's acceptance of these implications would be his simply responding with actions conforming to the slot indicated for him to fill within that same convention. On the other hand, this process need not proceed so smoothly. Friedrich (1972) provides vivid examples in his data of interactions in which the respective situations of the two participants clearly do not match. One of his less subtle examples follows, preceded by Friedrich's (1972) general description of the conventions involved:

> All classes of Russians interjected "brother," "little mother," and other terms when consciously or subconsciously trying to create an informal, congenial atmosphere with nonrelatives. And there were numerous combinations of proper names, ranging from nicknames, to diminutives, to the first name alone, to the first name plus a fixed epithet ("Mikhail the Wolf"), to the name plus an informal or formal patronymic (Ivanych as against Ivanovich), and so on up the line. These means of address had to be calibrated with each other. For example, "Aren't *ty* joking, Foma?" "In the first place, I am not *ty* . . . but *vy*, and don't forget it; and not Foma, but Foma Fomich" (Dostojevsky, *Stepanchikovo Village*, 472) [pp. 274–275].

To the extent that a partner responds in a manner indicating acceptance of the participant's situation, the participant's situation may be said to be *ratified* (Goffman, 1967, pp. 34 ff.). Because situations involve a number of assessments, there may be agreement or disagreement with any one or more of these assessments. In this sense, it is possible that ratification is a matter of degrees, rather than an all-or-none affair. Goffman (1971) discusses special "rituals of ratification," attending certain changes in the situation.

Changing Formulations of Situation

Let us assume for purposes of discussion that the participants in a given interaction have indeed found that their respective situations are mutually acceptable. There is no reason to believe that these participants are irrevocably committed throughout their interaction to these initial situations. Although they might elect to stay solidly with the initial situations, there seem to be at least two interesting ways in which an initial situation can be changed in the course of a single interaction.

One of these ways would be to modify the initial situation by adding or subtracting entities and–or categorizations applied to the social event. A second way of changing the initial formulation would be by making outright shifts in a correspondence (the actual result of an assessment). That is, a change is made in the categories selected from the applicable categories. Both of these methods of changing a situation are discussed in greater detail below.

If initial situations may be changed, then there seems to be no reason why any subsequent situation might not similarly be changed. In this sense, it becomes possible to regard situation as a dynamic affair, with the potential of accurately reflecting changes, both subtle and gross, in the participants' respective perceptions of various aspects of the interaction.

To illustrate some points on the process and effects of changing situations, data will be drawn from Ervin-Tripp's (1972) Fig. 7.1, "American address." This figure presents a flow chart of assessments involved in decisions regarding some American forms of address, as mentioned above. In developing Fig. 7.1, Ervin-Tripp uses a somewhat simplified version of Geoghegan's general model, in that (a) entities and categorizations are not distinguished in the chart (but may be inferred from it); and (b) categories for each categorization are confined to binary choices (+ or –).

Table 12.1 has been prepared from Ervin-Tripp's Fig. 7.1 by simply tracing the flow-chart paths leading to the following address forms: ϕ (no form used); kin title plus first name; and first name. (Ervin-Tripp presents data on three other address forms.) Despite the manner of preparation of Table 12.1, it should be regarded merely as an illustration for purposes of discussion, adapted from Ervin-Tripp's data, and not as a representation of her data. Each plus and minus in the table represents in yes–no terms a correspondence (in Geoghegan's sense) with respect to the entity-categorization indicated in each row. Each column in the table represents a distinct situation. Columns a–e represent the variety of situations in which a first name is appropriately used. Column f represents the single situation in which kin-title-plus-first name is appropriately used, and Column g represents the single situation in which no explicit address form is appropriately used.

Shifting a Correspondence

An immediately apparent way in which a situation may be changed would be that of changing a correspondence: the value assigned to a given assessment of entity and categorization. Table 12.1 suggests that a change in any one correspondence potentially results in (a) an entirely different form of address in the interaction, and, by extension, (b) an entirely different set of other conventions.

TABLE 12.1
Entities and Categorizations Applying to Certain
Address Forms as Reported by Ervin-Tripp (1972)

Entities and categorizations	First name					Kin title + first name (f)	ϕ (No address form used) (g)
	(a)	(b)	(c)	(d)	(e)		
Adult	−	+	+	+	+	+	−
Status-marked setting	−	−	−	−	−		
Name known	+	+	+	+	+	+	−
Kin		+	+	−	−	+	
Friend or colleague				+	+		
Alter higher rank				−	+		
Alter 15 years older				−			
Dispensation					+		
Ascending generation		+	−			+	
Older		−				+	

Obviously, not all assessments would be equally susceptible to change. Some assessments would appear to be relatively fixed, both for any single interaction, and potentially for more than one interaction between two given participants. Such relatively fixed assessments might involve such entity categorizations as relative ages, kinship status, and whether or not the generation was ascending.

On the other hand, correspondences for other entity categorizations may be free to shift for any given pair of participants during the course of a single interaction and–or between interactions. Examples of these more flexible entity categorizations might be status-marked setting and dispensation. Friedrich (1972) shows in his data how entity categorizations such as emotional solidarity might shift frequently during the course of a single interaction. Similarly, categorizations applying to an entity such as "type of interaction" (which might include categories such as joking, formal, hostile, polite, etc.) would also potentially be subject to this type of shifting.

、 It follows from the nature of flow-chart diagrams that the effect of shifting any single correspondence depends (a) on the organization of the entire set of assessments making up a situation; and (b) on the relationship of one situation to another. On the basis of these two factors, there is at least theoretically a continuum upon which assessments may be placed, relating to the reverberations in the repertoire of conventions appropriately used in an interaction caused by a change in the associated correspondence. The effects of shifting a correspondence located nearer the entry point of the diagram are potentially extensive, introducing dramatic changes in the assessments in-volved in developing a situation, and thus potentially dramatic changes in the conventions appropriately used within that interaction. On the other hand, the effect of shifting correspondences located nearer the termination of the flow-chart path may be slight, introducing more subtle, but perhaps no less meaningful changes in the situation and its corresponding conventions.

Modifying the Formulation of Situations

It seems theoretically possible to effect change in a prevailing situation without any outright shift in correspondences. This alternative means of changing the situation would be through adding assessments to, or subtract-ing them from, those involved in the prevailing situation. Let us consider the case of adding assessments to the situation, letting the reverse of this discus-sion be implied for subtracting assessments. Adding assessments might occur (a) because the conventions indicating the prevailing situation were ambigu-ous; and–or (b) because the original situation might be further specified through the use of additional social categories.

A clear case of ambiguous specification of situations by a convention may be found in Table 12.1 with respect to the use of first name. The table indi-cates that such a usage, considered alone, is consistent with five different sit-uations (Columns a–e). Based solely upon consideration of use of first name by a participant, it would not be clear whether or not the addressee was con-sidered by the participants to be adult, older, kin, of ascending generation, and so on. To the extent to which these ambiguities are to be clarified on the basis of participant's actions, it would be necessary to consider the situations implied by other conventions used by the participant, in addition to that re-garding form of address.

As considered above in the discussion of generality–specificity of conven-tions, there may be variation among conventions in the number of assess-ments included in their situations. An example of this may be found in Table 12.1 when the situation for the zero address term is contrasted with that for kin-title plus first name. (Neither of these address forms is ambiguous in the sense used immediately above.) The number of assessments applying to the use of the zero address term is two, while the use of kin-title-plus-first name requires six assessments. If the zero address term is used by a participant, he might subsequently bring into play other conventions that carry a greater number of assessments in their respective situations, thereby indicating a more specific situation.

Developments in the formulation of situation have been discussed in terms of decreasing ambiguity or of increasing specificity. Both of these modifica-tions of some previous situation have been in the direction of more sharply defining the situation. There is no theoretical reason, however, why modifi-cation of the situation might not proceed in the opposite direction along the two continua: increasing ambiguity, or decreasing specificity. The actual occurrence and implications for the interaction of modifications in either direction along these two continua are empirical matters. Research on these phenomena appears to have the potential of providing highly specific and subtle information on the course of the interactions studied.

Conclusion: Dynamics of Situation

Consideration has been given to ways in which a participant's perception of various aspects of an interaction event—that is, his formulation of situation—might change. Two general types of change were suggested: (a) shifting the values assigned to one or more assessments, and (b) modifying the situation by adding or subtracting assessments. Although for purposes of discussion these two types of change were treated separately, it seems reasonable to expect that in actual interaction, changes involving simultaneous use of both types of change might commonly be found.

Because conventions are indexed according to the situations in which they are appropriately used, both a participant's prevailing formulation of the situation, and his changes in this formulation, are potentially readable through his convention-based actions. This potential visibility of certain perceptions is of immediate practical value to his partner in the interaction, because of the wealth of information conveyed concerning the participant's perceptions of himself, the partner, the relationship between them, the type of interaction they are engaged in, and the like. With respect both to the initial formulation of situation and to any possible changes in that formulation by each participant, the requirement of ratification by the partner applies.

On this analysis, all of these phenomena are at least in principle accessible to the investigator of face-to-face interaction, subject to two empirical limitations and one theoretical one. Empirically, it is obvious that the conventions must be well formulated with regard to both (a) their constituent elements (actions, signals, and rules and the like); and (b) situations in which they are appropriately used. The theoretical limitation lies in the fact that underlying formulations of situation are not uniquely specifiable to the extent that the conventions observed in the interaction are ambiguous.

VARIATION IN CONVENTION-BASED ACTIONS

No convention rigidly constrains every detail of the actions to which it applies. There is always room for variation in the manner in which a given convention is actually performed. To behave in accordance with a convention is not to be deprived of individual choice and initiative.

This observation has been made by other authors. For example, Hayek (1962) comments:

> The rules of which we are speaking, however, generally control or circumscribe only certain aspects of concrete actions by providing a general schema which is then adapted to the particular circumstances. They will often merely determine the limit or range of possibilities within which the choice is consciously made. . . . Like scientific laws, the rules which guide an individual's action are better seen as determining what he will not do rather than what he will do [p.35].

Similarly Lewis (1969) writes: "No convention determines every detail of behavior. . . .[A given convention] restricts behavior without removing all choice. There is more choice, and more important choice [in some cases] than in others; but there is no difference in kind [p. 51]."

Lewis (1969) provides the following example. "If using Welsh is to be a convention, it must be a regularity in behavior. It is not, of course, a regularity that fully determines a Welshman's behavior. He can say a variety of things, or remain silent, and he can respond to utterances in a variety of ways, and still be conforming to the conventional regularity [p. 50]."

There are at least four sources of variation in the performance of a given convention: (a) the manner in which signals in the convention are defined; (b) permissible variation in the display of signals; (c) the availability of response alternatives within the convention's contingency plans; and (d) violation of the convention. Discussion of these sources of variation will be based on examples drawn from the proposed convention for speaking turns.

Definition of Signals

It does not seem reasonable to expect that the definition of a signal leaves no room for variation in the actions to which it applies. At least, such exhaustive definition did not appear to be necessary with respect to turn signals. For example, the definition of the gesticulation signal may be considered.

Recognition of the gesticulation signal as defined above requires, broadly speaking, a sequence of two discrete discriminations: (a) that of at least one hand being tensed, or of at least one hand and arm being in motion, as opposed to being at rest; and (b) if motion is noticed, then the identification of that motion as a gesticulation, as opposed to a self- or object–adaptor.

The discriminations required for the proper recognition of the gesticulation signal within the convention do not require taking into account many aspects of hand and arm movement that are physiologically possible and that may have considerable importance for the interaction. For example, not considered in the definition of the signal are such factors as: (a) the actual gesture employed; (b) the entire range of actions associated with self- and object–adaptors and other hand activity possible outside the signal; (c) whether one or both arms are used, and if one is, which one; and (d) various parakinesic (Birdwhistell, 1971) aspects of the gesture, such as extent or intensity.

Thus, a speaker in a conversation may be in full conformity to the gesticulation–signal aspect of the proposed speaking-turn convention and still retain considerable freedom of action with respect to hand–arm movements, both when the signal is active and when it is not. This is not to say, however, that if an aspect of gesturing is irrelevant to the definition of the gesticulation signal, that aspect is similarly irrelevant in all other respects in the interaction. It is reasonable to assume, for example, that other conventions have something to say about the type of gesture used, its parakinesic aspects, its location in the stream of interaction, the type and location of self- or object–adaptors, and so on.

Similar analyses might be made of other signals within the proposed turn convention and presumably of other convention-based actions in everyday life.

Permissible Variation in the Display of Signals

At several points within the proposed speaking-turn convention there are various parameters along which display of a given signal may vary. Here are some immediately apparent parameters:

1.   Variation is possible in the repertoires of cues and signals used in the interaction, drawn from larger sets of cues and of signals available within the convention. For example, a participant might never use some of the six turn cues or might never use the gesticulation signal.

2.   Variation is possible in the use of cues and signals in characteristic sequences or simultaneous clusters. For example, a participant might tend to activate certain combinations of turn cues more frequently than others. Thus, the combination of (a) drawl, (b) intonation, and (c) sociocentric sequence, might be found more frequently activated by a participant than would be predicted on the basis of the frequency of activation of each individual cue.

3.   ·Variation is possible in the relative frequency or extent of use of cues or signals. For example, participants might vary in the proportion of their speaking time that they use the gesticulation signal, or in the frequency with which they use sociocentric sequences, or in the frequency and–or duration of head nods.

Response Alternatives

It was said that certain turn signals were permissive, not coercive. Participants were apparently free to choose whether or not to respond with given signals and–or actions (such as attempts to take the turn) at specific points in the stream of action of the partner. For example, some participants might have the tendency to claim the speaking turn after certain cues or only after the activation of very large numbers of turn cues.

It was this type of permissible variation in response alternatives that was described in Chapter 11 as "optional sequences of action." The apparent operation of this type of optionality lay behind the way the research problem was formulated for turn-system signals. For example, for the speaker within-turn signal the problem was not to predict the occurrence of auditor back channels. Rather, as stated in Chapter 11, the problem was defined as that of finding some set of speaker cues that consistently preceded on a nonchance level the auditor back-channel signal.

Violation

Finally, variation is possible in the degree to which interactants violated the speaking-turn convention. For example, some participants might have a tendency to disregard the partner's activation of the gesticulation signal, or to fail to yield the speaking turn after the partner claimed the turn in response to a turn signal. The notion of violation of convention will be considered further in the next main section.

Significance of Variation in Performing Conventions

Given the variations possible in the performing of conventions, what significance might a variation have? To what extent might a variation be considered "free," having no noticeable significance in the interaction, as opposed to "bound," having appreciable significance?

As has been mentioned at several points above, on this analysis there are two general effects an action may have in interaction: an effect on the course of the interaction itself, and an effect on the impressions of all those in a position to observe the interaction directly, and potentially on the impressions of those who later hear about it. In this section the discussion will focus on effects on the course of the interaction. In order to assess the interactional significance of a given variation in the performance of a convention, several factors would have to be considered. These would include at least: (a) the type of variation involved; (b) the interaction rules attaching to the actions (including signals and cues) involved in the variation; and (c) the partner's tendency to respond to those actions.

For example, for a given conversation we may ask what sort of significance there might be in variation of (a) the extent to which (b) the gesticulation signal within the speaking-turn convention is used, (c) given the partner's strict observance of the interaction rules attaching to that signal. On the basis of the turn convention as presently formulated, and given the partner's strict observance, as long as the speaker keeps the gesticulation signal activated, the auditor is prevented from claiming the speaking turn. Thus, in the extreme case, through continuous use of the gesticulation signal a speaker might turn a potential dialogue into a monologue. (Research may show, however, other interesting effects stemming from variations such as extensive use of the gesticulation signal. For example, there may be found for some auditors an increasing tendency to violate the interaction rule and claim the turn, as the signal continues in heavy use. In this manner, a given type of variation by a participant may be found to have effects on the partner's tendency to respond over the course of an interaction.)

Similarly, if a given participant as auditor has a strong tendency to attempt to take the speaking turn in response to the activation of very low numbers of turn cues by the speaker, then the effect of this tendency would probably be at the least an increase in the number of speaking turns in the conversation, given the speaker's strict observance of the applicable interaction rules. It would be of interest to researchers, however, to observe whether or not this tendency had certain effects on the partner as speaker, such as an increased use of the gesticulation signal or an increased tendency to fail to yield the turn in response to the auditor's claims.

In contrast, as the speaking-turn convention is presently formulated, there can be no comparable impact on the conversation as a result of a speaker's tending to activate certain turn cues as opposed to others. All of these cues are apparently equivalent components of the turn signal. (There might, of course, be other conventions applying to the use of actions comprising the turn cues, so that predominant use of certain cues might acquire a significance apart from the turn system.)

With respect to the formation of impressions, and using the gesticulation signal as an example once again, given the interaction rules attaching to the signal, a more continually gesticulating speaker might be considered to be more dominant or aggressive or the like, than a speaker who makes less use of this signal. It is possible, however, that impressions may be formed as a result of a given variation in the performing of a convention, even when that variation does not have observable effects on the course of the interaction. For example, a partner through "civil inattention" (Goffman, 1963, 1971) may ostensibly ignore a given type of variation by a participant, even while forming impressions of that participant.

Limits on Variation in the Performance of Conventions

The speaking-turn convention as presently formulated does not specify limits within which the several types of variation may appropriately occur. It does not seem reasonable, however, to expect that conventions have nothing to say with regard to such limits on convention-related action. Rather, upper and lower bounds for specific types of variation may be set by convention. An act that involves exceeding any one of these various conventional limits would, to that extent, constitute a violation of the convention.

As Linton (1945) suggests, variation in convention-related actions along various parameters ". . . will ordinarily be found to fall within certain easily recognizable limits. . . .Behaviors which fall within the effective range will be considered normal, while those which fall outside of it will be regarded as queer and, frequently, as reprehensible [pp. 44–45]."

Generating Information
on Variation in the Performance of Conventions

It may be worth noting at this point that the observation of variation in the performance of convention implies making a comparison between at least two different observations of action, each observation being over a specified stretch of interaction, defined in terms of time or interactional events. The type of comparison made in order to yield information on action variation would seem to be limited only by the interests, acuity, and resources of the observer.

Comparisons may be made between observations of action during stretches of interaction, either within a single interaction, or in two or more interactions. Similarly, comparisons may be made between different observations of the action of a single participant, or between observations of two or more participants (including the case of simultaneous actions on the part of two or more participants, for example, Duncan & Niederehe, 1974). This discussion of variation is intended to be general with respect to the type of comparison made.

VIOLATION OF CONVENTIONS

The data presented in Chapter 11 suggested that, while regularities in actions attributable to the hypothesized turn system were strong, they were not perfect. There were some clear instances in the observed conversations in which the proposed turn-system rules were not followed. To the extent that the turn system or any other proposed convention is properly formulated, these failures to behave in accordance with the rules may be interpreted as violations. The discussion to this point suggests two somewhat different ways a convention may be violated: (a) a violation of an interaction rule; and (b) exceeding the permissible limits on variation in the performance of a convention. There are probably other types of violation.

In this general discussion of the violation of conventions, it is perhaps prudent to stick close to the basics. Respect for this topic is reinforced by Goffman's (1971) example of the running of a red traffic light, quoted above. That example illustrates graphically that there is considerable potential for complexity even in a seemingly straightforward rule violation.

It will be recalled that conventions are considered to be embodied cognitively as systems of expectation. I follow a given convention because I expect that other parties to the convention have a reasonable expectation that I do so, and so on. That is, I believe they may reasonably believe that I ought to follow the convention. In this sense, conventions may be seen as at least one type of norm. In Lewis's (1969) terms, "Any convention is, by definition, a norm which there is some presumption that one ought to conform to [p. 99]." Feather (1971), considering cognitive structure, sounds a similar note: ". . . the underlying abstract structures involved in the representation of social reality have a *normative* function. They specify sets of rules making up internally consistent theories about what *ought* to be the case in any given social situation that has been experienced over time [p. 374, original italics]."

Lewis (1969) extends the argument to claim that a convention "is also, by definition, a socially enforced norm: one is expected to conform, and failure to conform tends to evoke unfavorable responses from others [p. 99]." This is due to the advantage attached to the following of conventions. My use of a convention is held to be both to my advantage and to the advantage of other parties to the convention. The failure to conform can only be construed as an action contrary to our mutual advantage. If I am seen failing to conform to a convention, other parties to the convention "will be surprised, and they will tend to explain my conduct discreditably. The poor opinions they form of me, and their reproaches, punishment, and distrust are the unfavorable responses I have evoked by my failure to conform to the convention (Lewis, 1969, p. 99)."

Goffman (1967) expresses a similar notion: "In general then, when a rule of conduct is broken we find that two individuals run the risk of becoming discredited: one with an obligation, who should have governed himself by the rule; the other with an expectation, who should have been treated in a particular way because of this governance. Both actor and recipient are threatened [p. 51]."

Thus, on this analysis all conventions carry a normative aspect, but there is much to know about the nature and use of conventions beyond this normative aspect. For this reason, the terms "convention" and "norm" are not coextensive.

Certainly, conventions may vary enormously in the strength of their attending normative aspect and in the type of social censure applied when a convention is violated. For some conventions, there may merely be entirely implicit disapproval, perhaps quickly forgotten if the violation is not repeated, or quietly accumulated if it is. On the other hand, for other conventions there may be loud public outcry and invocation of civil authorities. Penalties may range from personal disfavor to the most stringent punishment.

The effects of violation of convention may include directly observable action, less extreme than public outcry or invocation of civil authority. For example, Scheflen (1963, 1968) mentions the notion of "monitors," actions presumably functioning to express disapproval of some perceived violation of appropriate conduct, with the aim of correcting that violation. Apart from the possibility of specific monitors, other effects on the respective actions of the participants, and thus on the course of the interaction itself, may be uncovered as a result of careful empirical study. One less subtle effect on the interaction would be a termination of that interaction, a phenomenon several investigators have observed in connection with presumed violations of conventions (Ellsworth, Carlsmith, & Henson, 1972; Felipe & Sommer, 1966).

Regardless of whether or not a violation of convention has some directly observable effect, it seems inevitable on this analysis that such violation will entail some effect on the partner's opinion of the violator, either to change or to confirm the opinion existing just prior to the violation. This effect might be on one or more of the partner's assessments with respect to the violator, or on the degree to which the partner judges the violator to possess some attribute, such as friendliness. Other actions by a participant, not entailing violation, might also have the effect of confirming or changing the partner's opinions. The distinctive result of a participant's violation of a convention held by the participant would simply be that the effect(s) would be uniformly negative with respect to that participant.

These considerations suggest that violation of convention constitutes a potentially complex phenomenon, worthy of study in its own right. In any event, information on violation is clearly essential to the complete description and understanding of any given convention.

DESCRIPTION OF CONVENTIONS

For research purposes, what would constitute a complete description of a convention or of a related set of conventions? Stated differently, what would be the elements of an entry for a convention in a dictionary of conventions— a conventionary, as it were? Clearly, given the present state of development of this area, this question cannot now be answered with authority. But, on the basis of the discussion to this point, it is possible to suggest certain elements that would most likely be a part of such a description. The following broad aspects of convention have been considered in this chapter: (a) convention substance and organization; (b) situation; (c) variation in convention-related actions; and (d) effects of violation of convention. These aspects will be briefly summarized below.

Convention Substance and Organization

The material presented in Chapter 11 was an attempt to describe the substance and organization of some conventions related to speaking-turn phenomena. The convention "substance" detailed in Chapter 11 included such elements as postulated states, hypothesized states, hypothesized signals and cues, definitions of signal and cue display and activity, and other actions related to the convention (such as attempts to take the speaking turn). The "organization" of the convention was stated in terms of "rules" describing hypothesized relationships between the various elements of substance: states, signals, etc. In this respect, signal-definition rules were distinguished from interaction rules. A signal-definition rule was said to describe the relationship between (a) a given signal; and (b) either another signal, or some state associated with the convention. An interaction rule was said to describe permissible sequences of action within the convention, given the currently active signal(s) and in some cases certain preceding actions by the participants. Certainly inclusion of a given convention's substance and organization is essential to its adequate description.

Given the present paucity of empirical results, it seems premature to advocate any single approach to describing the various elements of substance and of the organization of a convention. There is no compelling reason at this point to model the description of either rules or substantial elements after the prevailing practices in other fields, such as linguistics. There needs to be more information on the actual descriptive requirements of various conventions. This consideration influenced the decision not to present the turn system in a more formalized manner.

In Part III systematic efforts to describe the conventions relating to speaking-turn phenomena did not extend beyond those conventions' substance and organization. However, the discussion in this chapter suggests that there is a variety of other types of information, potentially significant to the understanding of the use of convention in face-to-face interaction. These further elements will be considered next.

Situation

It seems reasonable to expect that many conventions may not be appropriately used by all members of a culture or in all occurring social occasions. Rather, these conventions will be restricted to certain participants who are interacting with certain partners in certain social occasions. These restrictions were termed *situational requirements* in the discussion. It was said that a participant formulates the situation for himself by classifying himself, his partner, and other elements of the interaction event in terms of a set of applicable social categorizations. The results of this classifying process are then matched with the situational requirements of various conventions, in order to select an appropriate set of conventions for use in that interaction event.

As mentioned in the discussion, the systematic study of such simple conventions as those applying to forms of American address and the second-person pronoun forms in Russian, have produced interesting information both on the classification systems applied by the users of these forms and on the situational requirements for each of the particular forms. Clearly, information on its situational requirements must be included in any complete description of a convention or set of interrelated conventions.

Variation in Convention-Related Actions

It was emphasized that no convention constrains every detail of the actions to which it applies. Substantial elements of a convention, such as signals, may be defined in ways that leave considerable room for variation in their enactment. And the rules associated with these substantial elements may provide a participant with a choice of two or more alternative actions at various points in the performance of the convention.

At the same time, it is reasonable to expect that there are limits on the variation permissible within a convention. For example, to respond in the back channel is an action that a participant may take at points of his choosing. But to so respond virtually never, or almost continually, probably lies outside the convention's appropriate limits for rate of back-channel response. Thus, it becomes necessary to describe as accurately as possible the limits for important kinds of variation with a convention.

Effects of Violation of Convention

In the terms of this discussion there are two distinguishable ways a convention can be violated: (a) acting in a way directly contrary to the convention's rules; and (b) exceeding in the performance of a convention the limits on permissible variation along one or more dimensions. Because it was held that all conventions have a normative aspect attaching to their proper performance, it becomes necessary to include in any complete description of a convention the effects attending violation of these norms.

It was suggested that violation of convention by a participant always results in some negative effect on the partner's opinion of the violator (provided that the partner holds to the convention in question). This effect may be either to change or to confirm the opinion existing just prior to the violation.

In some cases violation of a convention may be observed to have regular effects, perhaps on the ensuing interaction. If such were the case, it would be of great relevance to the description of the convention.

Conclusion

It does not seem likely that any single study would provide all of the information discussed above for any single convention or set of related conventions. This is in part because different research strategies would probably be necessary to generate the several different types of information. More likely, particular studies might be designed to gather information on one of the several aspects of convention, such as violation, or situation, and the like. Such a study might gather this selected information on more than one convention. In any event, understanding of face-to-face interaction stands to gain much, both from "small, ideally cumulative extensions in the borders of the known" (Adams, 1974, p. 256), and from innovative breakthroughs in technique, analytic method, or conception.

INTERACTION STRATEGY

The discussion to this point has focused on convention as an important source of regularity in the actions observable in face-to-face interaction. But no adequate description of face-to-face interaction can be built on the basis of convention alone. In this section another important source of regularity in interaction will be considered: patterns of action resulting from a participant's exercising choice and initiative with respect to the options provided by convention. The term used to denote descriptions of these patterns will be *interaction strategy*.

Convention and Interaction Strategy

The notion of interaction strategy arises directly as a consequence of the formulation of convention presented in this chapter. It will be held that the performance of a convention inevitably involves a concomitant interaction strategy. This necessary connection exists because of the options available both in the initial formulation of situation (and in any subsequent dynamics of situation), and in the actual performance of convention. These options will be considered in greater detail below. Given the degrees of freedom available in the formulation of situation and in the performing of a convention, any performance of a convention commits the participant to a choice on each of the available options. (Of course, this logically necessary choice need not be a conscious one.) The data for the study of interaction strategy are provided by the description both of the conventions actually performed, and of option-related actions in the performance(s) of a convention or of some set of related conventions, either within a single interaction or in more than one interaction.

Convention was discussed in terms of cooperation: persons voluntarily achieving coordination of action, the results of that coordination being seen as mutually beneficial in some respect. In contrast, interaction strategies need not be confined to cooperation. An individual strategy in an interaction may indeed involve at least in part an effort to cooperate. Such a course of action may also involve an attempt to defeat the partner in a struggle, to influence the partner in some way, to maintain "face" or some other self-presentation (Goffman, 1959), to deceive, to express clearly the individual's perceptions of his own inner states, to express allegiance or solidarity, to transmit information on events removed in space or time from the immediate interaction, or any combination of these, and so on.

A convenient, though limited, analogy for the relationship between convention and interaction strategy is provided by games such as chess and football. We may speak of the game of face-to-face interaction, the "rules" for this game being provided by convention. The particular sequence of moves taken, the patterns of initiative and of response to the partner's initiatives, may be described in terms of one or more interaction strategies.

Care must be taken, however, not to carry the game analogy too far. A game implies some conflict between participants or "sides," each of which is striving to win the game. As mentioned above, interaction strategies need not involve conflict. In addition, it seems that the set of moves and rules provided by convention may be changed as a result of the strategies adopted by the participants, a property not commonly encountered in games. Finally, it is difficult to imagine the existence of a game without a set of rules for the game. However, it is possible to imagine an interaction taking place without conventions. For example, consider two individuals meeting, and these individuals are members of highly disparate cultures, and each has no knowledge of the other's culture. They may still effect an interaction through various devices and ingenuity. (It is not likely, however, that they will interact for long without developing a set of conventions for their continuing interaction.) Thus, conventions are not necessary for interaction in some absolute sense. But they are virtually ubiquitous in continual interactions because of their facilitating effect.

An interesting illustration of the relationship between convention and interaction strategy is provided by Birdwhistell's (1970) example of the military salute:

> During World War II, I became at first bemused, and later intrigued, by the repertoire of meanings which could be drawn upon by an experienced United States Army private and transmitted in accompaniment to a hand salute. The salute, a conventionalized movement of the right hand to the vicinity of the anterior portion of the cap or hat, could, without occasioning a court martial, be performed in a manner which could satisfy, please, or enrage the most demanding officer. By shifts in stance, facial expression, velocity or duration of the movement of salutation, and even in the selection of inappropriate contexts for the act, the soldier could dignify, ridicule, demean, seduce, insult, or promote the recipient of the salute. By often imperceptible variations in the performance of the act, he could comment upon the bravery or cowardice of his enemy or ally, could signal his attitude toward army life... [pp. 79–80].

While this example does not have the interaction-sequence emphasis that will be attached to the notion of strategy in the discussion below, it does illustrate the individual's capitalizing on the options available in the performance of a convention.

Preliminary Distinctions

Before proceeding with more specific description of interaction strategies, it is useful for the sake of clarity to draw distinctions between interaction strategies and other types of strategies, and between interaction strategies and their cognitive substrate, including goals.

Interaction and Other Strategies

It may be briefly noted that there are a large number of types of strategy distinguishable from that set designated "interaction strategy." Examples of strategies not considered to be interaction would be those involving (a) sequences of chess moves; (b) aspects of international diplomacy not involving face-to-face interaction; (c) financial investments; (d) survival in a hostile physical environment; (e) design and execution of scientific research; (f) completion of a jigsaw puzzle; (g) dealing with one's own moods or reactions, such as depression or anger, when one is alone; (h) patterns of betting in a game of chance, and so on. None of these strategies is directly concerned with the conduct of face-to-face interaction.

Action and Cognition

Care was taken in the discussion of interaction strategy to refer exclusively to certain patterns of action in face-to-face interaction. Such patterns may be distinguished from the undoubtedly complex cognitive processes that underlie and direct them. Some of these processes are considered extensively by cognitive psychologists (e.g., Newell & Simon, 1972) and are not be treated here.

This sort of issue arises when, for example, Whitten and Whitten (1972) in their review article use the term "social strategy" to denote "dynamic individual, group, or aggregate plans of action carried out over a specified time period [p. 248]." They note that social strategies "are abstractions derived from observations of social interaction and may be conscious or unconscious, explicit or implicit [p. 248]." This approach may be judged to fail to draw a sufficiently sharp distinction between cognitive processes and patterns of resultant action. This distinction may be preserved by defining interaction strategy in terms of patterns of action, and by placing the more abstract plans referred to by Whitten and Whitten squarely in the cognitive domain.

A rough analogy here would be the distinction between (a) a description of the moves in a chess game, together perhaps with some generalizations about these moves in terms of "patterns" or the like; and (b) the complex cognitive processes underlying these moves.

Similarly, the term "strategy" strongly implies the notion of a goal or goals which the strategy is aimed at obtaining. It will be assumed that goals of various sorts give direction to most, if not all, of the action patterns describable as strategies. (It is worth noting that Newell and Simon, 1972, p. 809, point out that not all directed action need involve goals.) However, even when action is goal directed, it is not necessary to specify these goals in order to describe the resulting action pattern. Indeed, the prudent investigator might do well to approach the description of goals in face-to-face interaction with great caution. There are several reasons for this judgment.

Some of these reasons have to do with technical difficulties. It has often been noted that the same goal may be approached through a number of different lines of action (the principle of equifinality). And conversely, essentially the same line of action might be used in order to approach different goals. For example, one person might engage in an exchange of courteous greetings with a partner for the sake of friendliness, while another person might do the same in order to deceive. Further, as Whitten and Whitten point out, it seems reasonable to assume that not all goals may lie within an individual's awareness and–or ability to articulate them. Thus, self-report must be used with care.

But there is another, more compelling reason to exercise caution in attempting to describe the goals directing interaction strategies: It seems clear that such an attempt requires the contemplation of the full complexity of human personality and motivation. The process of drawing connections between interaction strategies and human goals runs the constant danger of superficiality. Any given interaction strategy may reasonably be presumed to be influenced by multiple goals, some perhaps mutually compatible, others perhaps in conflict.

For all of these reasons, description of the goals to which interaction strategies are directed may be seen as concerning the field of human motivation, as well as cognitive psychology. In research on cognitive psychology, the goal—typically the solution of a clearly defined problem—is given, and the processes leading to the solution of that problem are studied. In the case of social interaction, the strategies used may be empirically described, but the goals underlying the strategies are not immediately apparent and must be hypothesized on the basis of various lines of evidence.

In any event, it is entirely possible to attempt to describe interaction strategies as such, without including their presumed goals. On the other hand, careful study of interaction strategies and their effects on interaction may provide useful information for investigators of motivation.

Elements of Interaction Strategies

Interaction strategies may be described specifically in terms of the elements from which they may be constructed. The preceding discussion of convention suggests two areas particularly well suited for taking individual initiative and thus for developing interaction strategies: (a) the dynamics of situation; and (b) variation in the performing of convention.

Interaction Strategy Through the Dynamics of Situation

Because the formulation of situation need not be entirely fixed for any given interaction, and because such a formulation entails an active classifying process by each participant, the general area of situation has potentially much to offer in the construction of interaction strategies. The use of situation in the construction of strategy will be discussed in terms of initial formulation, collaboration, change, and deceit.

Initial formulation.   It was stressed in the discussion of situation that each participant, upon approaching or engaging in an interaction, must develop an initial formulation of the situation. This formulation will include a classifying of various elements of the interaction event, including the participant himself, the partner, the type of relationship between them, the physical setting in which the interaction is taking place, and so on. Further, at least part of this initial classification becomes evident upon the participant's first actions in the interaction. This initial formulation, together with its consequent actions, represents the participant's initial interpretation of the interaction event and thus becomes an element of his strategy in the interaction.

Collaboration.   All formulations of situation by a participant are subject to ratification by the partner. The partner may refuse to ratify by simply not taking the slot alloted to him within the convention introduced by the participant. Or, the partner may counter with an alternative convention, implying an alternative formulation of situation. Thus, it is not necessary that any convention introduced by a participant be accepted by the partner. It is conceivable that differences in the respective formulations by the two participants may never be resolved in the course of a given interaction. An entire interaction might be carried out in which one participant behaves in accordance with a given slot in one convention, while the partner behaves in accordance with a given slot in another convention. In any event, the decision to collaborate in (ratify) the prevailing or the preferred convention is an element of strategy.

Change.   It may serve a participant's strategy to attempt to effect a change in a prevailing situation, either by shifting the value of one or more correspondences in the situation, and—or by adding assessments to, or subtracting them from, the situation. For example, a salesman's strategy on first contacting a potential client might be to move as quickly as possible from a situation in which the interactants are classified as strangers, to one in which they are classified as trusting, mutually beneficial friends. Such an attempt to change the situation would be made through introducing new conventions in the interaction, the situational requirements of these new conventions including the new classifications desired by the salesman. These attempted changes are, of course, subject to ratification by the partner.

Deceit. It is clear that a participant may use deceit in his formulation of situation. His ostensive formulation of the situation may not match that which he has in fact formulated. That is, a participant may perform conventions that imply assessments that are at variance with those that he has actually made. For example, a participant may select conventions that imply a friendliness or a respect or an emotional distance that he does not feel. This deceit may or may not involve a change in the initial situation. A given deceit may apply to each and every interaction a participant has with a given partner or may be introduced as a change in the course of an interaction, or as a change from one interaction to the next. Goffman (e.g., 1969, 1971) provides extensive discussion of the techniques and ramifications of various forms of deception.

All of these elements of interaction strategy are based on the cognitive operations involved in the formulation of situation, but the description of the strategy itself is made entirely on the basis of the actions eventuating from these operations.

Interaction Strategy Through Variation in the Performing of Convention

There are a number of ways, previously considered, in which the performance of a convention may vary. One of the more obvious ways of varying such a performance is in terms of the relative frequency or extent of use of cues and signals. It is not difficult to imagine that, in a given interaction, an individual's strategy might include much or little use of smiling, or interrupting, or gazing at the partner, or the like.

In a similar manner, an individual might make use of other sources of variation as elements of a strategy: selection of particular cues and signals from larger repertoires, display of characteristic sequences or clusters of cues and signals, and violation of the prevailing conventions.

An obvious element of interaction strategy would be the tendency to respond or not to respond in various ways to the partner. For example, within the proposed turn system, the auditor may or may not (a) claim the turn upon the speaker's display of a turn signal; or (b) respond with a back channel upon the speaker's display of a within-turn signal. Further, upon the concurrent display of both turn and within-turn cues by the speaker, the auditor may respond with a turn claim, or a back channel, or neither. When a signal (such as the turn signal) has multiple, optional cues, an auditor may tend to defer claiming the turn until larger numbers of cues (say, four or five) are displayed, or alternatively, attempt to seize the turn immediately upon the display of any single cue.

Summary: Elements of Interaction Strategy

From these considerations it will be apparent that participating in a convention inevitably involves an interaction strategy, and that this strategy necessarily includes both elements mentioned above: dynamics of situation, and variation in the performing of a convention.

Dynamics of situation is a necessary element of strategy because there is always an aspect of active choice in the initial formulation of situation, even if both participants arrive at the same formulation, and even if the tactics of deceit, change, and collaboration are not brought into play. Similarly, there is always room for appropriate variation in the performance of a convention. For example, within the turn system, use of the gesticulation signal by the speaker may theoretically range from 0 to 100% of his speaking time.

Whenever either a formulation of situation or a performance of a convention involves optionality, then those options exercised are inevitably a part of an interaction strategy. In this sense, convention and interaction strategy are inextricably related: two sides of the same coin. Clearly, both interrelated aspects must be included in any complete account of interaction.

For research purposes, actual observation takes precedence over theoretical considerations. Some theoretically possible options (such as the 100% gesticulating mentioned above) might never be used by participants, and—or certain elements of conventions may be violated while others are not. In this sense, interaction strategy ultimately becomes formulated in terms of the range of variation actually observed among interactants. (Research approaches to interaction strategy are considered further in Chapter 13.)

And similarly, while an interaction strategy potentially includes all elements of permissible variation in the selection and performance of convention, for research purposes it is not necessary or even particularly interesting to include all such possible elements of an interaction strategy in its description. The task for research is to identify those elements of strategy that have the most significant effects on interaction.

Effects of Interaction Strategy

It has been suggested that a given interaction strategy is based on use of both the dynamics of situation, and variation in the performing of a convention. A naturally ensuing question concerns the possible effects of interaction strategies. On this analysis there are two distinguishable but clearly related effects, applicable to all interactions: (a) the course and outcome of the interaction; and (b) the formation of impressions by each participant in the interaction.

The outcome of an interaction is typically evaluated in terms of criteria particularly interesting to the investigator: the outcome of a bargaining session; the prevalence of a point of view; ratings of success of psychotherapy; the extent of conflict, cooperation, reconciliation and the like; the winning or loss of allegiance; the nature of the relationship formed; and so on. Careful formulation of a convention, however, permits a less arbitrary and more specific evaluation of the effect of an interaction strategy on the course and outcome of an interaction. This alternative evaluation would be in terms appropriate to the convention(s) within which the interaction strategy is operating. For example, a participant's interaction strategy within the turn system might be evaluated in terms of such summary measures of interaction effects as percentage of conversation time spent speaking, number of simultaneous turns, and percentage of simultaneous turns "won." Such evaluation by criteria appropriate to the applicable convention would appear to have the advantage of considering conversational phenomena relatively more in their own terms, as opposed to terms borrowed by the researcher from other frames of reference. It will be recognized that this general research strategy is a basic constituent of the approach to research on face-to-face interaction being advocated in this monograph.

A second general effect of interaction strategy on face-to-face interaction has to do with the formation of impressions of the participants. These impressions seem inevitable because of the classifying process involved in all use of convention. It has been emphasized that the process of a participant's selecting and performing a convention inescapably involves a prior classifying of the participant himself, the partner, the type of interaction they are engaged in, and so on. Further, the results of this classifying process will be evident to all nonparticipating observers of the interaction, whether that observation is perceptually direct, or indirect through the accounts of others.

Similarly, strategy based on permissible variation in the performance of the conventions chosen may also give rise to the sort of impressions mentioned above. To repeat an example used above, a more continually gesticulating speaker might be considered to be more dominant, aggressive or the like, than a speaker who makes less use of that signal.

Both of these general effects are, of course, accessible to research. Research issues on the effects of performance strategies will be further considered in the next chapter.

Initiative and Response in Interaction

Interaction strategies do not occur in a social vacuum. It seems on principle to be impossible to examine a participant's interaction strategy independently of the social matrix within which it occurs. This fundamental understanding has underlaid the discussion of strategy to this point, but it deserves more explicit consideration.

Let us imagine two previously unacquainted individuals meeting at some location and time and carrying on a conversation. And let us permit each individual the opportunity to arrive at a formulation of situation prior to their actually beginning any aspect of their interaction. This initial formulation would be, in terms of this discussion, the first element of each individual's performance strategy.

At some point, one of the individuals must take some first move in the incipient interaction. This first move can be at least tentatively indexed to one or more conventions and thence to elements of a formulation of situation. Further, within the indicated convention(s) this first participant's choices with respect to appropriate action variations will be apparent to some degree. All of these elements have been discussed in terms of interaction strategy. And all of the implications of this first action can be used by the second participant to compare with his own formulation of situation (and intended first action), permitting him to make any adjustments he deems desirable.

It is now the second individual's turn to act. This second action carries, on this analysis, information with respect to the same phenomena: choice of convention(s) (and therefore formulation of situation), and action variation within the convention(s). But there is also a further significant implication of this second action: the degree of ratification (or total lack thereof) of the first participant's initial action.

Figure 12.1 illustrates some essential elements in this general train of events. In greatly simplified form, the figure shows the proposed process leading to the respective first action(s) by each of two participants in an interaction. The figure is arranged from left to right in terms of sequences of decisions and events logically entailed in the metatheory. For purposes of clarity, many possible complications are omitted, such as decisions to deceive, or to change a prevailing definition of situation. Similarly, the various components of those decisions are not detailed. No claim is made, of course, that the figure represents actual sequences in terms of information processing by the two participants.

To the extent to which the two formulations of situation, as evidenced by the respective observable actions of the two participants, are found to agree, the interaction may proceed to whatever its next stage might be. To the extent to which the two formulations are found to disagree, something must be done. It is not of concern in this discussion precisely what happens, whether there is mutual or unilateral accommodation, open conflict, termination of the interaction, subsequent scrupulous avoidance of those elements of situation on which there is disagreement, or some other tack. The handling of such discrepancies in ostensive formulations of situation is an empirical question.

The point of the present discussion is this: subsequent to the first action taken in an interaction between previously unacquainted individuals, each successive action can be interpreted as both a response and an initiative: a

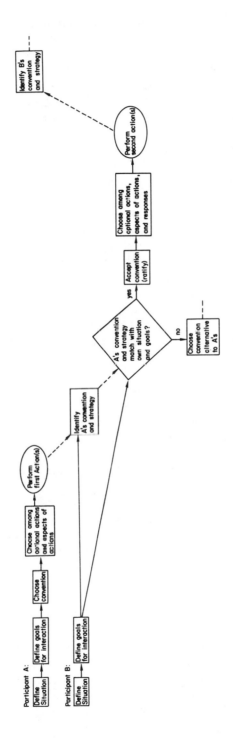

FIGURE 12.1 A Logical Model of Some Essential Elements in the Interaction Process.

response because it is accurately interpretable only in the light of those actions that preceded it; and an initiative because on this analysis all aspects of that action cannot be fully determined, either by the preceding action(s) or by the convention(s) from which the action derives.

The first action of an interaction has been distinguished from all others in that it was considered to be an initiative only, and not a response. This interpretation was based, however, on the stipulation that the interactants be previously unacquainted. If they are acquainted through previous interaction, however, a first action in any subsequent interaction may well be both an initiative and a response—a response to aspects of that previous interaction. Further, because of situation markers such as clothes, grooming, the decoration of a room, and the like, any number of important classifications by an incipient participant and by others may be clearly evident to the partner prior to interaction. In this case also, a first action in an interaction may be both a response and an initiative. Therefore, it will be said that virtually all actions occurring in interaction are both a response and an initiative.

For example, it is not sufficient merely to note that a participant as auditor attempted to take the speaking turn at some point in an interaction. Similarly, it is insufficient merely to count the number of times such attempts were made over some stretch of interaction. Rather, given the context of the turn system, it is necessary to know whether or not the speaker had switched on the turn signal at the time of the attempt (while not switching on the gesticulation signal). Thus, an auditor turn attempt ($+$) or the absence thereof (-) is interpretable in terms of a two-action sequence: (a) $\pm$ speaker turn signal, $\pm$ gesticulation signal' (b) $\pm$ auditor turn attempt.

Of course, sequences longer than two actions may be necessary for adequate interpretation of a given action within the context of convention. Drawing an example once again from the hypothesized turn system, the presence of absence of a speaker continuation signal in interpretable in terms of a three-action sequence potentially involving both participants: (a) $\pm$ speaker within-turn signal; (b) $\pm$ auditor between-unit back channel, or $\pm$ auditor early back channel; (c) $\pm$ speaker continuation signal.

These two examples also help illustrate the point that the absence of the appropriate action at some point in the sequence is both a response and an initiative that is fully as significant as the presence of the action. It is in this sense that Birdwhistell's (1971) dictum, "nothing *never* happens [p. 90 ms., original emphasis]" is interpretable within the framework of this discussion.

From this viewpoint, an interaction is a continually developing series of response-initiatives by both participants. As such, an interaction is interesting even when it follows the most unexceptional, predictable course, for with the possibility of initiative at each successive point in the interaction, it might have been otherwise. Further, this continual process of initiative and response is potentially accessible to research, just as it is accessible to the interpretations of the participants themselves.

In summary, a participant's action at any given point in an interaction may be viewed as an end point in a sequence of actions involving at least the preceding action by the partner, but potentially expandable, as required by convention, to include longer sequences and both participants. The significance of the participant's action (or lack thereof) can be properly understood only in the light of that sequence within the framework of the applicable conventions.

Locating the Context of an Action

If virtually every action in an interaction is both a response and an initiative, and if any adequate description of that action must include at least the preceding action(s) by the partner to which it is a response, then it becomes important to be able to locate the preceding action(s). This problem may be rendered incapable of solution by asserting the commonplace wisdom that an action may be considered in the broader sense to be a response to all that had preceded in the interaction, or perhaps even in the participant's life.

However, it seems possible in empirical studies to locate in a specific and nonarbitrary way some preceding action by the partner to which a subsequent action by the participant may be linked as a response. On this analysis an action is linked to preceding action(s) through the convention(s) of which both actions are a part. For example, within the turn system an auditor attempt to take the speaking turn may be linked to the presence or absence of speaker signals considered to be switched on when the turn attempt was made.

There is no need, however, for such an immediate temporal connection between an action and some other action to which it is considered to be a response. A hypothetical example will have to suffice here. Let us assume that somewhere there is a convention in which the form of one participant's leave-taking at the end of an interaction is linked to the form of the partner's greeting at the beginning of the interaction. And this connection through convention remains regardless of the nature or length of the interaction. Once that convention is known, there can be no difficulty in locating the preceding action to which the leave-taking is a response, even though the two events may be separated by considerable time and many intervening actions.

Thus, adequate knowledge of applicable conventions is required in order to locate properly an action to which a later action may be said to be a response. The same notion may be stated in a somewhat more abstract way: fully adequate research on interaction strategy cannot proceed apart from adequate knowledge of the convention(s) within which the strategy is operating. This is not to say, however, that prior knowledge of relevant convention(s) is required for the pursuit of studies aimed at the discovery of behavioral regularities from which both conventions and performance strategies may be inferred.

Regularities in Interaction Strategies

In the terms of this discussion, a participant's action or absence of action at any given point in an interaction, considered together with appropriate preceding action(s) by the partner and perhaps also by the participant, is a single element of the participant's interaction strategy.

A raw description of an interaction strategy, or of selected aspects of it, would require only a simple itemizing of its elements. However, both investigators and interactants will be more interested in the extent to which there are discoverable regularities within a strategy of either an individual participant or some group of participants. These regularities may then be used to characterize in a more general way the strategy of individuals or groups in specified types of interaction. On this analysis, it is precisely such regularities in interaction strategies that account, for example, for the consistent group differences found by investigators of "nonverbal communication."

An example here would be the consistent sex differences found in studies of gaze direction in a variety of situations (e.g., Ashear & Snortum, 1971; Beekman, 1973; Exline, 1963; Exline, Gray, & Schuette, 1965; Libby & Yaklevich, 1973; Russo, 1975). It appears that the females' greater amount of gazing at the partner (when male) is part of a greater "attentiveness," in the sense of both gazing more and speaking less. But a better understanding of findings such as these awaits a fuller description of the action sequences in which the gazing at and gazing away occur.

The value of research on regularities in interaction strategies lies in their presumed importance for interaction—for example, their potential effectiveness for participants in handling specifiable types of interactions, for characterizing the interactional styles of individuals and groups, and for permitting the planning of strategies by a participant to cope with a partner's anticipated regularities on the basis of previous observation.

For research purposes, a minimal requirement for a description of a regularity in a participant's interaction strategy must include each element of the relevant action sequence, as well as general information on the interaction situation. An optimally complete description of a strategy would additionally include such elements as the conventions within which the strategy operates and the situational classifications implied by these conventions.

Interaction Strategy to Convention

It was mentioned near the beginning of this discussion of interaction strategy that the set of signals, moves and rules provided by a convention may be changed as a result of the strategies adopted by the participants. It is now possible to elaborate on this notion.

A strategy might be adopted to deal with a one-time, short-term interaction. For example, an individual may act immediately to rid himself as quickly as possible of the importunings of a person he perceives to be a confidence man. The individual must adopt some strategy tailored to that situation, even if he has never before encountered such a person and has never considered what to do should such a situation arise. Consequently, it is possible that, in the strategy devised to deal with that situation, the individual may engage in certain actions, and–or construct certain combinations of actions that he has never used before. And it is possible that he may never encounter that situation and–or use that strategy again.

On the other hand, it seems more usual that a participant may repeatedly find himself in interactions for which he formulates roughly the same situation and repeatedly employs the same general strategy in dealing with that situation. This state of affairs would generate the regularities in interaction strategy considered above.

The regularities resulting from an individual's consistent adoption of a given strategy may be noticed by a partner, giving rise to some firmness of expectation on his part as to the participant's probable strategy in future, similar situations. This expectation by the partner may, in turn, lead to regularities in the partner's actions, in response to the participant's strategy. The partner's regularities may then be noticed by the participant, giving rise to firm expectations of the partner's future actions. Further, each individual may view the respective strategies as a desirable state of affairs. At this point, the basic requisites for convention are met. What began as two strategies is now coalesced to form a convention. In the case of the example, the convention is an entirely local one arising between two individuals. But it is easy to see that it might have arisen in essentially the same way among larger numbers of persons, or that what was once an entirely local convention may spread to other members of the culture over a period of time.

Whitten and Whitten (1972) have cited Bennett (1969) as pointing out that "adaptive strategies," aimed at coping with the environment, may become conventionalized in the same way. Bennett (1969) points out that "the many separate adjustments that have become patterned as strategies can also enter into culture . . . as repetitive patterns of action they can be viewed by the people as traditions [p. 16]." In this way, interaction strategies not only derive from variations in the performance of conventions, but also may lead to the development of new or modified conventions.

Interaction and Self-Concept

A final step in this theoretical discussion is necessary to prepare for the consideration of research in the next chapter. This step has to do with the relationship between interaction, including both convention and interaction strategy, and perception of self and of one's own action.

Bateson (1971) emphasizes that interaction of the sort we have been considering " . . . is not only between persons and about the pacts which they form, it is also and more strangely a dialogue which governs what each person *is* . . . . In communicational terms, we may translate this into a statement that the very rules of self-perception, the rules governing the formation of a self-image, are modified by the way in which others receive our messages [p. 26 ms., original emphasis]."

In addressing this intuitively appealing notion Goffman provides an elaborated formulation more accessible to research. He states (1971) that:

> ... the treatment that an individual gives others and receives from them expresses or assumes a definition of him, as does the immediate social scene in which the treatment occurs. This is a "virtual" definition; it is based upon the ways of understanding of the community and is available to any competent member, whether or not such interpretations are actually made. ... The ultimate referent here is a tacit coding discoverable by competently reading conduct, and not conceptions or images that persons actually have in their minds [p. 340].

Goffman goes on to say that "virtual definitions of an individual may be 'accorded'—that is, readable in the conduct of agencies seen as external to the individual himself. ... Corresponding to these accorded assumptions about him there will be virtually 'acted' ones, projected through what is seen as his own conduct [p. 340]."

In the terms of this discussion, virtual definitions correspond precisely to elements of the formulation of situation. An acted definition is composed of those classifications made by a participant of himself, and an accorded definition of that participant is composed of those classifications made of the participant by the partner. The point at stake here is that these definitions undoubtedly interact in turn with the way in which an individual actually perceives himself, although, as Goffman (1971) points out, "the psychological relation [an individual] sustains to his accorded and acted definitions is enormously complex [p. 341]." Thus, for a given individual it is not clear to what extent each element of accorded and acted definitions of self has been internalized, and to what extent the individual maintains role distance (Goffman, 1961).

The issues mentioned arise for investigators when relationships are found between an individual's conduct in an interaction and his responses on self-description inventories. What rationale exists for such relationships? On the basis of this brief discussion it appears reasonable to suggest that an individual's responses on self-description inventories may be influenced by, among other things, (a) the individual's experiences of being classified in terms of formulations of situation by both himself and others (his acted and accorded definitions); and–or (b) the actual way that the individual perceives himself (to the extent to which these two elements differ). Thus, the connection between response to self-description inventories and conduct in interaction lies in the classifying process required for formulations of situation. It remains for further research to clarify the nature and extent of this potential connection.

Our attempt to link summary scores for acts with scores from self-descriptive inventories, as described in Part II, was not very fruitful. That result does not provide evidence contrary to the view in the preceding paragraph for two reasons. On the one side, we did not have a way of determining systematically what the participants' formulations of the situation were. On the other side, our inventories yielded scores associated with global constructs rather than scores pertaining to how each participant saw himself in interactions like those we studied.

SUMMARY AND CONCLUSION

In this chapter an attempt has been made to describe some basic elements of a conceptual framework for understanding the processes of face-to-face interaction. This framework is designed specifically for the needs of research in this area. For this reason, greatest emphasis is placed on sources of regularity in the respective actions of each participant in face-to-face interaction. To the extent that such a framework is effective, it may contribute to interpreting existing research, including suggesting present limitations of that research, and to guiding the design of future research.

In outline, the proposed framework is quite simple. Convention provides a general "structure" of rules and the like within which face-to-face interaction takes place in a given culture. This structure facilitates the coordination of action among members of the culture by providing a certain, widely known, way to do things that the members feel need to be done. The structure also provides researchers with an important source of regularity in the actions observable in interaction.

But conventions appear to leave much to the discretion of the participants using them. Options of several sorts appear available in both the selecting and the performing of conventions. These options provide the possibility of another source of significant regularity in interaction: interaction strategy. More strictly speaking, the existence of various options within conventions requires participants to make, implicitly or explicitly, choices with respect to each of the available options. To the extent that there is any regularity in the manner in which these options are exercised, either across participants or across interactions, convention and interaction strategy become inextricably related in the study of face-to-face interaction. As opposed to the desire for cooperation that is reflected by the existence of conventions, interaction strategies may be used to serve virtually any human end.

Because the existence of an interaction strategy is possible only within the structure provided by convention, proper description (and interpretation) of an interaction strategy is possible only within that structure. Thus, it may be said that, from a conceptual viewpoint, interaction strategy derives in part from convention. But such a statement should not be allowed to detract from an appreciation of the deep significance that each element of strategy has for the conduct of actual interaction. In general, a full description of interaction would have to include consideration of both sources of regularity in the participants' actions.

The discussion of convention and of interaction strategy has, for the most part, been confined to their most essential elements. This deliberate limitation of the discussion was adopted for two main reasons. First, while it would be possible to increase the amount of detail by pursuing the logical development of various points, this sort of elaboration seems generally routine, yielding only a minimum gain in substantial information. Second, the discussion was designed to provide a general conceptual framework for research in the area of face-to-face interaction. It would seem that the further development of the framework would require input from empirical research on the description of convention and interaction strategy. A conceptual framework for research should not indulge itself in extended, autonomous, logical development.

In the next chapter the framework is applied to the consideration of specific research issues.

13
A Research Program
For Face-To-Face Interaction

In this final chapter we attempt to integrate the diverse elements considered at various points in the preceding chapters. We review the essential conceptual and methodological features of the approach to research that we have been advocating, and we reconsider the research presented in Parts II and III in the light of the conceptual framework presented in Chapter 12. This attempt at overview and integration leads to programmatic recommendations regarding the future course of research on face-to-face interaction, which touch on all aspects of the research process: the conditions for collecting data, the kind of data to be obtained, appropriate processing and analysis of these data, and the conceptual framework that both guides the research process and provides a generalized rationale for results.

It should be noted that, although the following discussion is based on an integration of the methodological recommendations with the conceptual framework, such an integration is not a logically necessary one. A researcher might, for example, follow most or all of the methodological recommendations, while casting obtained results in some alternative conceptual framework.

Types of Studies

After the proposal of certain general research methods, there will be a more specific discussion of studies of convention and of interaction strategy. Contrasts will be made at various points in the chapter with external-variable studies. In an earlier review article (Duncan, 1969) it was said that there were two general sorts of studies in the area of "nonverbal communication": the structural study and the external-variable study. These terms have already been described at length in earlier chapters.

It was stated above that the study described in Part II was designed as an external-variable study, and that the study described in Part III was designed as a study of structure. It is now possible to reconsider this dichotomy in terms of the conceptual framework described in the preceding chapter.

It is readily apparent that the study of structure is virtually identical to the notion of convention, although the notion of convention has been expanded somewhat beyond the single element of rules. In fact, the terms "structure" and "organization," when used with reference to the process of face-to-face interaction, may be considered to be comparable to the more specific term "convention," especially in the service of expository convenience. These two terms were so used in the discussion to this point, and this practice will continue.

It is tempting to draw a similar parallel between external-variable studies and the notion of interaction strategy presented in Chapter 12. Both are concerned with variation over persons. But this situation is somewhat more complicated. To begin with, it should be noted that there was an inconsistency present in the review article (Duncan, 1969). The notion of structure referred to a phenomenon of interest in face-to-face interaction: the operation of "rules." But the notion of an external-variable study referred to a methodology. This inconsistency was due in part to the incomplete conceptual development lying behind the review. But this incomplete development may have been facilitated by the fact that studies of interaction strategy as a phenomenon in face-to-face interaction, in the sense discussed in the preceding chapter, did not exist at the time that the review was written. Nor, to our knowledge, do they exist at this writing, at least in terms of the methodology which we shall be describing.

All considered, it seems appropriate not to discard the term "external-variable study," but to retain that methodologically based label. We shall continue to use it to refer to the studies described as such in the review article, to comparable studies appearing in the literature since that review, and to the study described in Part II. We choose to retain this term because it will be held that in these studies it is impossible to identify the relevant conventions. This being the case, it is impossible to obtain information on the concomitant interaction strategies. For these reasons, it is difficult to provide a unitary label based on their subject matter. Thus, it is simpler to use a label indicating their common methodology.

CONDITIONS OF DATA COLLECTION

Naturalistic Setting

If behavioral science has learned anything, it is that action varies with the situation in which it occurs. A crucial corollary is that action in a laboratory or testing room is influenced by those particular settings. All of us assume that there are general principles that explain action, principles that can be applied to action in any situation. It is clear, nevertheless, that the generalizations derived from settings established by the investigator may not hold in more natural conditions. Hence, even the researcher who prefers to study action in laboratory settings must eventually demonstrate that the principles derived from his findings are not restricted to those particular settings and do apply in the outside world. We take it for granted that in behavioral science the ultimate objective is to understand action as it occurs under natural conditions.

For these reasons, research on face-to-face interaction should ideally be studied under naturalistic conditions. This is even more important at the early stages of the research when hypotheses are being generated. Any steps representing departures from such conditions should be undertaken reluctantly and only when other considerations make these departures unavoidable. Research decisions involve tradeoffs (Runkel and McGrath, 1972), and steps away from natural conditions involve losses which are tolerable only when they are more than offset by gains in other respects.

One reason for departing from the ideal is the ethical consideration of obtaining permission from individuals prior to observing their interaction. Obtaining permission involves informing the persons that they will be observed. Such knowledge clearly can affect their actions. In the long run, it will be necessary to establish that research findings obtained with persons who knew that they were being observed also hold when the persons do not know. Such studies of generalizability might use actions which were quite public, that is, which occurred in the presence of other persons; it would seem necessary, however, to obtain from these persons permission to use the observations, after the observations had been made.

Although knowledge that one is being observed can and presumably does affect some aspects of one's action, it need not affect the aspects which the researcher is investigating. It is most improbable, for instance, that a person's signature will be different when written in the presence of others. Thus, there may be some aspects of action which are quite consistent across situations, including acts which are both inside and outside the focus of attention. In addition, it is reasonable to expect that the interaction itself makes definite demands on a participant's attention and conduct. But this is not a question on which we need to speculate. The susceptibility of various specific actions or patterns of actions to situational factors, including the presence of observers, is an empirical issue. Also empirical issues are the extent and speed of individuals' adapting to being observed as they interact.

Avoidance of Intervention

Even though the persons observed must be informed about the observation, the observed sequence of actions can be allowed to occur without manipulation or intervention. It is true that the subjects must be told not only that they are being observed but also why the observations are being made.

It seems sufficient to state the simple truth, that the objective is to study what happens when people talk to each other and interact. This information can be given in a manner which has minimal or no effect upon the participants' subsequent actions.

Beyond this general orientation, the experimenter need not affect the interaction in any way. He need not ask participants to role-play (such as "Pretend you are applying for a job"), and he need not introduce any stimuli during the observed sequence of actions. The participants can provide their own stimuli for themselves and for each other. Instead of asking what response follows a given experimental stimulus, the question becomes: What acts precede a given act, and what acts follow it? The investigator can follow the guidance of Egon Brunswik (1943) who urged the study of organismic achievement in the presence of environmental probabilities and who advocated the design of research which represented natural experience.

Recording the Interaction

It is clear that the data-generation requirements of research on face-to-face interaction can no longer be met solely on the basis of observations of the live interaction itself. There are still studies reported in which data are based on such observation of the live interaction: for example, indications of aspects of body motion such as gaze direction, and trackings of speech–silence intervals via manual operation of the interaction chronograph. Data generation of this sort may be judged to be excessively inflexible and susceptible to errors of perception and omission.

More deeply flawed is the approach to live observation that requires the observer to look for manifestations of an abstract category or to make post-observation judgments about the frequency, extent, or intensity of certain attributes of the actions or the participants observed. In procedures such as these there is still greater room for error in classification or interpretation. The exact degree of error cannot be readily assessed; it can only be roughly estimated by comparing the data records for two simultaneous observers.

The electronic recording of the interaction being studied has great advantages. The major advantage is, of course, that the phenomena themselves are not lost: they can be retrieved by replaying the recording. Thus, if the investigator wishes to change his rating categories or to look for new ones, he can do so readily, without seeking new interactions to observe. Another advantage is the possibility of observing each act by itself: the recording can be scanned separately for each act, thus minimizing errors of omission. Of considerable importance is the opportunity for playing the recording at slower speeds, even stopping the action if necessary, permitting the detection and accurate description of physical acts which may be too rapid for observers to rate accurately at normal speeds. Also at slower speeds, the observer can locate each act more precisely in chronological time and in its temporal order within ongoing sequences of other acts.

The recording of the phenomena will usually impose some limits on the activity of the participants. When a single camera is used, it should be placed so that the whole of each person is included in the picture and yet the recording provides sufficient detail for the purpose of the study.

In principle, with a number of cameras set up to catch the actions wherever they occurred within a fairly large physical area, very little restriction would have to be imposed upon participants. An investigator may depart from optimal conditions, especially in initial explorations of a class of phenomena, for reasons of economy or convenience. That choice may well be a sound allocation of limited resources. What is crucial to keep constantly in mind is the fact that restrictions have been placed on the population of actions from which the sample observations are drawn; these restrictions may place limitations on conclusions obtained from the study.

Making arrangements for recording phenomena and making the recording are relatively easy. The intensive examination of the recording is more demanding. The playing and replaying of the tape, the repeated scrutiny of troublesome passages, require concentrated effort, especially when the investigator is working inductively and not restricting his attention to acts chosen a priori.

ACTS AS DATA

A basic issue for research on the conduct of face-to-face interaction concerns the generation of data from the "stream of behavior" (Barker, 1963) observable in that interaction. We have recommended use of discrete units of observation, defined as closely as possible in terms of physical parameters. We have termed such units "acts," and we have noted that they are in increasingly wide use by investigators working in areas such as "nonverbal communication," human ethology, and the like.

We have defined the act as the smallest unit of observation used by an investigator, not further subdivided or analyzed in a given study. Clearly, what would be considered an act by a given investigator in one study might be more or less fine grained in his next study or in a study by another investigator. For example, in Part II one of our acts was the smile; another investigator might wish to categorize smiles into several classes. Again, we distinguished between gestures and self-adaptors; someone else might treat hand movement as a unit. And clearly, different investigators will often focus on different types of action observable in face-to-face interaction.

We have noted that acts have certain highly desirable properties as data. They are defined as concretely as possible. This permits observers to transcribe acts using a minimum of inference and to focus their observations on a narrow band of physical activity, such as hand movements or paralinguistic pitch, during a given pass of the recording. (This assumes that raters are required to transcribe only one type of act at a time—a recommended procedure.) Acts are treated as discrete, having defined onsets and offsets. In addition, it is desirable that these onsets and offsets be relatively instantaneous: "Now it is there. . .now it isn't." Thus, "turning the ignition key" seems preferable to "starting the car," the latter being an action that is harder to pinpoint in time because it is actually a series of actions. The opportunity to locate rather precisely the moment of onset and the moment of offset is quite important when one approaches actions as extending over time. Further, this on–off property of acts requires of observers a minimum of summarizing their judgments over time, a more complex cognitive process than a simple yes–no decision.

We do not claim, however, that the use of acts has the effect of reducing observers to the status of mere transducers of physical phenomena—a kind of metabolizing oscillograph. The definition of acts often includes certain culturally based categories (discussed in Chapter 2) that observers must apply in order to make their judgments. The distinction between gestures and self-adaptors as different hand acts (on one level of analysis) is a subjectively compelling one, presumably because of its close reflection of cultural categories applying to hand–arm movement. But the distinction ultimately requires validation in research. Such validation is already accumulating (e.g., Freedman, 1972; Freedman, Blass, Rifkin, & Quitkin, 1973; Freedman & Hoffman, 1967; Freedman, O'Hanlon, Oltman, & Witkin, 1972; Mahl, 1968; Rosenfeld, 1966; in addition to the research reported in Part III).

Cultural (perhaps in some cases universal) categories used in the definition of acts typically are extremely difficult to make fully explicit. The gesture–self-adaptor distinction remains a good example of this point. Nevertheless, definitions using such categories are readily understood both by investigators (at least by those of sufficiently similar cultural background) and by raters, for whom the definition may often be communicated ostensively. Our experience has been that the gesture–self-adaptor distinction and many other comparable ones are quickly and accurately grasped by raters as soon as they are verbally described in general terms and a few examples pointed out.

The exactness of this sort of process for defining acts—emphasizing shared knowledge and ostensive definition—is evidenced by the very high degree of agreement between observers routinely obtained by investigators using acts, a degree often approaching perfect consensus. Interjudge reliability obtained for acts contrasts sharply with reliability obtained by observers required to interpret action by making extensive inferences about unobservable properties or characteristics of the participants or of the interaction, and–or to summarize their judgments over time. The observer of acts is more a recorder than interpreter. The data generated through the observation of acts provide a substantial empirical base for ensuing analyses.

It should be pointed out, however, that the use of cultural categories in defining acts can be expected to be effective only when the observed participants are members of a culture with which the investigator and his observers are highly familiar. This is because the investigator and observers are simply using themselves as informants when they define the acts to be used in their study. When the investigator is unfamiliar with the culture observed, it of course becomes necessary to rely heavily on native informants and—or to define acts on a more truly physical ("etic") basis.

Temporal Location of Acts

In the research reported in Parts II and III acts in the stream of interaction were not located in chronological time. In Part II the duration of various acts was noted, but the respective locations of acts within the five-minute conversations were not recorded. In Part III the accurate location of acts was a central concern, but this location was accomplished in terms of an act's sequential position with respect to other acts or to the pauses between acts.

We believe, however, that the consideration of temporal factors would be a valuable addition to the study of interaction. There is clearly much to be learned concerning the temporal aspects of action sequences. One can imagine a kind of interaction chronograph study that took into account a wide variety of speech and body—motion actions, rather than focusing exclusively on temporal parameters of speech and silence. One might ask, for example, are there minimum and—or maximum time intervals associated with the appropriate activation of, and response to, given signals? Further information on this sort of issue is of potential interest, not only to investigators of interactions, but also to investigators of reaction time and human information processing. It appears, however, that considerable attention has to be given to problems of analyzing the temporal aspect of face-to-face interaction.

EXPLORATORY RESEARCH

We have reiterated at various points in this monograph the present need for exploratory research in the area of face-to-face interaction. This argument is based on notions concerning the orderly development of science, together with an assessment of the current stage of development of this research area. Despite the welcome proliferation of various types of studies of face-to-face interaction within the past 15 years, we believe the area to be at a relatively primitive stage of development. Empirical studies have focused on a somewhat limited set of actions. Investigators are still testing a variety of research methodologies.

For investigators accustomed to working within an experimental paradigm, there has been and continues to be a dearth of hypotheses for various phenomena of face-to-face interaction. For some, it has been an irresistable temptation to fill that relative void with hypotheses derived from intuition. After all, the phenomena in question are those with which each of us deals continually throughout each day.

We have argued that use of intuition-based hypotheses is not likely to be an optimally productive research strategy. Common-sense notions of face-to-face interaction, pursued without the benefit of systematic, disciplined observation and analysis, may be no more enlightening with respect to face-to-face interaction than would be a similar approach applied to language. In any event, experience has taught us humility with respect to our own hunches. Many a "brilliant insight" has quickly crumbled when tested against hard data in an exploratory analysis. But perhaps others' intuitions of these phenomena may enjoy higher survival rates.

There is a place for intuitive judgments, hunches, and "trial balloons, " but we hold that that place lies much more in the province of exploratory studies, aimed at the discovery of phenomena and ultimately at the formulation of detailed, explicit, and empirically based hypotheses. But along with the initial testing of intuitions there is also a place for a relatively open-minded perusal of exploratory data and for systematic data analyses, both aimed at the discovery of previously unsuspected relationships. We believe that investigators may be amply rewarded in such efforts—there is much to be discovered. And on the basis of existing research, some of the regularities encountered may be expected to be substantial.

We do not accord hunches and other intuitive notions the status of hypotheses, although at present most hypothesis-testing research in this area must begin with such hunches and intuitions. We suggest that hypotheses be regarded as more formal statements based on empirical results. We suggest that it become standard practice in this research area to expect of an investigator a description of research procedures and results leading to the positing of a hypothesis, no less than it is presently a practice to expect such a description with respect to the testing of a hypothesis.

Finally, exploratory efforts may be given structure and direction when pursued within some integrating conceptual framework. It is within this perspective that such a framework was offered in the preceding chapter to promote further discussion of conceptual issues.

In advocating the approach to data generation and the emphasis on exploratory research described above, we do not view these positions as unique. For example, in Chapter 8 the strong influence of *The natural history of an interview* (McQuown, 1971) was considered at length. Most of the contributors to the volume edited by Kendon, Harris, and Key (1975) share a similar research orientation. And very much in the same spirit is Blurton Jones' (1972) characterization of ethology, which includes, among other things: "(1) emphasis on the use of a large variety of simple observable features of behaviour as the raw data; (2) emphasis on description and a hypothesis-generating, natural history phase as the starting point of a study; (3) a distrust of major categories of behaviour whose meaning and reality have not been made clear . . . [pp. 4–5]."

Induction and Controlled Abstraction

In urging an inductive approach at this point in the study of face-to-face interaction, we have in mind a process in which the data, transcribed in terms of acts, are examined and reexamined in various ways with the aim of discovering significant relationships obtaining in sequences of acts (some of the acts in a sequence possibly occurring simultaneously). As these sequential relationships are discovered and then verified through appropriate analysis, these results may lead the investigator to develop concepts that are designed to apply directly to the observed relationships. In the first instance each such concept may refer precisely to one set of relationships. Because the data themselves involve a minimum of abstraction and the discovered relationships are between these data, it seems natural and desirable, but not necessary, that the first set of hypothesized concepts be at a low level of abstraction.

As research continues and a broader network of relationships is discovered, further sets of concepts may be hypothesized, each set being at a successively higher level of abstraction and tied explicitly to the lower level. Specifying the connections between one level and the next is essential to prevent the intrusion of loose global concepts that are deceptively attractive because of their familiar rich connotations. In this manner, a careful inductive study may provide not only a set of empirically based hypotheses, but also a set of hypotheses that is appropriately controlled and graduated with respect to abstractness.

The turn system is to some extent an example of the inductive generation of hierarchically ordered constructs. At roughly the lowest level is the notion of "signal," which includes in its definition both a set of component cues and a set of appropriate responses by the partner. The notion of "speaking turn" connects several sets of signals and responses. Finally, the full "turn system" attempts to integrate hypotheses relating both to interaction during speaking turns, and to the exchange of speaking turns.

We do not mean to suggest that an investigator should work in a rigidly unidirectional order of increasing abstraction. It seems natural that scientific investigation involves recurring oscillations from one level of abstraction to an adjacent one and then, later, a return to the first level, as research continues. But we are arguing that it is advantageous in relatively new areas of research for initial sets of hypotheses to be constructed at the lowest possible level of abstraction, and for each successively higher level to be developed cautiously and related rigorously to the next lower level. And of course the development of hypotheses may often lead to the deduction of further associations between observable variables.

It is to the careful control of abstraction in hypotheses that we referred in Chapter 1 when we mentioned the notion of "intermediate-level concepts," following the use of that term by Riskin and Faunce (1972). They criticized the loss of such control by investigators who immediately spin theories of dominance and the like, based on analysis of acts.

ACTION SEQUENCES

The notion of action sequences has been mentioned at a number of points in this monograph. It is appropriate now to consider this notion in greater detail. For research on the conduct of face-to-face interaction, we consider the use of action sequences to be as central to the formulation of variables as the use of acts was to data generation.

Interaction cannot be regarded simply as the respective display of (well-formed) signals by two or more individuals. An interaction is not produced when two television sets are each tuned to a different news commentator and then turned toward each other. Clearly, face-to-face interaction, at least in its normal forms, is created through organized sequences of action involving both participants, and the taking of successive actions in such sequences must be dependent in some manner on the preceding actions. Research on the conduct of face-to-face interaction must provide information on these action sequences.

The extreme form of sequential dependency between actions occurs when each action in the sequence is entirely fixed. One can imagine some rigidly "ritualized" action sequence that requires that: Participant A take Action 1; Participant B then take Action 2; A then take Action 3; B then take action 4; and so on. Action 3 must occur and may only occur on the completion of Actions 1 and 2. If this sequence is based on a known convention, the proper use of the sequence by the participants provides information on the situational aspect of interaction strategy, through the fact that that convention was chosen and ratified by the participants. We also know that the convention was performed properly without violation.

When the convention provides for optionality in an action sequence, as with the turn system, each action in the sequence provides additional information. Because each optional action might have been otherwise, it has the potential for yielding information on the state of the participant who takes it, including that participant's reaction to the preceding actions in the sequence. Also, the partner's preceding action(s) may exert an influence on the participant's action in the sense of affecting the probability of its occurring (but not in the sense of determining the action). Such a nondetermining influence was shown to be operating at several points in the turn system.

In an optional sequence, the significance of a participant's action for his interaction strategy cannot be properly evaluated apart from information on (a) the signal-definition rules and the interaction rules in the convention(s) applying to the action; and (b) the convention-relevant preceding and–or concurrent action(s) by the partner. For example, given the turn-system rules, it has been pointed out that the significance of an auditor's switching to the speaker state cannot be evaluated apart from information on whether or not the turn signal is active at the time of the switch, and on whether or not the gesticulation signal is currently active.

Considerations such as these led to the description of each action in an optional sequence as being both a response and an initiative: a response in the sense of taking into account (or failing to do so) the preceding actions of the partner, and an initiative in the sense of representing a positive choice in the presence of alternatives. This characterization of each element in optional action sequences gives conceptual meaning to the study of interaction strategy. It also carries both important implications for the development of such studies, and a critique of existing external-variable studies.

External-Variable Studies and Action Sequences

We have defined external-variable studies as those studies of face-to-face interaction which fail to preserve information on action sequences. We judge this failure to be a crucial but avoidable defect. As mentioned in the discussion of Part III, when information on action sequences is omitted from studies describing participants' actions in face-to-face interaction, this omission has the effect of preventing a meaningful interpretation of results based on analysis of those actions. It is simply not enough to know how many times or for how long during a stretch of interaction a given action occurred, regardless of the sophisticated treatment that is subsequently given to that information. We have applied this criticism to the external-variable research reported in Part II.

We therefore recommend that investigators of the conduct of face-to-face interaction abandon external-variable studies, replacing them with studies based on analysis of action sequences.

It is incontestable that external-variable studies have to date been a primary vehicle for the empirical study of face-to-face interaction, particularly in the study of "nonverbal communication." As such, these studies have made a basic contribution to our understanding of the interaction processes addressed. We are convinced, however, that it is time for the field to move to a more powerful paradigm, one that makes more efficient and effective use of the observable events in face-to-face interaction. We believe that that paradigm should be based in part on the analysis of action sequences.

Before the discussion proceeds further, let us point out the obvious: like most ideas in social science, the notion of action sequences is not a new one.

Action sequences have played a prominent role in the studies of other investigators. Examples of such work would be Altmann (1965), Chapple (1970), Jaffe and Feldstein (1970), Kaye (1976), Kendon (1967,1975b), McQuown (1971), Meltzer, Morris, and Hayes (1971), Sacks, Schegloff, and Jefferson (1974), and Schegloff and Sacks (1973).

Formulating Action-Sequence Variables in Exploratory Studies

We have been advocating research in which variables are formulated in terms of action sequences. But what would an action-sequence variable look like? How would an investigator go about setting up such variables? What elements would be included in their description? We shall consider these issues and then provide some examples of this kind of variable.

Our account will be couched entirely in the terms of the conceptual framework described in Chapter 12. The study of action sequences is not, however, restricted to that particular framework: the phenomena of action sequences can be rationalized from a number of different theoretical perspectives. When extensive hypotheses are not available for action-sequence variables in the type of interaction under study, we have suggested taking an exploratory, discovery-oriented approach. In the following discussion we assume that the investigator has chosen some set of actions to observe and has made the necessary transcriptions showing the location of each action in the stream of interaction.

Response initiatives.   As described above, when action sequences involve optionality of any sort, a given action may be considered to be both a response and an initiative. In that it follows other actions, it may be considered a response. In that other actions follow it, it may be considered an initiative. This being the case, the same action can be separately analyzed in its capacity as a response, and in its capacity as an initiative. Thus, the investigator can attempt to discover the actions systematically preceding a given action, and–or the actions systematically following it. That is, in the exploratory analysis of sequences there is no a priori "first" action. The designation of some action as being "first" in some sense is a hypothesis. (Examples of such hypotheses would be (a) the "first pair parts" in specific types of "adjacency pairs" proposed by Sacks, Schegloff, and Jefferson (1974) and Schegloff and Sacks (1973); and (b) the activation of the turn signal as the first step in the three-action sequence required for the smooth exchange of speaking turns.)

Separation of sequence-related acts.   Although time was not an aspect of the hypothesized turn system, it is clear that speaker signal display and auditor response in that system were separated by relatively brief time intervals: generally less than a second. This need not be the case for every action sequence. In Chapter 12 a hypothetical example is given of a structural linkage in a conversation between the form of the initial greeting and the form of the final leave taking, regardless of the length of the intervening conversation. Similarly, one might find certain relationships between the posture of one participant and the subsequent posture of the partner. These shifts might, however, be separated by considerably more than a fraction of a second. It is reasonable to expect that, when applicable conventions are not known, the discovery of sequence-related acts will become more difficult (a) as these acts are more widely separated by time and–or other interactional events; and (b) when the acts involve different sorts of actions (such as smiling and self-adaptors), as opposed to the same action (such as smiling). On the other hand, when the applicable conventions are known, identifying the related acts is routine, regardless of their separation or dissimilarity.

Describing action-sequence variables.   In the following sections, four elements, necessary to the description of action-sequence variables, will be considered: (a) the participants involved; (b) the aspects of actions relevant to the variable; (c) the type of linkage obtaining between the actions; and (d) the identification of actions as either dependent or independent.

Participants.   In the initial stages of data collection and analysis, data on the two participants in an interaction should not be pooled. The discussion below will assume that Participant A's responses to Participant B are distinguished from Participant B's responses to Participant A. It is of course entirely possible that these initially separate data sets might at some later point be pooled for certain research purposes.

Aspects of actions.   Formulating variables on the basis of the observed actions necessarily takes into account various aspects of the respective actions, such as onset, offset, and duration, as well as parameters of the action sequences, such as temporal intervals, and perhaps location of the entire action sequence in the stream of interaction. Part of the purpose of the exploratory study is to discover those aspects of the actions and those parameters of the sequences that are relevant to the phenomena being investigated. For example, it is important to ascertain whether it is the beginning, ending, or simply the occurrence of a participant's act that is related to aspects of other acts in the sequence. (For the sake of convenience, we refer below to "acts" rather than to "aspects of acts." We hope that this ellipsis will not be confusing. For example, it should be apparent that the statement, "act X precedes act Y," means that the onset of X preceded the onset of Y.)

Linkages between acts.   Crucial to the description of the successive acts in an action sequence is a statement of the manner in which a subsequent act is connected, or linked, to the preceding one. To be considered part of the same action sequence, the linkage between two or more acts must be described in terms of some time interval, or in terms of interactional events of some sort, or in terms of some combination of these two parameters. Careful analyses leading to the explicit definition of such temporal and–or event-based linkages between acts in a sequence appear to be a necessary element of any action-sequence study.

Independent and dependent actions.   It seems appropriate to label each action in an action-sequence variable as either independent or dependent. Independent actions are those that either must or must not occur in order for the variable to be observed. Dependent actions are those that may or may not occur in each instance of the variable. It will be apparent that the identification of an action as independent or dependent is always specific to the particular action-sequence variable being examined. The same action may be identified as independent in one such variable and as dependent in another. Independent and dependent actions are indicated in the examples of action-sequence variables that immediately follow.

Action-Sequence Variables: Some Examples

Given the preceding discussion, it may be well to consider a few examples of action-sequence variables, as we presently envision them. It will be seen that one of these examples is drawn from the turn system, while the others have not been investigated as such at this writing, serving merely as convenient examples.

1.   *Rate of auditor attempts to take the speaking turn, given the activation of x turn cues by the speaker, when the gesticulation signal is not concurrently activated.*   This variable has, of course, been considered above. It involves three actions; but because two of these actions are simultaneously considered (turn cues and gesticulation signal), the sequence has only two parts. The turn cues and gesticulation signal are independent actions, in that the turn cues must occur, and the gesticulation signal must not. The auditor attempt to take the turn is a dependent action because it either may or may not occur. (This is because the variable is concerned with rate of occurrence of attempts.) The variable involves event-based linkages both between turn cues and gesticulation signal, and between these and the turn attempt. (Of course, further specification is required of (a) the various acts and aspects of acts contained within the terms "turn cue," "gesticulation signal," and "attempt to take the speaking turn"; and (b) the nature of the linkage. But these need not be reiterated here.)

The preceding example views the situation from the auditor's point of view, positing the speaker's signal display as the independent action, and the auditor's response as the dependent action. The perspective may be reversed by positing the auditor's response as independent and the speaker's display as dependent. From this perspective the preceding auditor response would be treated as the antecedent of the subsequent speaker display. We might then ask such questions as, Does a high rate of auditor attempts tend to affect the number of turn cues subsequently activated by the speaker?

2.   *Rate of participant's smiling in response to, and during, the partner's smiling.*   This presently imaginary variable involves an event-based linkage

("during the partner's smile"). The partner's smiling is an independent action; the variable cannot be observed unless the partner smiles. The participant's smiling is a dependent action; the variable is a rate variable. The sequence of actions is indicated by the term "response," indicating the partner must smile first. As aspects of actions, the variable involves the duration of the partner's smiling, but only the initiation of the participant's smiling.

3. *Duration of partner's smiling after participant's smiling in response to, and during, the partner's smiling.*   This variable, awkward in its statement, merely considers a further aspect of the preceding variable: how long the partner keeps smiling after the participant responds by smiling. Here, both smiles are independent actions, in that both must occur in order for the variable to be observed. The dependent element of the variable is, of course, the duration of the first smile, after the initiation of the second. The linkage between the two actions remains an event-based one. And the variable involves the same aspects of actions as the preceding one: the duration of the partner's smiling, and the initiation of the participant's smiling.

4. *Rate of participant's averting gaze from the partner within the first six seconds of the partner's smiling, when that smiling is not during the participant's prior smiling.*   This presently imaginary variable involves two different actions: gaze aversion and smiling. The three-part action sequence includes two independent actions: (a) the partner's smiling, and (b) the participant's not smiling before the partner's smile. There is one dependent action: (c) the participant's averting gaze or not doing so. The aspect involved in Action *b* is duration; in Actions *a* and *c*, onset. The linkage between *b* and *a* is an event-based one; between *a* and *c*, a temporal one.

Evaluation of Action-Sequence Variables

An action-sequence variable becomes interesting for further research through the discovery of some empirical relationship between acts that are (a) linked by some explicit temporal and–or event-based factor; (b) occur in sequences; (c) involving both participants. This relationship may be expressed through any appropriate statistical procedure.

A simple example of such a relationship would be the correlation found between auditor attempts to take the speaking turn, and number of active speaker turn cues at a unit boundary (when the gesticulation signal is not concurrently active). This correlation is based on the data shown in Tables 11.3 and 11.4 and suggests the action-sequence variable given as the first example in the preceding section. The variable as stated is meaningful only when the turn-system convention (or one similar to it) is being used by the participants; the variable is useful only to the extent to which the turn system cues have been adequately and accurately described. Being based on the turn-system convention, this variable directly reflects interaction strategy (considered further in a later section).

On the other hand, it has already been stressed that action-sequence variables are considered the appropriate vehicle for exploratory studies of face-to-face interaction, aimed at hypotheses concerning conventions and–or interaction strategy.

Summing Observations of an Action-Sequence Variable

Once data have been generated by observing the course of a series of action sequences relevant to a variable, these data may of course be summed over any stretch of interaction or over any interactions that are of interest. For example, action-sequence variables could have been summed over the five-minute stretches of interaction studied in Part II. The error in the Part II study was not in summing data over stretches of interaction, but in ignoring action sequences.

When constancies in certain parameters of action sequences are found for a number of subjects, such findings may be strongly suggestive of conventions and–or strategies operating in the observed interactions. The turn-system study, especially in its early stages, may be taken as an example of an action-sequence study when conventions are not known.

Action-Sequence Variables and Partitions of the Data

Although action-sequence variables appear to have the potential of considerable precision with respect to the events of face-to-face interaction, this precision may carry a concomitant difficulty. More differentiated variables imply a greater selectivity from the available data and more partitions of the data. This situation is clearly illustrated by the speaker turn cue–auditor turn claim correlation. As indicated in Table 11.3, analyzing this variable required 13 partitions of the data: 7 (for the activation of 0–6 turn cues when the gesticulation signal is not concurrently active), plus 6 (for the activation of 0–5 turn cues when the gesticulation signal is concurrently active.) For this variable and other similar variables, our transcriptions were insufficient in extent to provide reliable estimates of data points for individual participants. Certainly, other variables may require fewer partitions of the data, and there may be ways to combine the data so as to provide more entries for each data point. But in general, it appears that there will always have to be some sort of tradeoff between precision in specifying the variable and extent of required transcription.

Notice in this regard that, strictly speaking, to increase data points on an action-sequence variable, one does not need transcriptions of longer temporal stretches of interaction, but rather more instances of the sequence in question. Thus, the information available on a given action-sequence variable depends on the frequency of occurrence of the independent action(s) in the transcription, not on the number of minutes transcribed.

External-Variable Studies and Action-Sequence Variables

The wealth of results available in the reports of external-variable studies provides an excellent source of leads on potentially productive action-sequence variables. For example, in the study presented in Part II a correlation was reported between amount of subject's smiling and amount of partner's smiling in the five-minute conversations. This correlation suggests that there was some tendency toward mutual smiling in the conversations, although, because of the way the data were handled, this need not be the case. In any event, this result suggests that it would be interesting to formulate and to test a series of action-sequence variables related to mutual smiling. Several examples of such variables were described in a preceding section. In this manner, the extensive available results of published external-variable studies may be used as a valuable resource for developing action-sequence studies.

It is also interesting to note that external-variable studies not infrequently contain action-sequence variables that are incompletely specified, observed, and rationalized. We may draw once again on the study reported in Part II. Indiscriminately included in that external-variable study was an action-sequence variable: "rate of interruptions." This variable involved observing a series of actions, making discriminations concerning turn beginnings versus auditor back channels, and the like. It is clear that a proper description of the variable would include a description of the sequence involved and of the relevant discriminations. It is also clear that it would be better not to require raters to make such a complex set of observations, even when working with film or videotape. A preferable procedure would be to make a transcription of the relevant actions and then to tabulate instances of the variable (and perhaps of other related variables) from the transcription.

Another action-sequence variable frequently found in external-variable studies is that of mutual gazing. This variable necessarily involves the action of both participants, as well as a sequence of actions. (A simultaneous occurrence of respective actions may be considered a special case of a sequence.) Of course, more information on the mutual-gaze sequence would be useful, such as which participant looks first at the other, which one looks away first, and the like. Findings on these action-sequence variables in external-variable studies are, of course, of considerable interest to more explicit studies of action sequences.

CRESCAT: A Program for Analyzing Action Sequences

In order to facilitate research on action sequences, a computer program is being developed by Duncan and Kenneth Kaye (also at the University of Chicago). The most important aspect of CRESCAT (not an acronym) is its on-line capability of finding complex patterns in sequences of data. This program is briefly described in Appendix B.

STUDYING CONVENTIONS OF FACE-TO-FACE INTERACTION

Part III reported a study that eventuated in the hypothesis of a "turn system" operating in the two-person, face-to-face interactions observed. As mentioned above, this study was described as being concerned with elements of the structure or organization of face-to-face interaction, but these terms may now be interpreted as referring to elements of convention. The study itself is referred to as the "turn-system study" in this discussion.

It is now possible to consider the turn-system study in the light both of the general research principles described above, and of the metatheoretical discussion of convention and strategy in the preceding chapter. This examination can serve to illustrate and clarify the metatheoretical analysis; it can also provide a critique of the current status of the proposed turn system.

General Research Principles

It may be readily seen that the turn-system study embodied many of the general principles considered earlier in this chapter.

Induction

The inductive strategy of the study has already been repeatedly emphasized, to a sufficiency. Clearly, the initial, exploratory study was not designed to test hypotheses. But hypotheses stemming from the exploratory study received an initial test in the ensuing "replication" study. It should be clear at this point that the emphasis on inductive research is not meant to imply an abandonment of hypothesis testing. Rather, the benefits of developing strong, focused, empirically based hypotheses have been stressed.

Acts

Within the context of the inductive strategy, data were generated in terms of acts, as we have defined that term. In general, raters transcribing these acts were required to attend closely to the physical aspects of the events observed, using a minimum of inference. The "meaning" or "intention" lying behind the acts played essentially no part in the transcribing process. The acts were considered to be discrete, and an important aspect of their transcription was the careful indication of the beginning and end of each act.

It was judged that a productive tactic for an exploratory study is to cast as wide a data net as possible. Accordingly, acts in both speech and body motion were transcribed. And within each of these "modalities" every effort was made to be inclusive. Certainly, the investigator cannot discover relationships between actions that have not been transcribed. The limits of the transcription were dictated mainly by human, financial, and technical considerations, as opposed to cryptohypotheses. (An example of cryptohypotheses operating in exploratory research would be the decision by Duncan & Rosenthal, 1968, in their study of experimenter bias to analyze the speech stream of experimenters for potential cues mediating the bias effect, and to neglect, at least initially, the visual record. Of course, if speech events had failed to account for an appreciable proportion of the variance in subjects' responses, it is likely that the body motion would have been examined.)

Once hypotheses are generated as a result of exploratory work, studies designed to test the hypotheses will follow a more economical transcription procedure. The identification of the acts in this case would be determined by the hypotheses being tested. This contrasting transcription procedure is illustrated in the replication study, in which only those acts involved in the definition of signals and—or in the creation of unit boundaries were transcribed. These acts comprised a relatively small part of the acts transcribed in the exploratory study and were more broadly defined than they had been in the first study.

But what about those acts transcribed in the exploratory study that did not figure in the turn system? The resources invested in transcribing those acts need not be considered wasted. In the first place, a number of acts were tested as potential cues in various signals and were explicitly rejected as such. This is useful information on that particular set of acts. In addition, as further exploratory studies of other conversational phenomena are carried out, previously "unimportant" acts may prove to be of central importance for these phenomena.

Interaction

The emphasis on interaction in the turn-system study resulted not only in the transcription of acts by both participants in the two-person conversations, but also in careful location of the beginning and end of each act in the stream of interaction.

The full inclusion of both participants in the study was made possible by three simple steps. First, both participants were considered to be "subjects" in the study, neither participant being a confederate or the like. Second, both participants were equally represented in the visible and audible portions of the videotape recording. Third, the same transcribing system was applied to the actions of both participants. These points seem straightforward, needing no further elaboration.

In addition to including both participants, the analysis of sequences of acts is an essential element in the study of face-to-face interaction (as has been discussed above). It is possible to analyze sequences of acts only when the location of the beginning and of the end of each transcribed act is carefully recorded. As noted earlier, it is possible to indicate the location of, say, the beginning of an act either (a) with reference to absolute chronological time, using film or videotape frame numbers (a laborious process when done by hand) or perhaps an event recorder; or (b) with reference to other transcribed acts—the approach used in the turn-system study. This latter approach preserves the sequence of actions but loses information on actual chronological time separating the beginnings and–or ends of the acts being studied.

We now believe that temporal information on various aspects of the turn system would be of considerable interest in the study of convention. For example, is there a "window" of time through which a would-be speaker must pass in order to make an appropriate claim of the speaking turn? Jaffe and Feldstein's (1970) study of temporal aspects of certain action sequences indicates that there are strong regularities in the timing of various conversational phenomena. It seems potentially valuable to relate such temporal regularities to the display of, and response to, turn-system cues and signals. Thus, the omission of chronological time (as contrasted to relative temporal positions) may be judged to be a potentially significant omission in the formulation of the turn system.

Use of Statistics

Mentioned in Chapter 9 but not in the preceding discussion was the use of statistics to document the interactional regularities claimed in the turn system. This practice departed from the strong linguistic influence that shaped much of the turn-system study. It is perhaps the more common practice in linguistics and in anthropology simply to describe the regularities in language or in custom found in a particular study, together with some examples of the phenomena in question.

But it seems legitimate to inquire about such issues as the extent of the transcribed materials upon which observation was based, the types of violation of the regularity together with their respective rates of occurrence, and the extent to which occurrence of the regularity exceeds that which may be expected on the basis of chance alone. Calculation of such rates requires a corpus of systematically developed observation. The statistics required for issues of this sort appear to be often quite simple; at least they were so in the turn-system study. And the claimed regularities benefit from the additional support of public evaluation. Finally, as mentioned in Part III, the regularities produced by convention may be expected in most cases to be quite strong, relative to those typically encountered in social-science studies that do not benefit from a data base of acts on which convention operates.

Seeking Relationships between Sequential Acts

The purpose of an exploratory study of action sequences is to discover and document relationships between sequential acts. One approach to such a study would be to seek acts that serve as "predictors" of subsequent acts. This seems to be a natural approach, in that action sequences inevitably involve some temporal ordering of events. However, the notion of prediction seems to be an inexact characterization of what has been said to be happening in optional action sequences. In the case of the turn system, for example, the activation of a turn signal by the speaker provided an appropriate point in the interaction for the auditor to act to take the speaking turn if the auditor was so inclined. When this turn-taking option attaching to the prior signal is used infrequently by the auditor, analyses may show that signal to be a very weak predictor, despite the fact that the relationship between the acts in the sequence is a highly regular one, in that virtually all attempts to take the turn by the auditor were preceded by the turn signal. From this viewpoint, it may be argued that data analysis based on behavior prediction is an inefficient approach to discovering the relationship in question.

A more effective discovery technique would seem to involve the analysis of the antecedents of the later acts. In such an analysis the question would be, Given the occurrence of some act, what act(s) typically precede it? This was the discovery procedure used for the turn system. Thus, we recommend a sort of "backwards" approach to exploratory analysis of optional action sequences.

Once exploratory analyses yield some potential relationships between sequential acts, these relationships must, of course, be verified by further analyses aimed at weeding out those relationships occurring on the basis of chance, and at ascertaining the precise nature of the relationship in question.

The final set of relationships obtained may include some results most directly relevant to conventions applying to the observed actions, while other results may be most directly relevant to associated interaction strategy. Part of the investigator's task is to disentangle these two sets of results by hypothesizing conventions, including relevant optionalities. It may be noted that this disentangling process was not complete in the first report of turn-system results (Duncan, 1972). The correlation between number of turn cues displayed and auditor attempts to take the turn was described as evidence directly supporting the hypothesized signals. It is true that that evidence supports the hypotheses, but only indirectly. The correlation appears to stem from regularities in the participants' interaction strategy within the context of the turn-system convention. Thus, the correlation is directly related to the convention-based interaction strategy and only indirectly to the convention.

Description of Conventions

Convention Substance and Organization

Apart from the general principles of research on the conduct of face-to-face interaction, what of the more specific problems of describing regularities in action that are hypothesized to be convention based? The turn system itself now may be evaluated in terms of the conceptual framework presented in Chapter 12.

It is clear that the proposed turn system focused on the convention substance and organization. Convention "substance" included the following elements: (a) postulated states, both of the participants and of the interaction, necessary to provide a rationale for the operation of signals and the like; (b) certain states of the participants, hypothesized in order to provide a more adequate description of the regularities encountered; (c) a series of signals and, as necessary, their attendant cues, hypothesized to represent in an observable manner the relevant states of the participants; and (d) certain moves relevant to the convention that may or may not be accompanied by signals.

The hypothesized signals and cues required definition in two respects:

1.   Definitions of signal display described the actions that constituted a display of the signal and in some cases the locations at which those actions must occur in order to be considered a signal.

2.   Definitions of signal activity described the stretch of interaction over which the signal was considered to be active, once it had been displayed.

Convention organization was described in terms of rules. In general, rules stated the relationship between any two or more elements of the turn system. It seemed useful to make a distinction between signal-definition rules and interaction rules. Signal-definition rules were said to describe the relationship between a given signal, and either a turn-system state, or some other signal. Interaction rules were said to describe permissible sequences of actions within the turn system, given the currently active signal(s), and in some cases, certain preceding actions by one or both participants.

Variation in the Performance of Convention

In the preceding chapter several types of variation in the performance of convention were noted. These included permissible variation in the display of signals (several types of display variation were mentioned), response alternatives deriving from optional sequences of action provided for by the convention, and outright violation of the convention. In general, these sources of variation were described in the turn system, although this sort of information was not an initial objective of that study. Types and rates of violations of the proposed rules are documented in the various tables. Response alternatives within the convention at each step in action sequences were enumerated. And the variety of ways a given signal might be displayed in terms of its constituent cues was indicated. It seems as important to acknowledge these aspects of convention-related actions that are not constrained by a convention, as to describe those aspects that are so constrained.

Turn-System States

The description of the turn system included several sets of internal "states," some sets postulated prior to analysis, and some hypothesized on the basis of results. The inclusion of these unobservable states in the turn system should make it clear that our approach, while heavily emphasizing the observation of relatively concrete acts, is not in any sense behavioristic. We do not hesitate to contemplate phenomena that are internal to the participant. The turn-system signals were considered to be about precisely such internal phenomena. It will be recalled that in Chapter 2 we argued strongly against attempts to generate data by requiring raters to "observe" unobservable states such as anxiety and the like. We did not, however, argue against all reference to unobservables. They have their proper place as postulated or hypothesized entities in the description of the organization of interaction.

Emotions as States

One set of internal states that has been considered extensively in the "nonverbal-communication" literature is the emotions. There has always been a substantial interest in nonverbal actions as being expressive of emotional states. In comparing the conceptual basis of the research on the expression of emotional states with that of the research on the turn system, two coordinate distinctions may be drawn.

In the first place, the focus of the turn-system research is clearly different: the organization of interaction, as opposed to the expression of emotion. But a proper description of the organization of interaction may in many instances include the postulation or hypothesis of internal states. In this case, however (our second distinction), these states arise directly from and are fully integrated with the organization being described.

It seems reasonable to expect that, as research on the organization of interaction continues, a variety of internal states will be proposed. Some of these states will be unsuspected prior to the discovery of the organization in question; some of the states may resemble, or be identical to, current notions of emotional states. In any event, the present course of research on face-to-face interaction seems substantially different from that of research on emotion that uses various "nonverbal" actions, such as facial expressions (e.g., Ekman, 1974; Ekman, Friesen, & Ellsworth, 1972). From the perspective of research on the expression of emotion, there is much in face-to-face interaction research that is irrelevant or uninformative. From the perspective of research on face-to-face interaction, the emotions may be viewed as a very special type of state, hypothesized primarily on some basis other than research on the process of face-to-face interaction. Further, the practical effect of research directed solely at the expression of emotion is to ignore other essential aspects of the interaction system, such as signals, rules, sequences of action involving both participants, and the like.

Thus, these two lines of research, often regarded as essentially the same sort of endeavor, may be seen as contrasting in many respects. It is difficult to anticipate the extent to which the two lines will tend to converge in the future.

Elements of Convention Not Included in the Present Description of the Turn System

In light of the discussion in the preceding chapter there are a number of aspects of a full description of a convention that were not included in the turn system. In this sense the turn system as presented cannot be considered a complete description of a convention.

Time. It was mentioned just above that chronological time was omitted from the transcriptions that served as data for the study and thus was not an element of the turn system. Only further investigation will establish the seriousness of this omission. However, it seems reasonable to expect that, for example, both time and interactional events may play a part in the active periods of cues and the like. It may be noted that, just as a structural study of face-to-face interaction may be deficient without the consideration of time, a careful study of temporal factors in interaction, such as is provided by investigators using the interaction chronograph in various forms (e.g., Jaffe & Feldstein, 1970; Matarazzo & Wiens, 1972), may benefit from consideration of a broader range of actions and aspects of actions. It seems that it is no longer appropriate for these two types of studies to continue as quasi-independent lines of research.

Situational requirements. The greatest single omission of the turn-system study was the failure to specify the situational requirements of convention(s) represented by the turn system. Within the conceptual framework presented in the preceding chapter, the situational requirements, regardless of whether broad or narrow, are a necessary element of the description of any convention. These requirements have to do with the sorts of persons who may appropriately take slots in a convention, the social settings in which the conventions may appropriately be used, and the like. In weak defense of this omission at this stage of the research, it may be pointed out that situational requirements are impossible to establish in advance of the formulation of the convention in question. However, pursuit of this issue should now be possible for the turn system, just as it has been for other conventions that were previously well understood, such as the *ty–vy* forms in Russian and the American forms of address mentioned in the last chapter. Research of this sort potentially provides multiple benefits: information is developed on the situational requirements of conventions, on possible variations in conventions in different situations, and on the nature and organization of the social categories and categorizations used by the individuals participating in the convention.

Sanctions attaching to violation.   Despite the fact that all violations of the turn system in the observed conversations were noted, careful study was not made of the sanctions attaching to these violations. As mentioned in Chapter 12, for a convention of the turn-system type there seem in general to be two potential effects of one or more violations: an effect on the subsequent course of the interaction, and an effect on the opinions concerning the violator by those who observe the violation (including the violator) or those who hear about it. The most direct approach to studying the sanctions attaching to specific convention violations would seem to be through analysis of the course of the subsequent conversation. The techniques for studying interaction strategies, considered in the next section, may prove to be useful for evaluating the effect of violations.

STUDYING INTERACTION STRATEGIES IN FACE-TO-FACE INTERACTION

Within the conceptual framework described in Chapter 12, the study of interaction strategy in face-to-face interaction is a necessary complement to the study of convention. In Chapter 12 it was said that there are two basic sources of interaction strategy: the dynamics of situation, and variation in the performing of convention. These two elements of interaction strategy are discussed immediately below.

Dynamics of Situation

An appropriate convention or set of conventions can be chosen by a participant only after that participant has formulated the situation in which he is interacting. According to the metatheory, this formulating process involves a classifying of various aspects of the situation, including the participant himself, the partner, other parties to the interaction, the social setting in which it occurs, and so forth. Once the situation has been formulated, conventions appropriately used in that situation can be brought into play. In this manner, formulation of situation is a necessary precedent of convention-based action. Through the conventions that a participant uses in an interaction, that participant's formulation of situation (or at least his ostensive formulation) becomes manifest to some degree to the partner.

It was held that formulation of situation may also be used in the service of interaction strategy. This strategy-related use of situation was considered in the section of Chapter 12 on "Interaction Strategy through Dynamics of Situation." Four potential components of situation-related strategy were mentioned. (Obviously, there may be more.)

Initial Formulation.   A participant's initial classification of various aspects of the situation apparently involves a series of decisions in which the participant makes some real choices. As has been repeatedly stated, if choice or optionality is involved, then resulting action is necessarily a strategy; for whatever the participant does, he might legitimately have done otherwise. Thus, it is possible that a participant's initial formulation of situation, as evidenced through the conventions he uses, may be developed in such a manner as to serve the participant's interaction strategy, implicit or explicit.

Collaboration.   By responding in a manner appropriate to a convention initiated by a participant, the partner implies acceptance of at least some portion of the participant's formulation of situation. Such acceptance was termed "ratification," following Goffman (1967, 1971). On the other hand, it was said that the partner may refuse to ratify simply by not taking the slot allotted to him within the convention introduced by the participant. In any event, this ratifying or nonratifying response, where it involves viable choices by the partner, necessarily becomes a strategy, paralleling the choices involved in the participant's initiation.

Change.   A change in the prevailing conventions in an interaction can only be the result of a change in the formulation of situation, except in the probably rare instance in which two alternative conventions for handling the same coordination problem have the same situational requirements. Changes in the formulation of the situation may clearly be used for strategic purposes.

Deceit.   None of the three potential aspects of situation-related strategy mentioned above—initial formulation, collaboration, and change—need involve actual deceit. Each may simply represent the choice of one of two or more real alternatives in the classifications applicable to a situation. But deceit may of course be used. A participant may strategically use conventions that carry situational requirements at variance with the classifications that the participant has actually made.

Summary: Dynamics of Situation

Because we have no personal experience with research related to describing the situational requirements of conventions, our discussion of research practices in this area is necessarily limited. But several brief and general comments may be made.

We view dynamics of situation and related interaction strategies as more advanced research topics. To investigate them, some foundation of information is needed on the substance and organization of the conventions used, and on the situational requirements for those conventions. Further, the possibility of such research depends on the existence of alternative conventions for handling the same or highly similar coordination problems. Here the examples may be those studies cited in the discussion of situation: Ervin-Tripp's

(1972) study of such forms of address as first name, kin title plus first name, title and last name, etc.; and Friedrich's (1972) study of the *ty–vy* forms in Russian. In both of these studies the general problem was that of using an appropriate mode of address with respect to the partner, and alternative forms were available. But these two studies are also examples of the fact that such research need not wait on the discovery and documentation of relatively unfamiliar conventions, such as those applying to the exchange of speaking turns, although such conventions may of course be used for studies of situation. The studies by Friedrich and by Ervin-Tripp suggest that a number of interesting conventions are already sufficiently well understood to be used effectively in situation research by enterprising researchers.

Finally, a careful reading of Friedrich's paper suggests that the study of strategy through situation may well be the most subtle and sensitive approach to interaction dynamics presently available.

Variation in Performing Conventions

The discussion of strategy through the dynamics of situation was concerned with the variations possible in the choice of conventions, and with the implications of these choices for the prevailing formulation of situation. As described in Chapter 12, once conventions are chosen, there is still room for variation in the way in which they are actually performed. In general, this variation stems from aspects of the convention that provide for specific options in their performance. A choice of any one of the optional alternatives would, of course, be entirely appropriate within the convention. A special, but presumably not rare, case of variation in the performance of conventions would be the violation of one or more of a convention's interaction rules.

The availability of options within the conventions used in an interaction provides both the possibility and the necessity for interaction strategy with respect to their enactment. More concretely, the options actually available within the conventions prevailing in an interaction define the specific nature and range of strategies that participants may appropriately use. Further, the absence of excessively harsh (as perceived by the participants) sanctions provide the possibility, but not the necessity, of an interaction strategy involving convention violation.

Of the types of variation in the performance of conventions mentioned in the preceding chapter, the following seem most relevant to the construction of strategies:

1. *Variation in the display of signals.* Permissible variation in the display of signals include such aspects as the repeated use of certain signals and cues drawn from larger signal and cue sets, use of cues in characteristic sequences or simultaneous clusters, and the relative frequency or extent of use of certain cues or signals. As examples, a given participant's turn signal may

frequently include the drawl cue, while never including the sociocentric-sequence cue. Or a participant may make repeated use of the following cluster of turn cues in the display of the turn signal: drawl, intonation, sociocentric sequence, and paralanguage on sociocentric sequence. Or a participant may make extensive use of the gesticulation signal, relative to that signal's use by other participants.

2. *Response alternatives.* Response alternatives are available when a convention's interaction rules indicate that participants have the option of responding or not responding with given signals and–or moves at various points in the enactment of the convention. For example, in the turn system an auditor may or may not act to take the speaking turn upon the activation of a speaker turn signal.

3. *Violation.* Violation refers to action contrary to the convention's rules. An example within the turn system would be the auditor's interrupting the speaker: that is, acting to take the turn when the turn signal is not activated.

These types of variation in the performance of conventions may be used by a participant as elements of an interaction strategy. It has been emphasized, however, that the strategy itself can be adequately described only in terms of action sequences.

Convention-Based Studies of Interaction Strategy

Earlier in this chapter it was stated that an entirely exploratory study of action sequences might typically yield information on both convention and strategy. A distinguishable type of action-sequence study would be one in which some of the conventions applying to the actions under investigation are known. Let us term this sort of study a convention-based study. Such a study would ordinarily be designed to produce evidence primarily on interaction strategy, although it might further clarify aspects of the convention as well.

Knowledge of the signals, rules, and other elements of a convention greatly facilitates the formulation of action-sequence variables. Such convention-based, action-sequence variables would be formulated taking into account specific types of permissible variation (or of violation), for given signals and–or moves of a convention. For example, on the basis of the turn system it is possible to formulate such action-sequence variables as (a) "rate of auditor interruptions per minute of speaker's talking time, when the gesticulation signal is not active"; (b) "rate of auditor's head nods per display of within-turn signal by the speaker"; and (c) "rate of violations of speaker turn signal by auditor." (The use of terms in these examples assumes the fuller specification of the relevant actions, as given in Chapter 11.)

A variable would be considered properly relevant to the performance of a convention if the variable is based on actions of functional significance within the convention. The variables mentioned in the preceding paragraph are intended to be examples of variables relevant to the turn system. But variables that are formulated using aspects of actions such as "number of different types of gestures used" or "parakinesic intensity of gestures", do not refer to aspects of actions that are relevant to the turn system in its present form. (These aspects may, of course, be relevant to other conventions applying to the use of gestures in conversations. They may also become relevant to the turn system on the basis of additional evidence on that convention.)

The number of relevant action-sequence variables that may be developed for a convention is a function of (a) the number of actions—cues, signals, and moves—involved in the convention; (b) the number of relevant ways in which each action may vary; and (c) the number of rules (that is, relationships) connecting these elements. Variables may be based both on action variation permissible within the convention, and on variation in violation of the interaction rules, such as interruptions.

Knowledge of a convention permits considerable precision in the formulation of action-sequence variables. An example may be drawn from the turn and gesticulation signals within the turn system. With regard to the gesticulation signal, gross time spent using the signal or the extent of signal use (time of signal use, divided by time spent speaking) would not be a proper element of an action-sequence variable based on the turn system. Within that system it is of importance only that the gesticulation signal is active near the end of unit of analysis, where auditors may properly act to take the turn if a turn signal is active. It is important to know, therefore, the number of unit boundaries at which both the turn signal and the gesticulation signal are active. An action-sequence variable might then be formulated in terms of the auditor's response at such points. This example suggests the potential benefits, for studies of interaction strategy, of capitalizing on the knowledge of rules operating in the convention. This knowledge permits the proper specification of "linkages" (as discussed in an earlier section) between elements of an action-sequence variable.

It will be noted that the study reported in Part II did not take unit boundaries into account but rather made use of the gross time and extent variables mentioned above. The practice in that study of ignoring unit boundaries was purposefully adopted in order to save time, but it, together with the failure to use action-sequence variables, was probably a central factor explaining the dearth of useful results for the gesture variables.

Discussion of action-sequence variables based on the turn system has focused on sequences that (a) are initiated by the speaker; and (b) involve a sequence of two actions. Turn-system variables, and presumably variables based on other conventions, need not be limited by these specific characteristics.

Sequences of three actions have already been mentioned in connection with the speaker continuation signal in the turn system. Action-sequence variables relevant to this signal took into account two independent actions: (a) whether or not a speaker within-turn signal had been activated; (b) whether or not the auditor responded with a back channel; and the dependent action: (c) whether or not a continuation signal ensued. Once again, analyses in this case required a number of partitions of the data. Another example of a three-action sequence (not yet analyzed for our data) would include information on (a) number of speaker turn cues; (b) presence or absence of auditor turn claim as independent actions; and (c) number of turn cues on next subsequent turn-cue display (when there is no auditor turn claim) as the dependent action.

As indicated immediately above, action-sequence variables based on the turn system might treat the auditor's actions as independent. For example, one might examine such actions as the number of speaker turn or within-turn cues displayed or the probability of gesticulation-signal activation, following such actions as an auditor turn claim, an auditor interruption of some sort, or an auditor back channel.

Description of Interaction Strategies

Prior to intensive research on interaction strategies, it is perhaps inappropriate to engage in speculation concerning the description of interaction strategies. However, certain general observations may be made.

The first task of the investigator of interaction strategy would seem to be the identification of those action-sequence variables most effective in the description of a strategy. Each effective variable relates to one element of a participant's interaction strategy, for example, tendency for an auditor to interrupt following some action by the speaker. But it can be shown that an element of strategy cannot be fully described in terms of a single action-sequence variable. Rather, that strategy element for a participant would be described in terms of an action-sequence variable, given some pattern of action by the partner.

The frequently used example of the gesticulation signal may serve as an illustration of this point. Imagine a conversation in which a partner as speaker gesticulates across a large proportion of boundaries at which the turn signal is also active. In this situation it may become something of a strategy issue for the participant as auditor whether to continue respecting the gesticulation signal, or to begin "breaking in" by claiming the turn at such points in order to get a word in edgewise. Let us say that the participant chooses to break in frequently. In contrast, imagine a partner as speaker using the gesticulation signal over a very moderate proportion of unit boundaries at which the turn signal is also active, but once again the participant as auditor breaks in at a large number of these points.

In both interactions we are looking at the same action-sequence variable: turn claims when both turn and gesticulation signals are active; and in both interactions there is a similar, high rate of such turn claims. Nevertheless, it seems reasonable to interpret the participant's frequent turn claims in these two situations as reflecting two distinguishable strategies: the first as a more straightforward effort to maintain a certain balance in the conversation, given a somewhat difficult situation; the second as a more "grabby," aggressive strategy. In this manner, a difference in a participant's strategy in two interactions may be observed, even when that participant's rate of response is essentially the same in the interactions.

The examples suggest that an action-sequence variable such as "proportion of auditor turn claims near boundaries where the speaker has activated both gesticulation and turn signals" fails to provide the necessary information to describe and potentially to interpret that element of interaction strategy, even though the variable is highly precise. What is needed, rather, is a statement that incorporates two variables, one of which is the action-sequence that expresses some rate of response to an action of the partner (such as the action-sequence variable described above). The second variable would express the rate of at least that action by the partner. In the case of the example, the expanded description of an element of an interaction strategy might be expressed as follows: "Proportion (x) of auditor turn claims near boundaries where the speaker has activated both gesticulation and turn signals, given the proportion (y) of boundaries at which such joint activations occur." It is anticipated that each element of interaction strategy will be describable in terms of at least two coordinate variables.

Thus, in order to describe a participant's strategy across some given stretch of interaction, it is necessary to summarize in some appropriate manner not only the participant's actions in response to the partner's actions, but also the partner's actions to which the participant is responding. Stated in the more general terms of the discussion of action-sequence variables, in order to summarize data on an interaction strategy, it is necessary to summarize not only for the dependent action in the variable, but also for the independent action. This general point appears to be a direct extension of the general position regarding action sequences as involving both participants.

As information is accumulated on a series of single elements of interaction strategy, it becomes an obvious task for the investigator to develop ways of combining these single elements in order to obtain a more comprehensive and integrated picture of a participant's interaction strategy, and to develop appropriate concepts for characterizing these multi-element strategies.

The discussion to this point has focused on describing an interaction strategy for a single participant. Of course, research on strategies need not have such an individual focus; investigators may be interested in describing strategy for an individual or for some group, over the course of a single interaction or of multiple interactions, and within the same general situation or across varying situations.

Description of Interactions in Terms of Strategies

Assuming for the moment a mutual ratification of prevailing conventions by the two participants in an interaction, it is consistent with the discussion to this point to view their interaction in terms of two interacting strategies, and to describe their interaction with some precision in terms of these strategies, including their fluctuation and–or stabilization over the course of the interaction.

Generalizing With Regard to Conventions
and Interaction Strategy

Given some positive results stemming from a study of either convention or interaction strategy, to what extent can the results be generalized? At this writing, and in view of the discussion in this and the preceding chapter, it appears that the generalizability of findings should be treated as a purely empirical question.

The discussion of convention suggested that conventions can range from the most local, used by the members of a single small group, to the most general, used by every member of the culture. On the basis of observing a single two-person interaction, one cannot on principle know how widespread conventions formulated for that interaction may be. It remains for more systematic observation based on properly constructed samples to locate the convention in question on the local–general continuum.

But there are other factors that further complicate the question of generalizability. It was stressed that the social situation in which the interaction occurs is a basic consideration with respect to the conventions appropriately used. Thus, for any given coordination problem, the same two participants who use one convention in one situation may well use another convention in another situation. Similarly, for the same coordination problem, a participant may use different conventions when interacting with different partners. And so on. For these reasons, it was said that a full description of a convention must include not only its substance and organization, but also its situational requirements.

Similar considerations may be applied to the generalizability of interaction strategies. The description of a strategy potentially begins with the actions of a given participant in an interaction. It is tempting to state that some strategies may be found to be essentially idiosyncratic to a participant, while others may be entirely general in the culture. But, as with conventions, the problem cannot be stated quite that simply. It has been emphasized that the description of interaction strategies must, like the description of conventions, include consideration of both participants. Thus, it may be said that a given participant adopts a certain strategy, given a specifiable set of actions by the partner. (This qualification may be limited by the case of the individual who uses the same interaction strategy, regardless of the actions of the partner.

But this case of extreme social insensitivity might well be studied as a phenomenon in its own right.)

Further, like conventions, interaction strategies may be affected by situational considerations. For example, a participant, may adopt a "push-back" strategy when interacting with peers who are interactionally "pushy" in some way, but that same participant, may acquiesce with pushy partners of higher status. Or a participant may acquiesce with a partner in public situations but push back with the same partner in private situations, and so on. For these reasons, it may be found on the basis of research that proper descriptions of interaction strategies must include not only the actions of the partner, but also relevant situational information.

Obviously, the same considerations affecting the extent to which a result in face-to-face interaction research may be generalized also affect the interpretation of a failure to replicate a given result. Such a failure may suggest faulty methods and–or hypotheses. But a failure to replicate may also occur when methods and–or hypotheses are sound but the convention in question is a relatively local one not used by the participants in the replication study, or the situation has changed in some unanticipated manner precluding use of the convention, or the like.

All of this is to observe only that the phenomena of face-to-face interaction are obviously social. The operation of the phenomena is subject to the complexity of the social structure within which they exist, and, in the case of interaction strategy, to the respective complexities of the participants in the interaction.

A LOOK AHEAD

Other Actions

In the studies reported in Parts II and III, the set of acts transcribed and analyzed was intended to be of relatively broad scope. But that set is obviously far from exhaustive, either of those acts observable in interactions, or of those acts studied by other investigators. Facial expressions, for example, were considered only superficially or not at all. Foot and leg movements and various aspects of "posture" might have received more attention, particularly in the turn study. As indicated in Chapter 11, it seems likely that the class of "back-channel" actions extends well beyond those reported here. Furthermore, some of the acts in our studies represented relatively gross categories. For example, gesticulating can be described in any number of more differentiated ways.

Other Conventions

The turn-system study was convenient as an example of research aimed at the careful description and documentation of conventions. Repeated use of that study in examples may help dramatize our belief that there is a serious need for increased investigation of convention-related phenomena. It is obvious to us that the research on the turn system reported in Part III reflects only a single, small set of related conventions; probably many other conventions are operating in the conversations observed for the turn study, as well as in other types of interactions. It seems a massive understatement to say that the field is wide open. Other aspects of conversations, such as greetings or other types of initiations of interaction (Cary, 1974; Kendon & Ferber, 1973) , terminations of the interaction (Schegloff & Sacks, 1973), topics of conversation, laughing and smiling, and posture shifts may be further explored. There are surely more rules applying to gestures than those hypothesized in Part III. And what about the use of self- and object–adaptors? For the turn system these existed only in the sense of being excluded. As indicated in Chapter II, it seems likely that the class of "back-channel" actions extends well beyond those investigated there. Facial expressions, given only the most cursory treatment in the research presented here, have been more extensively studied by a number of investigators (e.g., Buck, Savin, Miller, & Caul, 1972; Ekman, Friesen, & Ellsworth, 1972). To date, facial expressions have primarily been investigated in terms of their possible universality and their function in the expression of emotion. Might they play a part in conventions applying to face-to-face interaction? Vine (1970) has raised a similar question, and Kendon (1975b) has studied the face in just this manner.

Other Paradigms

We have noted at several points that the methodological approach we have urged is not necessarily limited to use within the conceptual framework described in Chapter 12. While this is generally true on principle, it is also true that aspects of the proposed methodology have been traditionally used by other groups of investigators. Very fine-grained acts in the form of phonetic transcriptions are a stock in trade of linguists. Most of the behavior units (or items, or categories) described by ethologists (most relevantly, the human ethologists) clearly conform to our definition of acts. In addition, ethologists have consistently emphasized determining the significance of an act from its interactional context, taking into account both sequences of acts and the general situation in which they occur. Further, it appears that some investigators working within the behavior-theoretic paradigm use units of behavior at approximately the same level as that defined for acts.

Finally, the many investigators of "nonverbal communication" are in most cases clearly using acts, although not necessarily taking into account sequences of acts or both participants in two-person interactions. And there are a number of theoretical orientations represented by these investigators.

Other Interactions

Other types of interaction need to be studied: interactions involving different sorts of persons; interactions in different sorts of social situations; interactions that rely less heavily on verbal productions; highly specialized interactions such as psychotherapy; commonly occurring types of interactions such as those occurring in the family and in work situations; and so on. Goffman (e.g., 1971) provides extensive and provocative consideration of a wide variety of conventions applying to a wide variety of interactions. Of particular interest is work being done on interaction between children (e.g., Grant, 1969; McGrew, 1970, 1972), and on mother-infant interaction (e.g., work in progress by Kaye, 1976, and Fogel, 1976).

Interaction Strategy

Studies of strategy are a natural concomitant of studies of convention. And as strategies are described, research will be directed at the effects of these strategies, both on the course and outcome of the interaction in which they are used, and on the impressions made regarding those using the strategies. Investigators are not likely to overlook the possibility that interaction strategies provide a natural and potentially effective approach to the description of persons.

In Conclusion

We stated in Chapter 1 that research on face-to-face interaction belongs entirely to no currently established academic discipline. As Kendon (1975b) observes: "The study of the organization of behavior in face-to-face interaction is neither linguistics nor anthropology, neither psychology nor ethology [p. 14]." Yet it has drawn investigators from these and other disciplines. This seems appropriate, in that observed regularities in face-to-face interaction provide a data source for research on issues in virtually all facets of social science. The conduct of face-to-face interaction must be at least one of the starting points for the study of society and of individuals within society.

It is clear that we believe that there is much work to be done in the study of conduct in face-to-face interaction. We have intended in the monograph to contribute to the discussion of effective approaches to studying this area. As we return to the development of transcriptions and the analysis of data, we hope that the interest in this domain will continue to grow.

Transcription and Reliability
for the Replication Study

Transcription

The purpose of the replication study was to provide an initial test of the hypotheses regarding the turn system as developed in the exploratory study. For this reason, only those actions were transcribed that were directly relevant to testing the turn-system hypotheses. The definition of each action was the same as that used in the exploratory study. The transcription for the replication study contained the following elements: (a) a careful rendering of the speech of each participant, including filled pauses, various types of non-fluencies, audible inhalation, and the like; (b) intonation, according to the Trager and Smith (1957) scheme, as modified for the purposes of the exploratory study, including primary stress, three pitch levels, and terminal junctures; (c) sociocentric sequences; (d) paralinguistic pitch and–or intensity on the sociocentric sequences, relative to the pitch and intensity on the syllables immediately preceding the sociocentric sequence; (e) paralinguistic drawl; (f) the syllables over which head nods occurred; (g) the syllables over which the head was directed at the partner; and (h) the syllables over which a gesticulation and–or tensed hand position occurred.

In addition, the following phenomena were identified in the replication transcriptions: (a) points at which the utterances were grammatically complete; (b) vocal back channels; and (c) instances of simultaneous turns and of smooth exchanges of the turn.

Reliability

It was not anticipated that reliability would present a problem in this transcription because of the straightforward, concrete nature of the actions involved, and because of previous results on reliability for these sorts of actions, reported both from this laboratory and from others.

The following procedures were used in checking interjudge reliability for the replication transcription.

1.   Actions checked for reliability were: gaze direction, head nods, gesticulation and–or tensed hand position, primary intonation stress, phonemic-clause boundaries, and deviation from the 22 → intonation pattern (the "intonation-marked" phonemic clause). Other actions used in the replication study were not checked, either because it was difficult to imagine how significant disagreement on them might occur among members of the research team, or because the actions carried relatively little weight in the analysis, or because the actions occurred relatively infrequently, or some combination of these reasons. Thus, actions not included in the reliability study were: completion of a grammatical clause, sociocentric sequences, paralanguage on sociocentric sequences, and paralinguistic drawl.

2.   Reliability was checked on only those actions directly relevant to turn-system signals. For example, even though intonation was fully transcribed for the replication study, agreement was checked on only the location of syllables over which the primary stress occurred, and of clauses that were "intonation marked."

3.   Because it is important within the turn-system research, not only to observe the occurrence of an action, but also to locate that occurrence with some accuracy, the unit for assessing agreement was for most actions the syllable. Reliability was not based on counts or timings of actions transcribed over extended stretches of speech, but rather on the presence or absence of the action on brief stretches of interaction. Thus, for head direction, head nods, gesticulation, and primary stresses, interjudge agreement was examined for each syllable, with regard to the occurrence or nonoccurrence of the action in question. For two actions—clause boundaries and intonation-marked clauses—the word rather than the syllable was used as the unit for assessing agreement. This slightly larger unit was used for these two actions because they were not considered to occur within the boundaries of words; therefore, the use of syllables would provide a slightly inflated measure of agreement.

4.   Regardless of whether syllables or words were used as units for measuring agreement, no margin for error was allowed the judges. For example, for any two successive syllables *a* and *b*, if one judge placed a primary stress on *a* and not *b*, and the other judge placed a stress on *b* and not *a*, the judges were considered in disagreement on both syllables.

5.   In measuring agreement for primary stresses, intonation-marked clauses, and clause boundaries, nonfluencies such as stutters were removed from the analysis because such nonfluencies do not play a part in the turn system.

6.   The statistical measure of interjudge agreement was *kappa* (Cohen, 1960). *Kappa* "is directly interpretable as the proportion of joint judgments in which there is agreement, after chance agreement is excluded. Its upper

limit is + 1.00, and its lower limit falls between zero and -1.00, depending on the distribution of judgments by the two judges . . . (Cohen, 1960, p. 46)." As such, *kappa* is a particularly stringent measure. The standard error for *kappa* (σ_{κ_0}) may be calculated, and the hypothesis that the obtained *kappa* is significantly different from zero may be tested by dividing kappa by σ_{κ_0}, and referring the result to the normal curve. In this connection, Cohen (1960) appropriately observes that "it is generally of as little value to test κ for significance as it is for any other reliability coefficient—to know merely that κ is beyond chance is trivial since one usually expects much more than this in the way of reliability in psychological measurement. It may, however, serve as a minimum demand in some applications [p. 44]."

Table A.1 presents the results of the reliability study. Shown for each type of action are (a) the type of unit used and the number of such units over which reliability was checked; (b) the gross percentage of agreement, calculated simply by dividing the number of units for which agreement was obtained, by the total number of units observed; and (c) *kappa*, together with σ_{κ_0} and *kappa* $/\sigma_{\kappa_0}$.

TABLE A.1
Interjudge Reliability on the Replication Transcription

Action	Units type	N	agree-ment (%)	Kappa	σ_{κ_0}	$\dfrac{\kappa}{\sigma_{\kappa_0}}$
Head direction	Syllable	1288	95.9	.801	.055	14.56
Head nods	Syllable	1289	95.5	.820	.048	17.08
Gesticulation	Syllable	1292	96.3	.963	.031	31.06
Stresses	Syllable	295	94.2	.819	.085	9.61
Clause boundaries	Words	244	85.7	.678	.071	9.50
Intonation-marked clauses	Words	244	89.8	.615	.106	5.78

CRESCAT:
A Program for Analyzing
Action Sequences

The CRESCAT system is being designed to identify complex sequential patterns which may be embedded in extensive (and possibly "noisy") data files, and to transform identified patterns in a number of useful ways. Currently implemented in the IBM 370, the CRESCAT system is intended to be a user-oriented, "friendly" system of considerable generality.

In studies of action sequences a major objective is that of discovering and verifying sequential patterns, a task that must be accomplished between the more typical research tasks of data generation and final analysis. CRESCAT (not an acronym) is intended to facilitate discovery and initial testing of potential action-sequence patterns. It is clear that transcriptions of face-to-face interaction readily yield unusually complex and rich data pools. Rapid scanning for promising sequential patterns would seem ideally consigned to a computer. CRESCAT can search raw data files for patterns specified by the investigator. When the data conform to the specified pattern, CRESCAT can create new data arrays reflecting the occurrences of the pattern, make counts of occurrences and nonoccurrences of the pattern, insert desired information in the original raw data, and the like. Laborious and error-susceptible hand searches and tabulations of the data may be eliminated at considerable potential savings of time and money.

There are no program-based limits on the length or complexity of the patterns being searched. CRESCAT patterns may involve character strings within an event (that is, ordered characters all at the same time or sequence number) and–or across events. Thus, patterns may involve simultaneous and–or sequential entries in a file. The search can span an entire file or prescribed set of files, or it can be limited to parts of files determined by parameters which can be either strings or sequence numbers.

343

CRESCAT is designed to be extremely flexible in the type and format of data which it accepts. (It is not, of course, limited to use in research on face-to-face interaction.) The data may include information on the absolute or relative time of events. CRESCAT will automatically accept the input of several types of event recorders. There is a wide variety of program options and packages. Users can readily sort, edit, update, create, and delete files. Files can be displayed in a number of formats. Certain often-used statistical operations are included; but data resulting from pattern searches can be produced in a manner acceptable to other statistical packages the user may prefer, e.g., SPSS (Nie, Hull, Jenkins, Steinbrenner, & Bent, 1975). There are also numerous options for output in terms of tables, graphs, and data arrays.

If the user's task is sufficiently idiosyncratic to render CRESCAT packaged functions inconvenient or unusable, the user may design (and retain in the form of executable programs in CRESCAT) a personal package, using lower-level CRESCAT elements, such as pattern ranges, program branches, and conditionally performed procedures. That is, CRESCAT can be used on both a "normal" and an "expert" level. (User programs are read by CRESCAT in the same way as data, so that such programs are subject to all the same operations as data.)

In short, CRESCAT has been designed to provide a practical analytic tool for implementing the research techniques advocated in this monograph and elsewhere. Investigators wishing to obtain more information on the CRESCAT system may contact either Duncan or Kenneth Kaye at the University of Chicago.

References

Adams, R. McC. Anthropological perspectives on ancient trade. *Current Anthropology,* 1974, 15, 239–258.

Altman, I. Territorial behavior in humans: An analysis of the concept. In L. A. Pastalan & D. H. Carson (Eds.), *Spatial behavior of older people.* Ann Arbor, Michigan: University of Michigan–Wayne State University Institute of Gerontology, 1970.

Altmann, S. A. Sociobiology of rhesus monkeys. II: Stochastics of social communication. *Journal of Theoretical Biology,* 1965, 8, 490–522.

Arensberg, C. M. Culture as behavior: Structure and emergence. *Annual Review of Anthropology,* 1972, 1, 1–26.

Argyle, M. *Social interaction.* New York: Atherton Press, 1969.

Ashear, V., & Snortum, J. R. Eye contact in children as a function of age, sex, social and intellective variables. *Developmental Psychology,* 1971, 4, 479.

Austin, W. A. Non-verbal communication. In A. L. Davis (Ed.), *Language resource information for the culturally disadvantaged.* Champaign, Illinois: National Council of Teachers of English, 1967.

Bales, R. F. *Interaction process analysis: A method for the study of small groups.* Reading, Mass.: Addison-Wesley, 1950.

Barker, R. G. *The stream of behavior.* New York: Appleton-Century-Crofts, 1963.

Bateson, G. Communication. In N. A. McQuown (Ed.), *The natural history of an interview.* Microfilm Collection of Manuscripts on Cultural Anthropology, Fifteenth Series. Chicago: The University of Chicago Joseph Regenstein Library Department of Photoduplication, 1971.

Baxter, J. C., & Rozelle, R. M. Nonverbal expression as a function of crowding during a simulated police–citizen encounter. *Journal of Personality and Social Psychology,* 1975, 28, 40–54.

Becker, F. D. Study of spatial markers. *Journal of Personality and Social Psychology,* 1973, 26, 439–445.

Beekman, S. J. Nonverbal behaviors in dyadic conversations in relation to subject sex and partner sex. Unpublished doctoral dissertation, University of Chicago, 1973.

Bennett, J. W. *Northern plainsmen: Adaptive strategy and agrarian life.* Chicago: Aldine, 1969.

Bernstein, B. Social class, linguistic codes, and grammatical elements. *Language and Speech,* 1962, 5, 221–240.

Birdwhistell, R. L. *Kinesics and context.* Philadelphia: University of Pennsylvania Press, 1970.

345

Birdwhistell, R. L. Body motion. In N. A. McQuown (Ed.), *The natural history of an interview*. Microfilm Collection of Manuscripts on Cultural Anthropology, Fifteenth Series. Chicago: The University of Chicago Joseph Regenstein Library Department of Photoduplication, 1971.

Blurton Jones, N. G. Non-verbal communication in children. In R. A. Hinde (Ed.), *Non-verbal communication*. Cambridge, England: Cambridge University Press, 1972.

Bock, R. D. *Multivariate statistical methods in behavioral research*. New York: McGraw-Hill, 1975.

Boomer, D. S., & Dittmann, A. T. Hesitation pauses and juncture pauses in speech. *Language and Speech*, 1962, 5, 215–220.

Brand, M. *The nature of human action*. Glenview, Illinois: Scott, Foresman, 1970.

Brannigan, C., & Humphries, D. Human non-verbal behavior: A means of communication. In N. G. Blurton Jones (Ed.), *Ethological studies of child behavior*. Cambridge, England: Cambridge University Press, 1972.

Brown, R., & Ford, M. Address in American English. *Journal of Abnormal and Social Psychology*, 1961, 62, 375–385.

Browning, D. *Act and agent*. Coral Gables, Florida: University of Miami Press, 1964.

Brunswik, E. Organismic achievement and environmental probability. *Psychological Review*, 1943, 50, 255–273.

Brunswick, E. *Systematic and representative design in psychological experiments*. Berkeley: University of California Press, 1947.

Buck, R. W., Savin, V. J., Miller, R. E., & Caul, W. F. Communication of affect through facial expression in humans. *Journal of Personality and Social Psychology*, 1972, 23, 362–371.

Campbell, N. R. *An account of the principles of measurement and calculation*. London: Longmans, Green, 1928.

Cary, M. S. Nonverbal openings to conversation. Paper presented at the meeting of the Eastern Psychological Association, Philadelphia, April, 1974.

Chapple, E. D. *Culture and biological man*. New York: Holt, Rinehart & Winston, 1970.

Chapple, E. D., & Coon, C.S. *Principles of anthropology*. New York: Holt, Rinehart & Winston, 1942.

Cohen, J. A coefficient of agreement for nominal scales. *Educational and Psychological Measurement*, 1960, 20, 37–46.

Condon, W. S., & Ogston, W. D. A segmentation of behavior. *Journal of Psychiatric Research*, 1967, 5, 221–235.

Crystal, D. *Prosodic systems and intonation in English*. Cambridge, England: Cambridge University Press, 1969.

Crystal, D., & Quirk, R. *Systems of prosodic and paralinguistic features in English*. The Hague: Mouton, 1964.

Dittmann, A. T., & Llewellyn, L. G. The phonemic clause as a unit of speech decoding. *Journal of Personality and Social Psychology*, 1967, 6, 341–349.

Dittmann, A. T., & Llewellyn, L. G. Relationship between vocalizations and head nods as listener responses. *Journal of Personality and Social Psychology*, 1968, 9, 79–84.

Dittmann, A. T., & Wynne, L.C. Linguistic techniques and the analysis of emotionality in interviews. *Journal of Abnormal and Social Psychology*, 1961, 63, 201–204.

Draper, P. Crowding among the hunter-gatherers: The !Kung bushmen. *Science*, 1973, 182, 301–303.

Duncan, S. D., Jr. Nonverbal communication. *Psychological Bulletin*, 1969, 72, 118–137.

Duncan, S. D., Jr., Some signals and rules for taking speaking turns in conversations. *Journal of Personality and Social Psychology*, 1972, 23, 283–292.

Duncan, S. D., Jr., & Niederehe, G. On signalling that it's your turn to speak. *Journal of Experimental Social Psychology*, 1974, 10, 234–247.

Duncan, S. D., Jr., Rice, L. N., & Butler, J. M. Therapists' paralanguage in peak and poor psychotherapy hours. *Journal of Abnormal Psychology*, 1968, 73, 566–570.

Duncan, S. D., Jr., Rosenberg, M. J., & Finkelstein, J. The paralanguage of experimenter bias. *Sociometry,* 1969, 32, 207–219.

Duncan, S. D., Jr. & Rosenthal, R. Vocal emphasis in experimenters' instruction reading as unintended determinant of subjects' responses. *Language and Speech,* 1968, 11, 20–26.

Ebel, R. L. Estimation of the reliability of ratings. *Psychometrika,* 1951, 16, 407–424.

Edney, J. J. Human territoriality. *Psychological Bulletin,* 1974, 81, 959–975.

Eibl-Eibesfeldt, I. *Ethology: The biology of behavior.* New York: Holt, Rinehart & Winston, 1970.

Ekman, P. *Darwin and facial expression: A century of research in review.* New York: Academic Press, 1974.

Ekman, P., & Friesen, W. V. Nonverbal behavior in psychotherapy research. In J. Shlien (Ed.), *Research in psychotherapy* (Vol. 3). Washington, D.C.: American Psychological Association, 1968.

Ekman, P., & Friesen, W. V. A tool for the analysis of motion picture film or video tape. *American Psychologist,* 1969, 24, 240–243.

Ekman, P., Friesen, W.V., & Ellsworth, P. *Emotion in the human face.* New York: Pergamon, 1972.

Ekman, P., Friesen, W. V.,& Tomkins, S. S. Facial affect scoring technique: A first validity study. *Semiotica,* 1971, 3, 37–58.

Ellsworth, P. C., Carlsmith, J. M., & Henson, A. The stare as a stimulus to flight in human subjects: A series of field experiments. *Journal of Personality and Social Psychology,* 1972, 21, 302–311.

Ervin-Tripp, S. On sociolinguistic rules: Alternation and co–occurrence. In J. J. Gumperz, & D. Hymes (Eds.), *Directions in sociolinguistics.* New York: Holt, Rinehart & Winston, 1972.

Ex, J., & Kendon, A. A notation for facial positions and bodily postures. In M. Argyle, *Social interaction.* New York: Atherton Press, 1969.

Exline, R. V. Explorations in the process of person perception: Visual interaction in relation to competition, sex, and need for affiliation. *Journal of Personality,* 1963, 31, 1–20.

Exline, R. V. Visual interaction: The glances of power and preference. In J. K. Cole (Ed.), *Nebraska Symposium on Motivation* (Vol. 19). Lincoln: University of Nebraska Press, 1971. (Republished in S. Weitz (Ed.), *Nonverbal communication.* New York: Oxford University Press, 1974).

Exline, R. V., Gray, D., & Schuette, D. Visual behavior in a dyad as affected by interview content and sex of respondent. *Journal of Personality and Social Psychology,* 1965, 1, 201–209.

Feather, N. T. Organization and discrepancy in cognitive structures. *Psychological Review,* 1971, 78, 355–379.

Felipe, N. J., & Sommer, R. Invasions of personal space. *Social Problems,* 1966, 14, 206–214.

Fiske, D. W. *Measuring the concepts of personality.* Chicago: Aldine, 1971.

Fogel, A. Temporal organization in mother-infant face-to-face interaction. In H. R. Schaffer (Ed.), *Studies in mother-infant interaction.* London: Academic Press, 1976, in press.

Freedman, N. The analysis of movement behavior during the clinical interview. In A. W. Siegman & B. Pope (Eds.), *Studies in dyadic communication.* New York: Pergamon, 1972.

Freedman, N., Blass, T., Rifkin, A., & Quitkin, F. Body movements and the verbal encoding of aggressive affect. *Journal of Personality and Social Psychology,* 1973, 26, 72–85.

Freedman, N., & Hoffman, S. P. Kinetic behavior in altered clinical states: Approach to objective analysis of motor behavior during clinical interviews. *Perceptual and Motor Skills,* 1967, 24, 527–539.

Freedman, N., O'Hanlon, J., Oltman, P., & Witkin, H. A. The imprint of psychological differentiation on kinetic behavior in varying communication contexts. *Journal of Abnormal Psychology,* 1972, 79, 239–258.

Friedrich, P. Social context and semantic feature: The Russian pronominal usage. In J. J. Gumperz & D. Hymes (Eds.), *Directions in sociolinguistics*. New York: Holt, Rinehart & Winston, 1972.

Fries, C. C. *The structure of English*. New York: Harcourt, Brace, 1952.

Futrelle, R. P. GALATEA, A proposed system for computer-aided analysis of movie films and videotape. *The University of Chicago Institute for Computer Research Quarterly Report*, 1973, No. 37, I-E.

Geoghegan, W. Information processing systems in culture. In P. Kay (Ed.), *Explorations in mathematical anthropology*. Cambridge, Mass.: MIT Press, 1971.

Goffman, E. *The presentation of self in everyday life*. Garden City, New York: Doubleday, 1959.

Goffman, E. *Encounters*. New York: Bobbs-Merrill, 1961.

Goffman, E. *Behavior in public places*. New York: Free Press, 1963.

Goffman, E. *Interaction ritual*. Garden City, New York: Anchor, 1967.

Goffman, E. *Strategic interaction*. Philadelphia: University of Pennsylvania Press, 1969.

Goffman, E. *Relations in public*. New York: Basic Books, 1971.

Goldschmidt, W. An ethnography of encounters: A methodology for the enquiry into the relation between the individual and society. *Current Anthropology*, 1972, 13, 59–78.

Goodenough, W. H. On cultural theory. (Review of *The interpretation of cultures* by C. Geertz.) *Science*, 1974, 186, 435–436.

Gough, H. G., & Heilbrun, A. B. *The Adjective Check List manual*. Palo Alto, California: Consulting Psychologists Press, 1965.

Grant, E. C. Human facial expression. *Man*, 1969, 4, 525–536.

Gross, N., Mason, W. S., & McEachern, A. W. *Explorations in role analysis*. New York: Wiley, 1958.

Gumperz, J. J., & Hymes, D. *Directions in sociolinguistics*. New York: Holt, Rinehart & Winston, 1972.

Haggard, E. A. *Intraclass correlation and the analysis of variance*. New York: Dryden Press, 1958.

Hall, E. T. A system for the notation of proxemic behavior. *American Anthropologist*, 1963, 65, 1003–1026.

Hall, E. T. *The hidden dimension*. Garden City, New York: Doubleday, 1966.

Hayek, F. A. Rules, perception, and intelligibility. *Proceedings of the British Academy*, 1962, 48, 321–344.

Heyns, R. W., & Lippitt, R. Systematic observational techniques. In G. Lindzey (Ed.), *Handbook of social psychology* (Vol. 1). Cambridge, Mass.: Addison-Wesley, 1954.

Hinde, R. A. (Ed.) *Non-verbal communication*. Cambridge, England: Cambridge University Press, 1972.

Hockett, C. F. Vocal activity. In N. A. McQuown (Ed.), *The natural history of an interview*. Microfilm Collection of Manuscripts on Cultural Anthropology, Fifteenth Series. Chicago: The University of Chicago Joseph Regenstein Library Department of Photoduplication, 1971.

Hume, D. *Treatise of morals*. Boston: Ginn, 1893.

Hymes, D. Models of the interaction of language and social life. In J. J. Gumperz & D. Hymes (Eds.), *Directions in sociolinguistics*. New York: Holt, Rinehart & Winston, 1972.

Jaffe, J., & Feldstein, S. *Rhythms of dialogue*. New York: Academic Press, 1970.

Jakobson, R. Discussion of "Factors and forms of aphasia" by A. R. Luria. In A. V. S. de Reuck & M. O'Connor (Eds.), *Ciba foundation symposium on disorders of language*. Boston: Little, Brown, 1964.

Jakobson, R., Fant, C. G. M., & Halle, M. *Preliminaries to speech analysis: The distinctive features and their correlates*. Cambridge, Mass.: MIT Press, 1952.

Kaye, K. Infants' effects upon their mothers' teaching strategies. In J. C. Glidewell (Ed.), *The social context of learning and development.* New York: Gardner Press, 1976, in press.

Kendon, A. Some functions of gaze-direction in social interaction. *Acta Psychologica,* 1967, 26, 22–63.

Kendon, A. Movement coordination in social interaction: Some examples described. *Acta Psychologica,* 1970, 32, 101–125.

Kendon, A. The role of visible behavior in the organization of social interaction. In M. von Cranach & I. Vine (Eds.), *Social communication and movement.* New York: Academic, 1972. (a)

Kendon, A. Some relationships between body motion and speech. An analysis of an example. In A. Siegman & B. Pope (Eds.), *Studies in dyadic communication.* New York: Pergamon, 1972. (b)

Kendon, A. Review of A. E. Scheflen, *Body language and the social order. Contemporary Psychology,* 1974, 19, 526–527.

Kendon, A. Introduction. In A. Kendon, R. M. Harris, & M. R. Key (Eds.), *The organization of behavior in face-to-face interaction.* The Hague: Mouton, 1975. (a)

Kendon, A. Some functions of the face in a kissing round. *Semiotica,* 1975, in press. (b)

Kendon, A., & Ferber, A. A description of some human greetings. In R. P. Michael & J. H. Crook (Eds.), *Comparative ecology and behavior of primates.* London: Academic Press, 1973.

Kendon, A., Harris, R. M., & Key, M. R. (Eds.) *The organization of behavior in face-to-face interaction.* The Hague: Mouton, 1975.

Krout, M. H. Autistic gestures: An experimental study in symbolic movements. *Psychological Monographs,* 1935, 46 (4, Whole No. 208).

Lennard, H. L., & Bernstein, A. *Patterns in human interaction.* San Francisco: Jossey-Bass, 1969.

Levine, D. N. *Georg Simmel on individuality and social forms.* Chicago: University of Chicago Press, 1971.

Lewis, D. K. *Convention.* Cambridge, Mass.: Harvard University Press, 1969.

Libby, W. L., Jr. Eye contact and direction of looking as stable individual differences. *Journal of Experimental Research in Personality,* 1970, 4, 303–312.

Libby, W. L., Jr., & Yaklevich, D. Personality determinants of eye contact and direction of gaze aversion. *Journal of Personality and Social Psychology,* 1973, 27, 197–206.

Lieberman, P. *Intonation, perception, and language.* Cambridge, Mass.: MIT Press, 1967.

Linton, R. *The cultural background of personality.* New York: Appleton-Century, 1945.

Maclay, H., & Osgood, C. E. Hesitation phenomena in spontaneous English speech. *Word,* 1959, 19, 19–44.

Mahl, G. F. Gestures and body movements in interviews. In J. M. Shlien (Ed.), *Research in psychotherapy* (Vol. 3). Washington, D.C.: American Psychological Association, 1968.

Malinowski, B. *A scientific theory of culture.* Chapel Hill: University of North Carolina Press, 1944.

Markel, N. N. The reliability of coding paralanguage: Pitch, loudness, and tempo. *Journal of Verbal Learning and Verbal Behavior,* 1965, 4, 306–308.

Markel, N. N. Relationship between voice-quality profiles and MMPI profiles in psychiatric patients. *Journal of Abnormal Psychology,* 1969, 74, 61–66.

Matarazzo, J. D., & Wiens, A. N. *The interview.* Chicago: Aldine, 1972.

McGrew, W. C. Glossary of motor patterns of four-year-old nursery school children. In S. J. Hutt & C. Hutt (Eds.), *Direct observation and measurement of behavior.* Springfield, Ill.: Charles C. Thomas, 1970.

McGrew, W. C. *An ethological study of children's behavior.* New York: Academic Press, 1972.

McGrew, W. C. Interpersonal spacing of pre-school children. In K. Connolly & J. Bruner (Eds.), *The growth of competence.* New York: Academic Press, 1973.

McQuown, N. A. (Ed.) *The natural history of an interview*. Microfilm Collection of Manuscripts on Cultural Anthropology, Fifteenth Series. Chicago: The University of Chicago Joseph Regenstein Library Department of Photoduplication, 1971.

Mead, G. H. *Mind, self and society*. Chicago: University of Chicago Press, 1934.

Mehrabian, A. Relationship of attitude to seated posture, orientation, and distance. *Journal of Personality and Social Psychology*, 1968, 10, 26–30.

Mehrabian, A. *Nonverbal communication*. Chicago: Aldine, Atherton, 1972.

Mehrabian, A., & Friar, J. T. Encoding of attitude by a seated communicator via posture and position cues. *Journal of Consulting and Clinical Psychology*, 1969, 33, 330–336.

Meltzer, L., Morris, W. N., & Hayes, D. P. Interruption outcomes and vocal amplitude: Explorations in social psychophysics. *Journal of Personality and Social Psychology*, 1971, 18, 392–402.

Newell, A., & Simon, H. A. *Human problem solving*. Englewood Cliffs, N.J.: Prentice-Hall, 1972.

Nie, N. H., Hull, C. H., Jenkins, J. G., Steinbrenner, K., & Bent, D. H. *SPSS: Statistical package for the social sciences* (2nd ed.). New York: McGraw-Hill, 1975.

Pastalan, L. A., & Carson, D. H. (Eds.) *Spatial behavior of older people*. Ann Arbor, Michigan: University of Michigan—Wayne State University Institute of Gerontology, 1970.

Pedersen, D. M., & Shears, L. M. A review of personal space research in the framework of general system theory. *Psychological Bulletin*. 1973, 80, 367–388.

Popper, K. R. *The logic of scientific discovery*. New York: Basic Books, 1959.

Poyatos, F. Cross-cultural study of paralinguistic "alternants" in face-to-face interaction. In A. Kendon, R. Harris, & M. R. Key (Eds.), *The organization of behavior in face-to-face interaction*. The Hague: Mouton, 1975.

Riskin, J. M., & Faunce, E. E. An evaluative review of family interaction research. *Family Process*, 1972, 11, 365–456.

Roberts, J. M. Three Navaho households: A comparative study in small group culture. *Papers of the Peabody Museum of American Archeology and Ethnology*, 1951, 40(3).

Rosenfeld, H. M. Instrumental affiliative functions of facial and gestural expressions. *Journal of Personality and Social Psychology*, 1966, 4, 65–72.

Rosenthal, R. *Experimenter effects in behavioral research*. New York: Appleton-Century-Crofts, 1966.

Ruesch, J., & Kees, W. *Nonverbal communication*. Berkeley: University of California Press, 1956.

Runkel, P. J. & McGrath, J. E. *Research on human behavior: A systematic guide to method*. New York: Holt, Rinehart & Winston, 1972.

Russo, N. F. Eye contact, interpersonal distance, and the equilibrium theory. *Journal of Personality and Social Psychology*, 1975, 31, 497–502.

Sacks, H., Schegloff, E. A., & Jefferson, G. A simplest systematics for the organization of turn-taking for conversation. *Language*, 1974, 50, 696–735.

Sapir, E. Communication. In D. G. Mandelbaum (Ed.), *Selected writings of Edward Sapir*. Berkeley and Los Angeles: University of California Press, 1968.

Scheflen, A. E. Communication and regulation in psychotherapy. *Psychiatry*, 1963, 26, 126–136.

Scheflen, A. E. Natural history method in psychotherapy: Communicational research. In L. A. Gottschalk & A. H. Auerbach (Eds.), *Methods of research in psychotherapy*. New York: Appleton-Century-Crofts, 1966.

Scheflen, A. E. Human communication: Behavioral programs and their integration in interaction. *Behavioral Science*, 1968, 13, 44–55.

Scheflen, A. E. *Communicational structure: Analysis of a psychotherapy transaction*. Bloomington: University of Indiana Press, 1973.

Schegloff, E. A., & Sacks, H. Opening up closings. *Semiotica*, 1973, 8, 289–327.

Schelling, T. G. *The strategy of conflict*. Cambridge, Mass.: Harvard University Press, 1960.

Schleidt, W. M. Tonic communication: Continual effects of discrete signs in animal communication systems. *Journal of Theoretical Biology*, 1973, 42, 359–386.

Schultz, W. C. *FIRO: A three-dimensional theory of interpersonal behavior*. New York: Rinehart, 1958.

Searle, J. *Speech acts*. Cambridge, England: Cambridge University Press, 1969.

Shwayder, D. S. *The stratification of behaviour*. London: Routledge & Kegan Paul, 1965.

Sommer, R. *Personal space*. Englewood Cliffs, N.J.: Prentice-Hall, 1969.

Taylor, R. *Action and purpose*. Englewood Cliffs, N.J.: Prentice-Hall, 1966.

Thorndike, R. L. *Thorndike Dimensions of Temperament manual*. New York: Psychological Corp., 1966.

Trager, G. L. Paralanguage: A first approximation. *Studies in Linguistics*, 1958, 13, 1–12.

Trager, G. L., & Smith, H. L., Jr. *An outline of English structure*. Washington, D.C.: American Council of Learned Societies, 1957.

Tyler, S. A. *Cognitive anthropology*. New York: Holt, Rinehart & Winston, 1969.

Vine, I. Communication by facial-visual signals: A review and analysis of their role in face-to-face encounters. In J. H. Crook (Ed.), *Social behavior in animals and man*. London: Academic Press, 1970.

Webb, E. J., Campbell, D. T., Schwartz, R. D., & Sechrest, L. *Unobtrusive measures: Nonreactive research in the social sciences*. Chicago: Rand McNally, 1966.

Weick, K. L. Systematic observational methods. In G. Lindzey & E. Aronson (Eds.), *Handbook of social psychology* (2nd ed.) (Vol. 2). Reading, Mass.: Addison-Wesley, 1968.

Werner, O. Ethnoscience 1972. *Annual Review of Anthropology*, 1972, 1, 271–308.

White, A. R. *The philosophy of action*. London: Oxford University Press, 1968.

Whitten, N. E., Jr., & Whitten, D. S. Social strategies and social relationships. *Annual Review of Anthropology*, 1972, 1, 247–270.

Wilson, E. O. Review of R. A. Hinde (Ed.), *Non-verbal communication. Science*, 1972, 176, 625–627.

Yngve, V. H. On getting a word in edgewise. *Papers from the sixth regional meeting Chicago Linguistic Society*. Chicago: Chicago Linguistic Society, 1970. Pp. 567–577.

Yngve, V. H. *An introduction to human linguistics*. Book in preparation, 1975.

Author Index

353

Subject Index